CAMBRIDGE
ENGLISH
for schools

Teacher's Book One

ANDREW LITTLEJOHN & DIANA HICKS

CAMBRIDGE
UNIVERSITY PRESS

Published by the Press Syndicate of the University of Cambridge
The Pitt Building, Trumpington Street, Cambridge CB2 1RP
40 West 20th Street, New York, NY 10011-4211, USA
10 Stamford Road, Oakleigh, Melbourne 3166, Australia

© Cambridge University Press 1996

First Published 1996

Printed in Great Britain at the University Press, Cambridge.

ISBN 0 521 42177 2 Teacher's Book
ISBN 0 521 42169 1 Student's Book
ISBN 0 521 42173 X Workbook
ISBN 0 521 42181 0 Class Cassette Set
ISBN 0 521 42130 6 Workbook Cassette

Contents

Map of *Cambridge English for Schools 1*

Introduction

Who is the course for?

Cambridge English for Schools (*CES*) is a four level course, plus a Starter for complete beginners, aimed at young students. Level 1 is for students who have done some English before or who have used the *CES* Starter Level.

For what type of teaching situations is it intended?

CES has been designed with a variety of possible situations in mind – from small classes with flexible furniture arrangements to fairly large classes with furniture fixed to the ground, from schools with considerable resources to schools with limited funds. The realities of many classes – with learners of varying abilities and varying levels of motivation and cooperation – have been given serious consideration and have shaped the approach and philosophy of the course (see *Rationale*, page 7).

What does it aim to do?

CES contains four different syllabuses.

1 At the centre of the course is the *language syllabus*. Through it, students develop their knowledge of English and their abilities to use English in various ways.

2 Complementing this, the course has an *education syllabus*. The materials aim to broaden the students' knowledge of the world and to build on what they are learning in other areas of their school life. Topics presented in *CES*, therefore, contain *curriculum links* with History, Science, Geography and so on. The materials also aim to develop *cross-curriculum* attitudes and abilities, such as working independently, caring for the environment, working with others and so on. In addition, the materials focus on *cross-cultural* topics, aiming to develop the students' knowledge of English-speaking societies and, through them, learn about their own society.

3 At the same time, a *learner-involvement syllabus* aims to help the learners to take more responsibility for their own learning and to feel that their classes are 'their own'.

4 In addition to these aims for the learners, *CES* also aims to offer *support for teachers* in a number of ways:

- Detailed practical suggestions in an easy-to-use *A to Z of methodology* (see page 116).
- Easy-to-use Unit notes (see page 21).

- Additional Unit notes on teaching classes with mixed abilities (see any *Topic* or *Language focus* Unit).
- Photocopiable language and pronunciation worksheets (see page 153).
- Advice on how the course may be lengthened or shortened (see page 16).
- Suggestions for investigating classroom language learning (see any *Topic* or *Language focus* Unit).
- A list of useful classroom phrases (see page 172).

How long does the course take?

Each level (except the Starter) of *CES* is intended for approximately 80–100 hours of classroom work. However, the course has a flexible design enabling it to be made either shorter or longer (see pages 16–17, for more details).

What does the course consist of?

Each level has six components:

A Student's Book	A Teacher's Book
A Workbook	A Class Cassette Set
A Workbook Cassette	A classroom Video

See *CES 1 at a glance*, page 12, for more details of each component.

This Teacher's Book contains:

- A detailed rationale for the course (pages 7–11).
- *CES 1 at a glance*: a visual overview of the course (see pages 12–15).
- Some introductory notes on using the course (see pages 16–17).
- A special note on *A Parcel of English* (see page 18).
- Guidance on using the Units and planning lessons (see pages 21–115).
- An A to Z of practical suggestions for teaching (see pages 116–144).
- Supplementary photocopiable language and pronunciation worksheets (see pages 153–171).
- A list of useful classroom phrases (see pages 172–173).

Please turn to the section which interests you most!

Rationale

Summary

Cambridge English for Schools has been based on a reconsideration of the possibilities of English language teaching with secondary aged students and the part that teaching materials can play. It offers a new approach in which wider educational goals, student involvement, and support for teachers combine to provide a significant step forward in English language teaching. This introduction describes the *aims, syllabus,* and *methodology* of the course and the role of *evaluation*.

English, language learning and education

For many teachers, the teaching of young adolescents poses some of the greatest and most rewarding challenges. For the students, a new school, new circles of friends, new interests and new experiences can all combine to make the period both exciting and demanding. It is also a time when the basis of their approach to learning, perhaps for the rest of their lives, is formed. This is especially true in the learning of foreign languages, where their first experiences define, for them, what language learning is all about and if it is something at which they can succeed.

In many classrooms all over the world, the initial experience of learning English is one of tremendous energy and imagination, in which the students feel that a whole new world is opening up for them as they learn to express themselves in another language. It is, however, also a sad fact that for other students it is sometimes a time of failure and disappointment in which they gradually feel left behind, often resorting to misbehaviour in the classroom and a gradual rejection of the work that the teacher is doing for them. It is thus important for everybody involved in teaching adolescents to try to determine the routes to success. In the pages which follow this introduction, we have set out what we believe, in our experience, is the basis for success in teaching and learning English and the basis on which *Cambridge English for Schools* is built. We will describe this under four main headings:

1 **Aims**, which describes the purposes of the course.
2 **Syllabus**, which describes what the students will be learning about.
3 **Methodology**, which describes the types of activities included.
4 **Evaluation**, which describes how learning and learning activities will be assessed.

1 AIMS

Summary

The main aims of *CES* are:
- to develop the students' abilities to use and understand English.
- to broaden the students' understanding and knowledge of the world.
- to involve the students and to develop their abilities to manage their own learning.
- to support teachers in developing their own teaching abilities and understanding of language learning.

1.1 Learning English and learning about the world

At the centre of the course is the aim of developing the students' abilities to use and understand English. For the vast majority of students, however, whether of secondary or adult age, language itself *is simply not interesting enough* to command their continual attention. Many courses have thus drawn on what are seen as exciting teenage topics (pop music, fashion, discos, fast food and so on) in order to try to motivate the students. It is our view, however, that there is a much greater potential for language teaching. For secondary aged students, this period in their lives is one when they have a great hunger for knowledge, want to learn about the world and want to learn to be able to do different things for themselves. As a subject without a clearly defined 'body of knowledge' (apart from grammar, words, etc.), learning English thus presents a unique opportunity to meet this eagerness to learn by offering both a broader *educational* approach to teaching the language and a rich variety of topics from which the students can learn. It is precisely this which *CES* aims to provide.

Example: the *Topic* Units and the Themes in the Student's Book.

1.2 Student involvement

One of the keys to successful learning, however, is *involvement*. Whilst interesting topics and richer, meaningful content are very important, the vital element in learning anything is that the students feel that the learning is *theirs*, and that they feel they are a part of what goes on in the classroom. Without this, it is very difficult for the students to sustain any motivation they may have or which the teacher or course materials may try to bring. All too often, we see the results of a lack of involvement: bored, seemingly tired students, some of whom resort to misbehaviour and make teaching an uphill struggle. In *Cambridge English for Schools,* we have thus given careful thought to ways of involving the students. Throughout the course, there are points at which they can make decisions, think about what they have just done, and gradually take more responsibility for their own learning.

Examples: Unit 3, Exs. 8 and 10; Unit 5; Unit 7, Ex. 8; Unit 18, Ex. 3; Workbook Units 6, 12, 17, 22, 27 and 32.

1.3 Support for teachers

English language teaching, however, offers opportunities not only for the students to learn, but for teachers to develop their own teaching. Through the course, therefore, we aim to provide both clear guidance in using the materials and support in understanding and thinking about some key areas in language teaching. Our purpose in doing this is to assist teachers in understanding why particular ways of working in *their* classes appear to succeed or fail and to thus make their teaching a more rewarding experience for both the students and themselves.

Examples: the *A to Z of methodology*, notes on mixed-ability classes in the *Topic* and *Language focus* Units, the 'overview' sections before each Theme and Unit, and the subsequent detailed Teaching Notes.

2 SYLLABUS

> **Summary**
>
> *CES* contains four principal syllabuses: i) a language syllabus, mainly of structure, vocabulary, reading and writing; ii) an educational syllabus of educational topics and abilities; iii) a learner-involvement syllabus which requires students to make decisions about learning; iv) a teacher support syllabus which provides ideas for teaching and for classroom research.

From the outline of the aims of the course, one can see that four different syllabuses underlie the structure of *CES.* They are: i) a language development syllabus; ii) an educational syllabus; iii) a learner involvement syllabus; and iv) a teacher support syllabus.

2.1 The language development syllabus

At the heart of the language syllabus in *CES* lies a **structural progression**. The course moves, in the familiar way, from the present tenses, through to the past tenses, future tenses and so on. All of this is made explicit to the students in the *Language focus* Units, with students either being presented with explanations or being encouraged to work out their own rules for forming and using language. We have chosen to use a structural language syllabus for a number of reasons. In our view, it provides a systematic 'mapping out' which enables students to generate an infinite number of new utterances and eventually use language to express what they wish to say. It is also a familiar means of organising language which allows teachers and learners either to come to *CES* from other courses or to go on to other work. The language syllabus, however, is not a narrow 'step by step'

one. Our aim is not that students master each new structure the first time it appears but that they *notice* it, since the course returns to each language point several times with numerous opportunities to learn.

At the same time, however, the course stresses **vocabulary development** right from the start, continually recycling vocabulary items through new texts, exercises and record pages. At the end of each *Topic* Unit, the students can draw together the vocabulary they have learnt and record the meanings on a *Language Record* page. In addition, the student's Workbook contains further work on vocabulary and a *picture dictionary*.

In terms of the **'four skills'**, *CES* draws on each of the skills in as natural a way as possible. Writing, for example, may be used as a means of preparing for a spoken task; listening and reading as a basis for sharing reactions and ideas. Writing, in particular, features quite a lot in *CES* since, in our experience, used appropriately, writing can give students the chance to plan, to reflect and ask for help. Spoken, 'social English', however is also highlighted in special '*Out and about*' sections and drawn together in a short phrase book section in the *Language Records*.

In the initial stages of the course, listening is mainly treated as a means of consolidating language already presented to students, rather than as 'listening comprehension' in the traditional sense. We have approached it in this way as, in our experience, the circumstances under which many teachers teach (with classroom and outside noise, and limited audio facilities) frequently makes listening work very difficult to undertake. 'Listening comprehension' work is thus postponed until the students have developed some basic abilities in producing language and in understanding the language of the coursebook texts and of the classroom.

Examples: the *Map of CES 1*, pages 4–5; *Language Records* pages 29 and 35; *Out and about*, page 33; Workbook page 26.

2.2 The educational syllabus

In addition to the language aims of the course, *CES* also aims to make a direct contribution to the students' general educational development. The course therefore also has an *educational* syllabus which has three main aspects: *curriculum links* with other subject areas; *cross-curriculum* abilities and attitudes and *cross-cultural* topics.

In terms of *curriculum links*, the topics in *CES* have direct connections with the work the students will do in other school subjects, but in a fresh, innovative way. These links mean that students are given the opportunity to broaden their knowledge and understanding of the world and to contribute what they already know. There is therefore a natural, *real* reason for communicating and for working with the language.

Examples: *Topics* in Themes A–F in the Student's Book.

In connection with *cross-curriculum* abilities and attitudes, the course contributes in a number of different ways. Through the presentation of different kinds of texts (such as graphs, maps, diagrams and newspaper style articles) the students become familiar with understanding and presenting ideas in a variety of modes. The course also shows the students how they can gather, develop and organise their own ideas through, for example, 'brainstorming' aspects of a topic. The ability to work independently is supported through practical advice on how they can help themselves learn. Broader concerns such as health education and animal welfare also feature as topics for language work.

Examples: text presentation: Unit 4, Ex. 1; Unit 9, Ex. 6; Unit 16, Exs. 1 and 5; brainstorming: Unit 16, Ex. 2; Unit 29, Exs. 3–4; *Help yourself* Workbook Units 6, 12, 17, 22, 27, 32; Broader issues: Units 9 and 14.

The third element in the educational syllabus is *cross-cultural* awareness. The *Culture matters* Units in the Student's Book aim to develop the students' understanding of life in Britain and how this compares with their own country. In addition, numerous tasks within other Units ask the students to compare across cultures, for example, in connection with school life and climate. A further feature is the *Parcel of English* scheme, which is intended to bring students in different parts of the world into contact with each other.

Examples: *Culture matters* Units 6, 12, 17, 22, 27 and 32; Unit 3, Ex. 1; Unit 25; *Parcel of English*: Unit 8 and notes on page 18 here.

2.3 The learner-involvement syllabus

In *CES*, the direct, personal involvement of the learners plays a very important part. An important element of the course is the involvement of the students in **decisions** over *what* they will work on and *how* they will work. The intention with this, as explained earlier, is to give the students a greater sense of ownership in language learning, such that they feel that what they learn is 'theirs'.

Recognising, however, that students may not have experience in thinking about such things, the course approaches this very gradually. In each of the *Topic* Units, *Decide* tasks ask the students to make a choice over what they will do next. As the course progresses, however, students become involved in making their own exercises (and in building up an *Exercise Box* for the class) and, later in devising their own tests. In addition, **evaluation** tasks re-occur at various points in the course, asking the students to consider what they did in particular tasks (see section 4 below).

A further aspect of the course is that topics have been chosen which give the possibility for students to contribute their own **personal ideas and experience**. The *cross-curriculum* aspect of this is important, as we have said, but further examples are in relation to family life, personal memories, writing poems, and so on.

Examples: Unit 3, Ex.10; Unit 5; Unit 7, Ex.8; Unit 33, Ex. 3.

2.4 The teacher support syllabus

As was mentioned in 1.3 above, an important aim of the course is to support teachers in working with a particular class and in developing their teaching abilities. To a certain extent, any coursebook will help teachers learn more about teaching by introducing them to types of exercises and ways of approaching classroom work which they have perhaps not met before. In *CES*, however, this is taken one step further.

At the back of this Teacher's Book, there is an ***A to Z of methodology***, outlining some of the main aspects of teaching and giving practical classroom suggestions. Cross-references to this *A to Z* are given in the Teaching Notes for each Unit but we hope that teachers will consult the *A to Z* at their leisure as a means of refreshing or developing their knowledge of teaching. In addition, at the beginning of the *Language focus* Units, there are some questions to stimulate your thinking about aspects of teaching. These are followed up in the relevant *A to Z* entry with notes on *Researching the classroom*.

Additional support is also given for teaching classes of **mixed–ability** students. In the Teaching Notes for the *Topic* and *Language focus* Units, there are ideas for how to give more support for particular exercises or how to make them more demanding. For students who require further practice, there are **Supplementary worksheets** which you may photocopy.

Examples: the *A to Z of methodology*, pages 116–144; notes on 'What happened with Units …?' and *Researching the classroom* in Unit 4; photocopiable worksheets pages 153–171.

3 METHODOLOGY

Summary

Tasks in *CES* aim to encourage the students to use English creatively, not only reproductively, and to contribute their own ideas and experiences. The instructions in the Student's Book provide clear indications for both the teacher and the students. In general, 'larger' tasks are included in order to give the students more 'space' and more control over their work. Tasks allow students with different levels of ability to work on the same topic and additional support is also provided for classes with mixed abilities. Initially, an active role for the mother tongue is also suggested.

A number of aspects of *CES* come under the general heading of 'methodology' which we will briefly describe here. They are: 1) a creative approach to language learning; 2) personalisation; 3) transparency; 4) learning centredness; 5) catering for classes with mixed abilities; and 6) use of the mother tongue.

It would probably be fair to say that language teaching generally emphasises what we would call '*reproductive*' approaches to language learning. These include various forms of repetition (choral, substitution, reading aloud and so on) and other tasks where students are expected to *reproduce* the information and language presented to them (for example, traditional comprehension questions) as in the traditional 'Presentation-Practice-Production' model of teaching. There is no doubt reproductive tasks are an important part of classroom language learning. We believe, however, that if we want students to develop the ability to express what they wish to say in English, then we also need to provide tasks which encourage the students to use the language **creatively** and not simply reproductively. This means that classroom tasks need to provide opportunities for the students to contribute their own ideas, share experiences and reactions. In *CES*, therefore, we have included tasks throughout the course which aim to do this, for example, by encouraging them to give their personal opinion or ideas about something, to write short texts for other students to read, and to design their own practice exercises, without following a tightly controlled model.

Examples: the *Activity* Units: 5, 11, 16, 21, 26, 31.

Creativity as an aspect of methodology is also closely related to personalisation. By **personalisation** we mean the process of bringing about 'ownership' which we referred to earlier. This happens in two main ways in *CES*. Firstly, wherever possible, students are asked to contribute their own ideas and content (for example, accounts of personal experiences, photos, and so on). Secondly, as the course progresses, the students are brought further and further into making decisions about their learning, within the clear constraints laid down by the teacher and the coursebook. This, as we mentioned earlier, includes the various 'evaluation' tasks in the course which ask the students to think back over what they have done and how they can improve it next time, and tasks where the students have to decide what they wish to do next.

Examples: Unit 14, Exs. 1–3; Unit 24, Exs. 1–3; Unit 7, Exs. 1 and 8; Unit 9, Ex. 10.

A third aspect of the course, in terms of methodology, is what we call **transparency**. This means that it should be clear to everyone (teacher and students) what the materials are suggesting. This, we believe, is particularly important for the students, since greater learner involvement depends on understanding what is going on in the classroom. In addition, experience tells us that it is difficult – if not impossible – for many students to maintain 100% concentration 100% of the time. For this reason, the Student's Book includes full instructions for each task, such that both the teacher and the students have the same information. Initially, of course, the students' language level may mean that they are not always able to benefit from this, but as the course develops we hope that this enables them to have a clearer understanding of what they are doing and why.

Examples: the instructions for tasks in the Student's Book.

In general, *CES* includes few of the conventional 'paced' oral activities, such as drills and choral repetition, that one often finds in course materials. In contrast, the tasks in the course centre on **'learning'** (rather than 'teaching'). In addition, they are generally 'larger', in which, for example, students have to write something, read something or share ideas with a neighbour, before being called upon to produce language to the whole class. Our purpose in designing such tasks is to allow students more time to think, plan, and ask questions and thus approach language learning in a more relaxed fashion.

Examples: Unit 15, Ex. 3.2; Unit 19, Ex. 2; and the *Activity* Units.

Larger tasks also make it easier for students to respond at their own level of ability. In addition, however, *CES* includes further support for classes with **mixed levels of ability**. Some students may require further practice exercises than the ones in the Student's Book and Workbook, and for these students additional **Supplementary language worksheets** are given at the back of this Teacher's Book. We recognise, however, that using one particular unit of materials in the same way with an entire class may not always be appropriate and for this reason, the Teaching Notes for the *Topic* and *Language focus* Units include suggestions for how more support can be given to students or how the tasks can be made more demanding. The *Time to spare?* and the *Revision Box* sections also offer further support for students.

Examples: Language worksheets, pages 154–168; Teaching Notes for all *Topic* and *Language focus* Units; *Time to spare?* Units 3, 4, etc.; *Revision Box* Unit 4, etc.

A final aspect of methodology is the **use of the mother tongue**. In *CES* the mother tongue plays an important role in two main ways. Firstly, a number of tasks, particularly in the *Language focus* Units, ask the students to think about the structure of their language and to compare it with English. Secondly, as the Teaching Notes make clear, we anticipate that some of the initial tasks and the evaluation stages will take place in the mother tongue, particularly in the early stages of the course. There are a number of reasons why we have designed the course in this way.

When people are learning they always try to make sense of 'what is new' by comparing it with what they already know. This means that, whatever the teacher or the coursebook says, students *will* translate the foreign language into their own language and it is therefore best if this is done explicitly so that misconceptions can be avoided. In addition, we believe that many students feel completely powerless and lost in language classes, especially in the initial stages, and thus the use of the mother tongue can ease them into language learning. Use of the mother tongue also gives the students an opportunity to participate more fully in making decisions over their own learning.

Examples: Unit 10, Exs. 3.1 and 4.1; Unit 15, Exs. 3.1 and 4.1; *Language Record* pages.

4 EVALUATION

Summary
Evaluation of the students' learning takes the form of tests in the Workbook and student-produced tests. Evaluation also focuses on *how* the students are working, in the form of brief discussion tasks set out in the Student's Book.

As we have already suggested, evaluation plays an important part in *CES*. There are two main ways in which it does so: evaluation of how much language the students have learnt and evaluation of the actual process of learning.

In terms of **evaluation of language**, the Student's Book includes an initial test in Unit 2 and a number of self-tests in the Workbook. The Student's Book also includes some simple tests which are intended as examples for students to write their own tests. We have included student-designed tests since we feel that self-assessment is a vital part of successful language learning. Too often students view tests as a very negative experience in which someone else makes judgements over them. Making tests available to the students and involving them in designing their own class tests is intended to reduce this fear and encourage them to view tests as a potentially useful part of their learning.

Examples: Student's Book Units 18, 23 and 33; Workbook Units 7, 13 and 28.

In terms of **evaluation** of *how* the students are learning, the course includes tasks (particularly at the end of a Theme and a large *Activity*) which asks the students to think about how well they worked, the problems they had and how they might do it better next time. As suggested earlier, the purpose of doing this is to raise the students' awareness of how they are learning and to make them feel more involved in their language course and able to participate in making decisions over both what they need and would like to do.

Examples: the last exercise in the *Revision and evaluation* Units and in the *Activity* Units.

We hope that you enjoy using *Cambridge English for Schools* and that both you and your students find it a rewarding course to work with. We welcome any comments on the materials – whether negative or positive. Please write to us:

Andrew Littlejohn and Diana Hicks
c/o English Language Teaching
Cambridge University Press
The Edinburgh Building
Shaftesbury Road
Cambridge CB2 2RU
England

You can also send a fax to: ++44 1223 325984
Or you can send an e-mail message to:
aldh@cup.cam.ac.uk

Cambridge English for Schools 1 at a glance

THE STUDENT'S BOOK

The course contains six Themes.

THEME **A** **A Parcel of English**	THEME **B** **The natural world**	THEME **C** **The way we live**	THEME **D** **Planet Earth**	THEME **E** **Natural forces**	THEME **F** **Living history**

Each Theme contains five Units, with approximately the following number of lessons.

TOPIC UNIT	LANGUAGE FOCUS UNIT	ACTIVITY	CULTURE MATTERS	REVISION
3 lessons	2–3 lessons	1 lesson	1 lesson	1–2 lessons

In each Theme, there is a TOPIC Unit which focuses on different aspects of the theme. Students read, write, listen and talk about the topic. There is particular emphasis on vocabulary.

This box shows you the topic in the Unit and its links with other school subjects.

Topic In the wild

Animals and how they live; curriculum links with Biology, Zoology and Science

1 What is it?

With your neighbour, write the correct letter by each word.

☐ a kangaroo   ☐ an elephant

Names of animals
Extra practice • WB Ex. 1

Following each *Topic* Unit, there is a LANGUAGE FOCUS Unit. Here the students focus on grammar, functions and social English.

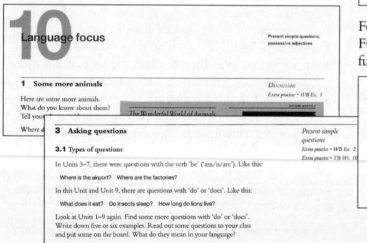

10 Language focus

Present simple questions; possessive adjectives

1 Some more animals

Here are some more animals. What do you know about them? Tell your...
Where d...

Discussion
Extra practice • WB Ex. 1

The Wonderful World of Animals

NATURE MONTHLY

3 Asking questions

3.1 Types of questions

In Units 3–7, there were questions with the verb 'be' ('am/is/are'). Like this:

Where is the airport?   Where are the factories?

In this Unit and Unit 9, there are questions with 'do' or 'does'. Like this:

What does it eat?   Do insects sleep?   How long do lions live?

Look at Units 1–9 again. Find some more questions with 'do' or 'does'. Write down five or six examples. Read out some questions to your class and put some on the board. What do they mean in your language?

Present simple questions
Extra practice • WB Ex. 2
Extra practice • TB Ws. 10

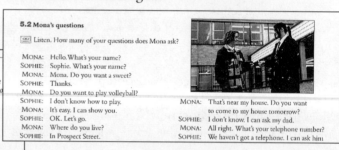

5.2 Mona's questions

Listen. How many of your questions does Mona ask?

MONA: Hello. What's your name?
SOPHIE: Sophie. What's your name?
MONA: Mona. Do you want a sweet?
SOPHIE: Thanks.
MONA: Do you want to play volleyball?
SOPHIE: I don't know how to play.
MONA: It's easy. I can show you.
SOPHIE: OK. Let's go.
MONA: Where do you live?
SOPHIE: In Prospect Street.

MONA: That's near my house. Do you want to come to my house tomorrow?
SOPHIE: I don't know. I can ask my dad.
MONA: All right. What's your telephone number?
SOPHIE: We haven't got a telephone. I can ask him

At the end of the *Topic* and *Language focus* Units there is a LANGUAGE RECORD. Here, the students can note down the meanings of the words and phrases they have learnt and complete some examples of the grammar points.

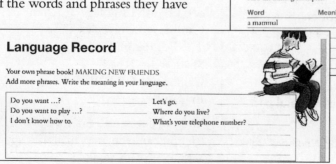

Language Record

Your own phrase book! MAKING NEW FRIENDS
Add more phrases. Write the meaning in your language.

Do you want ...?
Do you want to play ...?
I don't know how to.

Let's go.
Where do you live?
What's your telephone number?

Language Record

Write the meaning of the words in your language.
Add the missing examples.

Word	Meaning	Example
a mammal		A whale is a mammal.
		There is a bird in the tree.
		Do you like fish?
		Mammals give their babies milk.
		Insects have six legs.
		Bees are insects.

After the *Language focus* Unit, there is an ACTIVITY UNIT. This involves the students in using the language they have learnt and to work with other students to share their ideas for a larger piece of work.

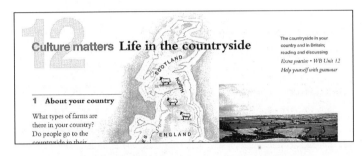

Each Theme also contains a CULTURE MATTERS Unit. This teaches the students about life in Britain and encourages them to compare it with life in their own country.

The last Unit in each Theme is REVISION AND EVALUATION. This asks the students to think about *how much* they have learned and revises the language they have covered. In some *Revision* Units they can also make a test for themselves. The last part of the Unit asks the students to think about *how* they are learning.

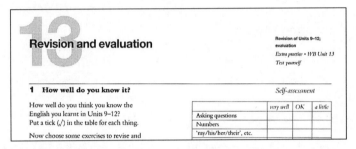

Theme A includes two special Units. These should be done as soon as possible so that students can make use of them throughout their course.

Unit 5 is an *Activity* Unit MAKING AN EXERCISE BOX. An *Exercise Box* is a collection of exercises that students can devise themselves and build for the whole class to use for homework, extra classwork or when they have time to spare. At the back of the Student's Book is a list of ideas to help them design their own practice exercises.

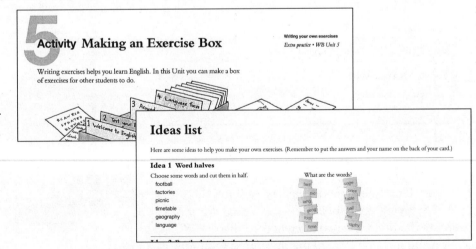

Unit 8 is A PARCEL OF ENGLISH. A *Parcel of English* is a package of work which the students produce and which describes their school, their class, where they live and so on. You can exchange parcels with another school or class and so continue to use English for genuine communication. Cambridge University Press offers a registration scheme to link *CES* classes in different countries. (See page 18 in the Teacher's Book.)

THE TEACHER'S BOOK

The Teacher's Book contains a RATIONALE for the course. This explains why the course is the way it is, the aims, the content and the methodology of the course and the way in which evaluation is treated.

Rationale

Summary

Cambridge English for Schools has been based on a reconsideration of the possibilities of English language teaching with secondary aged students and the part that teaching materials can play. It offers a new approach in which wider educational goals, student involvement, and support for teachers combine to provide a significant step forward in English language teaching. This introduction describes the *aims, syllabus,* and *methodology* of the course and the role of *evaluation*.

In many classrooms all over the world, the initial experience of learning English is one of tremendous energy and imagination, in which the students feel that a whole new world is opening up for them as they learn to express themselves in another language. It is, however, also a sad fact that for other students it is sometimes a time of failure and disappointment in which they gradually feel left behind, often resorting to misbehaviour in the classroom and a gradual rejection of the work that the teacher is doing for them. It is thus important for everybody involved in teaching adolescents to try to determine the routes to success. In the pages which

---

Some notes on the Units are included in USING *CES 1*. This also explains how the course can be lengthened or shortened.

Using *Cambridge English for Schools 1*

This section gives an overview of what the different units do and some ways in which the course can be shortened or extended.

What do the different Units do?

As the 'at a glance' section shows, there are five types of Units in the Student's Book: *Topic* Units, *Language focus* Units, *Activity* Units, *Culture matters* Units and *Revision and evaluation* Units.

Topic Units

such as some writing, a dialogue, or a poster. We anticipate these units taking approximately one fifty minute lesson each, though this may be extended. These units are important for three main reasons:
- Firstly, they provide an opportunity for the students to say what they wish to say, and thus develop the ability to express *themselves* in English.
- Secondly, extended work in small groups gives the students time to learn from each other and to ask each other questions without feeling embarrassed in front of the whole class.

There is also a SPECIAL NOTE ON *THE PARCEL OF ENGLISH* registration scheme.

Special note on 'A Parcel of English'

The first Theme in the book is called *A Parcel of English*. A *Parcel of English* is a package of work which the students produce and which describes their school, their class, where they live and so on. The actual production of this package takes place in Unit 8. (Note: if you decide not to work on the parcel, this will not affect any of your other work with the course.) Once the package has been produced there are a number of things which you can do with it:
- you can exchange the package with another class in your school

If your teaching situation makes it difficult to produce a *Parcel of English*, you can still participate in the link-up with other schools. In place of students' work, you can send photographs of your class and your school, postcards, and information about the place where you live.

It is hoped that this will enable teachers and students in different countries to make contact with each other and to develop continuing links.

See the Teacher's Notes for Unit 8 for more details.

Detailed guidance on teaching English with *CES* is provided in a handy *A TO Z OF METHODOLOGY* at the back of the book. This gives practical ideas and explanations.

An A to Z of methodology

This section contains details of some of the key areas of language teaching, particularly in relation to teaching with *CES*. You will find references to this section in the Teaching Notes for each Unit (for example: **AtoZ MOTHER TONGUE**). However, it is *not* intended that you should read all of the relevant references just to prepare one lesson or that you should read the entire section all at once! This section is for *reference*: for you to read at your leisure, as and when you wish.

Cross-references to other entries in the section are also shown in small capitals, LIKE THIS.

AtoZ AUTONOMY

What and why?   • The Workbook Cassette provides a good support for

---

9 Topic In the wild

Animals and how they live; curriculum links with Biology, Zoology and Science

1 WHAT HAPPENED WITH UNITS 3–8?

Some questions to think about before you start Unit 9.
- Look back at the content boxes for Units 3 and 4. Are there some areas where you think the students need extra practice? Do only *some* students need extra

- Is it possible for you to plan a time in the coming lessons where those students can get extra practice?
- Did it take longer or shorter than you thought to complete Units 3–8? If it took longer, are there

MIXED ABILITIES

More support can be given by
- giving students a list of questions. You can then give them a few minutes to find the answers before they ask each other in pairs.
- asking students first to ask each other questions about what animals eat, then about how long they live, then about how many hours they sleep.

The task can be made more demanding by
- asking students to make a matching exercise for other students to do. They can write eight questions and eight answers to match them to.

7 Ask about the animals

AtoZ PATTERN PRACTICE, PAIRWORK and **PRONUNCIATION**

Before beginning the exercise, draw the students' attention to the *Say it clearly!* box. Ask them to repeat each word after you. Additional words to pronounce are:
- 's' sound: cats, whales, bats, sharks, parrots.
- 'z' sound: cows, lions, dolphins, tigers, penguins, bees.
- 'iz' sound: horses, fishes, ostriches.

You could divide the class into teams for the exercise. One point for a correct question and answer. First team to 10 wins.

For every Unit, there are detailed TEACHING NOTES, giving suggested timings and notes for the exercises. It also gives cross references to the *A to Z* section and ideas on how to use the course with mixed-ability classes.

The Teacher's Book also contains NOTES ON THE WORKBOOK AND WORKBOOK ANSWERS.

Notes on the Workbook and Workbook answers

1 USING THE WORKBOOK

The Workbook and Workbook Cassette provide supplementary exercises for the work covered in the Student's Book.

As it is often difficult to do listening tasks and pronunciation work thoroughly and clearly in class, there

- Before you set Workbook exercises for homework, explain clearly what they have to do in each one. Write on the blackboard which exercises they are to do.
- After they have done the exercises, go through the answers with the class as a whole.

At the back of the Teacher's Book, there are SUPPLEMENTARY WORKSHEETS. These give additional practice in the main grammar points from the *Language focus* Units in the LANGUAGE WORKSHEETS and in pronunciation in the SAY IT CLEARLY! WORKSHEETS.

There is also a CLASS CASSETTE SET to use in the classroom.

Supplementary worksheets

This section includes 18 supplementary worksheets which you may photocopy for your classes. There are two types of worksheets.

LANGUAGE WORKSHEETS

The *Language worksheets* give extra support to those students who need further practice with the grammar areas presented in the *Language focus* Units. There are two worksheets for each *Language focus* Unit: one for each area

The *Language worksheets* are:
Ws. 2.1: 'be', 'live', personal details, social language
Ws. 2.2: 'There is/are', adjectives, negatives

THE WORKBOOK

The Workbook has the same structure as the Student's Book.

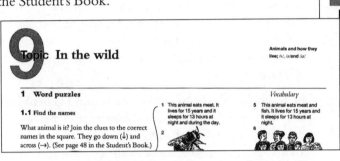

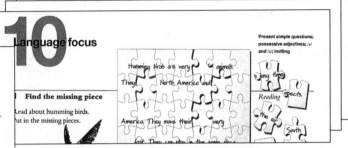

For each Theme, there is also a HELP YOURSELF Unit which shows the students how they can get more practice.

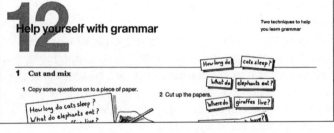

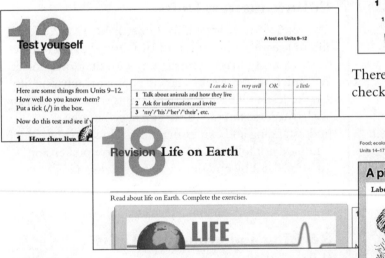

There are three TEST YOURSELF Units for students to check how much they know and three REVISION Units.

After those Units, there is a PICTURE DICTIONARY for students to record vocabulary.

At the back of the Workbook, there are the LANGUAGE SUMMARIES containing a grammar summary and a summary of the *Out and about* sections from the Student's Book.

There is also a WORKBOOK CASSETTE. This contains extra listening passages, 'open dialogues' to talk to, pronunciation exercises and the songs from the Student's Book.

Language summaries

Grammar summary		
Units 1 and 2	Negatives and questions are easy:	
'A' OR 'AN'?	**Subject + 'be' + 'not'**	**+ ...**
You use 'a' with most nouns:	I'm not (am not)	very happy today.
a book a pen a table a car	You aren't (are not)	
	She	
You use 'an' with nouns that begin with a vowel	He isn't (is not)	here.
	It	

Using *Cambridge English for Schools 1*

This section gives an overview of what the different Units do and some ways in which the course can be shortened or extended.

What do the different Units do?

As the 'at a glance' section shows, there are five types of Units in the Student's Book: *Topic* Units, *Language focus* Units, *Activity* Units, *Culture matters* Units and *Revision and evaluation* Units.

Topic Units

In the six *Topic* Units (Units 3, 9, 14, 19, 24, 29), the focus is on an aspect of the Theme, each one taking, very approximately, three fifty minute lessons. The intention with the *Topic* Units is to stimulate the students' ideas and develop their understanding and knowledge of the Theme. The focus is not on language itself but on using language to understand and express ideas. While the students work on the *Topic* Units, we anticipate that they will be trying to use language they have not yet fully learnt or which they have only a hazy idea. The teacher's role in this case would be to help the students to express their ideas (e.g. by explaining, rephrasing, supplying vocabulary as needed, translating etc.). The *accuracy* of the students' language is thus not of vital concern here. The important point to get across to the students is that they *can* be 'English language users'.

Language focus Units

In the six *Language focus* Units (Units 4, 10, 15, 20, 25, 30), the focus moves from the topic to the language itself. We anticipate these Units taking approximately two 50 minute lessons each. In these Units, the students have the opportunity to look closely at what they have been reading about or saying (or trying to say). The focus is thus on the students' understanding of how the language works and, as far as is possible, to 'get it right' in their own speech or writing. Although the emphasis is on accuracy in these Units, we do not expect students to learn everything first time: language learning is a slow process. However, *CES* has an open structure such that the same language will reappear in later Units. The *Language Record* page after the *Language focus* Units is designed to focus the students' understanding.

Activity Units

In the six *Activity* Units (Units 5, 11, 16, 21, 26, 31), the students work together to produce a larger piece of work

such as some writing, a dialogue, or a poster. We anticipate these Units taking approximately one fifty minute lesson each, though this may be extended. These Units are important for three main reasons:

- Firstly, they provide an opportunity for the students to say what they wish to say, and thus develop the ability to express *themselves* in English.
- Secondly, extended work in small groups gives the students time to learn from each other and to ask each other questions without feeling embarrassed in front of the whole class.
- Thirdly, they strengthen the social element of the lesson.

The teacher's role during this work is thus likely to be one of encouraging and supporting the students by suggesting ideas rather than fully directing them. The activities encourage the use of both accurate and fluent language. Once students have gathered together some ideas and produced a draft of their work, they can be asked to check it for spelling, grammar, and vocabulary before you look at it.

Culture matters Units

The six *Culture matters* Units (Units 6, 12, 17, 22, 27, 32) aim to present some aspects of Britain and to encourage the students to make comparisons with their own society. We anticipate these Units taking approximately one fifty minute lesson. The aim in these Units is thus, once again, not on accuracy in the use of language but on understanding and expressing ideas. Thus the texts in the Units are not followed by traditional 'comprehension questions' but by questions which require an understanding of the texts by asking the students what *they* think.

Revision and evaluation Units

In the six *Revision and evaluation* Units (Units 7, 13, 18, 23, 28, 33), the focus moves back to the language itself. We anticipate these Units taking one or two fifty minute lessons, depending on how much revision the students require. The *Revision and evaluation* Units offer the students another chance to see and learn the language that has been covered in the preceding Units. Each Unit opens by asking the students to self-assess what they have learned. Three Units (Units 7, 13, 28) then provide revision exercises which you can either direct them to do or let them choose, depending on where you think they need further work. Returning to the self-assessment *after* they have done the revision exercises should help them to see if their own estimations are correct. The other three revision Units (Units 18, 23 and 33) involve the students in designing part of a test for the whole class. Test-writing is a very effective way of developing the students' understanding for three main reasons:

- Firstly, it requires them to do some investigation, to focus carefully on the structure of the language and to use it.
- Secondly, it also helps to break down the fear of tests which many students have and instead to see tests as an opportunity to find out how much they know.
- Thirdly, it helps to integrate the class as it provides a means of students challenging each other.

The *evaluation* part of these Units gives the students an opportunity to look back at the Units in the Theme and to consider the level of difficulty of the tasks. This will provide useful feedback for you.

(For notes on the Workbook Units see page 145.)

How can the course be extended or shortened?

Level 1 is intended to provide material for about 80–100 classroom hours. However, the open and flexible design makes it relatively straightforward to shorten or extend the course. Each Unit is self-contained and there is no continuing story-line which forces you to do particular Units. Although the Units are placed in a logical order, it is possible to omit particular Units or change the order for your particular classes. Bearing in mind that a shorter course will not be able to take full advantage of all that *CES* contains, it is possible to **shorten** the course in the following ways:

- omit the *Extension* section of Unit 2, if the test in Unit 2 shows the students do not need to do it. If you are short of class time, the students can do all or part of the *Extension* at home.
- omit some of the *Activity* Units.
- omit the *Revision* Units 18, 23, and 33 (or ask the students to do them at home).
- omit the *Culture matters* Units.
- omit Theme A if your students already know the language which it covers.
- omit some of the exercises in each of the *Topic* and *Language focus* Units.

In terms of *extending* the course, the following components in the course provide enormous potential for extended work:

- the *Parcel of English*
- the *Exercise Box*
- all the *Activity* Units
- student test-writing
- *Out and about* sections.

In addition, the topic-based nature of the course provides an ideal basis for additional project work, supplementary reading, investigations, drama etc. and for working with other subject teachers. The *A to Z of methodology* gives many practical suggestions in this respect.

Special note on 'A Parcel of English'

The first Theme in the book is called *A Parcel of English*. A *Parcel of English* is a package of work which the students produce and which describes their school, their class, where they live and so on. The actual production of this package takes place in Unit 8. (Note: if you decide not to work on the parcel, this will not affect any of your other work with the course.) Once the package has been produced there are a number of things which you can do with it:

- you can exchange the package with another class in your school.
- you can exchange it with another school in your area.
- you can put it on display in your classroom.
  or
- you can send it to another class in another country.

Sending the Parcel to another country: what to do

The *Parcel of English* provides an ideal way to build contacts in different parts of the world and adds an extra dimension to *Cambridge English for Schools*. To help in this, Cambridge University Press offers a registration scheme to link schools together. Here's what to do:

1 Complete the **registration card** contained in this Teacher's Book (or if it has already been used, copy the form from the inside front cover).
2 Post this card to Cambridge University Press. From Cambridge, you will receive the name and address of a class in a different country, which is also working with *Cambridge English for Schools 1*.
3 Once your parcel is complete, you can then send it (or a copy) to the other school. You should similarly receive a parcel in return. (You can, of course, continue your correspondence with the other teacher and class.)

If your teaching situation makes it difficult to produce a *Parcel of English*, you can still participate in the link-up with other schools. In place of students' work, you can send photographs of your class and your school, postcards, and information about the place where you live.

It is hoped that this will enable teachers and students in different countries to make contact with each other and to develop continuing links.

See the Teacher's Notes for Unit 8 for more details.

Important Notes

1 Once you have received the name and address of the other teacher and school, please contact them at once to confirm that you will be sending them a *Parcel of English*.
2 *Please* ensure that you complete your side of the arrangement and that you reply to the letters and parcels that you receive. Students and teachers put a great deal of effort into producing the parcels and eagerly await a reply.
3 After registering, please contact the other school directly **not** Cambridge University Press. Unfortunately, the Press does not have sufficient staff to handle individual queries, problems, etc.

Good luck!

Welcome to *Cambridge English for Schools 1*

THE COVER PAGE

Each Theme in the course has a cover page to raise the students' interest and to give them an overview of what they will be learning. The first cover page, however, refers to the whole book. It aims to introduce the students to the topics covered in the Units and to 'invite' them into learning English.

Here is a suggested procedure for using the cover page. Note that Exercise 6 of Unit 1 asks the students to carry out this task.

Suggested time: 15 minutes

1 Allow them a few minutes to look through their book. They can do this with their neighbour.
2 Next, with the students, look through the pictures on the cover page. Tell them that these are *some* of the things they will be learning about *while* they are learning English. Ask them what they think the pictures are about.
3 Working in pairs, ask them to look through the book and to find the correct Unit for each picture. As you go through their answers, look at the relevant Unit with them.

Answers			
Stars:	Unit 19	African school:	Unit 3
Cavepeople:	Unit 29	Exercise Box:	Unit 5
Food basket:	Unit 14	Shop:	Unit 4
Chinese dragon:	Unit 32	Dolphin:	Unit 9
Collapsing hotel:	Unit 22		

What's in *Cambridge English for Schools 1*?

The activities in the 'What's in …' section help your students get to know the Student's Book and the Workbook before you start using the course fully. (See also see the 'at a glance' section in this Teacher's Book.) The students can discover the main Themes of the books and find out about the different kinds of Units. Note that Exercise 6 of Unit 1 asks the students to do these exercises at that point.

What you need

The Class Cassette for Exercise 7; the students need their Student's Book and Workbook.

1 Six Themes

Answers
Theme A: A Parcel of English;   Theme B: The natural world;
Theme C: The way we live;   Theme E: Natural forces;
Theme F: Living history.
Missing Theme: Planet Earth (Theme D).

2 The Themes

Allow students time to look through the book. Encourage them to look at the material at the front and the back of the book.

3 The Units

Answers
Missing numbers and words:
Line 1 29
Line 2 15
Line 3 'Activity'
Line 4 27
Line 5 'Revision'

Guidelines for Answers
The *Topic* Unit is about the subject of the Theme. The *Language focus* Unit presents new language and grammar. The *Activity* Unit gives an opportunity for the students to produce a larger piece of creative work. The *Culture matters* Units are about life in Britain and the *Revision and evaluation* Unit revises the vocabulary and grammar of the Theme.

4 Inside the Workbook

Allow students some time to look through their Workbook and to see the organisation of the book and to make comparisons with the Student's Book.

5 The Workbook Units

Answers
Unit 6: Help yourself with spelling (1);   Unit 12: Help yourself with grammar;   Unit 17: Help yourself with vocabulary;   Unit 22: Help yourself with spelling (2);   Unit 27: Help yourself with pronunciation;   Unit 32: Help yourself with fluency.

6 At the back

Answer
The *Language summaries* (a grammar summary and a summary of *Out and about with English*).

7 Listen to the page numbers 🔲

The Workbook and Class Cassettes always tell you which book and which page the recording comes from. This exercise gives the students practice in finding their way around with the cassette.

Answers/Tapescript
a Student's Book page 24 is Unit 3.
b Student's Book page 72 is Unit 15.
c Workbook page 21 is Unit 7.
d Workbook page 58 is Unit 21.
e Student's Book page 122 is Unit 28.
f Workbook page 84 is Unit 32.

1 Welcome to English!

SPECIAL NOTE ON UNITS 1 AND 2

Units 1 and 2 aim to provide a flexible starting point for the course, depending on your students' level of ability. Decide which of the following statements is true for you. You can then do the relevant parts.

'My students have recently completed the Starter level of the course.'
→ Move straight to Unit 3.

'They have studied English before and they have a good basic knowledge, including the verb 'be', 'have got', some nouns, verbs and adjectives in English.'
→ Do Unit 1 and then move to Unit 3.

'Some of my students know nothing, some of them know a little and some of them know quite a lot.'
→ Do Unit 1 and then the test in Unit 2 to find out who knows what! The weaker students can then do the all the Extension exercises and the Supplementary worksheets (see page 153). The better students can do some of the Extension exercises.

'I am not sure how much my students know.'
→ Do Unit 1 and then the test in Unit 2. Depending on the results, do all or some of the Extension exercises and Supplementary worksheets or move straight to Unit 3.

'I am certain that my students know nothing.'
→ The Starter level of the course will be more appropriate for your students.

TEACHING NOTES FOR UNIT 1

Overview of the Unit

Unit 1 aims to introduce the students to the course and to help you see how much they already know. It also teaches the students to say something about themselves, some classroom phrases, the numbers and takes the students on a 'guided tour' of their book.

> **Important!** If your students have just completed the Starter level of this course, they should not need to do Units 1 and 2.

Timing

Below are some suggested timings (in minutes) for each step. *These are only a rough guide and they may vary considerably from class to class.* You can note down your revised timings here as you go through the Unit and show how you think you will divide the material into lessons.

Important! The timings are our estimations for doing the exercises. You will need to allow extra time for settling the students down to work and moving them from one activity to another.

1	You know a lot of English!	15
2	A puzzle	10
3	Hello!	10
4	Talk about yourself	10
5	Make a poster	20
6	Find out about your book	25
7	Some useful phrases	10
8	What's the number?	15
9	Sing a song!	10
10	Your Language Record	10

What you need

The Class Cassette is needed for Exercises 3, 6 and 9 and, optionally, for Exercises 4, 7 and 8.

Blank sheets of A5 (half A4) paper, enough for one per student plus some spare (if possible coloured) for Exercise 5.

Workbook

The Workbook Unit 1 contains exercises to practise:

- Exercise 1: vocabulary (doing and making a puzzle).
- Exercise 2: reading.
- Exercise 3: writing.
- Exercise 4: speaking.
- Exercise 5: useful social phrases.
- Exercise 6: pronunciation /iːn/ and /iː/ in numbers.
- Exercise 7: singing a song in English.

For additional notes on the use of the Workbook and Workbook answers see page 145.

Guidelines

A word **LIKE THIS** with the symbol **AtoZ** shows that you can find more information in the *A to Z of methodology* (pages 116–144), for example, **AtoZ** **MOTHER TONGUE**. The *A to Z* is for you to read as you wish. You do not need to read all the sections referred to just to prepare one lesson!

A symbol like this 🔲 means that you need the cassette.

Cross-references to the Workbook are shown after the exercise notes like this:

- **WB Ex. 1: a vocabulary exercise.**

1   You know a lot of English!

The purpose of this exercise is to show the students that they already know a lot of English and to give them a sense of achievement.

Look through the pictures with the students and ask what each one is in English. Either you or a student can put the word on the board.

You can then ask for other words or phrases that they can say. Ask what they mean in their mother tongue.

Answers					
1	taxi	7	disk	13	television
2	cassette	8	sandwich	14	football
3	goal	9	chocolate	15	jet
4	jeans	10	tennis	16	zero
5	video	11	camping	17	telephone
6	radio	12	compact disc		

- **WB Ex. 1.1: a vocabulary exercise.**

2   A puzzle

The students can do this by themselves or in pairs. Give them a few minutes to do the puzzle before you go through the answers.

- **WB Ex. 1.2: make a vocabulary puzzle.**

3   Hello! 🔲

AtoZ LISTENING

Look through the pictures and ask the students what James and Martha are saying in each picture. (They can reply in their mother tongue or, if they can, in English.)

Next, play the recording all the way through.

For the second part (Who is who?), the students have to listen for the last sentence which each person says. Play the cassette at least twice so that everybody has a chance to find the answers.

Answers
James can swim very well. Martha can play football very well. Usha can draw very well. Emma can sing very well. Ali can run very well.

🔲 **TAPESCRIPT**

James:	My name is James. I'm 12 years old. I live in Hill Road. I can swim very well.
Martha:	Hello! My name is Martha. I'm 13 years old. I live in Park Road. I can play football very well.
Usha:	Hello! My name's Usha. I'm 11 years old. I can draw very well.
Emma:	Hello! My name's Emma. I'm 12 years old. I can sing very well.
Ali:	Hello! My name's Ali. I'm 10 years old. I can run very well.

- **WB Ex. 2: an exercise to practise introductions.**

4 Talk about yourself 📼

The students can now talk about themselves in a similar way. Read aloud the example sentences, the numbers and the phrases, or, if you prefer, play the cassette. Then, ask individual students to say a sentence about themselves.

- **WB Ex. 3: a writing exercise to practise describing a person.**

5 Make a poster

AtoZ POSTERS

This exercise reinforces the oral activity in Exercises 3 and 4. Students can draw their pictures and write about themselves on a piece of paper. You can then put them all on a bigger piece of paper and put it on the wall.

Alternatively, you can ask the students to draw their picture at home, before the next lesson.

6 Find out about your book 📼

See the notes on pages 19 and 20.

7 Some useful phrases 📼

Read each sentence aloud or, if you prefer, play the cassette. Ask the students if they know what the phrases mean in their language. Get them to write the phrases in their exercise books. Then ask the students to use the phrases to ask you questions.

- **WB Exs. 4 and 5: practice with useful phrases in writing and speaking.**

8 What's the number? 📼

AtoZ PATTERN PRACTICE

You could start by writing some numbers between 1 and 20 on the board to find out if they can tell you what they are called. Alternatively, say some numbers in English and ask the students to write them down ('seven' – 7, etc.). If

necessary, read the numbers aloud or play the cassette and get the students to repeat some of them. Emphasise the '-een' ending.

For the second part, you can draw a plan of the classroom on the board and number the chairs randomly with numbers between 1 and 100. Ask the students 'Who's in chair …?' a few times before you put them in pairs to practise.

- **WB Ex. 6: pronunciation practice with /iːn/ and /iː/.**

9 Sing a song! I'm so happy 📼

AtoZ SONGS

Play the cassette first and ask the students to sing along with it. You could then sing it again without the cassette. All the songs on the Class Cassette are also recorded on the Workbook Cassette. You could ask students to listen to the songs at home before you sing them in class.

- **WB Ex. 7: sing a song.**

10 Your Language Record

AtoZ LANGUAGE RECORD

There are *Language Records* after each *Topic* and *Language focus* Unit in the book. These give the students a summary and an easy way to refresh their memory. After the *Topic* Units, the *Language Record* summarises new vocabulary. After the *Language focus* Units, the *Language Record* summarises the grammar, provides some useful phrases and a *Revision Box*. Later, the students can complete the *Language Records* at home, but it is better to do the first *Language Records* in class.

Read through the words in the vocabulary list and the phrases and ask the students what each one means. Tell them to write the meaning in their language.

Test your English Around the English-speaking world

TEACHING NOTES FOR UNIT 2

Overview of the Unit

This Unit consists of a test, a photocopiable Student's Answer Sheet and a Teacher's Answer Sheet. The test will give you a good idea of what English your students already know so that you can decide whether to work on the **optional** Extension exercises or move straight to Unit 3. (See Scoring, below.)

The test is based on the idea of a trip around the world. The Extension section provides optional revision work in the form of 'Stopovers' at different places around the world. The test and the Extension section cover the following grammar and social language:

1 'To be'
2 Personal details
3 Personal subject pronouns
4 'Social' language
5 'There is/are'
6 Adjectives
7 Negatives
8 'have got' and 'has got'

Workbook

There are Workbook exercises to parallel each section of the Extension.

Guidelines for the test

Timing

The test is designed to last for one lesson. Let the students work at their own pace as much as possible. Students who finish early can perhaps be given a short written quiz in their mother tongue of things to find in their Student's Book (photographs, people, places, etc.).

Scoring

The total number of marks is 35, one mark for each answer.

When you have the results there are three ways you can go:

1 If all your students get 25–35 correct answers move straight on to Unit 3. They can do the Unit 2 Workbook exercises as revision.
2 If most of your students get 20–25 correct answers look at the sections on the test where they made errors, then put the students into groups to work on the appropriate 'Stopovers' sections in the Extension.
3 If most of your students get less than 20 correct answers work through all the 'Stopover' sections in the Extension. There are further exercises on the Supplementary language worksheets on pages 154–156.

What you need

Before you begin, make one copy of this answer sheet for each student. The test itself is in their Student's Book but it will be easier for you to mark if their answers are on a separate sheet. Before they begin the test, explain clearly what they have to do.

Name: .... Date: ....

Class: ....

Look at the test in your book. Put a circle around the answer here. For example:

a are   **b** am   **c** (is)

1 London to Dublin by boat

1 a are **b** am **c** is   **2 a** are **b** am **c** is   **3 a** are **b** am **c** is   **4 a** are **b** am **c** is

2 Dublin to New York by plane

> **JFK Airport Arrival Card**
>
> Name: ....   First Language: ....
>
> Address: ....   Age: ....
>
> ....   Colour of hair: ....
>
> Telephone number: ....   Colour of eyes: ....

3 New York to Vancouver by train

1 a you **b** they **c** it   **2 a** It **b** He **c** We   **3 a** it **b** he **c** she   **4 a** he **b** they **c** it

4 Vancouver to Sydney by submarine

1 a Fine, thanks.   **2 a** Peter Brown.   **3 a** Peter Brown.   **4 a** It's cold.
   b I'm Anna.   **b** Sydney.   **b** Vancouver.   **b** It's Tuesday.
   c I'm 12.   **c** I'm from Brazil.   **c** No, thanks.   **c** It's 4 o'clock.

5 Sydney to Perth by bus

1 a Are there   **2 a** Is there   **3 a** Is there   **4 a** Is there
   b There are   **b** There is   **b** There are   **b** There is
   c There is   **c** There are   **c** Are there   **c** There are

6 Perth to Calcutta by ship

1 a It's a big ship.   **b** It's a small ship.   **c** It's a fat ship.
2 a Yes, it's modern music.   **b** Yes, it's old music.   **c** Yes, it's very cold music.
3 a He's very green.   **b** He's very long.   **c** He's very fat.
4 a Yes, it's very cold.   **b** Yes, it's very hot.   **c** Yes, it's very bad.

7 Calcutta to Karachi by car

1 a I haven't got a car.   **b** I'm not a car.   **c** This isn't a car.
2 a There isn't a house.   **b** Here, it isn't a house.   **c** I haven't got a house.
3 a He isn't old.   **b** We don't swim.   **c** I'm not rich.
4 a He isn't a dog.   **b** I can't find my dog.   **c** He doesn't sleep.

8 Karachi to London by helicopter

1 Anna and Susan ....

2 Leo ....

3 Steven and Jack ....

4 Steven ....

Test your English: Teacher's Answer Sheet

Total 35 marks

1 London to Dublin by boat

1 **c** is   2 **b** am   3 **c** is   4 **a** are

2 Dublin to New York by plane

1 mark for each meaningful reply. (Ignore spelling mistakes.)
(Total: 7 marks)

3 New York to Vancouver by train

1 **a** you   2 **c** We   3 **a** it   4 **b** they

4 Vancouver to Sydney by submarine

1 **a** Fine, thanks.   2 **b** Singapore   3 **a** Peter Brown.   4 **c** It's 4 o'clock.

5 Sydney to Perth by bus

1 **b** Are there   2 **b** There is   3 **c** Is there   4 **c** There are

6 Perth to Calcutta by ship

1 **a** It's a big ship.   2 **a** Yes, it's modern music.   3 **c** He's very fat.   4 **b** Yes, it's very hot.

7 Calcutta to Karachi by car

1 **a** I haven't got a car.   2 **c** I haven't got a house.   3 **c** I'm not rich.   4 **b** I can't find my dog.

8 Karachi to London by helicopter

1 Anna and Susan have got the tickets.
2 Leo has got a guitar.
3 Steven and Jack have got a camera.
4 Steven has got a hat.
One mark for each sentence. Ignore spelling mistakes.
(Total: 4 marks)

Extension Around the world again

Optional revision exercises covering: 'To be'; personal details; 'social' language; 'have/has got'; 'there is/are'; negatives; adjectives; 'It is ...'; 'They speak ...'

To help you decide if your students need to do the *Extension* section, first correct the test and then look back at *Scoring* on page 24.

If most of the class gained less than 25 points, work on the *Extension* before starting Unit 3. Look at the sections in the test where the students were weakest. If possible, group together the students who seemed weakest in one area. Each section is a 'Stopover' in a different country and covers a particular language area. Some of the students may not need to do all the sections.

Timing

Once again, these times are only a rough guide. You can note down any revised timings here.

1	You're in England. Get ready to go!	
1.1	Play a game to go around the world!	5
1.2	Meet Martin Wilson	10
1.3	In Liverpool	10
2	Stopover in America!	
2.1	Martin Wilson arrives in New York	10
2.2	Your personal information	10
2.3	Martin telephones his friends	10
3	Stopover in Australia!	
3.1	Martin sends his family a postcard	5
3.2	Write part of Martin's postcard	10
3.3	A postcard of your town	15
4	Stopover in India!	
4.1	India is very different from Australia	15
4.2	Is it true?	15
5	Stopover in Pakistan!	
5.1	Meet some of Martin's friends in Pakistan	10
5.2	Describe yourself	10
5.3	Arrrrgh!	15
6	Welcome back to London!	
6.1	Other places and other languages	15
6.2	Brasília has got a population of 1 million people	10
6.3	Write part of an encyclopaedia!	15
7	Your Language Record	10

What you need

Class Cassette for Exercises 1.2, 2.1, 2.3, 5.1, and 6.2. Some postcards of their town for Exercise 3.3 (optional).

Supplementary worksheets

There are supplementary worksheets on each language area covered in the 'Stopover' sections. These are intended for particular students that need extra practice. See pages 17–21 in the Student's Book.

Workbook

The *Extension* Workbook Unit contains exercises to practise:

- Exercise 1.1: the verb 'to be'.
- Exercise 1.2: writing/speaking.
- Exercise 2.1: writing/speaking.
- Exercise 2.2: writing personal information.
- Exercise 3.1: reading ('there is/are').
- Exercise 3.2: writing about your town.
- Exercise 4.1: true or false (negatives).
- Exercise 4.2: writing negative sentences.
- Exercise 5.1: writing and speaking ('have/has got').
- Exercise 5.2: writing a description of a person.
- Exercise 6.1: listening ('to be', 'have/has got').
- Exercise 6.2: writing about cities.

Guidelines

1 You're in England. Get ready to go!

1.1 Play a game to go around the world!

AtoZ GAMES and **PHYSICAL MOVEMENT**
The purpose of this exercise is to give the students direct physical involvement with English, to reinforce vocabulary from the test and to practise listening skills.

Give students time to look at the pictures and check that they understand the words underneath. Let them practise the movements for each picture first. Then ask some students to mime some actions. The other students can then call out 'in a car', 'on a train' etc. as appropriate. Now explain in mother tongue that if you say 'YOU

ARE on a plane / in a car etc.' they must do the action. But if you say 'She/He is on a plane / in a car etc.' they must NOT do the action.

- **WB Ex. 1.1:** an exercise to practise the verb 'to be'. Language worksheet 2.1 gives further practice with 'be'.

1.2 Meet Martin Wilson 📼

Explain, in the mother tongue, that Martin Wilson is going around the world. Students read the sentences in the speech bubbles and listen to the cassette. Students can work alone or in pairs to write similar sentences about themselves. Let them say these to their partner or to the class.

- **WB Ex. 1.2:** an exercise to practise writing/speaking in an open dialogue.

1.3 In Liverpool

A to Z READING and WRITING

Students read the text. Ask them for some information about their town. Put the main points on the board. Students can work alone or in pairs to write some sentences about their town. Encourage the students to show their work to each other and note the differences.

2 Stopover in America!

2.1 Martin Wilson arrives in New York 📼

A to Z LISTENING

Give the students time to look at the card first. Play the cassette all the way through once and then with pauses so that they have time to fill in the details. Get them to check their answers with their partner.

📼 **TAPESCRIPT**

US Officer:	Welcome to New York.
Martin:	Thank you.
US Officer:	Can you tell me your name please?
Martin:	Martin Wilson.
US Officer:	And your address at home?
Martin:	25 Long Street, Liverpool.
US Officer:	And your telephone number?
Martin:	In New York?
US Officer:	No, at home.
Martin:	846732.
US Officer:	How old are you, Martin?
Martin:	I'm 12.
US Officer:	OK. And your first language is …?
Martin:	English.
US Officer:	Are your eyes blue or green?
Martin:	Green.
US Officer:	Your hair is black.
Martin:	Yes.
US Officer:	Thank you. Have a nice day …

- **WB Ex. 2.1:** an exercise to practise writing and speaking in an open dialogue.

2.2 Your personal information

A to Z PAIRWORK, MONITORING AND GUIDING

Explain that the students will be making a dialogue with their partner. Go through the phrases given under the card and then ask one student as an example. Tell them that one student plays the part of the Immigration Officer and asks questions and writes the information on the card. They then change parts. Go round and give help where necessary. When the students are ready, invite some pairs to act their dialogue for the class. If a pair does not want to speak in front of the class, do not force them.

- **WB Ex. 2.2:** an exercise to write about personal information; also, Language worksheet 2.1 gives further practice on personal details.

2.3 Martin telephones his friends 📼

A to Z LISTENING, PAIRWORK

Let students read the dialogue first and then listen to it on the cassette. Students can follow the dialogue in their books. Before practising the dialogue, ask students to suggest other cities and countries. Write them on the board. Students then work in pairs (you may want them to work in different pairs from Exercise 2.2) to practise the dialogue about different countries.

3 Stopover in Australia!

3.1 Martin sends his family a postcard

A to Z SPEAKING

Allow students time to look at the postcard. Ask students to label the postcard (in pairs or alone). Students then tell the class what they can see in the picture using the adjectives and phrases given. Write some of the sentences on the board for help with Exercise 3.2.

- **WB Ex. 3.1:** an exercise to practise reading and writing using 'there is/are'. Language worksheet 2.2 gives further practice with 'there is/are' and adjectives.

3.2 Write part of Martin's postcard

A to Z WRITING

Students can work in pairs or alone. Encourage them to look at each other's writing.

- **WB Ex. 3.2:** an exercise to practise writing about your town.

3.3 A postcard of your town

A to Z WRITING, MONITORING AND GUIDING

You can set this as a homework exercise or alternatively ask them to bring in some cards. As preparation, start by asking them about their town. Write some key words and phrases on the board. You could make a **POSTER** of their work with the postcards.

4 Stopover in India!

4.1 India is very different from Australia!

AtoZ READING, BRAINSTORMING, WRITING

Students read the text about India. Ask them to suggest some differences between India and Australia (e.g.: capital, languages, animals, location). In pairs, students write some negative sentences about Australia following the model. Students can compare their sentences when they have finished and then read them out. Insist on a clear pronunciation of '-n't'.

Possible sentences
1 The capital of Australia isn't New Delhi. It is Canberra.
2 There aren't 16 official languages in Australia. There is one official language – English.
3 Australia has not got tigers and lions. It has got kangaroos and koala bears.
4 Australia isn't in the Northern hemisphere. It is in the Southern hemisphere.
5 Australia isn't near China and Pakistan. It is near New Zealand.

• **WB Ex. 4.1:** an exercise to practise negatives.

4.2 Is it true?

AtoZ WRITING, SPEAKING, MONITORING AND GUIDING

Students work with a partner. Each pair writes 4 negative sentences about their town or country. Then, divide the class into two teams (A and B). Explain the 'game' to the students. Each team takes it in turns to say one sentence to the other team. The other team must reply 'True' or 'False'. The first team to get 10 correct answers is the winner. Keep a score on the board. Insist on the correct pronunciation of '-n't'.

• **WB Ex. 4.2:** an exercise to practise writing negative sentences. Language worksheet 2.2 gives further practice on negatives.

5 Stopover in Pakistan!

5.1 Meet some of Martin's friends in Pakistan

AtoZ LISTENING

Read through the words under the pictures and then ask the students what type of hair some of the people in the class have got. You can ask two types of question: 'What type of hair has Ali got?' 'Who's got short straight hair?'

Then ask the students to read the three short texts and match them to the pictures. To check their answers, you can either play the cassette or read it aloud.

Answers
From left to right, the texts correspond to pictures 3, 1 and 2. The missing description is for picture 4: Jane has got long, straight hair and blue eyes.

TAPESCRIPT
Ali is 11 years old. He's got short, curly hair and green eyes. James is 12 years old. He's got short, straight hair and brown eyes. Fatma and Muneera are 13 years old. They've got short, curly hair and brown eyes.

• **WB Ex. 5.1:** an exercise to practise writing and speaking in an open dialogue. Language worksheet 2.3 gives further practice with 'have/has got'.

5.2 Describe yourself

AtoZ GROUPWORK, MONITORING AND GUIDING

Ask some of the students to describe themselves, then put them in groups to tell each other. After 5–10 minutes, stop them and ask some students to describe another student. Insist on clear pronunciation (see *Say it clearly!*). Then get the students to continue in the same way in their groups.

• **WB Ex. 5.2:** an exercise to practise writing a description. See also Language worksheet 2.3.

5.3 Arrrrgh!

AtoZ SPEAKING, PAIRWORK

Read the instructions to the students, translating where necessary. Then give an example to the students – they have to guess which monster you are talking about. For example:

'It's got curly eyes, long straight green hair and blue eyes.'

Ask one or two students to describe a monster and then get them to continue in their groups.

6 Welcome back to London!

6.1 Other places and other languages

AtoZ SPEAKING, PAIRWORK

Explain to the students that they must join up the name of the country, with the name of the appropriate language. They do this in pairs if they want to.

Students work in pairs and ask each other questions. Go round and give help where necessary. Ask them for the names of some more countries, cities and languages and put them on the board. They can use these to extend their dialogues.

Answers
1 Brasília – Brazil – Bom dia!
2 Madrid – Spain – ¡Hola!
3 Tokyo – Japan – こんにちわ
4 Rome – Italy – Ciao!
5 Paris – France – Bonjour !

• **WB Ex. 6.1:** a listening exercise using 'be' and 'have/has got'.

6.2 Brasília has got a population of 1 million people 🔲

AtoZ **PAIRWORK**

Let students look at the chart first. Explain that the cassette will give the population figures for the cities. They work in pairs; one chooses column A, one chooses column B and they listen for their own information on the cassette.

Answers

List A: Brasília 1 million;   Madrid 3 million;
   Tokyo 11 million.
List B: Rome 3 million;   Mexico City 20 million;
   Paris 2 million.

🔲 **TAPESCRIPT**

Rome is in Italy. It has got a population of 3 million people. Tokyo is in Japan. It has got a population of 11 million people. Paris is in France. It has got a population of 2 million people. Brasília is in Brazil. It has got a population of 1 million people. Madrid is in Spain. It has got a population of 3 million people. Mexico City is in Mexico. It has got a population of 20 million people.

- **WB Ex. 6.2: an exercise to practise writing about cities.**

6.3 Write part of an encyclopaedia!

Give students time to look at the encyclopaedia pages and to read the sentences about Brasília. In pairs they choose three of the cities and write sentences about them. Some students may want to read out their sentences to the class. Ask them to write some similar sentences about some cities in their country.

7 Your Language Record
AtoZ **LANGUAGE RECORD**

Theme A
A Parcel of English

OVERVIEW OF THE THEME

Theme A, 'A Parcel of English', focuses on two important aspects in the *Topic* Unit and *Language focus*: the school where the students go and the area where they live. Unit 5 is the first *Activity* Unit of the book and asks the students to make their own *Exercise Box* to be used in the classroom for the rest of the year. Unit 6, *Culture matters* looks at different kinds of towns in Great Britain. Unit 7 provides revision activities to practise the language covered in Units 3–5. Unit 8 is *A Parcel of English* (see further details on page 18). The Theme provides cross-curricular links with Geography, Social Studies and Maths.

In Units 3 and 4, students are introduced to the Present simple negative and 'there is/are' and they learn the names of school subjects and places in a town. In the *Out and about* section (Unit 4) they practise phrases connected with shopping.

Using the cover page

Suggested time for the cover page: 10 minutes

The cover page visually summarises the Theme and raises the students' interest in the next six Units. Allow time for the students to look closely at the pictures and the Units which follow.

Students can work alone or in pairs to answer the questions and write the Unit numbers in the boxes at the side.

The Parcel of English (See also page 18.)

The cover page at the beginning of the Student's Book (page 7) shows a *Parcel of English* similar to the one which the students can produce in Unit 8. If you intend to do Unit 8, do the following activities now:

- Look through the pictures with the students and explain to them that you will be making a *Parcel of English* which will contain writing and pictures, maps etc. about their town, their school and their family.
- Ask them if they would like the *Parcel of English* to go to another school in another country – if your school is in agreement (you may need to ask the permission of your head of department or head of school) in order to make a school-to-school link up.
- Alternatively, the students may prefer to make a big display of all the work in the classroom, corridor or school hall. Or they may prefer to make a big 'scrap book' to keep in the classroom.
- Ask students to think about what they would like to put in the *Parcel of English* to describe themselves, where they live and their school.

Put a big piece of paper on the wall and write on it their suggestions as a reminder for them to start collecting things about their town and school for Unit 8 over the next few weeks.

Answers

jigsaw: Unit 3;   postcards, scissors, glue: Unit 8;
    beach scene: Unit 6;   map of Newport area: Unit 4;
    Exercise Box: Unit 5.
a puzzle: Unit 3, Ex. 5 and Unit 7, Ex. 5;   a song: Unit 3, Ex. 9;
    a game: Unit 3, Exs. 4 and 10.1;   Unit 4, Ex. 2.2.
On pages 29 and 35 there are the *Language Records* to revise
    grammar and vocabulary.
In Unit 5 they make an *Exercise Box*. In Unit 8 they make a
    Parcel of English.

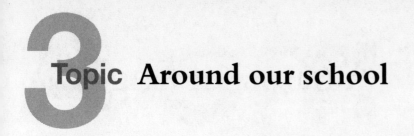

Topic 3 Around our school

1 WHAT HAPPENED WITH UNIT 1 AND UNIT 2?

Some questions to think about before you start Unit 3.

- Do you think you now have a good idea of how much English your students know? Are there many differences in level?
- Do you think you need to give particular students extra suppport (for further *Extension* or Workbook exercises)?
- Look at the test results again. Which were the strongest and the weakest areas (generally) of the students? Are there any areas you would like to focus attention on in Unit 3?

2 TEACHING NOTES FOR UNIT 3

Overview of the Unit

Unit 3 introduces compass points, place names in a town and school subjects. 'There is/are' are introduced by asking about places and students also practise the Present simple. Curriculum links with Geography involve scales, distances and compass points. A *Decide* exercise (Exercise 10) gives students a choice of speaking and listening or writing to practise new vocabulary and structures.

Timing

Below are some suggested timings (in minutes) for each activity. You can note down your anticipated timings here and mark your anticipated lesson divisions.

> **Important note:** The timings we give here are our estimations for *doing the exercises*. You will need to allow extra time for settling the students down and moving from one exercise to another.

1	Where is your school?	
1.1	Schools around the world	5
1.2	Where you live	5
2	Near your school	10
3	Where is it?	10
4	Where am I?	10
5	Find the places	15–20
6	A favourite day	10
7	Your favourite day	10
8	Make an exercise	5
9	Sing a song!	10
10	Decide …	10–15
11	Your Language Record	10

(See also **AtoZ** TIMING.)

What you need

The Class Cassette for Exercises 3, 5, 6 and 9.

Mixed-ability classes and supplementary worksheets

Exercises 5 and 8 have additional guidelines for mixed-ability classes.
Say it clearly! worksheet 1: provides practice of /æm/, /aɪm/, /θ/ and /ð/.
(See also **AtoZ** MIXED ABILITIES.)

Workbook

Unit 3 in the Workbook contains exercises to practise:

- Exercise 1: vocabulary.
- Exercise 2: reading about places in a town.
- Exercise 3: reading and writing about a school.
- Exercise 4: pronunciation of 'I'm' and 'I am'.
- Exercise 5: vocabulary.
- Exercise 6: reading.
- Exercise 7: singing a song in English.

For additional notes on the use of the Workbook and Workbook answers see page 145.

Guidelines

1 Where is your school?
AtoZ DISCUSSIONS

1.1 Schools around the world
Give the students time to look at the pictures of different schools and then ask the questions given. Ask them where they think the schools are. (They are from India, China, Spain, England and Africa.)

1.2 Where you live
Look at the map with the students. Read through the sentences and ask the students where they live. This is also an introduction to the children who appear in the book – Anne, Pat, David, Ali and Mona.

Additionally, you could draw a sketch map of your country on the board, ask the students to suggest some towns in their country and ask them to say where they are: 'X is in the north west', 'Y is in the south east', etc.

- **WB Ex. 1: a vocabulary exercise on places in the town and country.**

2 Near your school
AtoZ SPEAKING and PROCESSING TIME

Look through the pictures and read the names to them. Give one or two *true* examples of places near the school, for example, 'There is a park near our school'. Write some key vocabulary on the board if necessary. You could give the students time (alone or in pairs) to prepare some sentences. When they are ready ask them to tell the class their sentences.

> **Note:** In this exercise the students are practising the fixed phrase 'There are *some* ...'. It is not necessary at this point to explain 'some' and 'any'!

3 Where is it?
AtoZ LISTENING, VOCABULARY and CHECKING ANSWERS

Ask the students to guess where the sounds on the recording come from. Students can check their answers with each other by asking the question 'What's number 1?' and the reply, e.g. 'It's a restaurant', 'No, it's not. It's an airport.'

Answers		
1 a factory	3 a market	5 a restaurant
2 a park	4 a bus station	6 a river

- **WB Ex. 2: an exercise to look at and write about a map.**

4 Where am I?
AtoZ PHYSICAL MOVEMENT

You can give an example yourself to start the game. For example, do some typing with your fingers to mime 'office'.

5 Find the places
AtoZ READING PASSAGES and PAIRWORK

Allow the students time to read the letter silently before playing the cassette. Many students may want to listen to the cassette again. Let them decide if they would like to read the text at the same time as listening to the cassette.

Students can then work in pairs to match the jigsaw pieces to the text. Pairs of students can then compare their jigsaw puzzles.

Answers			
1 c	2 a	3 d	4 b

MIXED ABILITIES
More support can be given by
- providing a written translation of some phrases/sentences.
- asking them to read the letter and find a jigsaw piece for each paragraph.
- giving the answer for two or three pieces.
- giving them four questions about the text – one for each paragraph. In pairs they can answer two questions each. Then they can show each other the answers.

The task can be made more demanding by
- asking the students to prepare some comprehension questions on the text for their partner to answer.
- asking the students to choose a paragraph, write the sentences in a different order and ask their partner to put them in the right order.
- making a gap-fill text of one paragraph.
- asking them to choose a paragraph and write a similar paragraph about where they live.

- **WB Ex. 3: writing a letter about school plans.**

6 A favourite day
AtoZ LISTENING

Give students time to look at the timetable first and then play the recording all the way through, with half the class listening for Ali's information and half listening for Mona's information. Play the recording through again, this time listening for the other information.

Mona:	Hi Ali. Do you like the new timetable?
Ali:	Hi Mona. Yes, it's OK.
Mona:	What's your favourite day?
Ali:	Thursday. We've got two lessons of Sports on Thursday. Sports is my favourite subject.
Mona:	My favourite subject is Maths.
Ali:	So, is Tuesday your favourite day?
Mona:	Yes it is.

7 Your favourite day

AtoZ PAIRWORK and **SPEAKING**

Before putting the students in pairs, ask two or three students the questions, as an example. They can then work in pairs to make up a similar dialogue using the phrases given from the cassette. Go round the pairs giving help where needed while they prepare their dialogues and then ask some pairs to perform their dialogues for the class.

> ### MIXED ABILITIES
>
> *More support can be given by*
> - giving the students a copy of the tapescript or writing it on the blackboard so that they can look at it while they prepare their dialogue.
> - giving them a cut up version of the tapescript which they can put in correct order and read out in pairs.
>
> *The task can be made more demanding by*
> - asking students to talk about their favourite film, hobby, sport or book instead.
> - asking them to find out their partner's five favourite things (e.g. favourite colour, food, sport etc.). They can write this in dialogue form and perhaps act it for the class.

- **WB Ex. 4: an open dialogue.**

8 Make an exercise

AtoZ AUTONOMY and **EXERCISE BOX**

This exercise introduces the students to making their own exercises, an idea which is developed in Unit 5, *Making an Exercise Box*.

Students work alone to match the two sides of the words and then translate them into their mother tongue. They

then choose six new words from this Unit, divide them in the same way and give them to a partner to join and translate.

Go round and check how they are managing. If some students work more quickly than others you could ask them to look at the *Ideas list* to make another type of exercise.

- **WB Ex. 5: a vocabulary puzzle.**
- **WB Ex. 6: reading a letter.**

9 Sing a song! In my town, in the countryside

AtoZ SONGS

Play the cassette while the students read the words and then let the students sing along with the cassette.

- **WB Ex. 7: sing a song.**

10 Decide …

AtoZ DECIDE EXERCISES

In pairs, the students decide which task they would like to do next – speaking and listening, writing or something else. Go through Exercises 10.1 and 10.2 first so that they see what the choices are. While they are working go round and give individual help and advice.

If some students finish early you can get them to start work on their *Language Record* and the *Time to spare?* exercises on pages 28 and 29.

11 Your Language Record

AtoZ LANGUAGE RECORD

Students can fill in the *Language Record* as soon as they finish Exercise 10. Some students may need individual help but encourage them to work on it alone or with a partner.

Time to spare?
AtoZ TIME TO SPARE?

Preparation for Unit 5

Get students, for homework, to look back through Units 1, 2 and 3 and find an example of a vocabulary exercise, a reading exercise, a listening exercise and a writing exercise.

Language focus

1 RESEARCHING THE CLASSROOM: SPELLING

Some questions to think about during the coming lessons.

- Are there some words which the students often spell incorrectly? What are they? Do they fall into groups? Why do you think they have difficulty with those particular words?
- How important do you think spelling mistakes are?

- Do the students who have difficulty with spelling in their mother tongue have problems with English spelling?

Unit 6 in the Workbook gives students some ideas on how to help their spelling. (See also **AtoZ SPELLING** for more ideas.)

2 TEACHING NOTES FOR UNIT 4

Overview of the Unit

Unit 4 introduces the Present simple negative and parts of grammar in the context of maps and map symbols. There is also work on the third person 's' and the short answers 'Yes, I do' and 'No, I don't'. The *Out and about* section practises the language of shopping. The *Learn more about your book!* section allows students to become more familiar with the sections at the back of the Student's Book.

Timing

Below are some suggested timings (in minutes) for doing the exercises. You will need to allow extra time for settling the students down and moving from one exercise to another.

1	What's on the map?	
1.1	Maps	5
1.2	What can maps tell us?	10–15
1.3	Make a map	10
2	Nouns, verbs and adjectives	
2.1	What type of word is it?	10
2.2	Play a game!	5
3	No, I don't	
3.1	Sentences with 'not'	5–10
3.2	Describe the negative	5–10
3.3	Practice	10
3.4	More practice	10
4	Out and about with English	

4.1	Pocket money	5
4.2	Mona and Ali go shopping	10–15
4.3	Practice	10
5	Your Language Record	5

What you need

The Class Cassette for Exercise 4.2.

Mixed-ability classes and supplementary worksheets

Exercises 3.2, 4.2 and 4.3 have additional guidelines for mixed-ability classes.
Language worksheet 4.1: Present simple.
Language worksheet 4.2: Present simple negatives.
Say it clearly! worksheet 1: /æm/, /aɪm/, /θ/ and /ð/.
(See also **AtoZ MIXED ABILITIES**.)

Workbook

Unit 4 in the Workbook contains exercises to practise:

- Exercise 1: writing about location; vocabulary.
- Exercise 2: parts of grammar: adjectives.
- Exercise 3: reading, writing, speaking, 'don't/doesn't'.
- Exercise 4: pronunciation of 'th'.
- Exercise 5: speaking (an open dialogue in a shop).

> **Reminder:** This is the time to tell students that for Unit 8 they need a small photograph of themselves and if possible some pictures, photographs, postcards and maps of their town.

Also, for Unit 5, Exercise 1, they need to do a small amount of preparation.

Guidelines

1 What's on the map?

1.1 Maps

AtoZ DISCUSSIONS

Let the students share their ideas – in their mother tongue and English – about maps, the kinds of maps they know or use, what information is on maps, when they or their family uses a map. Put some key words on the board.

1.2 What can maps tell us?

AtoZ PROCESSING TIME

Students can work in pairs or alone for this task. Check that they understand the questions before they start the task.

> **Answers**
>
> 1 a castle and a museum
> 2 20 kms x 20 kms?
> 3 seven picnic sites
>
> 4 hospital, theatre, lake, information centre and woods.

1.3 Make a map

Ask the students to give you names of places in their area and write them on the board. Draw the grid on the blackboard and then agree with the students where the places should go. Ask them what they can say about the map on the board. For example, in the map below 'There is a school in square C4.'

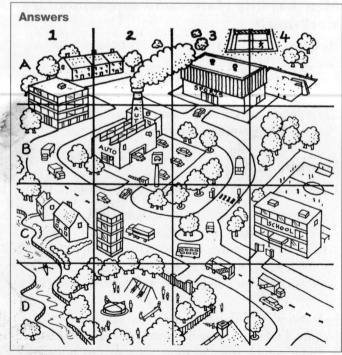

Answers

- **WB Exs. 1.1–1.3: provide further language work with maps; Language worksheet 4.1 provides practice with Present simple.**

2 Nouns, verbs and adjectives

2.1 What type of word is it?

AtoZ GRAMMAR

Before you run through the meanings of *noun*, *verb* and *adjective*, check whether the students know what they are called in their mother tongue. Get them to provide examples in the mother tongue. In pairs, get students to fill in the circles with the words given and any other words they can find in their *Language Record*.

Optional extra: if there is time, divide the class into three groups – nouns, verbs and adjectives, set a time limit and see which team can think of the most number of words of that kind.

> **Answers**
> Nouns: bicycle, history, country, river, timetable, map
> Verbs: dance, swim, go
> Adjectives: hot, good, small, beautiful

2.2 Play a game!

AtoZ GAMES and PHYSICAL MOVEMENT

This is a physical game and would be a good way to start or end a lesson as you may find it disruptive in the middle of a lesson. Make sure the students understand that noun = right hand, verb = left hand and adjective = shaking head. Use the words from the *Language Record* and get the students to respond accordingly.

Alternatively, the students can make noises: noun = cough; verb = clap their hands; adjective = hum.

- **WB Ex. 2: an exercise on adjectives.**

3 No, I don't!

3.1 Sentences with 'not'

AtoZ MOTHER TONGUE and GRAMMAR

Ask students to read the sentences to say how they say the same things in their mother tongue. If possible, write some examples on the board (or ask the students to write some) to show the differences between the negative construction in English and in their mother tongue.

3.2 Describe the negative

AtoZ GRAMMAR and INDUCTIVE GRAMMAR

Put the chart on the board and add some of the sentences from Exercise 3.1. Ask the students how they can describe negative sentences.

> **Answers**
> Subject + 'don't' + verb for sentences with 'I/you/we/they';
> Subject + 'doesn't' + verb for sentences with 'he/she/it'.

In pairs, the students can write some more negative sentences as examples.

- **WB Ex. 3: a reading and writing exercise with negative sentences.**

3.3 PRACTICE What does your neighbour do?

A to Z PAIRWORK and **MONITORING AND GUIDING**

Make sure that the students understand what they have to do. Get them to look at the list of verbs given in the exercise. Ask some students some questions as an example. Insist on a clear pronunciation of 'Yes, I do/No, I don't'. Ask them to continue in pairs.

You can make it into a game by saying that students cannot repeat a question that their partner has asked them.

In pairs, they find out information about each other and then report back about their partner around the class. Insist on correct use of the third person 's' ('He live**s** ...', etc.).

3.4 MORE PRACTICE Possible or impossible?

A to Z PROCESSING TIME

Students can work alone or with a partner to do this task. Give them time to look carefully at the map first.

> **Answers**
> 3 Impossible! Lanark isn't near the sea.
> 4 Possible! There is a river near Lanark.
> 5 Possible! There is a road to Carstairs.
> 6 Possible! There are lots of picnic places near Lanark.
> 7 Impossible! There isn't an airport in Lanark.
> 8 Impossible! The castle isn't near Lanark.

- **Language worksheet 4.2 gives further practice with Present simple negatives.**

4   Out and about with English

The *Out and about* sections offer listening, reading, and speaking practice in the use of social English. Mona and Ali are first introduced in Unit 3, Exercise 1. In subsequent *Out and about* sections, Mona makes friends with a new girl at her school, Sophie.

4.1   Pocket money

A to Z DISCUSSIONS

Discuss pocket money with the students: how much do they get? when do they get it? what do they do with it? This can be in the mother tongue or in English or in both languages, depending on the students' level of ability. You can put some key sentence beginnings on the board:

> 'I get ...'
> 'I get my pocket money on ...'
> 'I buy ...'
> 'I save it.'

4.2   Mona and Ali go shopping

A to Z LISTENING

Allow time for the students to look at the pictures. Check their answers and vocabulary items after they have heard the dialogue once. Play the cassette again.

You can then ask the students to practise the dialogue in pairs. Insist on a clear pronunciation of the 'th' sound in 'the', 'this', 'that', 'these', 'thanks'.

Note: British money is the pound (£) which has 100 pence (p). The £ symbol comes before the amount, e.g. £7.40.

> **Answers**
> Mona wants to buy a cassette and a box of chocolates.
> Ali wants to buy a computer magazine and some games.

- **WB Ex. 4 and *Say it clearly!* worksheet 1 offer more practice with 'th' words.**

4.3 PRACTICE

AtoZ PAIRWORK, SPEAKING and **MONITORING AND GUIDING**

Students work in pairs to practise the dialogue. Read through the phrases given and give the students some examples using the pictures in the exercise. Insist on a clear pronunciation of the 'th' words. Students can then use different items for their own dialogues.

When they are ready ask some pairs to act out their dialogue in front of the class.

Note: If some students are shy about performing their dialogue, do not force them to.

MIXED ABILITIES

The task can be made more demanding by

- asking students to think of the last time they went shopping. Alone or with a partner they recreate the dialogue which took place.
- asking the students to sit back to back. One is the customer telephoning a shop asking if a certain item is in the shop and how much it is.

- **WB Ex. 5: an open dialogue to practise speaking and writing.**

5 Your Language Record

AtoZ LANGUAGE RECORD

Students can move straight on to the *Language Record* when they have finished Exercise 4.3.

Remind the students to bring in their photos for Unit 8.

Time to spare?

AtoZ TIME TO SPARE?

Subjects in the word search are: English, Maths, Art, Sport, History, Science, Music, Geography.

The letters in green print spell 'Timetable'.

Learn more about your book!

This section aims to get the students to make full use of the contents of their book. It is probably best done in pairs. You can talk through the tasks first and then set them working with a time limit.

> **Answers**
> 1 Useful sets, Map of the world, Wordlist/Index
> 2 a Useful sets b Map of the world c Ideas list
>   d Wordlist/Index e Useful sets f Map of the world
>   g Wordlist/Index h Wordlist/Index i Songs
> 3 rise v.: Unit 24; rain n. and v.: Unit 24; tall adj.: Unit 2
>   Extension; elephant n.: Unit 2; possessive adjectives:
>   Unit 10; Present simple questions: Unit 10; asking for
>   information: Units 4 and 20 (travel information); making
>   plans: Unit 25.

5 Activity Making an Exercise Box

TEACHING NOTES FOR UNIT 5

Overview of the Unit

In Unit 5, the students work in groups to start a collection of exercises for class use. (This will be used throughout the course.) At the end, there is a short evaluation discussion focusing on how well they managed to work on making their own exercises.
(See also **AtoZ** EXERCISE BOX.)

Timing

The *Activity* Units are usually intended as one lesson. However, as this is the first activity the students will do, and as the *Exercise Box* will be important throughout the course, you may need to allow extra time. Suggested timings (in minutes) for each step are:

Before the lesson	
1 Look back	(at home)
In the lesson	
2 Types of exercise	10
3 The Ideas list	20
4 Take an exercise	15
5 Evaluation	5

What you need

A small cardboard box and some cards for making divisions in the box. A shoebox and blank postcards or record cards are ideal.

Mixed-ability classes

Exercise 3 has additional guidelines for mixed-ability classes.
(See also **AtoZ** MIXED ABILITIES.)

Workbook

Unit 5 in the Workbook contains further practice in making exercises:

- Exercise 1: looking at different kinds of exercises.
- Exercise 2: writing different kinds of exercises.

Guidelines

Before the lesson

Explain first to the students what they will be doing in Unit 5. They will be making their own exercises for other students to do. They will put these in a box so that other students will be able to do them in subsequent lessons, for revision or homework, or to test themselves.

1 Look back

Students look back through Units 1, 2, 3 and 4 to find examples of a vocabulary exercise, a reading exercise, a listening exercise and a writing exercise.

In the lesson

2 Types of exercise

Students work together and compare exercises. You can then ask for examples of each type of exercise that they found.

3 The Ideas list

AtoZ IDEAS LIST, GROUPWORK and MONITORING AND GUIDING

The first part of the exercise is best done with the whole class. Look through the three example exercises with them and then look at the *Ideas list*. Explain that this is a list of ideas for making their own exercises and then ask them if they can find the example exercises in the list. Give them a few minutes for this.

Before the students move into small groups (of two or three students) check that they know what they will be doing. Read through the instructions with them and either tell each group what type of exercise they must write or ask them to decide in their group.

As the students finish writing their exercises, they can give them to you to check before they are put into the *Exercise Box*. Remind them to write a title to the exercises and to put the answers on the back. Students who finish before others can produce another exercise of a different type.

> **MIXED ABILITIES**
>
> *More support can be given by*
> - asking the students to suggest words. You can then show them how to make a word halves exercise and a word puzzle with the words they suggested. You can then ask the students to take five more words from the *Language Record* to make a puzzle.
> - asking the students to say a few simple sentences about their school. You can then put one sentence on the board and show them how they can mix it up.
>
> *The task can be made more demanding by*
> - asking students to make a word puzzle only with adjectives or nouns or verbs.
> - asking students to write their own sentences to be mixed up (i.e. not ones from the book).

- **WB Ex. 1:** gives further practice in looking at different kinds of exercises.
- **WB Ex. 2:** gives further practice in writing different kinds of exercises.

4 Take an exercise

Remind them not to write on the paper! They can check their answers on the back.

5 EVALUATION

AtoZ EVALUATION

This will probably have to be done in their mother tongue. Get the students first to read the questions in their books (translate) and give them a few minutes to formulate some ideas either individually or in pairs/groups. As this is probably the first time they will have done an evaluation of an activity the response may be rather confused. Get them to focus on the 'How can I do it better next time?' question and see if they can suggest any ways of improving the writing of the exercises.

Alternatively, if the group is very large or noisy it may be better to get the students to write suggestions in their mother tongue about how they can improve next time, which they then put in a suggestion box. (See also **AtoZ** LEARNER INVOLVEMENT.)

Culture matters Life in the town

TEACHING NOTES FOR UNIT 6

Overview of the Unit

The main aim of the *Culture matters* Units is to give the students some understanding of how British society is different from their own. They do not introduce any new structures or language areas. This first *Culture matters* Unit focuses on different kinds of British towns. Students get an overview of the geography of Great Britain. The Unit provides listening and reading tasks.

Timing

The *Culture matters* Units are intended for one full lesson but you may decide to split it up over a number of lessons. Suggested timings (in minutes) are:

1	About your country	5
2	British towns	10
3	Are you right?	10
4	Where are the postcards from?	10–15

Important note: The timings we give here are our estimates for *doing the exercises* and will vary from class to class.

What you need

The Class Cassette for Exercises 3 and 4.

Mixed-ability classes

Exercise 3 has additional guidelines for mixed-ability classes. (See also **AtoZ MIXED ABILITIES**.)

Workbook

Unit 6 in the Workbook is the first *Help yourself* Unit: *Help yourself with spelling*. It focuses on ways in which the students can help themselves with spelling. The Unit contains three ways the students can practise their spelling at home:

- Exercise 1: look, cover, write, check.
- Exercise 2: word pairs.
- Exercise 3: spelling groups.

See page 145 for a special note on the *Help yourself* Units. (See also **AtoZ SPELLING**.)

Guidelines

1 About your country

AtoZ DISCUSSION

Ask these questions in English or their mother tongue. Accept replies in their mother tongue. Since the main aim of the Unit is to develop cross-cultural awareness, an 'English only' rule may defeat the purpose.

2 British towns

Give the students plenty of time to look at the map of Great Britain. They need to understand that it is an island with three countries; England, Wales and Scotland.

Note: the United Kingdom includes Northern Ireland

Make sure students understand the vocabulary 'farming areas', 'industrial areas', 'port', 'seaside town'. Let them work in pairs to find the towns and guess which kind of towns they are.

The main aim here is to familiarise students with Great Britain rather than insist on the correct answer.

> **Answers**
> 1 Newport : industrial town – South Wales
> 2 Wick : farming town – Scotland
> 3 Newquay : seaside town – South West England
> 4 Milton Keynes : new city – South East England

3 Are you right? 🔲

AtoZ READING and LISTENING

Divide the class into three groups: Wales, Scotland and England. Each group reads the tourist guide for their part. Check that they understand the vocabulary. Play the cassette pausing after each talk. Let the students from each group tell the others the correct answers.

4 Where are the postcards from?

A to Z READING

Students work alone or in pairs. They read the postcards and decide which postcard has which stamp.

Answers		
1 Wick	**2** Newport	**3** Milton Keynes

7 Revision and evaluation

TEACHING NOTES FOR UNIT 7

General note on the Revision and evaluation Units

CES contains six *Revision and evaluation* Units (7, 13, 18, 23, 28 and 33). Each Unit has two main purposes: to revise the language in the previous four Units and to give the students the chance to give you feedback on their English lessons. The first purpose is so that students check that they understand what has been covered before the course moves forward. The second purpose is to help you plan your next lessons, taking into account students' reactions.

The *Revision and evaluation* Units are linked (optionally) to Workbook Units 7, 13, 18, 23, 28 and 33, as follows:

	Student's Book	Workbook
Unit 7	Revision exercises	Self-test
Unit 13	Revision exercises	Self-test
Unit 18	Student test writing	Revision exercises
Unit 23	Student test writing	Revision exercises
Unit 28	Revision exercises	Self-test
Unit 33	Student test writing	Revision exercises

Overview of the Unit

Exercise 1 asks the students how well they think they know the English from Units 3–6. Revision exercises then follow. Students can do some or all of these exercises, depending on time and how much revision they need. In the last exercise, students think about what they found easy or difficult and provide you with written feedback.

Timing

The Unit is intended for one full lesson, with students doing Exercises 2–8 selectively. However, you may want all students to do all the exercises, in which case the Unit may be split up over a number of lessons. Suggested timings (in minutes) for doing the exercises are:

1	How well do you know it?	5–10
2	Say what's in a town	10
3	What do they do?	10
4	A problem to solve	15
5	New words	10
6	Who says what?	10
7	Were you right?	5
8	Evaluation	20

What you need

No special equipment or materials.

Mixed-ability classes and supplementary worksheets

Language worksheet 4.1: Present simple.
Language worksheet 4.2: Present simple negative.
(See also **A to Z** **MIXED ABILITIES**.)

Workbook

Unit 7 in the Workbook is a self-check test focusing on the language covered in the Theme:

- Exercise 1: describing a town.
- Exercise 2: negative sentences.
- Exercise 3: an open dialogue.
- Exercise 4: reading and comprehension; writing a letter.
- Exercise 5: shopping phrases.
- Exercise 6: grammar words.

A picture dictionary summarises the vocabulary presented in the Theme.

For additional notes on the Workbook and Workbook answers see page 145.

Guidelines

1 How well do you know it?

AtoZ TASKS IN BLOCKS and OVERVIEWING

The main aim here is to encourage the students to reflect on how much they have learnt.

Before asking students to complete the chart, look back with them at the relevant sections of the previous Units to remind them what they did. Give the students a few minutes to tick the box. You could encourage them to compare *briefly* with their neighbour.

Before the students start working, it is a good idea to go through the exercises with them, so that they know exactly what they have to do in each one. After this there are a number of possibilities:

- Let the students choose what they want to revise and practise – either to test themselves or to revise where they feel weakest.
- Ask the students to do *two* exercises: one that they ticked 'very well' and one that they ticked 'a little'.
- Get all the students to do all the exercises (requires more time, of course, but the students can complete the Unit for homework).

> **Relevant sections are**
> What is in a town: Unit 3, Ex. 2;   Present simple negatives: Unit 4, Exs. 3.1 and 3.2;   Talk about school subjects: Unit 3, Exs. 6 and 7;   New words: *Language Record* pages 13, 22, 29, 35;   Going shopping: Unit 4. *Out and about*: Ex. 4.

2 Say what's in a town

Students label the picture as shown.

> **Possible answers**
> There are some shops near the bus station. There is a bank near the park. There is a train station near the park. There are some flats near the shops. There are some houses near the school. There is a school near the flats.

3 What do they do?

The students need to write complete sentences.

> **Answers (example sentences)**
> 1 One student plays the piano. Seven students don't play the piano.
> 2 Seven students play football. One student doesn't play football.
> 3 Six students live in a flat. Two students don't live in a flat.
> 4 Seven students like Science. One student doesn't like Science.
> 5 One student rides a horse. Seven students don't ride a horse.
> 6 Seven students walk to school. One student doesn't walk to school.
> 7 Three students go to the library. Five students don't go to the library.

4 A problem to solve

The students can write out the timetable to help them solve the puzzle.

> **Answers**
> Their free lessons are Monday Lesson 3 and Tuesday Lesson 1.

Lesson	MONDAY	TUESDAY	WEDNESDAY	THURSDAY	FRIDAY
1	Maths	FREE	English	English	English
2	Geography	Maths	Geography	Geography	Geography
3	FREE	Music	Maths	Music	Music
	Lunch	Lunch	Lunch	Lunch	Lunch
4	History	History	History	Maths	Maths
5	Language	Language	Language	Sport	Science
6	Science	Science	Language	Sport	Science

5 New words

Students circle the words and then make a puzzle for the rest of the class.

Answers
LIBRARY
THEATRE
CASTLE
MUSEUM
WOODS

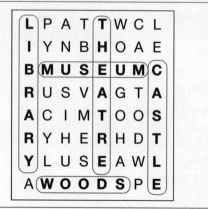

6 Who says what? 📼

Students write the number of the correct sentence in the empty speech bubbles.

> **Answers**
> **1** 10–4   **2** 8–6   **3** 3–1   **4** 9–7   **5** 2/5-5/2

> 📼 TAPESCRIPT
>
> *Anne:* Excuse me, how much is this please?
> *Assistant:* That's £9.40.
> *Anne:* That's expensive! How much is that?
> *Assistant:* That's £8.
> *Anne:* Can I have that bag, please?
> *Assistant:* Here you are.
> *Anne:* Thanks. Here you are. £10.
> *Assistant:* Thanks. £2 change.
> *Anne:* Bye.
> *Assistant:* Bye.

---

7 Were you right?

Once the students have done two or more exercises, ask them to look back at their chart in Exercise 1. Do they still think the same? Did they know more or less than they thought?

8 EVALUATION

A to Z **EVALUATION**

This section has two parts. 8.1 involves a small group discussion, while 8.2 asks students to note down their own reactions. You will need to allow a few minutes at the end of the lesson for students to write their own comments.

8.1 Talk about your English work

Divide the students into groups of three to four, and allocate a Unit to each group. Ask them to decide who will report back to the class.

For the reporting back stage, if more than one group is looking at a Unit, ask one group to report back and then ask the other group(s) if they have any other points to add.

8.2 Your own ideas

This is a very simple introduction for students to think about what they are doing in their English lessons. Students write the Unit and exercise numbers on a line (very easy – very difficult). If possible, ask them to write their own personal ideas in their own language what they think about their English lessons. You could give them some questions to stimulate their thoughts:

- What did they like best in their English lessons so far?
- Is it going too fast, just right or too slow?
- Do they have any suggestions for future lessons?

If you tell them that they don't have to put their name on the paper that they give you, you will get more honest and more useful feedback.

8 A Parcel of English

Writing about the
students' school and town
to send to another school

I Important: See the additional notes on the Parcel of English on page 18.

TEACHING NOTES FOR UNIT 8

Overview of the Unit

The *Parcel of English* provides an active context for revision and an opportunity for students to make contact with another school in another town or country. It also gives you, the teacher, an opportunity for professional contact with a teacher in a different town or country who is using the same textbook. It may be interesting to share classroom ideas and experiences. Cambridge University Press offers a registration service which links schools in different countries with each other. To get the maximum benefit from the *Parcel of English*, we suggest that you register as soon as possible. See page 18 for more information. (If you do not wish to exchange with another school, you can still use the *Parcel of English* Unit. See below.)

The 'Parcel' which the students produce in this Unit focuses on two important aspects: the place where the students live and the school they go to. Students can revise the Present tense and the vocabulary of description. Subsequent 'parcels' can include a variety of texts. (See below.)

Timing

Unit 8 is quite a large activity which will last more than one lesson in total. Additionally, you and the students may like to keep it going for a number of weeks so that more material may be included in it. The suggested timings (in minutes) are given below. You could break the Unit up over a number of lessons as follows:

step 1   steps 2–4   steps 5–6   steps 6–7   step 8

Before the lesson		
1	Pictures of you and your town	(at home)
In the lesson		
2	A Parcel of English	5
3	What's in the Parcel of English?	10
4	A picture and description of me	10
5	Writing in groups	25
6	Put it together	10
7	Your Parcel of English!	10

What you need

Small pieces of paper 10 cm x 10 cm (enough for the whole class). To get paper this size, fold a piece of A4 paper into six equal parts, or alternatively a sheet of paper for every six students. A4 paper, glue, scissors, sticky tape, postcards, maps, photos of the town and school in case students bring very little.

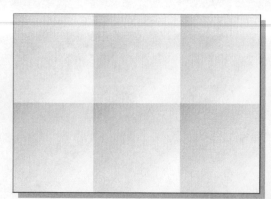

Mixed-ability classes

Exercise 5 has further guidelines for mixed-ability classes.

Workbook

Unit 8 in the Workbook is also called 'A Parcel of English' and gives the students some ideas for the letters and puzzles they can put into their own Parcel. The Workbook Unit also contains exercises connected to the Parcel.

Guidelines

Before the lesson

1   Pictures of you and your town

Remind students to bring in a photo of themselves and pictures of their town.

In the lesson

2   A Parcel of English

With the whole class, look at the picture of the *Parcel of English*. In English or in their mother tongue tell the students that the *Parcel of English* is a link with another school (possibly in another country) or a school/class display. Ask them what they can see in the Parcel and what they could do with their own Parcel.

3   What's in the Parcel of English?

Ask students to suggest – in the mother tongue or in English – things they could put in the Parcel. Make a list on the board under the three headings:

> You and our class
> Our school
> Our town

4   A picture and description of me

Pupils work alone for this part of the activity to write a short description of themselves. Remind them it must fit on to the small piece of paper! Refer students back to Unit 1, Exercise 5 for help if needed. Go round giving help where necessary. Students can exchange papers with a partner for checking. Give out to pupils a small (10 cm x 10 cm) piece of paper to write out the final version of their description. Stick six of these on to a piece of A4. (Alternatively you could pass one sheet of paper around for six students to write on.)

5   Writing in groups

A to Z **READING, WRITING, GROUPWORK** and **MONITORING AND GUIDING**

Point out to the students that there are four sections to the *Parcel of English* (a–d as given in the Student's Book).

Divide the class into four groups a–d. Each group reads the text about their topic. Go round and give help where necessary but encourage them to guess words and help each other.

Students decide what they are going to write about in their paragraph. Everyone shares ideas but **everyone must write**. Go round giving help where necessary.

Some more ideas:

- *Our class:* plan of class and names of students in each place; picture of view from window; pictures of games they play; comics; well-known children's characters in cartoons, etc.
- *Our school:* plan of the school; names of the classes and the teachers; photographs of important things in the school: paintings, displays, etc.
- *Our town:* maps, plans, postcards, bus timetables, restaurant menus, local newspaper advertisements for events, recipes of local dishes.

MIXED ABILITIES

More support can be given by
- making sure that there are students of different abilities and strengths in each group.
- breaking down one paragraph into single sentences on the board. Show students how these can be used as model sentences by substituting their own information.
- asking students to write one sentence each of the paragraph. When they have written it they pass it to the next person for corrections and additions.

The task can be made more demanding by
- asking some students to write more imaginatively about their town/region/school. They can create a brochure about the school, for example, or write a poem.

---

6   Put it together

7   Your Parcel of English!

Remind students to bring in more things for the Parcel of English if they have any.

Sending the Parcel of English to another country: some questions and answers

If you are unsure of how to organise your Parcel of English or can foresee difficulties, the following answers may help.

Q: *'It is too expensive. Our school doesn't have much money. How can we send a Parcel of English?'*

If there are financial reasons for not sending the *Parcel of English*, some of these ideas may be useful:

- stationery: Perhaps students could bring in paper, glue and other stationery from home.
- stamps: Perhaps each student could bring in a small stamp.
- lighten the load: Perhaps the Parcel could be made lighter by photocopying on both sides of the paper, writing on airmail paper or by photocopying the photographs instead of sending the originals.
- fund raising: Many schools in the UK now have fêtes, fairs and concerts to raise money for materials and computers. The children (and parents) make cakes and sell them at fairs to raise money. Perhaps your school could have an 'English evening' where students sing English songs, read some poems in English or tell stories. Parents and visitors pay a small amount for a ticket.
- sponsorship: Some local companies may pay for the cost of the postage, perhaps if you include some of their advertising material in the Parcel.
- ask the students for ideas!

Q: *'The postal system is unreliable. How can we send a Parcel of English?'*
If there are problems with the postal service in your area or country you could possibly:

- send two copies of the Parcel.
- send a postcard first to say that you are about to send the Parcel.
- send a reduced version of the Parcel by fax (if the school has a fax, it should be on the registration card).
- send the Parcel by computer on Electronic Mail if you have access to this. (Universities frequently have e-mail connections to other universities worldwide. A friendly person in your local university may be able to help.)
- use Registered or Special Delivery.
- investigate other (private) courier systems.
- If there is a Cambridge University Press office in your country, you could ask for their suggestions. They may have ideas about how your Parcel can be sent.

Q: *'My class is very weak! I am embarrassed about the quality of their work. What can I do?'*
The standard of students' work varies enormously for a wide variety of reasons: some students start studying English at eight years old, some at 11 or 12 years old; some students have two lessons a week, some have six or more lessons a week, some students have extra English lessons after school; some have a native speaker assistant in the school; some students are in very small classes. All these factors play a role in the 'standard' of students' work in English.

However, for the *Parcel of English* the standard of the English is not the most important factor. For the students the excitement and the benefit of the Parcel is in having contact with another school and learning about the way of life in another country. The students will be more interested in sharing real communication by discovering the similarities and differences in their lives, homes, school and hobbies than in analysing the quality of the English. Do not feel embarrassed about the quality of your students' work. It is probably not as low a standard as you think! Some other ideas are:

- include in the Parcel a lot of 'real' material from your town and school: maps, pictures, timetables, postcards, photographs, bus tickets, sweets or sweet wrappers, advertisements, menus from restaurants, cinema tickets, bus and train timetables, the front page of the local paper, a copy of a school magazine, etc.
- encourage the students to include their own drawings and pictures cut from magazines.
- persuade students to include the piece of work that they enjoyed doing most.
- encourage the students to draft their writing and to correct it themselves in a group (with a little help from you) before rewriting it.
- don't put too much emphasis on 'perfection' or the weaker students will be discouraged.
- the *Parcel of English* from a class is more than the sum of its individual parts!

Q: *'How often should I send it?'*
This will obviously depend on how many lessons each week you have with your class. However, it may be a good idea to negotiate with the students about:

- what should go in the Parcel. Let the students decide if they want to include a certain piece of work in the next Parcel. If they do, they can leave it in a box or drawer called 'The Parcel of English' until it seems there is enough variety of material to send.
- how often you should send it.
- who is to arrange it. Let the students decide who is going to help you do any photocopying, tape recording, wrapping up, etc.
- you don't need to wait to receive a Parcel before you send your next one (particularly where the postal services are slow).

Q: *'I've got many different classes using CES. How can I do the Parcel of English?'*
- the easiest way would be to exchange material between the classes. Decide which classes are to be linked and exchange pieces of work as a Parcel.
- the other way would be to send one *Parcel of English* which contains work from different classes to another school through the Cambridge registration system. Enclose a letter in the Parcel which explains which

classes are sending work and the Parcel which is returned can belong to all your classes.

Q: *'What else can I put in a Parcel of English?'*
There are many tasks in *CES* which are suitable for including in the *Parcel of English*:

- the students' work from the *Activity* Units.
- exercises and puzzles which they have written for the class *Exercise Box*.
- the tests which the students write themselves in Units 18, 23, and 33.
- dialogues from the *Out and about* sections in the *Language focus* Units be written or tape recorded for the Parcel.
- set aside 15 minutes every two weeks to prepare *Parcel of English* work.

In addition:

- students may like to include an audio (or video★) cassette of their 'talents'. Some may play a musical instrument, sing some songs, tell some jokes, read some poetry or record part of a radio or television programme which would be interesting for children in another school or country.
- it is always interesting to see school textbooks on History, Geography, Science and Maths from other schools and countries.
- if the school or any of the children have a video★ camera some of them may want to make a short video recording of a lesson, a sports match, 'a day in the life of a student', a local festival, a famous building or site in the region.
- some children may like to write recipes for their favourite meals or explain traditional dishes.

Q: *'What shall I do with the Parcel of English when it arrives?'*
Remember that the students will be looking forward to the arrival of the *Parcel of English* from the other school especially if it is in a different country about which they know very little.

- as soon as it arrives, please write and tell the teacher and class that sent it to you that you have received it and say, approximately, when you will be sending your Parcel.

In class:

- to avoid over-excitement and frustration in the lesson, open the Parcel and look at the contents *before* the lesson so you can see if you need to take in a tape recorder (if there are cassettes to listen to, for example). You could re-seal the Parcel and open it again in class.

- in order for the whole class to look at the material in the *Parcel of English*, it may be better to divide the class into groups and ask each group to look at one part of the contents.
- while they are looking at the contents go round and ask each group how they will respond to their part. They may have already done some work which they want to send. Some may want to write to individual students in the other class; others may want to answer questions asked in the Parcel.
- the Parcel may contain exercises and puzzles for your class *Exercise Box*. Some students may want to try these out and send the answers in your next Parcel.

Q: *'I think that it will take a lot of time. How useful is it really?'*
Much of the work that you and the students are doing in class can be included in the *Parcel of English* without doing any extra work. The *Parcel of English* adds an extra dimension to your course, the value of which is immense in terms of motivation, making English 'real', developing cross-cultural awareness, fostering friendships, peace education and more. Read through the notes on the *Parcel of English* to get an idea of what benefits it can bring.

Q: *'I don't think my students are very interested in the idea of the Parcel of English. What can I do?'*
The key to a keen class is undoubtedly a keen teacher! If you can present the *Parcel of English* as an exciting thing to do you will undoubtedly fire the students' imagination and energy. Some ideas:

- start by making sure that the students know what the *Parcel of English* contains and how it works.
- ask students what they know about other countries in the world and/or other regions or towns in their country.
- explain that the *Parcel of English* draws on the different talents of each student in the class. It is not expected that all the students will include the same things in the *Parcel of English*; they can be encouraged to choose what they would like to send.
- some students may be reluctant to write very much but they may be very good at finding pictures and postcards, or at drawing: others may prefer to send a cassette recording of a letter or story if they prefer to speak.
- some students may prefer to write to one of the students in a corresponding school on an individual 'pen-pal' basis.
- talk about what they will be able to do with their English. Many pupils do not realise how *international* English is. The fact that they will be able to communicate with pupils in another country through English will open up new worlds to them.

LINKING TEACHERS TO TEACHERS

In addition to the value of your students learning from and about students in another school or country, you may also find it worthwhile to use the *Parcel of English* as a means of sharing your teacher experiences and reactions with another teacher. Some regions have Teachers' Centres where teachers can discuss new methods or teaching issues with others, but many teachers can be very isolated in their subject and their school. The *Parcel of English* can offer an opportunity to discuss professional issues with another teacher in the same position as you.

- start by including in the Parcel a letter in English from you to the other teacher. This will give you a chance to use 'adult, communicative English' as a change from the classroom English you use every day.
- give information about yourself, your students, your school and region.

- you could share your ideas and reactions to the 'Researching the Classroom' sections. You could describe how you approach grammar, pronunciation, errors and fluency with your students.
- from the 'What happened in Units...' sections you may want to describe some successful lessons and say why they went well and some not so successful lessons and why you think they did not work.
- you can describe the differences between different groups and the different outcomes of the *Activity Units*.
- you may be able to share videos★ of different lessons.

★ You will need to check whether your TVs run on the same system (e.g. PAL, SECAM, NHTSC).

Theme B
The natural world

OVERVIEW OF THE THEME

Theme B, *The natural world*, focuses on animals and how they live and life in the countryside. In terms of grammar, the students learn to use Present simple question forms and possessive adjectives. The *Out and about* section in Unit 10 focuses on language for asking for information. They gain practice in listening comprehension (for general meaning and for detail), speaking (through preparing interviews), and writing (short descriptive texts and formal letters). They also become involved in making decisions about their learning (through *Decide* exercises and evaluation activities).

The Theme offers cross–curricular links with Biology, Zoology and Science.

Using the cover page

The pictures visually summarise what the students will be doing in the next five Units. Look through the pictures and ask them what they can see (names of animals, a puzzle and so on). Next, read through the tasks with them before they work in pairs to complete them.

In addition to completing the cover page tasks, you could build up a Question Poster with the students. Put a large sheet of paper on the wall and draw a circle with the word 'Animals' in it. Add lines out from the circle and on one line put a question (for example, 'What do giraffes eat?'). Ask the students what other things they would like to know about animals. Add their questions to the poster. (They can ask their questions in the mother tongue but you can write them in English.) Over the next few weeks, students can try to find the answers to some of these questions. Allow time at the end of some lessons for them to tell the class what they have found out.

> **Note:** It is *not* intended that *you* answer their questions! It is the *students'* responsibility to find the answers from books, friends, family, their other subject teachers and so on.

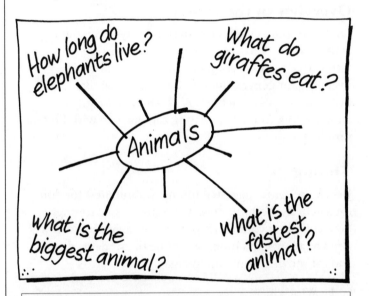

Answers
a word puzzle: Unit 13;   butterfly poster: Unit 11;
   parrot: Unit 9;   jigsaw: Unit 10;   activity poster: Unit 12.
a graph: Unit 9, Ex. 6;   a song: Unit 9, Ex. 5;   a letter: Unit 12.
In Unit 11 they can make a poster about animals.
In Unit 12 they can learn about life in the countryside.

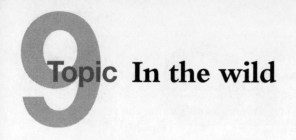

Topic **In the wild**

---

1 WHAT HAPPENED WITH UNITS 3–8?

Some questions to think about before you start Unit 9.

- Look back at the content boxes for Units 3 and 4. Are there some areas where you think the students need extra practice? Do only *some* students need extra help?

- Is it possible for you to plan a time in the coming lessons where those students can get extra practice?
- Did it take longer or shorter than you thought to complete Units 3–8? If it took longer, are there sections of Units 9–12 that you can drop?

---

2 TEACHING NOTES FOR UNIT 9

Overview of the Unit

Unit 9 introduces animal names and ways of classifying animal types. Present simple question forms are introduced through asking about graphs and charts. Listening for general understanding and making dialogues are also practised. A *Decide* exercise gives a choice between further writing and practice with Present simple questions.

Timing

Below are some suggested timings (in minutes) for doing each activity. You can note down any revised timings here and show your anticipated lesson divisions. You will need to allow extra time for settling the students down and for moving from task to task.

1	What is it?	5
2	Buzzz ...	10
3	Mammals, reptiles, insects, birds and fish	15
4	What are we?	5
5	Sing a song!	10
6	How do they live?	15
7	Ask about the animals	10
8	Which animal is it?	5
9	Your own radio programme	20
10	Decide ...	15
11	Your Language Record	10

(See also **AtoZ** TIMING.)

What you need

The Class Cassette for Exercises 2, 3 (optional), 5 and 8.

Mixed-ability classes and supplementary worksheets

Exercises 7 and 9 have additional guidelines for mixed-ability classes.
Say it clearly! worksheet 1: /s/, /z/, /ɪz/
(See also **AtoZ** MIXED ABILITIES.)

Workbook

Unit 9 in the Workbook contains exercises to practise:

- Exercise 1: vocabulary (doing and making a puzzle).
- Exercise 2: classifying animals.
- Exercise 3: sounds /s/, /z/ /ɪz/.
- Exercise 4: speaking.
- Exercise 5: reading and writing about animals.
- Exercise 6: singing a song in English.

For additional notes on the Workbook and Workbook answers see page 145.

Guidelines

1 What is it?

Before you do this exercise, you can ask the students (perhaps in their mother tongue) if they have animals at home, what their favourite animals are, which animals they don't like, etc.

Answers		
a monkey	**d** parrot	**g** shark
b bee	**e** elephant	**h** crocodile
c kangaroo	**f** whale	

2 Buzzz ...

For each animal noise, you can ask two or three students for their answers. Encourage them to use the phrases given in the book. Explain that the box with '?' in it contains a 'mystery' animal.

Answers		
1 a cow	4 a horse	7 a parrot
2 a sheep	5 a bee	8 a whale
3 a lion	6 a monkey	

- WB Ex. 1: names of animals.

3 Mammals, reptiles, insects, birds and fish

AtoZ TRANSLATION and PROCESSING TIME

Check the students understand what *mammals*, *reptiles*, *insects*, *birds* and *fish* mean and explain that they have to match the texts to the correct definition. Read through the sentences 1–5 for the students and then read through the sentences in boxes a–e, dealing with any vocabulary problems. Give the students a few minutes, in pairs, to match the definition to the names and then play the cassette once or twice for them to check their answers.

Answers
1 b 2 c 3 e 4 a 5 d

> **Note:** not included here are other types of animals, such as amphibians (e.g. frogs and toads) arachnids (e.g. spiders and scorpions), annelids (e.g. worms) and molluscs (e.g. octopuses, oysters, snails).

Give the students a few minutes to look back at the animals in Exercises 1 and 2. Encourage them to use the phrases in Exercise 2 when giving their answers.

Answers
Mammals: a kangaroo, an elephant, a whale, a monkey, a cow, a sheep, a lion, a horse;   Reptiles: a crocodile;   Fish: a shark;   Insects: a bee;   Birds: a parrot

- WB Ex. 2: classifying animals.

4 What are we?

AtoZ PROCESSING TIME

Answers
a ✓ b ✗ c ✗ d ✗ e ✓ f ✗   We are mammals.

5 Sing a song! Wimoweh

AtoZ SONGS

After listening to the song on the cassette, you could divide the class into two groups, with one group singing 'Wimoweh' and the other groups singing the verses.

- WB Ex. 6: sing a song.

6 How do they live?

AtoZ PROCESSING TIME

There is a lot of information here so the students will need time to become familiar with it before they work in pairs on Exercise 7. Read the questions to the students and ask for translations. Ask a few questions about each piece of information e.g. 'How long do cows sleep?' Encourage full answers e.g. 'They sleep for six hours.'

Then give the students a few minutes to find the answers to a–d.

Answers
a people b lions, giraffes and cows c bats d horses

7 Ask about the animals

AtoZ PATTERN PRACTICE, PAIRWORK and PRONUNCIATION

Before beginning the exercise, draw the students' attention to the *Say it clearly!* box. Ask them to repeat each word after you. Additional words to pronounce are:

's' sound: cats, whales, bats, sharks, parrots.
'z' sound: cows, lions, dolphins, tigers, penguins, bees.
'iz' sound: horses, fishes, ostriches.

You could divide the class into teams for the exercise. One point for a correct question and answer. First team to 10 wins.

> **MIXED ABILITIES**
>
> *More support can be given by*
> - giving students a list of questions. You can then give them a few minutes to find the answers before they ask each other in pairs.
> - asking students first to ask each other questions about what animals eat, then about how long they live, then about how many hours they sleep.
>
> *The task can be made more demanding by*
> - asking students to make a matching exercise for other students to do. They can write eight questions and eight answers to match them to.

- WB Ex. 3: practises these sounds. See also *Say it clearly!* worksheet 1 (page 169).

8 Which animal is it?

TAPESCRIPT

Expert: Yes that's right. Well, you see they sleep 19 hours during the day and then they look for food at night.

Interviewer: What do they eat?

Expert: Well, they eat small insects and fruit. They have to eat a lot.

Interviewer: Do they live very long?

Expert: Usually they live about five years. Sometimes six or seven years, but usually they live for five years.

Interviewer: They are reptiles, aren't they?

Expert: Oh no, they are mammals. In fact, they are the only mammals that can fly.

Interviewer: That's interesting.

---

9 Your own radio programme

AtoZ **TASK IN BLOCKS, MONITORING AND GUIDING** and **ROLE PLAY**

This exercise has two stages. It will probably save time if you explain to the students what they have to do for each section before they begin work. That way, they can move on to the second stage when they are ready.

Students do the first part by themselves (drawing and filling in the form) and the second part with their neighbour, using the questions on the form as part of the interview. You could leave the second part to another lesson, asking them to prepare their interviews before class.

- **WB Exs. 4 and 5: speaking, reading and writing about animals.**

10 Decide ...
AtoZ **DECIDE EXERCISES**

11 Your Language Record
AtoZ **LANGUAGE RECORD**

Time to spare?
AtoZ **TIME TO SPARE?**

Language focus

1 RESEARCHING THE CLASSROOM: GRAMMAR

Some questions to think about during the coming lessons.

- Are there points of grammar which the students seem to understand but which they do not use accurately most of the time? What are they? Why do you think that is?

- Are there areas of grammar which they use more or less correctly but which you haven't taught them? What are they? Why do you think that is?
- How important do you think their grammar errors are?

(See also **AtoZ** GRAMMAR for more ideas.)

2 TEACHING NOTES FOR UNIT 10

Overview of the Unit

Unit 10 opens with a brief discussion about the students' knowledge of animals and a listening task. It then provides practice with Present simple questions and possessive adjectives. The *Out and about* section focuses on asking for personal information and inviting. The *Revision Box* after the *Language Record* revises the names of the numbers.

Timing

Below are some suggested timings (in minutes) for doing the exercises. These may vary considerably from group to group and are given here only as a rough guide. (See also **AtoZ** TIMING.)

1	Some more animals	10
2	Which animal is it?	10
3	Asking questions	
3.1	Types of questions	15
3.2	Describe questions	5
3.3	Some more practice	15
4	'my, your, his, her' ...	
4.1	What do you say?	5
4.2	Complete the box	10
4.3	Practice using possessive adjectives	10
5	Out and about with English	
5.1	Mona makes a new friend	5
5.2	Mona's questions	10
5.3	Practice	15
6	Your Language Record	10

Important! Remember to allow time for students to discuss the posters they will make in your Unit 11 lesson. (See the Teaching Notes for Unit 11.)

What you need

The Class Cassette for Exercises 2 and 5.2.

Mixed-ability classes and supplementary worksheets

Exercises 3.3, 4.2, 4.3, and 5.3 have additional guidelines for mixed-ability classes.

Language worksheet 10.1: Present simple questions.
Language worksheet 10.2: possessive adjectives.
(See also **AtoZ** MIXED ABILITIES.)

Workbook

Unit 10 in the Workbook contains exercises to practise:

- Exercise 1: reading.
- Exercise 2: Present simple questions.
- Exercise 3: possessive adjectives.
- Exercise 4: sounds /s/, /z/, /ɪz/.
- Exercise 5: speaking (inviting).
- Exercise 6: numbers.

Guidelines

1 Some more animals

AtoZ DISCUSSION

Look at the pictures with the students, saying the name of each animal. Write the three questions on the board and read through the possible answers. Then ask the students for their answers for each animal.

Answers
pandas: in forests, plants (bamboo), Asia
hippopotamuses: in rivers, grass, Africa
humming birds: in trees, nectar from plants and very small insects, North and South America
tarantulas: in deserts and jungles, insects, in most continents of the world

2 Which animal is it? ▭

A to Z LISTENING

The purpose of this recording is to give the students more exposure to question forms. They can thus listen with their books open or closed. After they have listened and answered the questions, you can play the recording again and ask the students Anne's questions.

Answer
a humming bird

- **WB Ex.1: reading about animals.**

3 Asking questions

3.1 Types of questions

Put the two types of questions on the board so that you can draw your students' attention to the differences. When they have found more examples from Unit 1–9, you can then add them to the board under the appropriate type.

Some examples from Unit 9
What do elephants eat? How long do lions live? How many hours do cats sleep? What does it look like? What does it eat? Where does it live?

3.2 Describe the questions

A to Z INDUCTIVE GRAMMAR and GRAMMAR

After the students have thought about and perhaps discussed with their neighbour how to describe the question form, ask what they have put in their notes.

You can then write 'how long', 'how many' and 'where' on the blackboard and ask the students for examples of questions with those words.

Answers
'Do' + subject + verb
'Does' +
Possible points to note:
– the difference between question forms in English and question forms in the mother tongue
– the use of 'does' with he/she/it
– use of the infinitive verb form

3.3 SOME MORE PRACTICE

A to Z TASK IN BLOCKS, MONITORING AND GUIDING and EXERCISE BOX

Before the students choose an exercise, go through the three exercises with them so they know what to do. While they are working, you can then move round the room helping where necessary.

MIXED ABILITIES
More support can be given by
- giving the first word of each question in Exercise B.
- giving out cut up questions for students to put together for Exercise C, and answers to match them to.

The task can be made more demanding by
- asking the students to write a conversation between two animals in which they ask each other about where they live. They can then act this out.
- asking students to write eight questions in Exercise C.

Answers
Ex.A: How long do giraffes sleep? What do pandas eat? When do giraffes sleep? Where do pandas live? How many legs does a tarantula have? Does a hippopotamus lay eggs? Does a hippopotamus eat meat? Do tarantulas eat people?

Answers
Ex. B (in order): How long do giraffes sleep? When do giraffes sleep? What do pandas eat? Where do pandas live? Does a hippopotamus eat meat? Does a hippopotamus lay eggs? How many legs does a tarantula have? Do tarantulas eat people?

- **WB Ex. 2: further practice on questions. Also, Language worksheet 9.1.**

4 'my, your, his, her' …

4.1 What do you say?

If you put the sentences on the board, you can then ask for translations and write them over the appropriate word. You can then point out that these types of words are called *possessive adjectives* and ask for more examples.

4.2 Complete the box

Students can complete the box in pairs. All the missing possessive adjectives are given in the examples. Put a complete version of the box on the board.

In many languages, the same word may be used for two or more English possessive adjectives. This can make the table confusing for the students. If this is the case, you can first talk with the students about why they find it confusing or difficult and then, with them, put an explanation after each possessive adjective. For example:

he	his	*translation* (of 'a man')
she	her	*translation* (of 'a woman')
it	its	*translation* (of 'a thing' or 'animal')

Answers
you (sing.) – your/Write your answers;   it – its/A cow gives milk to its babies;   we – our /Our skin is thick;   they – their/Their blood is cold

4.3 PRACTICE using possessive adjectives

A to Z PATTERN PRACTICE and MONITORING AND GUIDING

This exercise requires quite a lot of careful thought, so it is probably best to go through some examples with the students before they do it in pairs.

- WB Ex. 3: further practice with possessive adjectives. Also, Language worksheet 9.2.

5 Out and about with English

5.1 Mona makes a new friend

This exercise can be done with the students' books closed so that they do not see the dialogue that follows.

Collect the students' suggestions of questions on the blackboard.

5.2 Mona's questions 🖭

Once the students have listened, you can look back at your list of blackboard questions and see if any of Mona's questions are there.

5.3 PRACTICE

A to Z ROLE PLAY

Before the students go into pairs, you can follow the basic dialogue and ask a few students around the class. Then get them first to practise the dialogue in pairs before they go on to invent their own.

- WB Ex. 5: further practice with speaking.

6 Your Language Record

A to Z LANGUAGE RECORD

Time to spare?

A to Z TIME TO SPARE?

Answers

1 bee	4 people	7 snake
2 lion	5 fish	8 cat
3 egg	6 bat	9 elephant

Revision Box

You could also then give a dictation of some numbers for them to write down and perhaps add up and take away. (This will have to be done slowly – numbers take time to work out.)

For the Bingo game, you can play the cassette (pausing if necessary) or read out the numbers yourself. The cards will be completed in this order: 5, 6, 3, 1, 2, 4.

▭ **TAPESCRIPT**

28 26 92 18 24 88 99 55 81 13 30 45 54 11 40
23 101 12 1 38 10 67 90 9 19 61 15 29 16 21
60 42 31 3 100 4 2 17 70 14 5 7

• **WB Ex. 6: further practice with numbers.**

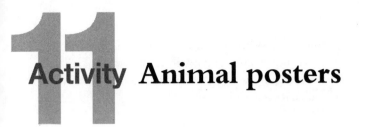

Activity Animal posters

TEACHING NOTES FOR UNIT 11

Overview of the Unit

In Unit 11, the students work in groups to produce posters about pictures of animals which they have collected. This involves them in writing short descriptive texts. At the end of the activity, there is a short evaluation discussion. (See also **AtoZ POSTERS**.)

Timing

Unit 11 is intended for one full lesson, but you may decide to split it up over a number of lessons. Suggested timings (in minutes) are:

Before the lesson	
1 Talk about your poster	10
2 Collect some pictures	(at home)
In the lesson	
3 Write about your pictures	30
4 Talk about your posters	10
5 Evaluation	10

What you need

Some large sheets of paper (e.g. A3) and some smaller sheets (e.g. A4). Some extra pictures of animals (in case students don't bring enough). Coloured pens, glue, scissors.

Mixed-ability classes

Exercise 3 has additional guidelines for mixed-ability classes.
(See also **AtoZ MIXED ABILITIES**.)

Workbook

Unit 11 in the Workbook contains exercises to practise:

- Exercise 1: reading about animals.
- Exercise 2.1: reading and finding information.
- Exercise 2.2: asking questions.

Guidelines

Before the lesson

1   Talk about your poster

AtoZ GROUPWORK and **DISPLAYING STUDENTS' WORK**
Before putting the students into groups, explain what they will be doing and what you want to do with the posters (e.g. display them on the wall, in the school corridor, etc.). You will need to allow 10 minutes or so for students to discuss in their groups what their poster will be about. If they can't agree, you could move students to another suitable group. Alternatively, you could ask the students to talk about the posters in their own time (at break, lunch, etc.).

2   Collect some pictures

Go through the types of pictures they can collect and the information they need to find out about the animals in their pictures. Ask them where they can find the information (parents, friends, libraries, encyclopaedias, etc.).

3 Write about your pictures

AtoZ INTERACTIVE WRITING

Students should do their work on rough paper first so that they can correct and revise it. They can then copy it on to another sheet to mount beside their pictures on the poster sheets, possibly using coloured papers (if available) to liven it up.

MIXED ABILITIES

More support can be given by
- dividing the students into groups with a mixture of student abilities in each group. Each student can write a sentence which the rest of the group can revise or develop.
- providing an outline on the board. For example: 'This is …', 'It is …', 'It lives in …', 'It lives for …', 'It eats …', 'It has …'
- sitting with the groups and discussing what they can write and perhaps writing it with them.

The task can be made more demanding by
- asking students to write about several animals.

- asking them to find out more details and to write about it. For example: habitat, how they look after their young, how many offspring they have, what the animal eats, and so on.

4 Talk about your posters

AtoZ DISPLAYING STUDENTS' WORK

The posters can be stuck on the wall or laid out on the desks. The students can then all stand and walk around the room looking at the other posters and talking to the people who wrote them. You could make a quiz (on the board) for this stage, based on what the students have written. Students then have to find the answers as they look at the posters. For example:

- What is Mozzi?
- How long do Monarch butterflies live?
- Where does a hippopotamus live?

5 EVALUATION

AtoZ EVALUATION

This can be done with the whole class. Emphasise the 'How can you do it better next time?' question and try to get them to suggest practical steps for the next activity they do.

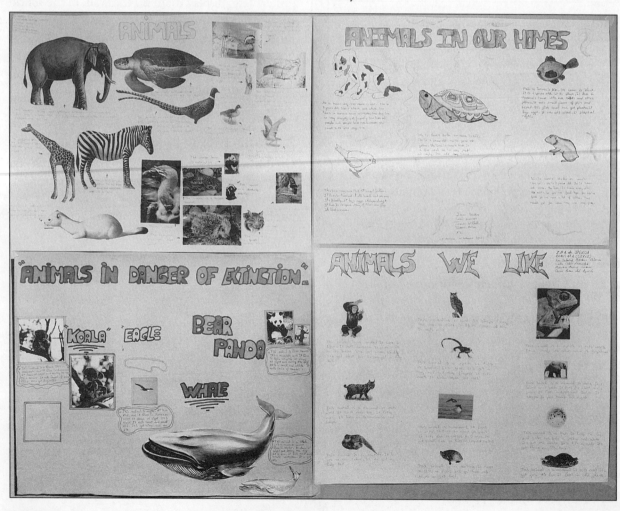

12 Culture matters Life in the countryside

TEACHING NOTES FOR UNIT 12

Overview of the Unit

The aim of the *Culture matters* Units is to give the students some understanding of how British society is different from their own. This Unit complements Unit 6 (Life in a town) with an emphasis on life in the British countryside. Students learn about two key roles of the countryside in Britain: as a workplace (farms) and as a leisure area. The Unit provides listening comprehension and letter-writing tasks. The letter-writing task is a real one – students can send for further information about the leisure activities in the British countryside.

Timing

The *Culture matters* Units are intended for one full lesson, but you may decide to split it up over a number of lessons. Suggested timings (in minutes) are:

1	About your country	10
2	Working in the country	15
3	Relaxing in the country	20–25

What you need

The Class Cassette for Exercise 2.

Mixed-ability classes

Exercise 2 has additional guidelines for mixed-ability classes.
(See also **AtoZ** MIXED ABILITIES.)

Workbook

Unit 12 in the Workbook is the second *Help yourself* Unit: *Help yourself with grammar*. The Unit contains three ways the students can practise their grammar at home:

- Exercise 1: making sentence jigsaws.
- Exercise 2: writing their own sentences following a model.
- Exercise 3: writing their own sentences to translate into English following a model.

See page 145 for a special note on the *Help yourself* Units. (See also **AtoZ** GRAMMAR and INDUCTIVE GRAMMAR.)

Guidelines

Note how the term 'country' has two meanings:
1) a nation e.g. England, France, etc.
2) a rural area.

1 About your country

AtoZ MOTHER TONGUE

You can ask these questions in English, but, at this stage, you may need to translate them and accept replies in the mother tongue. (You could translate these replies.) Since the main aim of the Unit is to develop cross-cultural awareness, an 'English only' rule may defeat the purpose.

2 Working in the country 📼

AtoZ LISTENING

Read the introductory sentences aloud, translating if necessary.

Look through the pictures with the students, reading the captions under each one. Students then number them in the order they think he does the activities. Play the cassette (probably two or three times) for them to write in the times and check their order. Point out that NOT ALL the times are given on the cassette.

You could continue by asking if farmers in your country have the same sort of day. If not, how is it different?

> **MIXED ABILITIES**
> *More support can be given by*
> - giving the students the tapescript to read beforehand.
> - putting the students into groups and asking different students in each group to listen for particular pieces of information.
> - telling the students to ask you to stop and replay the recording when they don't understand.
> - telling the students some of the times.

Answers

1 gets up (F): 6.00 a.m.
2 milks cows and cleans shed (D): between 6–7.30 a.m.
3 has breakfast (B): 7.30 a.m.
4 puts fertilizer on field (A): between 7.30–10.00 a.m.
5 checks equipment, does repairs (H): between 7.30–10.00 a.m.
6 goes to market (I): 10.00 a.m.
7 eats lunch (G): 12.00 p.m.
8 milks cows again (J): 4.00 p.m.
9 has dinner (E): 5.30 p.m.
10 goes to bed (C): 10.00 p.m.

🔲 **TAPESCRIPT**

Interviewer: So, what time do you get up, Henry?

Henry Wilson: Now, in April, I usually get up at about 6 o'clock in the morning.

Interviewer: And do you have breakfast then?

Henry Wilson: Oh, no, I milk the cows first and clean the milking shed. Then I come back to the house.

Interviewer: What time is that?

Henry Wilson: Well, I come back and have breakfast at about half past seven.

Interviewer: What do you do then?

Henry Wilson: After breakfast, I put fertilizer on the fields and then I check my machines and do repairs. Then, at about 10 o'clock, I usually go to the market.

Interviewer: Do you come back home for lunch?

Henry Wilson: No, I usually have a sandwich at the market at about 12 o'clock.

Interviewer: Then, what?

Henry Wilson: Then I come home at about four to milk the cows again. Then about half past five, I have my dinner.

Interviewer: And then?

Henry Wilson: And then I go to bed! It's a long day.

Interviewer: What time is that?

Henry Wilson: About 10 o'clock.

3 Relaxing in the country

A to Z WRITING and **MONITORING AND GUIDING**

Read the introductory sentences aloud to the students and then look through the leaflet with them. Ask individual students what they would like to do. Encourage full sentences: e.g. 'I would like to go climbing'. Then ask: 'Where can you do that?' (See map.)

Students now write letters asking for information about their chosen activity. They will need to write to the appropriate Tourist Board in England, Scotland or Wales. Emphasise the layout – this is how formal letters are normally laid out in English. While they are writing, circulate around the class helping where necessary. You can send a letter from your class to find out, asking for more information. Addresses:

English Tourist Board
Thames Tower
Black's Road
London W6 9EL
England
Great Britain

Scottish Tourist Board
23 Ravelston Terrace
Edinburgh EH4 3EU
Scotland
Great Britain

Welsh Tourist Board
8/14 Bridge Street
Cardiff CF5 2EV
Wales
Great Britain

Note: England, Scotland and Wales are three separate countries. Together, they form 'Great Britain', a geographical unit (Great Britain is a single island). The 'United Kingdom' consists of Great Britain and Northern Ireland, with one central government. The United Kingdom is therefore the political unit.

Revision and evaluation

TEACHING NOTES FOR UNIT 13

See Unit 7 for the 'General note on the *Revision and evaluation* Units'.

Overview of the Unit

Exercise 1 asks the students how well they think they know the English from Units 9–12. Revision exercises then follow. Students can do some or all of these exercises, depending on time and how much revision they need. In the last exercise, students think about how well they have understood the previous lessons and provide you with written feedback.

Timing

The Unit is intended for one full lesson, with students doing Exercises 2–5 selectively. However, you may want all students to do all the exercises, in which case the Unit may be split up over a number of lessons. Suggested timings (in minutes) are:

1	How well do you know it?	5–10
2	What's the question?	20
3	What's the number?	15
4	This is my family	10
5	What's the word?	10
6	Were you right?	5
7	Evaluation	
7.1	Talk about your English work	10
7.2	Your own ideas	10

What you need

No special materials needed.

Mixed-ability classes and supplementary worksheets

Language worksheet 10.1: Present simple questions.
Language worksheet 10.2: possessive adjectives.
(See also **A to Z** MIXED ABILITIES.)

Workbook

Unit 13 in the Workbook is a self-check test focusing on the language covered in the Theme.

Guidelines

1 How well do you know it?

A to Z TASKS IN GROUPS and OVERVIEWING

The main aim here is to encourage the students to reflect on how much they have learnt.

Before asking students to complete the chart, look back with them at the relevant sections of the previous Units to remind them what they did.

Give the students a few minutes to tick the box. You could encourage them to discuss/compare *briefly* with their neighbour.

Before the students start working, it is a good idea to go through the exercises with them, so that they know exactly what they have to do in each one. After this there are a number of possibilities:

  a Let the students choose what they want to revise and practise – either to test themselves or to revise where they feel weakest.
  b Ask the students to do *two* exercises: one that they ticked 'very well' and one that they ticked 'a little'.
  c Get all the students to do all the exercises (requires more time, of course).
  Students can work alone or in pairs.
(Students can also complete the Unit for homework.)

2 What's the question?

A Students match the question and answer.

> **Answers**
> 1 c 2 d 3 a 4 b 5 e

B   Students form their own questions.

> **Possible questions**
> Where do they live? What do they eat? How long do they live?
> How big are they? Do they lay eggs?

C   The reading passage should give answers to some of their questions!

3   What's the number?

A

> **Answers**
> ninety-seven   thirty-two   eighty-eight   nineteen   ninety

B

> **Answers**
> 12 + 12 = twenty-four   70–15=fifty-five
> 90–20=seventy   88+13=a hundred and one
> 60+30=ninety   35–17=eighteen
> 19+81=one hundred   97–26=seventy-one

4   This is my family

> **Answers**
> 1 my   3 my   his   5 my   its   7 your
> 2 my   her   4 my   their   6 our

5   What's the word?

Words go down through the puzzle.

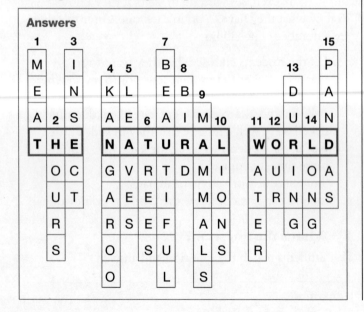

> **Answers**

6   Were you right?

Once the students have done two or more exercises, ask them to look back at their chart in Exercise 1. Do they still think the same? Did they know more or less than they thought?

7   EVALUATION

A to Z   EVALUATION

This section has two parts. 7.1 involves small group discussion, while 7.2 asks students to note down their own reactions. You will need to allow a few minutes at the end of the lesson for students to write their own comments.

For 7.1, divide the students into groups of 3–4, and allocate either Unit 8, Unit 9 or Units 10 and 11 to each group. Ask them to decide who will report back to the class.

For the reporting back stage, if more than one group is looking at the Unit, ask one group to report back and then ask the other group(s) if they have any other points to add.

For 7.2, the students write their own personal ideas in their own language about how they find their English lessons. You could give them some more questions to stimulate their thought:

- How do they feel in their English lessons?
- Do they have any suggestions of what they would like to do?
- Is there anything they would like to do again?
- Where do they think they need more practice?
- What did they like best in their English lessons so far?

Theme C
The way we live

OVERVIEW OF THE THEME

Theme C, *The way we live*, focuses on modern lifestyle – the kinds of food we eat, our leisure activities and where we live. Students learn about the value of different foods and the importance of a good diet (Units 14 and 15). In Unit 16 they write a questionnaire to find out about other students' leisure and eating habits. Unit 17, *Culture matters*, looks at different kinds of British homes.

In terms of language, the students learn to use 'some' and 'any' and object pronouns. 'Can' and the language of daily routines are also revised. The *Out and about* section (Unit 15) presents language for talking about likes and dislikes. Students practise listening (for general understanding and for detail), speaking (through 'brainstorming' and roleplay), and reading and writing short descriptive texts. The *Decide* exercises, use of the *Exercise Box* and evaluation stages continue to involve the students directly.

The Theme offers cross-curricular links with Health Education (Units 14 and 15) and Geography (Unit 17).

Using the cover page

Suggested time: 10 minutes

The pictures visually summarise what the students will be doing in the next five Units. Look through the pictures and ask them what they can see. Next, read through the tasks with them before they work in pairs to complete them.

In addition, you can build up a Question Poster with the students around the word 'Food' of things they would like to learn about food in the coming weeks (see notes on the Theme B cover page, page 51, for more details).

Answers
living room: Unit 17;   food text: Unit 14;   kitchen: Unit 15;   posters: Unit 18;   questionnaire: Unit 16.
something to make at home: Unit 15;   a game: Unit 14, Ex 5;   a song: Unit 14, Ex 9.
Revision Box: different exercises on 'can' and 'can't'.
Unit 16: make a questionnaire.

Topic Food matters

1 WHAT HAPPENED WITH UNITS 9–13?

Some questions to think about before you start Unit 14.

- Which parts of Units 9–13 went best, do you think? Why do you think this was? What do you think the students think? Did the student evaluation section in Unit 13 provide useful feedback to you?
- Which parts of Units 9–13 did not go so well? Why do you think this was? What do you think the students think?

- The students have now worked through two Themes. Do you think they understand the focus of the different kinds of Units (for example, *Topic* Units, *Language focus*, and so on)? Perhaps you could look back at an example of each kind of Unit and ask them what they think the purpose of each Unit was.

2 TEACHING NOTES FOR UNIT 14

Overview of the Unit

Unit 14 focuses on food and the nutritional value that different foods have. Students learn about different ingredients in food and the necessity of having a balanced diet. The vocabulary of food and shopping and the use of 'some' and 'any' are introduced. The *Decide* exercise gives a choice between revising vocabulary in a puzzle or writing about a menu.

Timing

Below are some suggested timings (in minutes) for doing each activity. These will vary considerably from class to class and are only given here as a rough guide.

1	The foods you like	5
2	The food you eat	15
3	How do you start the day?	10
4	Some more things to eat	10
5	Play a game: Dinner time!	10
6	Eat well, stay healthy!	20
7	In the supermarket	15
8	Decide ...	20
9	Sing a song!	10
10	Your Language Record	10

(See also **AtoZ** TIMING.)

What you need

The Class Cassette for Exercises 5, 6 (optional) and 9.

Mixed-ability classes and supplementary worksheets

Exercises 2 and 6 have additional guidelines for mixed-ability classes.
Say it clearly! worksheet 2: /iː/ and /e/.
(See also **AtoZ** MIXED ABILITIES.)

Workbook

Unit 14 in the Workbook contains exercises to practise:

- Exercise 1: vocabulary related to food.
- Exercise 2: an open dialogue about food.
- Exercise 3: reading about calories.
- Exercise 4: further reading about calories.
- Exercise 5: pronunciation: /iː/.
- Exercise 6: singing a song in English.

For additional notes on the use of the Workbook and Workbook answers see page 145.

Guidelines

1 The foods you like

AtoZ DISCUSSION and PROCESSING TIME
The first two questions are intended to get the students' opinions of what they like/dislike eating, while the

second set of questions focuses on facts about food. There may be some contradiction between their answers to the two sets of questions!

For the second set of questions, you could **BRAINSTORM** the answers. Put two circles on the board. In one write 'Foods that are good for you' and in the other 'Foods that are bad for you'. (This may be in the mother tongue; you can write their suggestions in English.) As they suggest foods, you can write them around the circles and also ask *why* they think they are good/bad. This should bring up some of the vocabulary in the text in Exercise 6 (minerals, protein, etc.). The basic point, however, which should become clear in your discussion is that there are few foods which are 'good' or 'bad' in themselves. What is more important is *the quantity* that is eaten and how the food is *balanced* with other foods. (Carrots, for example, are said to be good for you. However, an overdose of carrots can be disastrous!) This point is developed in Exercises 6 and 7.

2 The food you eat

AtoZ **PROCESSING TIME**

Allow the students a few moments to read and answer the questionnaire silently before you discuss it.

MIXED ABILITIES

More support can be given by

- working with the students through the questions one by one, explaining any vocabulary as necessary and giving time for some students to answer orally.
- checking that they understand 'How many' and 'How often' before they start the questionnaire.
- providing translations of the questions which the students first have to match to the English questions.

The task can be made more demanding by

- asking students to write some more 'food' questions.
- asking them to prepare a dialogue using the six questions.
- asking them to write exactly *what* they eat or drink for each question.

3 How do you start the day?

AtoZ **PAIRWORK** AND **MONITORING AND GUIDING**

With the students, read through the words under the pictures first. Students then work in pairs. Go round and listen to their exchanges. Ask a few students to tell the class.

4 Some more things to eat

AtoZ **PRONUNCIATION**

Students can work alone or in pairs for this exercise. Write the lists on the board and practise the pronunciation of the /iː/ sound.

- WB Ex. 1.1: an exercise to practise food vocabulary;
  WB Ex. 2: an open dialogue about food;
  WB Ex. 5: an exercise to practise pronunciation of /iː/.

5 Play a game: Dinner Time!

AtoZ **GAMES**

(We suggest that you do this game in the last five to ten minutes of the lesson. This may mean that you move on to Exercise 6 first.) Make sure the students understand how the game works before they start to play. The game is similar to Bingo but the students choose *two* cards. The students who hear five things on one card without a stomach ache shout 'Dinner Time!' This will only happen for the 'Spider Soup' cards. Play the cassette or read out the items in the following order:

> ▭ TAPESCRIPT
>
> some fruit   some eggs   some fish   some sugar   some bread   some potatoes   some butter   some sweets   some water   some rice   a crocodile sandwich   some meat   an old shoe   some vegetables   some juice   some cereal   and, to finish, some milk!

6 Eat well, stay healthy!

AtoZ **READING**

After reading through the text with the students, you can look back at their questionnaire in Exercise 2 and ask them if they think they eat healthy foods.

Students can also listen to the article on the cassette.

MIXED ABILITIES

More support can be given by

- going through the vocabulary in the *Language Record* first. Students can then refer to the translations as they read.
- showing students how to find key words. Write the first sentences from 'Protein' on the board. Ask students to say which are the important words in the sentence (protein and grow) and underline them. Do the same with sentence 2 (key words: meat, fish, milk). Write the key words at the side. Students can then work in pairs and choose another paragraph and underline the important words.

The task can be made more demanding by
- giving the students the key words from the text and asking them to write some sentences before they read it.
- dictating one of the texts once before the students read it. Students then compare their written version with the text. They can then work in pairs and dictate the other passages once to each other.

- **WB Exs. 3 and 4: reading exercises about calories.**

7 In the supermarket

AtoZ **TASKS IN BLOCKS**

Students can work in pairs to complete both parts of this exercise. They can then check their answers with the rest of the class.

Answers
From left to right, the correct labels are: (top shelf) carbohydrates, fats, fibre; (bottom shelf) water, protein, minerals, vitamins (also in all foods).
Food baskets: **1** mainly carbohydrates, some protein; **2** mainly fibre, some minerals; **3** mainly minerals, some carbohydrates; **4** all seven elements.
Basket 4 contains a balanced selection of foods.

- **WB Ex 1.2: an exercise about the important things in food.**

8 Decide …

AtoZ **DECIDE EXERCISES, AUTONOMY** and **OVERVIEWING**

Once again, go through the exercises with the students before you ask them to choose.

8.1 A puzzle

Answers

1	**C**	H	E	E	S	E	
2	W	**A**	T	E	R		
3	E	N	E	**R**	G	Y	
4			B	**R**	E	A	D
5	G	R	**O**	W			
6		H	**A**	I	R		
7	E	**Y**	E	S			
8	B	O	**D**	Y			
9	M	I	N	E	**R**	A	L	S
10	S	U	G	**A**	R		
11	M	E	A	**T**			
12	R	I	C	**E**			

8.2 Write a menu

AtoZ **WRITING**

Students can work alone or in pairs to prepare their menus. When they have finished let the rest of the class have a look to discuss their choices.

- **WB Ex. 6: sing a song.**

9 Sing a song! I love chocolate ▭

AtoZ **SONGS**

10 Your Language Record

AtoZ **LANGUAGE RECORD**

Time to spare?

AtoZ **TIME TO SPARE?**

Language focus

1 RESEARCHING THE CLASSROOM: VOCABULARY

Some questions to think about during the coming lessons.

- What do you think your students do to help themselves learn vocabulary? (Do they, for example, ask you the meanings of words? Do they write down translations? Do they make lists? Do they try to guess meanings?)
- Are there any ways you can get the students to learn vocabulary more actively?
- A week after a lesson, how many 'new words' do you think the students can still remember? What about two weeks or a month later? Why do you think they forget?

(See also **AtoZ** **VOCABULARY** for more ideas.)

2 TEACHING NOTES FOR UNIT 15

Overview of the Unit

Unit 15 opens with a brief discussion about whether the students like cooking and the recipes they know. A listening task then follows which contextualises use of 'some' and 'any'. A grammar discovery exercise for students to work when 'some' and 'any' are used. Practice exercises follow and revision exercises on object pronouns. The *Out and about* section focuses on talking about likes and dislikes. The *Revision Box* after the *Language Record* revises the different uses of 'can' and 'can't'.

Timing

Below are some suggested timings (in minutes) for doing the exercises.

1	Can you cook?	5
2	What are they making?	10
3	What have we got?	
3.1	What do you say?	10
3.2	A grammar puzzle	15
3.3	Practice with 'some' and 'any'	15
4	'them, it, her, him' …	
4.1	What do you say?	5–10
4.2	Practice	10
5	Out and about with English	
5.1	Sophie visits Mona's house	5
5.2	Are you right?	10
5.3	Practice	15
6	Your Language Record	10

What you need

The Class Cassette for Exercises 2 and 5.2. For the *Revision Box* after the *Language Record* you will need some objects in a bag.

Mixed–ability classes and supplementary worksheets

Exercises 3.1, 3.3, and 4.2 have additional guidelines for mixed–ability classes.
Language worksheet 15.1: 'some' and 'any'.
Language worksheet 15.2: object pronouns.
Say it clearly! worksheet 2: /iː/ and /e/.
(See also **AtoZ** **MIXED ABILITIES**.)

Workbook

Unit 15 in the Workbook contains exercises to practise:

- Exercise 1: reading.
- Exercise 2.1: 'some' and 'any'.
- Exercise 2.2: vocabulary.
- Exercise 3: object pronouns and possessive adjectives.
- Exercise 4: pronunciation /e/.
- Exercise 5: talking about likes and dislikes.

Guidelines

1 Can you cook?

AtoZ DISCUSSION

Students discuss their favourite recipes and the meals they can cook. Put the key words on the board. You could ask some pupils to make one of their recipes for the class to try next time.

2 What are they making? 📻

AtoZ LISTENING and PROCESSING TIME

First, read through the recipes with the students. Check that they understand the names of the ingredients. The students can listen to the cassette before, while or after they read.

- **WB Ex. 1: further reading practice about the recipes.**

3 What have we got?

3.1 What do you say?

AtoZ INDUCTIVE GRAMMAR and GRAMMAR

Elicit translations from the students and ask them what they think 'some' and 'any' mean.

> **MIXED ABILITIES**
>
> *More support can be given by*
> - writing the translations of the sentences on the blackboard.
> - asking students to find two examples of a 'some' and 'any' sentence in the dialogue and comparing them.
> - Using some objects from the classroom and making up sentences like this:
>   'I haven't got any chalk.'
>   'There aren't any books here.'
>   'There are some papers on my desk.'
>   Ask students to make up similar sentences about other objects.
>
> *The task can be made more demanding by*
> - asking the students to make up three more similar sentences about their bag or the classroom or their home.

> **Answers**
> 'some' and 'any' here mean 'an unspecified amount'. However, many languages do not have a direct equivalent that speakers would naturally use.

3.2 A grammar puzzle

AtoZ INDUCTIVE GRAMMAR and GRAMMAR

Students look at the examples and write down their rules.

You do NOT need to point this out here, but, specifically, 'some' is used for uncountables in positive sentences:

> 'There is some sugar on the table.'

and plural countables:

> 'There are some books in my bag.'

However, there are many exceptions to this basic rule. For example, if you are thinking about a specific amount, you might say 'some' in a question:

> 'Do you want some sugar?' (i.e. a small amount for your coffee).

The concepts of 'uncountable' and 'countable' are introduced in Unit 25.

Ensure the students have a clear pronunciation of 'any'.

> **Answers**
> The basic rule which the examples here follow is that 'some' is used with positive sentences and 'any' is used with negative sentences and questions.

- **WB Ex. 4: an exercise to practise the /e/ sound.**

3.3 PRACTICE with 'some' and 'any'

Check that students have labelled the picture correctly. Then allow time to look at the picture. Explain that you will say the names of some foods. Students write a sentence using 'some' and 'any' to describe the picture.

> **MIXED ABILITIES**
>
> *More support can be given by*
> - getting the students first to write four sentences using 'some' and 'any' about the picture. These may be true or not true. They then give them to their partner (or the class) to say if the sentences are true or not.
> - reading out only six words: tell the students that three are in the picture and three are not.
>
> *The task can be made more demanding by*
> - giving each student six magazine pictures. They write a 'some' or 'any' sentence about each picture and other students must guess which picture each sentence refers to.
> - writing out the dialogue from Exercise 2 with 'some' and 'any' removed. Students try to fill the gaps and then check their answers with the book.

> **Words to read out**
> bread   meat   butter   cheese   fruit   eggs   water   fish
> vegetables   sweets   milk   sugar

- WB Exs. 2.1 and 2.2, and Language worksheet 15.1 give further practice with 'some' and 'any'.

4 'them, it, her, him' ...

4.1 What do you say?

AtoZ MOTHER TONGUE

You could put some more sentences on the board to give the students more examples. For example:

'Here are some books. Do you want them?
That dog doesn't like us!'

4.2 PRACTICE

AtoZ PATTERN PRACTICE, PAIRWORK and **MONITORING AND GUIDING**

Check that students understand the phrases: 'I like', 'I don't mind', and 'I hate' before they start the pairwork. Students then look at the pictures and ask each other what they like.

> **MIXED ABILITIES**
>
> *More support can be given by*
> - working through the pictures with the students first to help them write 'it', 'him', 'her', 'them' under each one.
> - asking students to suggest some more items. Write them on the board with the appropriate object pronoun next to them and an adjective.
> - getting the students to take it in turns to ask you the questions first for you to reply.

- WB Ex. 3 and Language worksheet 15.2 give further practice in object pronouns.

5 Out and about with English

5.1 Sophie visits Mona's house

AtoZ DISCUSSION

Give students plenty of time to look at the pictures. Ask them what they talk about when they visit someone else's house. Put the key ideas and vocabulary on the board.

5.2 Are you right? 📼

AtoZ LISTENING

When the students have listened to the cassette, look back at the suggestions on the board. Check vocabulary if necessary.

5.3 PRACTICE

AtoZ ROLE PLAY

Before the students invent their own dialogues, ask them to practise the dialogue in 5.2 as an open dialogue in pairs first. One student reads one part, the other has the book shut and has to improvise some answers.

Using the items listed, you can then act out a dialogue with one or two students as an example. Encourage them to be as creative as they can with the language they know.

- WB Ex. 5: further practice talking about likes and dislikes.

6 Your Language Record

AtoZ LANGUAGE RECORD

Time to spare?

AtoZ TIME TO SPARE?

> **Exercise 2 answers**
> bread   butter   cheese   eggs   milk   potatoes   sugar

Revision Box

AtoZ REVISION BOX

For Exercise 3, you will need to have a few objects ready in a bag. You can play the game with the whole class. Before beginning, elicit some more questions that they can ask.

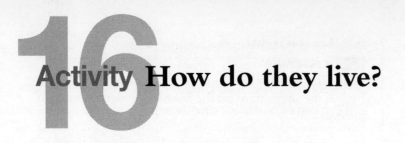

Activity How do they live?

TEACHING NOTES FOR UNIT 16

Overview of the Unit

In Unit 16, the students work in groups to write a questionnaire about different aspects of their lives, for example, daily routines, food, hobbies, sports, etc. They also learn about ways of presenting the information they get. At the end, there is a short evaluation discussion focusing on how well they managed to write their questionnaires.

Timing

The *Activity* Units are usually intended as one lesson. However, this *Activity* Unit will need to be done over two lessons (one complete lesson and part of another lesson a week or so later). Suggested timings (in minutes) are:

1	How do you live?	15
2	Other classes, other students	20
3	Write a questionnaire	20
4	Test your questionnaire	10
In the next questionnaire lesson		
5	What did you find out?	15
6	Evaluation	10

What you need

No special materials, but if you have the use of a computer, printer and an overhead projector the making of the questionnaires and the presentation of the graphs and information will be more fun.

Mixed-ability classes

Exercises 2, 3 and 5 have additional guidelines for mixed-ability classes.
(See also **AtoZ MIXED ABILITIES**.)

Workbook

Unit 16 in the Workbook contains exercises to practise fluency, first by drawing and writing about graphs and then by writing a questionnaire.

- Exercise 1: looking at / reading graphs.
- Exercise 2: writing about a graph.
- Exercise 3: reading and then drawing a graph.
- Exercise 4: writing a questionnaire.

Guidelines

Introduction

To raise the students' interest, you can tell them that they are going to find out about the way other people live. Explain that they will be designing a questionnaire together.

1 How do you live?

AtoZ READING and DISCUSSION
Let the students work alone to fill in the questionnaire and then compare their ideas with the rest of the class.

2 Other classes, other students

AtoZ BRAINSTORMING
Copy the diagrams on to the board and then ask the students for other questions they would like to ask. Encourage them to say these in English, but help them to form the questions correctly as you put the questions on the board. Encourage them to suggest other topic areas.

> **MIXED ABILITIES**
> *More support can be given by*
> - providing further ideas such as: the magazines they buy, the kinds of books they read, the clubs they belong to, places they like to visit, etc.
> - writing some examples of 'Wh' questions on the board first (what, when, where, etc.) from the topic.
> - writing some examples of 'Do you' questions on the board.

3 Write a questionnaire

AtoZ GROUPWORK and MONITORING AND GUIDING

Divide the students into groups and ask them to choose two or three topic areas. Point out the two kinds of questions (multiple choice and open questions).

Remind them to look back at the questionnaire in Unit 14 for some help with questions. Tell them to write clearly so everyone can read their questions.

> Note: If there is a computer and printer available the students could type the questionnaire and print out some copies.

MIXED ABILITIES

The task can be made more demanding by
- asking students to design a questionnaire to cover two different ages, for example, students and their parents or grandparents, or writing questions for boys and girls separately or a questionnaire for teachers!

4 Test your questionnaire

Students pass their questions to another group or groups for them to answer. They can then check to see if the questions were clear enough or if more possible answers need to be given in the multiple choice questions.

Once the students have revised their questions, they can then use them to ask people over the next few days. Agree with the students *when* you will continue with the questionnaire and which people or groups they should each ask (family, friends, other schools, other classes).

In the next questionnaire lesson

5 What did you find out?

AtoZ OVERVIEWING and GROUPWORK

Before you set the students working in groups, go through what they have to do. You may want to do this in stages:

a Students share the information.
b You ask for one group's information and show the class how they can make a graph. Students then make graphs in their groups.
c Using one group's information, show them how they can say it (as in the example in the book).

MIXED ABILITIES

More support can be given by
- putting some graphs on the board first and explaining how to draw them.
- asking the students to divide the questionnaire so that each person has some questions to work on.

The task can be made more demanding by
- giving students different examples of graphs – e.g. piecharts or line graphs: they can then present the same information in different ways.

- **WB Exs. 1–4 focus on graphs and questionnaires.**

6 EVALUATION

AtoZ EVALUATION

This can be done with the whole class. Emphasise the 'How can you do it better next time?' question and try to get them to suggest practical steps for the next activity they do.

17 Culture matters Life at home

At home in your country and in England; reading, listening and discussing

TEACHING NOTES FOR UNIT 17

Overview of the Unit

This *Culture matters* Unit focuses on different kinds of houses and homes in England. The students see inside an English living room and make comparisons with homes in their country.

Timing

The *Culture matters* Units are intended for one full lesson but you may decide to split it up over a number of lessons. Suggested timings (in minutes) are:

1	About your country	5
2	Two families in England	10
3	At home with the Sharmas	10
4	At home with the Greens	10–15
5	In the living room	10

What you need

The Class Cassette for Exercise 5. If you have more photographs or magazine pictures of English streets and houses they would make a useful addition.

Mixed-ability classes

Exercises 2, 3 and 5 have additional guidelines for mixed-ability classes.
(See also **AtoZ** MIXED ABILITIES.)

Workbook

Unit 17 in the Workbook is the third *Help yourself* Unit: *Help yourself with vocabulary*. The Unit contains two ways in which the students can practise their vocabulary at home:

- Exercise 1: making a word bag.
- Exercise 2: making a jigsaw.

See page 145 for a special note on the *Help yourself* Units.

(See also **AtoZ** VOCABULARY.)

Guidelines

1 About your country

AtoZ MOTHER TONGUE and DISCUSSION

You can ask these questions in English, but you may need to translate them and accept replies in the mother tongue. Put the key words in English on the board. You may need to explain words like *brick*, *stone* and *wooden* (houses) and *detached*, *semi-detached* and *terraced* houses.

2 Two families in England

AtoZ READING AND DISCUSSION

Ask students to read the texts and discuss the questions with their partner before you open it out for a class discussion.

> **MIXED ABILITIES**
>
> *More support can be given by*
> - asking students to look at the pictures of the two families before they read the texts and match them to the houses in Exercise 1.
>
> *The task can be made more demanding by*
> - getting students to work in pairs and read one text each. They share the information with each other. Encourage students to guess words they don't know and to focus only on the key words in the text.
> - asking the students to work in groups to discuss the questions first before discussing with the whole class.

3 At home with the Sharmas

AtoZ READING, TASKS IN BLOCKS and MONITORING AND GUIDING

Check that the students know the vocabulary of rooms in a house before they start reading. Ask students which rooms they have in their house and write key words on the board with translations if necessary.

74 Theme C Unit 17 Culture matters

Answers
a Mr and Mrs Sharmas' bedroom
b kitchen
c living/dining room
d bathroom
e bedroom

4 At home with the Greens

Students read the text and then choose the appropriate jigsaw piece.

Answers
Downstairs: television room and kitchen;
Upstairs: bedroom and bathroom.

5 In the living room 📻

AtoZ LISTENING

You can ask the students to label the picture before you go through the meaning of the words. This will help you see how much they know.

Answers

1 a carpet	7 a wall
2 a sofa	8 a fire
3 a chair	9 a lamp
4 a (dining) table	10 a bookcase
5 curtains	11 a (coffee) table
6 a vase	

📻 TAPESCRIPT

Interviewer: Tell me about your living room, Mrs Green.
Mrs Green: Well, we've got a small living room. It's got a sofa and a large, old bookcase. We've also got a small table in the window and ...
Interviewer: Have you got any plants?
Mrs Green: Oh yes! I love plants. I've got some very big plants.
Interviewer: What colour are the walls?
Mrs Green: Well, the walls are pink. They look very nice with the dark red curtains.
Interviewer: What colour is your carpet?
Mrs Green: Oh, we haven't got a carpet. We haven't got anything on the floor.
Interviewer: Isn't it cold?
Mrs Green: Oh no, we've got a big open fire. It's always very warm.
Interviewer: Oh I see.

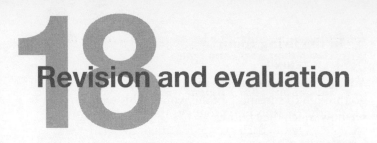

18 Revision and evaluation

TEACHING NOTES FOR UNIT 18

See Unit 7 for the 'General note on the *Revision and evaluation* Units'.

Overview of the Unit

Previous *Revision and evaluation* Units (Units 7 and 13) have included revision exercises for the students to do. This revision Unit, however, has a different structure which is repeated in Units 23 and 33. Instead of doing prepared revision exercises, the students build up their own test, using examples given in the Student's Book. The process of doing this has a number of important aims. It helps to make tests directly useful to learning; it helps to dispel the fear of tests which many students have; and it involves them in a deeper level of language and learning awareness.

The final part of the Unit involves an evaluation discussion of Units 14–17 and where the students think they need more practice.

Timing

The main part of the Unit (Exercises 1–3) is intended for one full lesson, with the students' own test being used in another lesson or as homework. (See below.) Suggested timings (in minutes) are as follows. To save time, students can do the example test (Exercise 2) for homework before the lesson.

1	How well do you know it?	5–10
2	Test yourself!	15–20
3	Write your own test (assembled later)	25
4	Evaluation	
4.1	Talk about your English work	10
4.2	Your own ideas	10

What you need

No special materials needed.

Mixed-ability classes and supplementary worksheets

Language worksheet 15.1: 'some' and 'any'.
Language worksheet 15.2: object pronouns.
(See also **AtoZ MIXED ABILITIES**.)

Workbook

Unit 18 in the Workbook provides further revision exercises around the topics of food and ecology and a *picture dictionary* of vocabulary from Units 14–17.

Guidelines

1   How well do you know it?

AtoZ OVERVIEWING and **AUTONOMY**

The main aim here is to encourage the students to reflect on how much they have learnt. Before asking students to complete the chart, look back with them at the relevant sections of the previous Units to remind them what they did.

Give the students a few minutes to tick the box. You could encourage them to discuss/compare *briefly* with their neighbour.

2   Test yourself!

This test is a simple model for students to write their own test.
Writing their own test is useful because:

1 In order to write the test students need to look back through what they have done and revise new vocabulary and structures.
2 Writing the test will encourage the students to think more deeply about the language.
3 Students are often terrified by tests. Showing them how they can write tests can help to break down this fear so that they can see tests as being another way to learn – rather than simply something imposed on them 'from above'.
As this is simply an example of a test, the answers are provided for students to correct.

Explain to the students that they are going to write their own test and that the test provided here is only an example. Point out where the answers are but encourage them to try doing the test without looking. After doing the test, they can look back at Exercise 1.

> Answers to the test are provided at the end of the Unit in the Student's Book.

3 Write your own test!

Divide the class into small groups (three is probably the best number) and ask each group to choose which of the four sections they want to prepare. The students can prepare a test section as in the example test or they might think of other ways to make a test.

Once the students have prepared their section, collect it in. Over the next few days, you can put the sections together to make a complete test. (You will need to ensure that the test is in correct English.) The test can then be given back to the students as *their* test, which they can do in class or for homework. (Experience shows that students also learn a lot from seeing the parts which they have written in fully correct English.)

4 EVALUATION: GROUP DISCUSSION

AtoZ **EVALUATION**

This section has two parts. 4.1 involves small group discussion, while 4.2 asks students to think about their own strengths and weaknesses in English and the kinds of language work they would like to do in future. Allow some time at the end of the lesson for the students to write down their own comments.

4.1 Talk about your English work

Divide the students into groups of three or four, and allocate a Unit to each group. Ask them to decide who will report back to the class.

For the reporting back stage, if more than one group is looking at a Unit, ask one group to report back and then ask the other group(s) if they have any other points to add.

4.2 Your own ideas

Students write their own ideas in their own language about where they would like more practice and what kinds of tasks they would like to do in the future. They can choose whether or not to put their name on the sheets. Collect them in to read later.

Extra activity – a letter to the authors

At this point, approximately halfway through the book, you and your students might like to consider writing to the authors and publishers to give your comments on the course. The authors and Cambridge University Press welcome all comments – whether negative or positive – as this helps to ensure that teaching materials respond directly to the views and needs of teachers and students. See Unit 33 in the Student's Book (and the appropriate Teacher's Notes) for some ideas on how you can get your students to write a letter.

OVERVIEW OF THE THEME

Theme D, *Planet Earth* focuses on the Earth as a planet and its relationship with the moon. Students learn about how the moon affects the sea, the first moon landing, and how eclipses happen (Units 19 and 20). Music introduces Unit 19 and Unit 21, where it is used as a stimulus for some simple poetry writing. Unit 22, *Culture matters*, looks at how the sea is important to life in Britain. The final Unit in the Theme, Unit 22, involves the students in test writing once again.

In terms of language, the students learn to use the Present continuous and comparative and superlative forms of short adjectives (long adjectives are covered in Unit 25). Use of prepositions is also revised. The *Out and about* section (Unit 20) presents language for asking for travel information.

The Theme involves the students in brainstorming, creative writing, listening and reacting to classical music, work in all four language skills, and continues to develop the students' autonomy in language learning.

The Theme offers cross-curricular links with Science and Geography.

Using the cover page

Suggested time: 10 minutes

The pictures visually summarise what the students will be doing in the next five Units. Look through the pictures and ask them what they can see. Next, read through the tasks with them before you ask them to work in pairs to complete them.

In addition, you can build up a Question Poster with the students around the word 'Space' or 'Our Planet' of things they would like to learn about space in the coming weeks (see notes on the Theme B cover page, page 51, for more details).

Answers

coastal area: Unit 22; lunar landing: Unit 19; test: Unit 23; shape poems: Unit 21; solar eclipse: Unit 20.

listening occurs in Unit 19, Exs. 1, 4, 6; Unit 20, Exs. 2 and 5.2; Unit 21, Exs. 1 and 4; Unit 22, Exs. 2 and 3.

reading occurs in Unit 19, Exs. 2 and 4; Unit 22, Exs. 2 and 3.

writing occurs in Unit 19, Exs. 2, 6.2 and 7.2; Unit 20, Ex. 2; Unit 21, Exs. 1–4; Unit 23, Exs. 2 and 3.

speaking is practised in Unit 19, Exs. 1, 3, 7.1; Unit 20, Exs. 3.3, 5.3; Unit 21, Exs. 2, 3; Unit 22, Ex. 4.

The students can have a balloon race. They can see how rockets work.

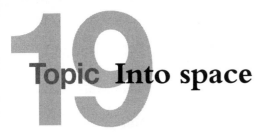

Topic Into space

1 WHAT HAPPENED WITH UNITS 14–18?

Some questions to think about before you start Unit 19.

- Theme A (Unit 5) introduced the *Exercise Box* and the *Time to spare?* sections in Units 14 and 15 referred to it. The *Exercise Box* is useful in involving the students directly with their own learning. Are the students actively contributing to the *Exercise Box* and using it? If not, perhaps you can plan some time to work on it during the coming lessons.
- Are there some particular students in your class who may be falling behind the others? Is it possible in the coming lessons to spend some time working with them while the others get on with something else?

2 TEACHING NOTES FOR UNIT 19

Overview of the Unit

Unit 19 introduces the topic of 'space' through music and a brainstorming activity and presents information concerning the moon and its effect on tides. An optional activity shows the basic principle on which rockets work. The Unit also introduces comparative and superlative forms and the Present continuous tense. A *Decide* exercise provides a choice between a writing task and preparing a dialogue.

Timing

Below are some suggested timings (in minutes) for doing each activity.

1	The planets	5
2	Our place in space	20
3	What do you know about the moon?	10
4	The moon, our nearest neighbour	15
5	Sing a song!	10
6	The first people on the moon	15
7	Decide ...	20
8	Your Language Record	10

(See also **AtoZ** TIMING.)

What you need

The Class Cassette for Exercises 1, 4 (optional), 5 and 6. Optionally for the Balloon activity (after Exercise 7): balloons, needle and thread, drinking straws and adhesive tape.

Mixed-ability classes and supplementary worksheets

Exercises 2, 4 and 6 contain additional guidelines for mixed–ability classes.
Say it clearly! worksheet 2: /eɪ/ and /ɪŋ/ sounds.
(See also **AtoZ** MIXED ABILITIES.)

Workbook

Unit 19 in the Workbook contains exercises to practise:

- Exercise 1: vocabulary and sentence building.
- Exercise 2: reading and writing.
- Exercise 3: speaking in an open dialogue.
- Exercise 4: reading (postcards from a fictional planet).
- Exercise 5: writing a postcard (from a fictional planet).
- Exercise 6: pronunciation of /eɪ/.
- Exercise 7: singing a song in English.

For additional notes on the use of the Workbook and Workbook answers see page 145.

Guidelines

1 The planets 📼
AtoZ MUSIC
This exercise is intended to invite the students into the Unit by giving them time to look at what they will be doing and to make their work on the topic more memorable through music.

In giving their opinion of the music, you could encourage the students to use the phrases they learnt in Unit 15, Exercise 6.

The music comes from *Mars*, part of the *The Planets Suite* by Gustav Holst (1916). A further extract (part of *Jupiter*) is available for Unit 20.

2 Our place in space

A to Z READING and DISCUSSION

Explain to the students what they have to do and then ask them to read silently by themselves and to make notes. After a few minutes, ask them to compare with their neighbour. You can then put the three headings on the board, read through each piece of information under the pictures, and ask what notes they made, at the same time checking that they understand the texts. Students may be able to add further details.

The texts introduce the comparative and superlative forms and the Present continuous. At this point, the emphasis should be on the meaning. The language rules, forms, etc. are covered in Unit 20.

MIXED ABILITIES

More support can be given by
- going through the vocabulary in the *Language Record* before they begin. They can then refer to the translations as they read. (Weaker students can be given their own list.)
- asking students to read in pairs and together put the information in their own language.
- working through the first two texts with the students to show them what to do.

The task can be made more demanding by
- asking the students to write a fifth text with some information that they know.
- asking the students to write four questions about the texts (these can be put in the *Exercise Box* or exchanged with other students).

- **WB Ex. 1: practice with reading, writing and vocabulary.**
- **WB Ex. 2: more vocabulary and writing work about stars and planets.**

3 What do you know about the moon?

A to Z BRAINSTORMING

'Brainstorming' is a method of collecting ideas as an initial step in doing something. Here the brainstorming activity aims to elicit what they know about the moon so that they approach the text in Exercise 4 more interactively.

Some of the points the students suggest are likely to be in the mother tongue but you can write some or all of them in English. (Just the key words are enough – for example, 'cold', 'no gravity', 'at night', 'the sea' and so on.)

4 The moon, our nearest neighbour ▱

A to Z READING

Once they have brainstormed their knowledge of the moon in Exercise 3, students can then read the text to see what further information they can add.

Once you have put the additional points that they suggest on the board, you can read through the text with them, checking any remaining language problems. Finally, students can listen to the text on the cassette.

MIXED ABILITIES

More support can be given by
- reading through the text with the students, asking for translations and suggestions for points to add to their ideas from Exercise 3.
- telling the students in their mother tongue what the text is about before they read it.
- giving the weaker students a list of translations of words and phrases from the text.
- giving the students translations of some of the more difficult sentences/phrases in the text and asking them to match them to the English.

The task can be made more demanding by
- asking the students to draw a diagram of the moon, the sun and the earth and to add the information in the text to it.
- asking the students to write some more sentences about the moon, using the information they collected in Exercise 3.

- **WB Ex. 3: an open dialogue about the moon, stars and planets. Ex. 6: pronunciation practice of /eɪ/.**

5 Sing a song! Space ▱

A to Z SONGS

- **WB Ex. 7: singing a song.**

6 The first people on the moon

6.1 On the moon 📼

A to Z LISTENING

The voice of the astronaut is from the actual recording made during the moon landing, 1969.

6.2 On television

> **MIXED ABILITIES**
>
> *More support can be given by*
> - writing the beginnings of each sentence on the board with gaps for the remaining words. You can also add '-ing' to emphasise the form they are to use. For example: 'They're p___ing __ __ ____.'
> - doing the sentence writing exercise with the students.
>
> *The task can be made more demanding by*
> - asking the students to find similar '-ing' sentences in Exercise 2.
> - asking the students to write some more sentences about things that are happening *now*.

> 📼 **TAPESCRIPT**
>
> *Narrator:* It's coming down. Slowly, slowly. The ship is landing on the moon. The Eagle is coming down … It's down now … That's Neil Armstrong … Neil Armstrong is opening the door … He's getting on the ladder … He's going down, going down the ladder … slowly, slowly … And he's, he's putting his foot on the moon.
>
> *Neil Armstrong:* That's one small step for man, one giant leap for mankind.

> **Answers**
>
> | | |
> |---|---|
> | He's putting up a flag. | He's going up the ladder. |
> | He's collecting rocks. | He's closing the door. |
> | He's driving his moon-car. | They're leaving the moon. |

7 Decide …

A to Z DECIDE EXERCISES; for **7.1: SPEAKING**; for **7.2: WRITING**

Optional activity

The text *How does a rocket work?* is intended for the students to look at at home. However, it is highly recommended that you try it in class. With a small amount of preparation, it takes about five to eight minutes to do and makes the lesson memorable as well as offering an authentic context for natural language use.

Preparation:
Bring to the class some balloons, some sticky tape, some drinking straws and some needle and thread. Before you do the activity, tie two long pieces of thread to a fixed object (e.g. door, window, table) and using the needle, pass each piece of thread through the drinking straw. (You can do this while the students are working on Exercise 4, for example.)

In class:
You can create a sense of mystery and excitement by saying nothing at first but simply blowing up a balloon and letting it go. Then ask one student to hold the thread tightly. Blow up a balloon and with the tape, stick it to the drinking straw. Repeat with another balloon. The two students can then let go of the balloons and have a race. While you are doing this you can use language naturally: checking names of colours (of the balloons), using comparatives (bigger? while blowing up the balloons), instructional language (hold this, take this, etc.). If you have time, you can have two or three races.

- **WB Exs. 4 and 5: reading and writing a postcard from a fictional planet.**

8 Your Language Record

A to Z LANGUAGE RECORD

Time to spare?

A to Z TIME TO SPARE?

> **Answers**
>
> Mercury is a planet.
> Our planet is called Earth.
> The sun is at the centre of our solar system.
> The sun is a star.
> Tides are changes in the level of the sea.
> You are lighter on the moon because the gravity is weaker.
> Nothing lives on the moon because there isn't any air.

Language focus

1 RESEARCHING THE CLASSROOM: SPELLING

Some questions to think about during the coming lessons.

- Are there some words that the students consistently misspell? What are they?
- Are there some misspellings that can be explained by the influence of the students' mother tongue?
- Are there particular sounds that the students misspell? What are they?
- Do the students sometimes misspell words which they normally get right? Why do you think that is?

Does the students' spelling seem to be influenced by other factors? For example, what they are writing about (are they thinking more about the meaning of the words than about the form?), time of day and day of the week (are they tired?) or, what they have just been doing (are they distracted?).

Units 6 and 22 in the Workbook provide additional ideas for improving spelling. (See **A to Z** SPELLING for more ideas.)

2 TEACHING NOTES FOR UNIT 20

Overview of the Unit

Exercise 1 introduces the topic of solar eclipses. This then gives the context for listening work in Exercise 2 where the Present continuous is used. Further work with the Present continuous then follows in Exercises 3.1–3.3. The focus moves to use of the comparative and superlative forms of short adjectives (long adjectives are covered in Unit 25). The *Out and about* section, Exercise 6, focuses on asking for travel information.

Timing

Below are some suggested timings (in minutes) for doing each activity.

1	Night in the day	10–15
2	Mexico, 1992	15
3	What are they doing?	
3.1	What differences do you notice?	10
3.2	How to form the Present continuous	10
3.3	Play a game: On the moon	10
4	Comparing things	
4.1	Pluto is smaller than Earth	10
4.2	Practice	10
4.3	A quiz: Back on Earth	10+
5	Out and about with English	
5.1	Mona, Sophie and Ali go to the circus	5–10
5.2	Listen	10
5.3	Practice	15
6	Your Language Record	10

What you need

The Class Cassette for Exercises 2, 4.2 (optional) and 5.2.

Mixed-ability classes and supplementary worksheets

Exercises 2, 3.3, 4.2, and 5.3 have additional guidelines for mixed-ability classes.

Say it clearly! worksheet 2: /eɪ/ and /ɪŋ/ sounds.

Language worksheet 20.1: Present continuous.

Language worksheet 20.2: comparative and superlative forms of short adjectives.

(See also **AtoZ** MIXED ABILITIES.)

Workbook

Unit 20 in the Workbook contains exercises to practise:

- Exercise 1: reading about tides.
- Exercise 2: Present continuous.
- Exercise 3: comparatives and superlatives.
- Exercise 4: asking for travel information.
- Exercise 5: pronunciation of /ɪŋ/.

Guidelines

1 Night in the day

AtoZ DISCUSSION

As you go through the descriptions of the eclipse of the sun and of the moon, it may help to put a diagram on the board.

- **WB Ex. 1: practice with reading.**

2 Mexico, 1992 🖭

AtoZ LISTENING

Play the cassette all the way through first and ask the students whether they think the woman is talking about an eclipse of the sun or an eclipse of the moon.

> **Answer**
> An eclipse of the sun

For the second part, there are a number of alternatives:

- play the cassette, stopping after each paragraph or after every two paragraphs so that the students can write.
- divide the calls into pairs. Tell one student in each pair to listen for times 1, 3 and 5, and the other student to listen for times 2, 4 and 6.

MIXED ABILITIES

More support can be given by

- giving the students some of the times.
- giving the students a copy of the tapescript. They can then read it before they listen.
- talking about the pictures of the sun first, making sure to use some of the language that is on the cassette. Put the key phrases on the board.
- giving the students all the times on the board, in both words and figures. They can then match the time to the numbers under the photograph.

> **Answers**
> 1 5.10   2 5.30   3 5.35   4 5.45   5 5.50   6 6.00   7 6.05

> 🖭 TAPESCRIPT
>
> Well, here we are in Yucatán, Mexico. It's ten past five and the sun is very clear. It's a beautiful day. We are all waiting for the eclipse to begin. It's very warm …
>
> It's now half past five and the eclipse is starting. We can see a very small shadow on the sun, but it's getting bigger …
>
> It's twenty-five to six and the shadow is much bigger now. Much bigger. We can only see half of the sun. The sun is …
>
> It's a quarter to six and it's night time! There isn't any light from the sun. This is fantastic! This is the most beautiful thing …
>
> Now, now we have some light. It's ten to six and the sun is coming back. The shadow is smaller now. Yes, it's *much* smaller …
>
> It's now, what time is it? It's six o'clock and we can see about half of the sun now. This is fantastic! Fantastic! The eclipse is finishing now.
>
> Five past six and it's finished. We can see all of the sun now. Beautiful! That was really beautiful!

3 What are they doing?

3.1 What differences do you notice?

AtoZ MOTHER TONGUE

You could do this section on the board rather than directly from the book. That way you will be able to introduce the points more slowly and, perhaps, ask for further examples.

> **Answers**
> The Present continuous has a form of 'be' + '-ing'. A basic rule is that the Present continuous is used to talk about actions which are happening at the time of speaking.

3.2 How to form the Present continuous

AtoZ INDUCTIVE GRAMMAR

Draw the students' attention to the *Say it clearly!* box. You could get them to repeat the words after you.

Ask the class for ideas on how to describe the Present continuous. The colour coding should help them.

> **Answer**
> Present continuous can be described as: subject + 'be' + verb + '-ing' (+ object).

- **WB Ex. 5 and *Say it clearly!* worksheet 2: practice with pronunciation of /ɪŋ/.**

3.3 Play a game: On the moon

AtoZ PHYSICAL MOVEMENT

> **MIXED ABILITIES**
>
> *More support can be given by*
> - putting some complete sentences on the board for the students to use during the game. You can use the phrases in the book and elicit further sentences when you demonstrate the game.
>
> *The task can be made more demanding by*
> - extending the game to include other actions.

- **WB Ex.2 and Language worksheet 20.1 provide extra practice with the Present continuous.**

4 Comparing things

4.1 Pluto is smaller than Earth

It may also be best to stress that you do not use 'more' with short adjectives. For example, the following are wrong:

~~Pluto is more small than Earth.~~
~~The sun is more big than Earth.~~

You could elicit further examples from the students about cities near them (big), people in the class (tall, old, young), books (big), lines on the blackboard (long, thin, thick).

The rules given here are for <u>short</u> adjectives. Unit 25 presents comparatives with long adjectives.

4.2 PRACTICE

AtoZ PROCESSING TIME

Once again, you could do this on the board which would enable you to check the students' understanding at each stage. You could then ask the students to do the exercise in writing as reinforcement.

Point out the double letters in the spelling when '-er/-est' follow a consonant preceded by a vowel.

> **MIXED ABILITIES**
>
> *More support can be given by*
> - giving further written exercises using the ideas listed in Exercise 5.1 above.
> - playing the cassette through once or twice before you ask the students to do the exercise in writing.

> **Answers**
> Mercury is hotter than Earth. The sun is the hottest.
> A year on Earth is longer than a year on Mercury. A year on Pluto is the longest.
> K2 is higher than Kilimanjaro. Mount Everest is the highest.
> A dog bite is bad for you. A snake bite is worse for you. A shark bite is the worst for you!
> Maths is good for you. History is better for you. English is the best for you!

- **WB Ex. 3 and Language worksheet 20.2: extra practice with the comparative and superlative forms.**

5.3 A quiz: Back on Earth

You could do this as a competition. Divide the class into small groups (teams). Give them a time limit. Ask them to write down their answers and then pass them to another group for correcting. One point for each correct answer. The group with the highest number of points wins.

> **Answers (correct in 1995)**
> 1 Sears Tower, Chicago, USA
> 2 Mexico City
> 3 a Giraffe
> 4 Mars
> 5 Vatican City
> 6 Cheetah
> 7 True
> 8 The population of England in 1995: 48 million
> 9 False

5 Out and about with English

5.1 Mona, Sophie and Ali go to the circus

Elicit questions for each of the four points and put them on the board.

5.2 Listen 📼

AtoZ LISTENING

5.3 PRACTICE

AtoZ ROLEPLAY and MONITORING AND GUIDING

Ensure that the students fully understand what they have to do before they work in pairs.

- **WB Ex. 4: practice with asking for information.**

MIXED ABILITIES

More support can be given by

- asking the students to act out the dialogue in the book first.
- giving students cards with information already on them.
- going through an example with them, using a completed card on the board.

The task can be made more demanding by

- asking the students to write 5 'true or false?' statements about the dialogue in the book (or about their own dialogue) for other students to answer, once they have completed the task.

6   Your Language Record

AtoZ LANGUAGE RECORD

Time to spare?

AtoZ TIME TO SPARE?

Revision Box

AtoZ REVISION BOX

Activity 21 Poems from the Earth and space

TEACHING NOTES FOR UNIT 21

Overview of the Unit

In Unit 21, students are shown how they can write simple poems about space. The Unit first involves the students in brainstorming what they can remember from Units 19 and 20 and then asks them to imagine that they are travelling in space. They then write simple poems about what they can see.

> **Note:** Some students may react negatively to writing poems so you could do the activity without actually referring to the book or using the word 'poem' until they have finished (if at all). This kind of activity is valuable because it develops a feeling for personal expression in English, focusing on the meaning and impact of words. (See also **A to Z** STUDENT INVOLVEMENT.)

Timing

Unit 21 is intended for one full lesson, but you may decide to split it up over a number of lessons. Suggested timings (in minutes) are:

1	The words in your head	5
2	Talk to your neighbour	5
3	Imagine ...	5
4	Write a poem	15
5	Show each other your poems	10
6	Evaluation	5

What you need

The Class Cassette for Exercises 1 and 4. If you intend to put their complete poems on the wall, you will need large poster paper (e.g. A3), scissors, glue, pens and (optionally) coloured A4 paper.

Workbook

Unit 21 in the Workbook contains ideas to stimulate more poem writing.

Guidelines

1   The words in your head 🖭

A to Z BRAINSTORMING

There are several ways you could do this:

- draw the ideas map from the book on the board and ask the students to work individually to complete their own. Play the music while they are working.
- put the ideas map on the board and ask students to come out to add to it. This could be done silently after the first person comes out (offer the chalk to different students). Play the music while they are writing on the board.
- ask students to imagine they are travelling in space. Play the music and let them think. When the music stops, introduce the ideas map on the board. Students then build up the map on the board or in their books.

The music is part of *Jupiter* from Holst's *The Planets Suite*.

2   Talk to your neighbour

If students have completed the ideas map individually, they can now compare.

3   Imagine ...

A to Z DISCUSSION

You can use the questions to lead a discussion. Try to ask different students for each question.

4   Write a poem

AtoZ MONITORING AND GUIDING

If you want to avoid referring to poems, you can say 'Let's write about space'. Look and put one of the examples on the board (or one of your own). Ask the students to write their ideas in a shape (e.g. a star, the sun, or a rocket). They can first write, then draw an outline and then copy the words around it.

While they are doing this (alone or in groups), go around the room. (If you do have students who don't want to do it, they can do a *Time to spare?* exercise, or something from the *Exercise Box*. See **AtoZ** STUDENT INVOLVEMENT.)

5   Show each other your poems

AtoZ DISPLAYING STUDENTS' WORK

Discuss with the students if they would like to put their work up somewhere, put it in a book or look at each other's work in a small group. Students may, however, wish to finish off their work at home first.

6   EVALUATION

AtoZ EVALUATION

The question to emphasise here is 'Would you like to do it again?' If there are only *some* students who would like to do it again, you could offer them a chance within the next few lessons when other students are working on something else.

22 Culture matters Life by the sea

TEACHING NOTES FOR UNIT 22

Overview of the Unit

This *Culture matters* Unit focuses on how the sea affects and has affected life in Britain. They learn about the importance of tides around the British coast and the good and bad effects that they have.

Timing

The *Culture matters* Units are intended for one full lesson but you may decide to split it up over a number of lessons. Suggested timings (in minutes) are:

1	About your country	5
2	Britain and the sea	15
3	The moon, the sun and the sea in Britain	20
4	Fun at the seaside	10

What you need

The Class Cassette for Exercise 2.

Mixed-ability classes

Exercise 3 has additional guidelines for mixed-ability classes.
(See also **AtoZ** MIXED ABILITIES.)

Workbook

Unit 22 in the Workbook is the second *Help yourself with spelling* Unit. The Unit contains two ways the students can use to improve their spelling:

• Exercise 1: putting their spelling mistakes into groups.
• Exercise 2: listing words according to their letter patterns.

See page 145 for a special note on the *Help yourself* Units. (See also **AtoZ** SPELLING.)

Guidelines

1 About your country

AtoZ DISCUSSION

You can ask these questions in English, but you may need to accept replies in the mother tongue. Put the key words in English on the board.

2 Britain and the sea

AtoZ READING and DISCUSSION

Look at the map with the students. You can perhaps ask them where there are similar industries, boats, etc. in their country.

Read through the text with the students. Then ask them which places on the map relate to each sentence in the text.

Play the cassette once or twice.

> **Answers**
> 1 fishing (a market)   2 beaches   3 shipbuilding
> 4 important ports   5 oil and gas platforms (a helicopter)
> 6 boats and hovercraft

3 The moon, the sun and the sea in Britain

AtoZ READING AND PROCESSING TIME

Give the students some time to read silently through the texts and find three good points and three bad points.

As you go through their answers, you can check vocabulary.

> **Note:** Tides are not so great in some parts of the world because the sea is enclosed. For example, Italy has very weak tides because the Mediterranean only has one very narrow opening which restricts the movement of water.

MIXED ABILITIES

More support can be given by

- giving the students a translated word list.
- asking the students to help each other in pairs.
- reading through the first two texts with them.

The task can be made more demanding by

- asking them to write 4 questions about the texts.
- giving the students some phrases from the text in their mother tongue. They have to find the English version.

Answers

Good points: you can walk, it cleans the beaches, tides make electricity.

Bad points: the ships can't go out, the tides make problems for towns near the coast, Britain is disappearing.

4 Fun at the seaside

AtoZ DISCUSSION

Revision and evaluation

Revision of Units 19–22;
test and making a test,
evaluation of the lessons
from the students' point of
view

TEACHING NOTES FOR UNIT 23

See Unit 7 for the 'General note on the *Revision and evaluation* Units'.

Overview of the Unit

See Teaching Notes for Unit 18.

Timing

The main part of the Unit (Exercises 1–3) is intended for one full lesson, with the students' own test being used in another lesson or as homework. (See below.) Suggested timings (in minutes) are as follows. To save time, students can do the example test (Exercise 2) for homework before the lesson.

1	How much do you know?	5
2	Test yourself	15
3	Write your own test (assembled later)	25
4	Evaluation	
4.1	Talk about your English work	10
4.2	Your own ideas	10

What you need

No special materials needed.

Mixed–ability classes and supplementary worksheets

Language worksheet 20.1: Present continuous.
Language worksheet 20.2: comparative and superlative forms of short adjectives.
(See also **AtoZ MIXED ABILITIES**.)

Workbook

Unit 23 in the Workbook provides further revision exercises around the topic of continental drift and a *picture dictionary* of vocabulary from Units 19–22.

Guidelines

For detailed notes see Unit 18.

Theme E
Natural forces

OVERVIEW OF THE THEME

Theme E, *Natural forces*, focuses on the weather. Music introduces Unit 24, and then the students go on to describe the weather in their country and look at how winds and rain occur. The Unit also includes two experiments to try at home. Unit 25 broadens the topic to the 'Midnight Sun' in Scandinavia. In Unit 26, the *Activity* Unit, students make weather maps of the world. Unit 27, *Culture matters*, looks at the effect of the seasons in Britain. The final Unit in the Theme, Unit 28, provides revision activities.

In terms of language, the students learn the difference between countable and uncountable nouns and the use of *much*, *many*, and *a lot of*, and how to form the comparative and superlative form with long adjectives. The *Out and about* section (Unit 25) presents language for making plans. The *Revision Box* at the end of Unit 25 revises the Present simple tense.

The Theme offers cross-curricular links with Science and Geography.

Using the cover page

Suggested time: 10 minutes

The pictures visually summarise what the students will be doing in the next five Units. Look through the pictures and ask them what they can see. Next, read through the tasks with them before you ask them to work in pairs to complete them.

In addition, you can build up a Question Poster with the students around the word 'The weather' of things they would like to learn about space in the coming weeks (see notes on the Theme B cover page on page 51, for more details).

Answers
map: Unit 26;   puzzle: Unit 28;   snowman: Unit 27;
    telephoning: Unit 25;   deckchair: Unit 24.
Music by Beethoven comes in Unit 24, Exercise 1.
A balloon experiment comes in Unit 24.
A song comes in Unit 24 Ex. 5.
The *Revision Box* contains practice with the Present simple tense.

Topic 24 The weather

1 WHAT HAPPENED WITH UNITS 19–23?

Some questions to think about before you start Unit 24.

- Theme D included two brainstorming activities (Unit 19, Exercise 3 and Unit 20, Exercise 5.8). Did the students respond well to brainstorming? Can you see any opportunities in the coming Units where you can use brainstorming?

- Did you try the balloon experiment in Unit 19? Unit 24 includes two similar experiments to try, possibly in class.
- Themes C and D both included student test writing (Units 18 and 23). How well did the students do it? Can you see any opportunities for students to write more tests for each other?

2 TEACHING NOTES FOR UNIT 24

Overview of the Unit

Unit 24 opens with a short musical extract which illustrates the weather. Students then learn the use of frequency adverbs to describe weather in their country, and some weather related adjectives. After a song, the students then move on to look at how weather conditions happen: specifically, rain and wind. A *Decide* exercise offers a choice between vocabulary or reading work. The Unit includes two simple weather-related experiments to try at home.

Timing

Suggested timings (in minutes) for doing each activity:

1	Musical weather	10
2	What's the weather like in your country?	15
3	We never have snow in June!	15
4	What's the weather like?	10
5	Sing a song!	10
6	Where does the weather come from?	10
7	Why do we have rain?	10
8	Why do we have winds?	10
9	Decide ...	15
10	Your Language Record	10

(See also **AtoZ** TIMING.)

What you need

The Class Cassette for Exercises 1, 4, 5 and 8. (If you would like to do the experiment after Exercise 9, see details below.)

Mixed-ability classes and supplementary worksheets

Say it clearly! worksheet 3: /ə/, /ɪə/, /ɪəst/. (See also **AtoZ** MIXED ABILITIES.)

Workbook

Unit 24 in the Workbook contains exercises to practise:

- Exercise 1: names of the months.
- Exercise 2: reading, writing and frequency adverbs.
- Exercise 3: weather adjectives.
- Exercise 4: reading and writing.
- Exercise 5: weather vocabulary.
- Exercise 6: an open dialogue about the weather.
- Exercise 7: pronunciation of /ə/.
- Exercise 8: singing a song in English.

For additional notes on the use of the Workbook and Workbook answers see page 145.

Advance notice! Unit 26 involves the students in making a world weather map. To do this, they need to collect some information beforehand so you will need to allow five minutes to tell them what to do. See the notes on Unit 26 for further details.

Guidelines

1 Musical weather 🔊

AtoZ MUSIC

The extract is the last part of the 4th movement (*Storm*) and the beginning of the 5th movement (*Calm after the Storm*) from Beethoven's 6th Symphony, known as the *Pastoral Symphony.*

2 What's the weather like in your country?

Read through the names of the months, checking that the students know what they mean. Then, before the students start working, check that they know the meanings of the weather types given in the list.

Put the sentence outline on the board and check that the students understand *always*, *usually*, etc. Before you ask them to copy and complete the calendar, you can ask them questions such as:

'When do we have strong winds?'
'Do we have cold weather in July?'
'What weather do we have in March?'

- WB Ex. 1: names of the months; Ex. 6: an open dialogue about the weather.

3 We never have snow in June!

AtoZ INTERACTIVE WRITING

Before the students begin writing in pairs, you could say some true and untrue sentences yourself for the students to correct as appropriate.

- WB Ex. 2: writing about the weather;
  Ex. 7 and *Say it clearly!* worksheet 3: pronunciation of '-er'.

4 What's the weather like? 🔊

AtoZ LISTENING

Check the students' understanding and pronunciation of each of the adjectives *foggy*, *chilly*, etc.

Answers		
1 a sunny day	3 a chilly day	5 a windy day
2 a rainy day	4 a foggy day	

🔊 **TAPESCRIPT**

1 Beautiful today, isn't it?
   Oh wonderful. I'm going for a swim.

2 What a terrible day!
   Yes, it's worse than yesterday. Take your umbrella.

3 Brrrrrr! It's terribly cold.
   Wonderful for skiing.

4 Gosh! I can't drive in this. I can't see anything.

5 Listen to that door. Can you go out and close it?
   Who me?

- WB Ex. 3: listening and writing exercise involving weather adjectives.

5 Sing a song! Singing in the rain 🔊

AtoZ SONGS

- WB Ex.8: sing a song.

6 Where does the weather come from?

AtoZ DISCUSSION and PROCESSING TIME

Answers	
1 true	4 false – high up in the sky
2 false – cold air falls	it is very cold
3 false – trees move	5 true
because of the wind	

- WB Exs. 4 and 5: reading and writing about weather processes, weather vocabulary.

7 Why do we have rain?

Answers
2 The water becomes vapour.
4 The wind blows the clouds.
5 The cold cloud meets a warm cloud.

8 Why do we have winds?

AtoZ TASKS IN BLOCKS

You may prefer to ask the students to do Exercises 7 and 8 together. Alternatively, you could do Exercise 7 with the whole class and ask them to do Exercise 8 in pairs.

> **Answers**
> 2 The ground becomes warm.
> 4 The air rises.
> 6 The wind blows.

9 Decide …

AtoZ DECIDE EXERCISES

Three experiments to try at home!

If have time, you may like to do one of the experiments in class. The third experiment, with a balloon and a bottle, is the best one to do in class as the effects are easily seen by a large group of children. You can take warm water in a vacuum flask and some plastic bottles and containers to do the experiment.

Encourage the students to try the experiments at home. In experiment C, the balloon should be sucked back into the bottle, and it will then burst.

> **Answers**
> 9.1: rain, water, cloud, vapour, blow, cold, wind, hot.
>
> 9.2: 1 rises 2 colder
> 3 falls 4 make
> 5 jumps, expands

10 Your Language Record

AtoZ LANGUAGE RECORD

Time to spare?

AtoZ TIME TO SPARE?

Language focus

1 RESEARCHING THE CLASSROOM: PRONUNCIATION

Some questions to think about during the coming lessons.

- How serious a problem do you think pronunciation is for your pupils? Do you think people will have problems understanding them?
- Poor pronunciation is often linked to shyness and lack of confidence in the foreign language. Do you think this is true for any of your students?

- Have you noticed any improvement in your students' pronunciation through use of the *Say it clearly!* worksheets? Do they spend any class time on the Workbook *Say it clearly!* exercises?

Workbook Unit 4 also focuses on pronunciation. (See **AtoZ** PRONUNCIATION for more ideas.)

2 TEACHING NOTES FOR UNIT 25

Overview of the Unit

Unit 25 opens with some basic information about the 'Midnight Sun' and weather in Norway. This is used as a context for use of 'much' and 'many'. A grammar problem solving activity then follows, with practice in using 'much', 'many' and 'a lot of'. Work on comparative and superlative forms of long adjectives comes next. The *Out and about* section focuses on language for making plans. The *Revision Box* after the *Language Record* revises the Present simple.

Timing

Below are some suggested timings (in minutes) for doing each activity.

1	The Midnight Sun	5
2	Near the North Pole	20
3	'How many rainy days …?' and 'How much rain …?'	
3.1	A grammar puzzle	10
3.2	Can you count?	10
3.3	Questions, negative sentences and positive sentences	5
3.4	Practice	15
4	It's sunnier and more beautiful than yesterday	
4.1	Adjectives with 'y'	10
4.2	Long adjectives	10
5	Out and about with English	
5.1	It's Sophie's birthday	5
5.2	Listen	10
5.3	Practice	15
6	Your Language Record	10–15

What you need

The Class Cassette for Exercises 3.4 and 5.2.

Mixed-ability classes and supplementary worksheets

Say it clearly! worksheet 3: /ə/, /ɪə/ and /ɪəst/.
Language worksheet 25.1: countables/uncountables.
Language worksheet 25.2: comparative and superlative
  forms of long adjectives.
(See also **A to Z** MIXED ABILITIES.)

Workbook

Unit 25 in the Workbook contains exercises to practise:

- Exercise 1: reading about the 'Midnight Sun'.
- Exercise 2: 'much', 'many' and 'a lot of'.
- Exercise 3: long comparatives and superlatives.
- Exercise 4: an open dialogue about making plans.
- Exercise 5: pronunciation of /ɪə/ and /ɪəst/.

Reminder: Remember to tell the students to collect information about the weather in different countries of the world for Unit 26.

Guidelines

This language study covers two small but important grammatical areas. To give variety to your lessons, you could break it up and devote some part of your lessons to Unit 26 or Unit 27 material.

1   The Midnight Sun

Note: Workbook Unit 25, Exercise 1 has an explanation of why we have seasons and why some countries get the 'Midnight Sun'.

- **WB Ex. 1: reading about the 'Midnight Sun'.**

2   Near the North Pole

From the information, we can see that Norway has a dry, bright summer with very little rain and a wet, dark, windy winter.

Other questions the students can ask are:

'How many rainy days do they have in December?'
'How many sunny days do they have in June?'
'How many windy days do they have in June?'

Point out that there are four weeks in the month so the answers for one week must be multiplied by four.

Answers			
1 720 mm	2 0 mm	3 92 hours	4 564 hours

3   'How many rainy days …?' and 'How much rain …?'

3.1   A grammar puzzle

A to Z INDUCTIVE GRAMMAR

Answers
'much' is used with things that you can't count (e.g. rain);
'many' is used with things that you can count (e.g. days).

3.2   Can you count?

Depending on the students' mother tongue, the distinction between countables and uncountables may be a tricky one for them. Some nouns may be uncountable in English but countable in other languages. It will probably be best, therefore, if you do this section with the class as a whole. Give the students a few minutes to put U or C and then ask for answers.

Answers
water U;   sunny days C;   clouds C;   snow U;
hours of sunshine C;   rain U;   windy days C;   ice U.

3.3 Questions, negative sentences and positive sentences

3.4 PRACTICE 🔊

🔊 TAPESCRIPT
1 We have a lot of rain here.
2 We don't have much snow.
3 We have a lot of windy days here.
4 We don't have much water.
5 We don't have many clouds here.
6 We have many hours of sunshine.
7 We have a lot of foggy days here.
8 We don't have much water.
9 We have a lot of water here.

- **WB Ex. 2: practice with 'much', 'many' and 'a lot of'.**

4   It's sunnier and more beautiful than yesterday

4.1   Adjectives with 'y'

- **WB Ex. 5: practice of /ɪə/ and /ɪəst/.**

4.2   Long adjectives

A to Z PATTERN PRACTICE

Adjectives are called 'long' adjectives if they contain more than one syllable. You can count the syllables with the students.

big: one syllable
cold: one syllable
expensive: three syllables
beautiful: three syllables

Remember to check that the students understand the adjectives.

- **WB Ex. 3: practice with comparatives and superlatives with long adjectives.**

5 Out and about with English

5.1 It's Sophie's birthday

Elicit three or four questions that Sophie can ask. For example:

'Can you come to my party on Sunday?'
'What are you doing on Sunday?'
'Would you like to come to my party on Sunday?'
'Are you free on Sunday?'

5.2 Listen 🔲

AtoZ LISTENING

5.3 PRACTICE

AtoZ ROLE PLAY and MONITORING AND GUIDING
Students first complete the 'Your Week' card with five activities before they work in pairs. As an example, you can put a 'Your Week' table on the board and ask a few pupils.

- **WB Ex. 4: an open dialogue about making plans.**

6 Your Language Record

AtoZ LANGUAGE RECORD

Time to spare?

AtoZ TIME TO SPARE?

Answers

Unit 3: David lives in the north – in Lanark;
Unit 4: Mona wants a box of chocolates;
Unit 9: Cows sleep for 6 hours;
Unit 10: Sophie lives in Prospect Street;
Unit 14: Fats are good for you because they make you strong
 and give you energy;
Unit 15: No, you don't need eggs for shortbread;
Unit 19: Earth to moon, 382,000 km;
Unit 20: See table, page 92;
Unit 24: It rises;
Unit 25: Countries near the North Pole.

Revision Box

AtoZ REVISION BOX

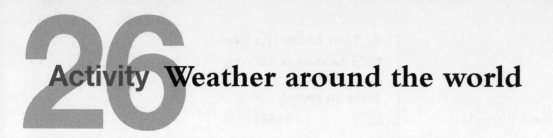

Activity Weather around the world

Making a poster

TEACHING NOTES FOR UNIT 26

Overview of the Unit

In Unit 26 the students collect information about the weather in different countries of the world and, in groups, draw a world weather map. At the end of the activity, there is a short evaluation discussion.

Timing

Unit 26 is intended for one full lesson, but you may decide to split it up over a number of lessons. Suitable breaks are as follows:

Before the lesson: Exercises 1 and 2.
Lesson 1: Exercise 3 and start on Exercise 4.
Lesson 2: finish Exercise 4 (put maps on the wall between lessons).
Lesson 3: Exercises 5 and 6.

Suggested timings (in minutes) are:

Before the lesson	
1 Copy the map	(at home)
2 Collect some information	(at home)
In the lesson	
3 Tell everybody your information	10
4 Make a poster	25
5 Show your maps to each other	10
6 Evaluation	5

What you need

Some large sheets of paper (e.g. A3) and some smaller sheets (e.g. A4). Some information about climate in other countries. Coloured pens, glue, scissors.

Workbook

Unit 26 in the Workbook contains fluency practice around the topic of Australia.

- Exercise 1: reading about Australia
- Exercise 2: reading and map reading
- Exercise 3: reading a postcard
- Exercise 4: writing a postcard

Guidelines

Before the lesson

1   Copy the map

2   Collect some information

Both steps 1 and 2 are to be done before the Unit 26 lesson. You could agree with the students which countries they want to find out about and then decide who will be responsible for each place.

In the lesson

3   Tell everybody your information

4   Make a poster
AtoZ WRITING and INTERACTIVE WRITING

5   Show your maps to each other
AtoZ DISPLAYING STUDENTS' WORK

6   EVALUATION
AtoZ EVALUATION

27 Culture matters Living with nature

TEACHING NOTES FOR UNIT 27

Overview of the Unit

This *Culture matters* Unit focuses on how the seasons affect the way people live in Britain and the games that children play at different times of the year. The students are encouraged to think about how the seasons are different in their country. They also learn two games that are very popular with children in Britain.

Timing

The *Culture matters* Units are intended for one full lesson, but you may decide to split it up over a number of lessons. Suggested timings (in minutes) are:

1	Seasons in your country	5
2	The seasons in Britain	15
3	Spring and summer	15
4	Games in the park	5

What you need

The Class Cassette for Exercise 3 (optional). Some hard nuts or beans and some pieces of string for Exercise 4.

Workbook

Unit 27 in the Workbook is the fifth *Help yourself* Unit: *Help yourself with pronunciation*. The Unit contains three ways the students can practise their pronunciation:

- Exercise 1: using a mirror.
- Exercise 2: stress in two syllable words.
- Exercise 3: stress in sentences.

See page 145 for a special note on the *Help yourself* Units. (See also A*to*Z **PRONUNCIATION**.)

Guidelines

1 Seasons in your country

Check that the students understand the names of the seasons. They should be able to give a lot of points in English by now.

2 The seasons in Britain

A*to*Z **READING**

After the students have had a chance to read the texts with their neighbour, you can read each one aloud to check their answers.

> **Answers**
> Autumn: The leaves on the tree go brown;   we have to wear warm clothes.
> Winter: we have a lot of snow;   it is already dark

(The poems are similar to *haikus*, a Japanese form of poetry in which the first line has five syllables, the second line has seven syllables and the third line has five syllables. As an extension to this Unit, you could ask the students to write their own haiku about seasons in their country. The actual number of syllables would not be very important for this.)

3 Spring and summer 🔲

Again, allow the students to read silently before you ask for answers. Alternatively, you could play the cassette first and then give them time to read it again.

The games shown in the photographs (for Exercises 1–4) are: making snowmen (winter), hopscotch (spring), rounders (summer), a game similar to baseball, and conkers (autumn).

4 Games in the park

These are traditional British children's games. You could get a few children out to the front of the class to try out the two games.

Revision and evaluation

Revision of Units 24–27;
evaluation of the lessons
from the students' point of
view

TEACHING NOTES FOR UNIT 28

See Unit 7 for the 'General note on the *Revision and evaluation* Units'.

Overview of the Unit

Exercise 1 asks the students how well they think they know the English from Units 24–27. Revision exercises then follow. Students can do some or all of these exercises, depending on time and how much revision they need. In the last exercise, students think about how well they have understood the previous lessons and provide you with written feedback.

Timing

The Unit is intended for one full lesson, with students doing Exercises 2–5 selectively. However, you may want all students to do all the exercises, in which case the Unit may be split up over a number of lessons. Suggested timings (in minutes) are:

1	How much do you know?	5–10
2	I never do that!	15
3	It's bigger and better	15
4	'How many ...?' or 'How much ...?'	10
5	What's the word?	15
6	What are you doing next week?	20
7	Evaluation	15

What you need

No special materials needed.

Mixed-ability classes and supplementary worksheets

Language worksheet 25.1: countables and uncountables. Language worksheet 25.2: comparatives and superlatives. (See also AtoZ **MIXED ABILITIES**.)

Workbook

Unit 28 in the Workbook is a self-check test focusing on the language covered in the Theme.

Guidelines

1 How much do you know?

AtoZ **TASKS IN GROUPS** and **OVERVIEWING**

The main aim here is to encourage the students to reflect on how much they have learnt.

Before asking students to complete the chart, look back with them at the relevant sections of the previous Units to remind them what they did.

Give the students a few minutes to tick the box. You could encourage them to discuss/compare *briefly* with their neighbour.

Before the students start working, it is a good idea to go through the exercises with them, so that they know exactly what they have to do in each one. After this there are a number of possibilities:

  a Let the students choose what they want to revise and practise – either to test themselves or to revise where they feel weakest.
  b Ask the students to do *two* exercises: one that they ticked 'very well' and one that they ticked 'a little'.
  c Get all the students to do all the exercises (requires more time, of course).
   Students can work alone or in pairs.
   (Students can also complete the Unit for homework.)

2 I never do that!

3 It's bigger and better

Answers		
2 more modern		6 smaller
3 heavier		7 lighter
4 newer		8 more expensive
5 more difficult to use		

4 'How many ...' or 'How much ...?'

Answers		
1 many	4 many	7 much
2 a lot of	5 many	8 many
3 much/a lot of	6 a lot of	

5 What's the word?

Answers

WATERS / ASSISTS / THUNDER / WINDY / CRYSTALS / RAIN / CLOUD / JUMPS / JOURNEY / AND / YES / JUICY / LIGHTNING / MARCH / SHOUT / APRIL / AUGUST

THUNDER AND LIGHTNING

6 What are you doing next week?

7 EVALUATION

7.1 Talk about your English work

7.2 Your own ideas

AtoZ EVALUATION

OVERVIEW OF THE THEME

Theme F, *Living history*, focuses on events in the past: first on the lives of cavepeople (Unit 29) and then on the life of the student, their family and friends (Unit 30). The *Out and about* section gives students practice in talking about events in their past. In the *Activity* Unit (Unit 31) the students make a booklet about their family. Unit 32, *Culture matters*, describes a variety of traditional celebrations in Britain.

The focus on the past gives the students a light introduction to the Past tense, with some regular and irregular verbs. The Past tense is covered more fully in Level 2.

In terms of educational content, students learn about family trees and life in the Stone and Bronze Age. These make cross-curricular links with History and Geography.

Using the cover page

Suggested time: 10 minutes

The pictures visually summarise what the students will be doing in the next five Units. Look through the pictures and ask them what they can see. Next, read through the tasks with them before you ask them to work in pairs to complete them.

In addition, you can build up a Question Poster with the students around the word 'History' or 'Cavepeople' of things they would like to learn in the coming weeks (see notes on the Theme B cover page on page 51, for more details).

Answers

girls in street: Unit 30;   cavepeople: Unit 29;
    envelope: Unit 33;   Chinese dragon: Unit 31;
    family tree: Unit 32

listening occurs in Unit 30 Exs. 2, 5.3;   reading is practised in
    Unit 29 Exs. 3, 7;   writing occurs in Unit 29 Ex. 4, Unit 31
    Exs. 2, 3, Unit 33 Exs. 2, 3, 5;   speaking is practised in
    Unit 29 Ex. 1, Unit 30 Ex. 5.1.

In Unit 31 they can make a booklet about their family or
    friends.

Topic 29 The cavepeople

1 WHAT HAPPENED WITH UNITS 24–28?

Some questions to think about before you start Unit 29.

- Unit 24 used music to introduce the topic. What effect did this have on the students? Did it make them more/less relaxed? embarrassed? more imaginative? Could you use music in your lessons on Theme F? (See **AtoZ** MUSIC for ideas.)
- Are there some particular students in your class who are falling behind the others? Is it possible in the coming lessons to spend some time working with them while the others get on with something else?
- Is there one particular language area you need to spend extra time on with the class? For example, pronunciation, writing, or some language point from an earlier *Language focus* Unit?

2 TEACHING NOTES FOR UNIT 29

Overview of the Unit

Unit 29 gives the students an initial contact with the Past simple forms of some regular and irregular verbs. (The Past simple is covered more fully in Level 2 of the course.) The Unit focuses on the life of Bronze Age and Iron Age people and compares their lives with our lives today. Brainstorming occurs in two exercises to stimulate the students' own ideas and three short texts present various facts about the life of the cavepeople (dangers, hunting and painting).

Timing

Below are some suggested timings (in minutes) for doing each activity.

1	15,000 years ago ...	10
2	In a cave	10
3	A dangerous life for cavepeople!	25
4	A dangerous life today	10
5	Differences Poster	15
6	Sing a song!	10
7	Cavepeople painted and hunted	25
8	Decide ...	20
9	Differences Poster	10
10	Language Record	15

(See also **AtoZ** TIMING.)

What you need

The Class Cassette for Exercises 2, 3, 6 and 7. Some large pieces of paper for the posters in Exercise 5. Dice and counters for the game in Exercise 8.1.

Mixed-ability classes and supplementary worksheets

Exercise 3 has additional guidelines for mixed-ability classes. *Say it clearly!* worksheet 3: /wə/, /t/, /d/ and /ɪd/. (See also **AtoZ** MIXED ABILITIES.)

Workbook

Unit 29 in the Workbook contains exercises to practise:

- Exercise 1: vocabulary.
- Exercise 2: 'was/were'.
- Exercise 3: regular past tense verbs.
- Exercise 4: reading, writing and listening.
- Exercise 5: writing.
- Exercise 6: singing a song in English.

For additional notes on the use of the Workbook and Workbook answers see page 145.

Guidelines

1 15,000 years ago ...

AtoZ DISCUSSION

Let the students respond to the pictures by saying what they know about cavepeople and their life. Put key words on the board as needed. Encourage them to try to use the adjectives given in the Student's Book and ensure a clear pronunciation of 'was' and 'were'.

- **WB Exs. 1.1 and 1.2:** adjectives.

2 In a cave 📼
A to Z LISTENING

> 📼 TAPESCRIPT
> Sounds of a cave: dripping water, hammering, wild
> animal noises, crackling fire, cutting/sharpening spears.

3 A dangerous life for cavepeople! 📼
A to Z BRAINSTORMING and READING

Students work in pairs and brainstorm dangers in the lives
of cavepeople. When they are ready, you can gather their
ideas on the board.

Important note: The focus here is on the ideas rather
than totally correct language use. The students will
undoubtedly produce incorrect sentences (particularly
with the past form) but you can put the correct form
on the board as you collect their ideas.

Remind the students that they are reading the text to find
out about dangers so they do not need to understand
every word in the text. They can then add the dangers to
their ideas map.

For the brainstorming stage:

MIXED ABILITIES
More support can be given by
- encouraging the students to brainstorm in their
  mother tongue.
- doing Exercise 4 first. 'Modern life' is closer to the
  students' experience and so may be easier for them
  to brainstorm.
- giving the students some key words: weather,
  animals, food, home, medicine and by giving them
  some ideas to start.
- asking each pair to work on one category only, e.g.
  food.

The task can be made more demanding by
- asking students to write about the dangers for cave
  children and for adults separately.
- asking students to work alone first and then to join
  with one or two other students and make one large
  ideas map.
- asking the students to write reasons for their ideas,
  e.g. 'It was very dangerous in the caves because they
  had no light'.

For the reading stage:

MIXED ABILITIES
More support can be given by
- looking at the pictures closely with the class before
  they read the text. Ask them what is happening and
  write the key words on the board.
- explaining that there are five dangers in the text.
  (wild animals, the deep river, cold weather, fire,
  poisonous nuts/fruit). Put them on the board in the
  wrong order and ask the students to say which
  paragraph of the text the dangers are in.
- building confidence: students underline or circle
  every word in the text which they know and
  compare their text with their partner's.

The task can be made more demanding by
- asking students to add one more sentence to every
  paragraph. They then compare texts with their
  partner.
- asking students to work in pairs. Each student takes
  one or two paragraphs and copies it out leaving a
  blank for the verbs. The partner then fills in the verbs
  without looking at the text.

- **WB Ex. 2:** practice with 'was/were'.
- **WB Ex. 3:** practice with regular Past tense verbs.

4 A dangerous life today
A to Z BRAINSTORMING

5 Differences Poster
A to Z BRAINSTORMING

Students can work alone, in pairs or in groups for this
task. Put a large piece of paper on the wall and write up
the questions as they suggest them. (Encourage them to
do this in English.) Leave the poster up – you can add
more questions during the lesson or over the next few
lessons if they suggest them.

6 Sing a song! Caveman rock 📼
A to Z SONGS

- **WB Ex. 6:** sing a song.

7 Cavepeople painted and hunted 📼
A to Z READING

Students work in pairs and read one text each. Ask them
to read through the questions before they start the text.
Encourage them to use their dictionary or guess the
meaning (or both). (The texts may suggest more points
for the *Differences Poster*.)

Answers

Text 1 (Cave Paintings)
1 They made paint from plants.
4 Mammoths, tigers and bears.
5 On the walls of the cave.
7 In animal bones.
8 To show they were dead.
9 Before and after a hunt.

Text 2 (Hunting and Cavepeople)
2 They killed animals with spears: they frightened animals with noise and lights.
3 Fat. To keep warm and to slip away from animals.
4 Mammoths, tigers and bears.
6 The soft part (the heart and the brains).
10 The animal skins.

- WB Exs. 4, 5, 6: more reading and writing work with regular Past simple verbs. *Say it clearly!* worksheet 3: pronunciation of '-ed'.

8 Decide ...

AtoZ **DECIDE EXERCISES** and **MONITORING AND GUIDING**

Make sure that the students know what they are expected to do in each of the choices. 8.1 involves speaking and writing in the Past tense through a game and 8.2 involves reading and writing about a timeline.

8.1 Play a game: Danger!

Tell the students to read the instructions first! Then, before they begin, check that they know how the game works and that 'Danger' cards are to be found at the back of the Student's Book on page 149. (Make sure they write one more 'Danger' card each before they start playing.)

8.2 What changed first?

Students can check their answers with you before they continue with the second part of the exercise.

Answers
1 b 2 d 3 a 4 e 5 c

9 Differences Poster

10 Your Language Record

AtoZ **LANGUAGE RECORD**

Time to spare?

AtoZ **TIME TO SPARE?**

Answers
Ex. 2: a false b true c true d false

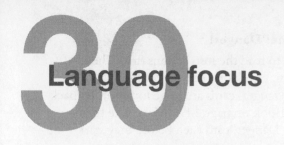

Language focus

1 RESEARCHING THE CLASSROOM: FLUENCY

Some questions to think about during the coming lessons.

- Do you notice that sometimes, when students are doing an exercise, they make mistakes that they don't normally make?
- Do you feel that some of your students are afraid to speak? How can you increase their confidence?
- This is the final *Out and about* section of the book. How successfully have the students been able to create their own dialogues?

- Are the students too concerned/not concerned enough about the accuracy of the language they produce?
- Do you think they are always translating when they are speaking/writing/reading/listening? Do you think this is a good thing or a bad thing?

Workbook Unit 32 is *Help yourself with fluency*. (See **A to Z** FLUENCY for more ideas.)

2 TEACHING NOTES FOR UNIT 30

Overview of the Unit

Unit 30 introduces the past form of regular verbs and of a few irregular ones (be, have, go and make). The question form of 'was/were' is presented and some fixed phrases with 'did'. The *Out and about* section focuses on talking about past events. The *Revision Box* after the *Language Record* returns to comparative and superlative forms of adjectives.

Timing

Below are some suggested timings (in minutes) for doing each activity.

1	Your own past: your first day at school	10
2	Sophie's first day	15
3	Were you older? Was it newer?	
3.1	'Was' and 'were'	10
3.2	Was it cold?	5
3.3	Spot the differences	10
4	Some more Past tense verbs	
4.1	What do you say?	5
4.2	What's the difference?	10
4.3	Past verbs	15
4.4	Some more practice	5
5	Out and about with English	
5.1	It was fun!	10
5.2	Sophie's party	5
5.3	Listen. Are you right?	10
5.4	Practice	15
6	Your Language Record	15

What you need

The Class Cassette for Exercises 2, 4.3 (optional) and 5.3.

Mixed-ability classes and supplementary worksheets

Exercises 3.1, 4.1 and 4.4 have additional guidelines for mixed-ability classes.

Language worksheet 30.1: Past tense of 'to be' and some regular verbs.

Language worksheet 30.2: some more regular and some irregular verbs.

The *Say it clearly!* worksheet 3: /wə/, /weə/ and /t/, /ɪd/ and /d/.

(See also **AtoZ** MIXED ABILITIES.)

Workbook

Unit 30 in the Workbook contains exercises to practise:

- Exercise 1: regular Past tense verbs.
- Exercise 2: 'was/were'.
- Exercise 3: pronunciation of '-ed'.
- Exercise 4: irregular Past tense verbs.
- Exercise 5: talking about past events.

Advance Notice: In Unit 31 students will make a booklet about their friends or family. They will need some photographs and some information about them so now is the time to tell them!

Guidelines

1 Your own past: your first day at school

AtoZ DISCUSSION, GROUPWORK and MONITORING AND GUIDING

You could begin by getting the students to ask you the questions at the start of this Unit (and add some more of their own). Students can then work in groups to ask each other the same questions.

2 Sophie's first day 📼

AtoZ LISTENING and PROCESSING TIME

Students could read through the dialogue in pairs first before listening to the cassette.

> **Answers**
> 1 In Scotland
> 2 Small
> 3 Crowded
> 4 Four and a half

3 Were you older? Was it newer?

3.1 'Was' and 'were'

AtoZ INDUCTIVE GRAMMAR, MONITORING AND GUIDING and TASKS IN BLOCKS

Students can work alone or in pairs through the next three exercises at their own pace. Check that they have all filled in the table and understand when to use 'was' and 'were'.

> **MIXED ABILITIES**
>
> *More support can be given by*
> - going through the sentences with them asking them to circle the 'was' sentences and underline the 'were' ones. Give them time to compare the sentences. If this is still difficult ask them to work in pairs and find the subject of each sentence.
>
> *The task can be made more demanding by*
> - asking them to choose one of the following sentences:
>   > I was 4 years old
>   > It was exciting
>   > It was difficult
>   > It was dangerous
>
>   and to write a little story which has that sentence as a title.
> - asking them to write a diary entry for Nogoba.

3.2 Was it cold?

Students can read these mini dialogues out in pairs if there is time. Remind them that the question comes after the statement.

> **Answers**
> a 6 b 3 c 4 d 2 e 1 f 5 g 7

3.3 Spot the differences

> **Answers**
> 1 The woman was in the cave.
> 2 There were six men in the cave.
> 3 There wasn't a fire.
> 4 The dog was in the cave.
> 5 There was a tiger on the hill.
> 6 There was a lot of food on the ground.
> 7 There were animals near the river.
> 8 There were people in the river.

- WB: Ex. 2: questions with 'was/were'.
- WB: Ex. 1: practice with regular Past tense verbs.

4 Some more Past tense verbs

4.1 What do you say?

AtoZ INDUCTIVE GRAMMAR, MOTHER TONGUE

> **MIXED ABILITIES**
>
> *More support can be given by*
> • checking that the students understand what 'past tense' means. Ask for some examples of Past tense verbs in their own language and write them on the board. Include the Past tense of the verb 'to be' if possible.

4.2 What's the difference?

AtoZ GRAMMAR

There are two points that the students should notice:

1 The verbs in List B are Present tense and those in List A are Past.
2 Some of the past forms are made with '-ed' and some seem to follow no rule.

• **WB Ex. 3** and *Say it clearly!* worksheet 3: pronunciation of 'was', 'were' and -ed;
• **Ex. 4**: irregular Past tense verbs.

4.3 Past verbs 📼

Both texts are on the cassette.

> **Answers**
> **Life of cavepeople:**
> 1 lived   5 killed
> 2 walked   6 cooked
> 3 used   7 painted
> 4 hunted
>
> **Cave music:**
> 1 made   5 used
> 2 had   6 went
> 3 played   7 saw
> 4 used   8 made

4.4 SOME MORE PRACTICE

AtoZ PAIRWORK and SPEAKING

Make sure students understand the formula 'What did you do on ...?' as a fixed phrase. Students work in pairs and ask each other about their days.

> **Note:** It is not necessary to explain the 'did' construction at this point.

> **MIXED ABILITIES**
>
> *More support can be given by*
> • collecting some answers on the blackboard.
> • getting the students to ask you some questions first.
> *The task can be made more demanding by*
> • asking a student to pretend that they are someone else answering the questions – a president, princess or pop star. The other students must guess who they are from the answers.
> • asking the students to write some questions for an interview with someone they want to meet.

5 Out and about with English

5.1 It was fun!

AtoZ DISCUSSION

You could begin by telling the class somewhere you went that was fun. Pause deliberately at the end of each sentence. Students can then ask you questions in each pause.

5.2 Sophie's party

5.3 Listen. Are you right? 📼

AtoZ LISTENING

Before they listen to the dialogue students may like time to read through it in pairs.

5.4 PRACTICE

AtoZ ROLE PLAY

• **WB Ex. 5.1**: talking about past events.

6 Your Language Record

AtoZ LANGUAGE RECORD

Time to spare?

AtoZ TIME TO SPARE?

> **Answers**
> a lived   c washed   e watched
> b cleaned   d stayed

Revision Box

AtoZ REVISION BOX

> **Reminder:** Remind the students to bring their photographs and some information about them to the lesson on Unit 31.

Activity 31 A book about your family and friends

TEACHING NOTES FOR UNIT 31

Overview of the Unit

In Unit 31, the students make a booklet about their family or their friends. It will involve writing about their lives and some research at home before the lesson. At the end there is a short evaluation discussion focusing on what they learnt about their friends and family and what they found easy/difficult in the activity.

Timing

Unit 31 is intended for one lesson but it may be worthwhile extending this activity over one or two lessons. The task may be done at several levels of ability – the stronger students can be expected to write more about their family. Suggested timings (in minutes) are:

Before the lesson	
1 When were they born? What did they do?	(at home)
In the lesson	
2 Your family tree	25
3 Write about some more people	15
4 Show your books to each other	10
5 Evaluation	10

What you need

Some glue, some scissors, some A4 paper, crayons. (Some magazine pictures of people for students who do not want to write about their family – they can invent some information.)

Mixed-ability classes

Exercises 2 and 3 have additional guidelines for mixed-ability classes.
(See also **AtoZ MIXED ABILITIES**.)

Workbook

Unit 31 in the Workbook contains fluency practice around the topic of families and family trees.

Guidelines

Before the lesson

1   When were they born? What did they do?

In the lesson

2   Your family tree
AtoZ   TASKS IN BLOCKS
You can put the family tree of one student on the board as an example. Students could go straight on to Exercise 3 when they are ready.

> **MIXED ABILITIES**
>
> *More support can be given by*
> • eliciting some information from the students and writing some more examples on the board.
> *The task can be made more demanding by*
> • asking students to write more about what each person did. It could be: something interesting, exciting, dangerous, unusual.
> • asking the students to write a short description of the person on the family tree.

3 Write about some more people

> **MIXED ABILITIES**
>
> *More support can be given by*
> - asking students to go and look at other students' work at this stage to get some ideas and inspiration.
> - focusing on information and events in the Present tense of current family members or friends.
>
> *The task can be made more demanding by*
> - asking the students to prepare for Exercise 5 (showing the books to each other) by writing some questions about their booklet which the other students can try to answer when they look at their booklet.
> - asking students to describe an event that happened in one person's life (for example, their wedding, first day in a new job, an important journey) from their point of view – as a letter to another family member for example.

4 Show your books to each other

`AtoZ` DISPLAYING STUDENTS' WORK

5 EVALUATION

`AtoZ` EVALUATION

32 Culture matters Living traditions

Celebrations in your
country and in Britain:
reading and discussing

TEACHING NOTES FOR UNIT 32

Overview of the Unit

Students learn about how Great Britain became a multi-cultural society and how and when the different groups celebrate important events. The final exercise encourages students to think about the characteristics of celebrations as a way of making comparisons with celebrations in their own country.

Timing

Suggested timings (in minutes): are:

1	Celebrations in your country	10
2	Who has celebrations in Britain?	10
3	When are the celebrations?	15
4	What is a celebration?	10

What you need

Optionally, the Class Cassette for Exercise 3.

Mixed-ability classes

Exercises 3 and 4 have additional guidelines for mixed-ability classes.
(See also **AtoZ MIXED ABILITIES**.)

Workbook

Unit 32 in the Workbook is the sixth *Help yourself* Unit: *Help yourself with fluency* and contains three techniques the students can practise:

- Exercise 1: making phrase cards to test themselves.
- Exercise 2: making their own 'open dialogue'.
- Exercise 3: roleplaying situation.

See page 145 for a special note on the *Help yourself* Units.
(See also **AtoZ FLUENCY**.)

Guidelines

1 Celebrations in your country

AtoZ DISCUSSIONS and OVERVIEWING

Get the students to discuss the celebrations they have in their country – when they have them, what they celebrate, what they do, what they eat/drink. Does everyone have the same celebrations? Get students to look at the pictures in the Unit and see if they have any celebrations like any in the pictures.

2 Who has celebrations in Britain?

Background information: Today, Britain contains a rich variety of people from different cultural backgrounds. Their foods, traditions, celebrations, styles of dress, religious and cultural values are now a permanent feature of British society. The presence of these different groups in Britain goes back to two main waves of immigrants to Britain. Between 1956 and 1962, West Indians came to work in hospitals and on London Transport. They settled mainly in London and Bristol. Between 1962 and 1968, Asians (Indians and Pakistanis) from East Africa who had British passports came. Most of these settled in London, the Midlands, Bradford and Leeds. There are also large Chinese (Hong Kong) communities in London and Manchester. In the past, groups of Vietnamese and Poles made their homes here. About 2% of the population of Great Britain are non-Caucasian.

3 When are the celebrations? 📼

AtoZ READING

The intention here is that the students should scan the texts, looking for the date to put on the calendar i.e. they should not be reading in detail (see Exercise 4). All they have to do is find the month in the text and circle it on the calendar. (To help them do this, you can tell them to focus on the words which begin with a capital letter. This will speed their search for the name of a month.) You can go through their answers before they read/listen further.

Before playing the cassette, students can read the texts silently.

MIXED ABILITIES

More support can be given by

- reading one text with the students first pointing out the key words.
- asking the students to work in pairs and to read two texts. Ask them to underline the key words.
- asking students to guess the words they don't know.
- Asking them to choose two texts to read and look for the answers to some questions on the board: Why are Diwali and Chinese New Year the same? When is Guy Fawkes night? Who has paper dragons? What happens in August? What is the festival of lights?

The task can be made more demanding by

- asking students to write about some of the similarities in the festivals.
- asking students to write 50 words about a festival in their country.

4 What is a celebration?

AtoZ GROUPWORK

Students work in small groups or in pairs, look back at the texts and fill in the chart from the information in the texts. Students then think of an important celebration in their country and fill in the last column of the chart accordingly.

MIXED ABILITIES

More support can be given by

- starting with a celebration/festival the students are familiar with. Discuss with students what happens during their festival. Work through the ten points on the list. They can tick the chart and add other features if necessary.

The task can be made more demanding by

- asking the students to write a letter – perhaps for the Parcel of English – describing the last festival that they went to.

Answers

	Carnival	Diwali	Guy Fawkes	Christmas	Chinese New Year	Eid	Your Celebration
1 Eat special foods		✓		✓		✓	
2 Give presents				✓		✓	
3 Wear new clothes		✓				✓	
4 Send cards				✓			
5 Visit people				✓			
6 Go on the streets	✓	✓			✓		
7 Stay at home							
8 Have a party			✓	✓	✓	✓	
9 Dance	✓	✓			✓		
10 Sing	✓				✓		

Revision and evaluation

Revision of Units 29–32;
evaluation of the lessons
from the students' point of
view; letter to the authors

TEACHING NOTES FOR UNIT 33

See Unit 7 for the 'General note on the *Revision and evaluation* Units'.

Overview of the Unit

Unit 33 has a similar structure to Unit 18 and 23. After asking the students to reflect on what they have learnt in Exercise 1 the students work through a short test (Exercise 2) which the students are then able to correct themselves, before they move on to devising their own class test in Exercise 3. The final part of the Unit involves an evaluation discussion about the students' opinions (Exercise 4) and a letter to the authors (Exercise 5).

Timing

The main part of the Unit (Exercises 1–3) is intended for one full lesson, with the students' own test being used in another lesson or as homework. (See below.) Suggested timings (in minutes) are as follows. You can note down your anticipated timings here and mark your anticipated lesson divisions (if any). To save time, students can do the example test (Exercise 2) for homework before the lesson.

1	How much do you know?	5–10
2	Test yourself	15–20
3	Write your own test (assembled later)	25
4	Evaluation	20
5	Write a letter to us! (discussion only)	15

What you need

No special materials needed.

Mixed-ability classes and supplementary worksheets

Language worksheet 30.1: the Past tense of 'to be' and some regular verbs.
Language worksheet 30.2: the Past tense of more regular and some common irregular verbs.
(See also **AtoZ MIXED ABILITIES**.)

Workbook

Unit 33 in the Workbook provides further revision exercises based on a topic ('Where did the dinosaurs go?') and a *picture dictionary* of vocabulary from Units 29 to 32.

Guidelines

See Teaching Notes for Unit 18 for guidance on the Unit.

5 Write a letter to us!

The authors and the publishers would be *delighted* to hear from you and your students concerning your reactions to *Cambridge English for Schools*. Feedback from teachers and students is very important in ensuring that published materials meet the needs, interests and wishes of those who use them.

Theme trail A revision game

TEACHING NOTES

This final Unit is an optional game to revise the language they have learnt during the book as well as the topic information.

Timing

The game is designed to last one lesson but may be played for half a lesson if time is short.

What you need

Each student will need a counter or button of a different colour from the rest of the group and one dice for each group (four students in a group).

Guidelines

AtoZ GAMES

Preparation

Check that the students know what they have to do before they divide into their groups. You may need to explain the rules in the mother tongue to speed the lesson up and ensure that everyone understands.

Playing the game

The rules for playing the game are given in the Student's Book. Before the students begin, you will need to give the Questioner the Answer key to the Unit questions on the next page.

The students together should be able to determine if an answer is correct or not, but the Questioner can resolve any problems.

Answers

UNIT 3
1 *personal response*
2 *personal response*
3 *personal response*
4 *personal response*

UNIT 4
1 adjective   adjective   noun   verb
2 I do not study music at school.
3 *personal response*
4 Excuse me, can I pay for this?
   Can I have a ...?
   How much is this / are these?

UNIT 9
1 An animal that gives milk to its babies and has warm blood.
2 An animal that has got cold blood and lays eggs. It has got thick skin.
3 They eat leaves.   They live in Africa.   They have got very long necks.
4 Africa and India.

UNIT 10
1 Where do Pandas live?   What do Pandas eat?
   How long do Pandas sleep?
2 When do they sleep?
   What do they eat?
   Where do they live?
3 your   his   her   its   our   their
4 What's your name?   Where do you live?   Would you like a ...?   Do you like ...?   Can you play ...?

UNIT 14
1 fats   vitamins   protein   water   minerals   fibre
2 *personal response*
3 nuts   beans   cereals
4 Because they give you energy.

UNIT 15
1 some   any   any
2 him   it   her
3 'some' with positive sentences, 'any' with negatives and questions (but there are exceptions).
4 you   him   her   it   us   them

UNIT 19
1 Because it takes many years for light from the stars to come to us.
2 It makes the tides. (It pulls the sea.)
3 It has very weak gravity. There isn't any air. It is dead.
4 Pluto   Mercury   Mercury

UNIT 20
1 *personal response*
2 Can you tell me which bus goes to East Town?
   How much is the ticket?   When does the bus go?
3 *personal response*
4 England is warmer than New Zealand. Saudi Arabia is the warmest.

UNIT 24
1 Because warm air rises from the ground and cold air comes to take its place.
2 Because water vapour rises into the air and becomes clouds. When a cold cloud meets a warm cloud, the water vapour becomes rain.
3 *personal response*
4 rise ... falls

UNIT 25
1 a much   b many   c many
2 uncountable   countable   uncountable   countable   countable   uncountable
3 *personal response*
4 This car is more expensive than that car. *or* This car is cheaper than that car.

UNIT 29
1 35,000 years ago.
2 They collected berries, got water from the river, cooked and made pots.
3 *personal response*
4 Mammoths, tigers and bears.

UNIT 30
1 'walked' and 'talked'
2 'went' and 'had'
3 *personal response*
4 Was it noisy?   Was it quiet?   Was it good?   Was there dancing?   Was there music?   Were your friends there?   Was it a birthday party?   Was the food nice?

An A to Z of methodology

This section contains details of some of the key areas of language teaching, particularly in relation to teaching with *CES*. You will find references to this section in the Teaching Notes for each Unit (for example: **A to Z** **MOTHER TONGUE**). However, it is *not* intended that you should read all of the relevant references just to prepare one lesson or that you should read the entire section all at once! This section is for *reference*: for you to read at your leisure, as and when you wish.

Cross-references to other entries in the section are also shown in small capitals, **LIKE THIS**.

A to Z AUTONOMY

What and why?

Autonomy has two main aspects in language teaching. The first concerns the students' *use* of the language. The ultimate goal of most language teaching is to develop the students' autonomy in their own language use. That is, to develop the ability to use the language as they need or want to. This has direct implications for the kind of tasks that students are asked to do. If students are only asked to do 'closed tasks' they are unlikely to develop the ability to use the language with ease. **OPEN-ENDED TASKS** are much more important in this respect.

The second aspect of autonomy, however, concerns how the students *learn*. If all the decisions about learning are always taken by the teacher, the students will not have the opportunity to decide things for themselves. This means that they will not develop the ability to learn by themselves or to work out what works best *for them* as individuals. In a rapidly-changing world, however, these abilities are increasingly important as people are continually required to learn new skills and absorb new information. Learning how to learn should thus be a vital component in any educational course.

Practical ideas

- *CES* incorporates numerous tasks which require students to decide things for themselves, to plan and to evaluate. You can discuss these tasks with the students so that they understand the value of them in helping them to learn without your direct supervision.

- The Workbook Cassette provides a good support for the students to exercise autonomy in learning. You can spend some time discussing with the students how they use the cassette, when they listen to it, and so on.
- The *Help yourself* Units in the Workbook offer practical support in developing the students' autonomy in learning. Once the students have done one of the Units, you can return to it after a week or so and ask how many of the techniques they have used, why/why not, and so on.
- The **DO IT YOURSELF** exercises ask students to make decisions. You can increase the number of these in order to encourage the students to take more responsibility. The 'Open Plan' sections after the *Revision and evaluation* Units (Level 2) can also be increased in frequency.
- After the students have decided something and then carried it out, it is important to **EVALUATE** what they have done. You can discuss what they did, how it went and how they could improve it next time.
- Stress to the students that there are a number of vital tools for learning. They need to have a bilingual dictionary, a grammar, notebooks, and a cassette player.
- You can discuss with the students different ways in which they can get practice (see the *Help yourself* Units).

A to Z BRAINSTORMING

What and why?

'Brainstorming' is the name given to a number of techniques used for generating and gathering ideas. The basic principle is that the students suggest ideas which may be collected, for example, on the blackboard. During the collecting of ideas, ALL ideas suggested are noted down – only after the brainstorming is finished are the ideas discussed, grouped, or eliminated. Brainstorming can encourage students to speak out and share ideas. It also gives the teacher an immediate impression of how much the students already know about something.

Practical ideas

There are a number of different ways you can approach brainstorming.

- Write 'What do we know about (name of the topic)?' in big letters on the blackboard. Place a circle round it and some lines out from the circle. Ask the students what they know about the topic. As they say things, write them around the circle.
- Write 'What do we know about (name of the topic)? in big letters on the blackboard. Give the students a few minutes to note down ideas by themselves. Then, collect their ideas on the board.
- As above, but students work in small groups.

- As above, but play some soft MUSIC while they are thinking/discussing.
- Students work in groups to generate ideas and then cross-group (see GROUPWORK) to compare. You can use different types of MUSIC during these stages.
- The brainstorming can be put up on a POSTER and referred to and added to over a number of lessons.
- Brainstorming doesn't have to be about things they know. It can be about things they would like to know. Students can build up a question POSTER.
- Brainstorming can be done in English or in the MOTHER TONGUE.

AtoZ CHECKING ANSWERS

What and why?

After students have done an exercise, it is important that they have an opportunity to check what they have done. This will give them FEEDBACK on their work. There are a number of ways in which you can do this.

Practical ideas

- You can go through the answers while the students look at their own work.
- Students can work together and then sit with another pair to check the answers.

- Small groups of students can go through their answers together. During this time, you can circulate around the class, helping and checking.
- You can provide an 'answer sheet' for students to check their own answers. (This can be circulated around the class while they are doing some other activity, pinned up on the board for students to check after the lesson, or written on the blackboard.)
- If students have incorrect answers, you can give hints or clues rather than simply give the correct answers. This can help them think through the task again and learn more (see ERROR CORRECTION).

AtoZ CURRICULUM LINKS

What and why?

One of the main features of *CES* is that it makes direct links between English language learning and the school curriculum. This happens in two ways. Firstly, there are links with broader educational aims, such as developing PROBLEM-SOLVING abilities, AUTONOMY, QUESTIONing, cooperative learning, and so on. Secondly, there are direct links with school subjects, such as Science, Geography, Language and so on. There are a number of reasons why this is important. Language teaching *is* a part of education, and needs to take its full educational responsibility. A cross-curricular approach also offers students an ideal opportunity to refresh and revise what they have done in other subject areas and to make links with what they have learned so that their knowledge becomes more active. This makes both learning *and* teaching English more interesting and more memorable. Working with subject knowledge that is important and interesting in its own right makes it more likely that students will remember the language associated with it. Finally, whether language teaching has explicit links with the curriculum or not, it is clear that it can have a role in

shaping the broader attitudes and abilities of students. It thus makes sense to take this fact into account and build it into our language teaching methodology.

Practical ideas

- Teaching English through a cross-curricular approach can mean that your role as a teacher changes. Many teachers report that cross-curricular teaching is more interesting, since it involves *their* learning as well. However, you are an *English* teacher and you cannot be expected to know all about Science, Geography and so on. Your role as a teacher, then, is to stimulate the students to find the information/answers/ explanations that they require for themselves.
- In the notes to the Units, you will find some background information on some of the topics covered in *CES*.
- You may find it useful to talk to teachers of other subject areas. As you approach a new Theme, you could find out what work the students will do or have done in that area.

- It may be possible to teach some lessons together with another subject teacher. For example, with some advance preparation, students could do Science experiments, Maths, Physical Education and so on in English. You could choose a new topic area together.

- As you begin a new Theme, you could start with a question POSTER. You can ask the students questions such as: 'What questions from History connect to this? How does Geography connect to this? Is Maths important for this topic? How?' and so on.

AtoZ DECIDE EXERCISES

What and why?

The *Decide* exercises come in each *Topic* Unit. They give the students a choice of what they can do next. One option is usually to decide for themselves what they want to do (see DO IT YOURSELF). The students can do the *Decide* exercises alone, in pairs or in small groups. The exercises are designed as a first step in the students taking responsibility for their own learning (see STUDENT INVOLVEMENT).

Practical ideas

- Explain the choices clearly to the class before they start. Allow enough time for them to decide which task to do and how to work (alone/in pairs, etc.).
- Make sure there is enough time left in the lesson to make a start.
- While the class is working go round and offer help if needed (see MONITORING AND GUIDING).

If students finish before the others, they can use the TIME TO SPARE?, LANGUAGE RECORD and the EXERCISE BOX.

AtoZ DISCIPLINE

What and why?

One difficulty frequently encountered by teachers of secondary aged students is the problem of maintaining discipline. There are two main aspects to consider in this. The first is to ask 'What kind of discipline do I want?'. The key should be to maintain a purposeful but relaxed atmosphere in the classroom, where certain students don't disturb other students. This may mean that some so-called discipline problems are not real problems at all. As long as the overall atmosphere is conducive to learning, it may not be worth making an issue out of minor acts of 'misbehaviour'. If students were 100% compliant, we would have reason to be worried! On the other hand, discipline can, at times, become a serious problem. The important question to consider here is '*Why* are they behaving like that?'. The cause of discipline problems may lie in difficulties at home, in school, or with friends. These are likely to be beyond your control. Some causes of discipline problems, however, may lie within your classroom and you may be able to resolve them.

Practical ideas

- If the problem reoccurs, try to discuss it with the students. Approach the issue as *their* problem as well as yours ('We've got a problem. Our lesson/groupwork, etc. is not working, is it? What can we do about it?'). This can give them a feeling of responsibility. For this, you will need to listen to their views and be ready to make changes.
- If you have a large class, discipline problems may be caused by students who feel left out or who don't

understand what is happening. Using GROUPWORK can help them feel more involved.

- Discipline problems may occur during listening activities. This may be because some students cannot hear the cassette very well. They may be 'lost' before the lesson really starts. Tell them to look at the words in the book while they listen if the room is noisy.
- If the students are restless or tired, you could start with some PHYSICAL MOVEMENT.
- The PACE and TIMING of the lessons may be too fast for some of the students and so they get lost, feel they can never catch up, and then begin to misbehave. These slower students may prefer to work individually.
- Make sure that the work of the weaker students has equal feedback.
- Try to bring about more STUDENT INVOLVEMENT, especially from those students who are causing disruption.
- To settle students down when they come into the class, you can use MUSIC or regular journal writing. A journal is a book that the students write in which you do not correct or look at unless invited to do so. The students may write anything they like about their day, their feelings, the things they have done, the things they have learned and so on. Initially, this will be in the MOTHER TONGUE but you can encourage them to try to write in English as the course goes on.

During group or pairwork:

- Give extra help to the troublesome students.
- Get the troublesome students to work on something you know they are good at and which will give them a

feeling of achievement. You can give them some other individual responsibility for a term. For example, being in charge of the **EXERCISE BOX**, collecting in **HOMEWORK**, helping with the **DISPLAYS**, leading the

singing in **SONGS**.
- Try not to give extra English homework as a punishment; it can create the view that English is boring or difficult or both!

AtoZ DISCUSSIONS

What and why?

Discussions can allow students the opportunity to give their own ideas and, in the later stages of the course, to practise using English to say what they want to say. They can also form a way into a topic which can stimulate the students' imagination and give the teachers an indication of how much the students already know. It is important, however – particularly when discussions are done in English – that the emphasis is always on the *ideas* which are being expressed, not on the accuracy of how it is expressed (grammar, pronunciation etc.). A heavy focus on form can block a discussion and prevent ideas emerging.

Practical ideas

- Discussions can be approached through **BRAINSTORMING**.
- In the initial stages of the course, brief discussions can be in the **MOTHER TONGUE**. The importance of this is that it can give the students the feeling that their ideas and contributions are valued.

- As the students' abilities in English develop, you can encourage them to express their ideas in English. If the students show resistance, you might ask them 'Would you like to know how to say that in English?' and show them how they can express the same idea in English.
- Discussions in the mother tongue can be used as a way to raise the vocabulary that they will meet in English. After a brief discussion, you can put words on the board and ask if they know how to say those things in English.
- Discussions of abstract topics do not usually work well with students of this age. Discussions need a clear, concrete focus – for example, what they know about something or what they think about something with which they are very familiar.
- Discussions are probably best kept short (maximum 10 minutes). Beyond that students may lose interest or the discussion may lose its focus.
- With a clear, concrete focus, students can work briefly in small groups. Some groups can then feedback to the whole class.

AtoZ DISPLAYING STUDENTS' WORK

What and why?

At the end of each *Activity*, students will have produced a large piece of work (e.g. **POSTERS**, a poem, the *Parcel of English,* etc.). To give students a sense of purpose about their work it is a good idea to display it.

Practical ideas

- Pin work up on the classroom wall for a week or so and then change it. Perhaps you can display work in the corridors, in the school hall, in the school foyer, in the canteen, in the staff room or in other subject rooms (for cross-curricular links). (You can also ask students for display ideas.)
- Take a photograph of the display for reference.
- Make sure you write on the display the students' names, their class, the subject of the work and a

description of the purpose of the work (in **MOTHER TONGUE**).
- When you take the work down the students can either keep their work in their own 'Activity file' or put their work in a large scrap book.
- Encourage students to help you display work.
- Display pictures as well as the writing – some students may be better at art than English!
- Some students may be sensitive about showing their work to others – it may be best to ask them if they want to.
- If a display is put up in the classroom or put out on the class tables, allow time for the students to walk around to read it. One member from each group can stand by their work to explain and talk about what they have done (see also **POSTERS**).

AtoZ DO IT YOURSELF

What and why?

'Do it yourself' is an important idea that occurs throughout *CES*. Encouraging students to do something

themselves, rather than simply using the exercises in the book, is to encourage them towards **AUTONOMY** – the ultimate goal of education. This also allows students room for the own individual interests, needs and abilities.

In Level 1, students are given the option of deciding what they want to do in each *Decide* exercise. In Level 2, this is taken one step further, where the DIY exercises in the *Language focus* Units require planning for what they will do in the 'Open Plan' section at the end of the *Revision and evaluation* Units. In these exercises, the students must decide what they wish to do, in consultation with you. Initially, it is likely that the suggestions that students make for what they would like to do are not ones that you think are particularly valuable. This may not be a problem for a number of reasons. Firstly, one of the aims of allowing students to suggest something else to do is to bring about greater STUDENT INVOLVEMENT and a feeling of 'ownership' of what they are learning. Secondly, it is *only* through making decisions that students can become better at making decisions. The important point is that any suggestion they make and which they actually do is followed up by some kind of EVALUATION. This can be simply asking the students how useful they found what they did.

Practical ideas

- If students cannot think of something to do, you can *propose* something. Have a list of ideas ready. For example: choose something from the EXERCISE BOX, do some READING, look back through the previous Unit, do something from the Workbook, do a TIME TO SPARE? exercise, play one of the GAMES in the book, write some GRAMMAR rules on a POSTER, prepare something for the PARCEL OF ENGLISH, listen to a SONG.
- One or two lessons before the students come to the DECIDE EXERCISES, point out the option for them to decide for themselves. Encourage them to think of something they might like to do. Give them suggestions (see above).
- You will need to insist that what they decide to do is related to learning English!
- You could also allow some time for students to tell other students (either in small groups or to the whole class) what they have been doing.
- There are six 'Open Plan' sections in Level 2. You can, however, allow the students an open space more frequently. You could, for example, allow 15 or so minutes every week or every other week. Build up a 'lesson plan' with them, on the board, a week or so before an 'Open Plan' time.

AtoZ ERRORS AND ERROR CORRECTION

What and why?

Making errors is an inevitable and necessary part of language learning. It is only through making errors, and hearing the correct forms, that students can develop their own understanding of how English works. It is thus important that students have as much opportunity as possible to produce language and, with the focus on using English creatively (rather than simply repeating language), the number of errors that students make will inevitably rise. Teachers thus need to think carefully about how they will respond to these errors.

The process of absorbing a new language structure takes considerable time. Teachers cannot, therefore, expect that simply correcting an error will produce immediate results. Some errors can remain even up to very advanced levels (such as the 's' in *she lives, he goes*, etc.). A strong emphasis on error correction cannot be expected to produce students who make few errors. In fact, an over-emphasis on error correction is likely to be counter-productive as students become deterred from using – and experimenting with – new language and vocabulary. But students *do* need to have their errors pointed out to them. The key is to limit correction to a small number of points at a time and to judge when the right moment for correction is.

Practical ideas

- Correcting students when they are in the middle of saying something may produce students who are afraid to talk. You can make a note of the errors students make and go through them at the end of the discussion/lesson.
- Limit yourself to only correcting a few errors in written work or after the students speak.
- For errors in WRITING, students can be encouraged to build up a short list of their most common errors. The list can be arranged to form a mnemonic of things to check (e.g. PATTIBS = Plurals, Articles, Tenses, 'there is/are', '-ing' form, 'Be', Spelling etc.).
- In monolingual classes most students will make the same errors. You may want to have 'an error of the week' game. Choose an error which most students make, tell them what it is and write the correct version on a piece of paper on the wall. This raises the students' consciousness about this particular error. Students then have to try not to make this error all week. The student who succeeds can choose the 'error of the week' for the next week.

AtoZ EVALUATION

What and why?

There are two main ways in which evaluation is important in learning. The first way is in relation to *what* and *how much* students have learned – such as through tests and quizzes (see TESTS). The second way, however, is in relation to *how* the students have been learning – whether groupwork, for example, is effective, whether they receive enough guidance, and so on. The first aspect of evaluation is the most common in language teaching. The second aspect is not often considered in much depth, although it is obviously extremely important. In *CES*, this second aspect of evaluation is introduced in a number of places, particularly in the *Revision and evaluation* Units, where students talk about their reactions to the preceding Units. The aim through this kind of evaluation is to involve the students more in thinking about how they are learning, to encourage them to take more control over their learning and to give you, the teacher, an insight into how the students see their English classes.

Practical ideas

- For practical ideas in the *what* and *how much* aspects of evaluation, see TESTS.

- Initially, it is likely that the students' evaluation of how they have been learning will be very superficial. Just like learning itself, evaluation requires practice. The more they do it, the better they will become at it, and the more able they will become to accept responsibility.
- Limit the time for an evaluation discussion and give the students a clear focus for any group discussion (for example, to come up with a list of their points).
- Evaluation by the students requires the teacher to be open to listen and discuss, and make changes if necessary.
- Evaluation can be done in writing directly to you. This can avoid problems with 'public' discussions.
- Avoid, initially at least, asking the students questions such as 'What things did you like?' 'What things didn't you like?' Negative questions will produce negative answers. It is better to ask 'What do you think about ...?'
- Evaluation of *how* the students have been learning/ working comes mainly in the *Revision and evaluation* Units. However, you can involve the students in evaluation (oral or in writing) after any major piece of work or period of time (for example, after a *Topic* Unit and *Language focus*, before they do the *Activity*).

AtoZ EXERCISE BOX

What and why?

The *Exercise Box* is introduced in Unit 5 in Level 1 and in Supplementary Unit B in Level 2. It is used for the entire course. Each class can have its own *Exercise Box* (a small cardboard box or shoe box with cardboard dividers) which, ideally, should be kept in the classroom or taken to every lesson.

The purpose of the *Exercise Box* is to encourage students to write their own exercises which they keep in the *Exercise Box* for other students to use later, particularly if there is TIME TO SPARE in a lesson. Students learn a great deal from writing exercises for each other.

Practical ideas

- Refer to the IDEAS LIST for examples of kinds of

exercises that students can write. Students can write a neat, correct version of their exercise on a blank postcard. They should put the answers on the back.
- The TIME TO SPARE? section gives students a chance to write an exercise and/or answer an exercise from the *Exercise Box*.
- Use the *Exercise Box* if some students finish a task before the others.
- The *Exercise Box* will gradually build up to offer a source of revision and/or remedial work.
- For easy reference, label the exercises, showing what Unit they come from. You can divide the box into sections for each Unit. You may want to colour code the exercises for difficulty.
- You can add your own exercises to the box, of course.

AtoZ FEEDBACK

What and why?

In learning, one of the most important factors is a feeling that you are getting somewhere. For some students, learning at school can seem like an endless list of exercises, in which they move from one task to the next.

This can lead to a lack of a sense of direction in their learning or a feeling that there is no value in it. It is important, therefore, that students receive feedback on what they have done and that their effort is recognised and valued. Feedback may focus on the *form* of what they have done (spelling, grammar, neatness, etc.) or on its *content* (its message, the opinions and ideas expressed). As teachers, we typically respond to the form aspect, but it is only through the content aspect that we can really recognise our students as individuals with their own ideas.

Practical ideas

- Feedback can come from other students as well as from the teacher. Allowing time for students to show their work to each other (if they wish – this may be a sensitive point) can allow them an opportunity to have pride in their work, ask questions about things they are unsure of, and share ideas.
- If the students are engaged in a large activity, such as in the *Activity* Units, allow some time at the end for them to DISPLAY THEIR WORK.

- Feedback between students is best done in pairs or threes with students who are friends with each other.
- Feedback between students can be given a clear focus by asking them to produce a *single* re-written version of their work which draws on what each of them have done. For example, if they have completed a guided piece of writing, they can produce a new version which has corrected spellings, grammar, extra ideas etc.
- In feedback to each other, students may be over-critical or focus only on the form aspect. One way to overcome this is to insist that they make positive suggestions for improvement. Comments may also be limited to two or three points.
- Feedback to you, as the teacher, can be gained through the EVALUATION activities.

AtoZ FLUENCY

What and why?

Many language learning tasks focus on accuracy. These are often 'closed' exercises in which there is only one correct answer. Fluency tasks, on the other hand, are more open. They encourage the learners to take risks and be more creative with the language because there is no 'right' or 'wrong' answer (see OPEN-ENDED TASKS). At lower language levels, language teaching has traditionally emphasised accuracy, believing that fluency comes once the grammar has been mastered. In *CES*, however, both accuracy and fluency are emphasised right from the beginning. Developing fluency is important in building up the students' confidence and maintaining a sense of achievement in being able to say something meaningful. Many students also learn more naturally through tasks which focus on *using* the language, rather than learning *about* the language. The *Topic* Units, *Activity* Units and *Culture matters* Units all aim at developing fluency. The *Language focus* Units, *Revision and evaluation* Units and exercises aim at developing accuracy.

In all four skills, confidence and fluency are linked and make the students more receptive to learning. Confidence and fluency in READING and LISTENING help students to deal with language without feeling the need to understand every word, encourages them to guess new words, and enables them to understand the main message, including the speaker/writer's attitude. Confidence and fluency in WRITING and SPEAKING allow students to get their ideas across without being restricted by an over-concern with form.

Practical ideas

- There are numerous fluency activities throughout *CES*. Compare, for example, the exercises in an *Activity* Unit with the accuracy exercises in a *Language*

focus Unit.
- In fluency exercises, the focus is on developing and expressing ideas. There is nothing wrong with correcting language ERRORS as they arise, but don't let this stop the main focus. Make a note of significant language errors and return to them later.
- There is only one way to becoming fluent and accurate at the same time: through using the language to express/understand ideas. This takes time, so you will need to expect and tolerate language errors as students develop this ability.
- In fluency focused exercises, try to react to *what* the students say, not *how* they say it. For example, if you are marking their written work, you can add something about what they have said, your opinion on the topic, and so on.

Researching the classroom

- Where possible, keep a record of what the students have produced in a fluency exercise (e.g. written work or a recording of a ROLE PLAY or DISCUSSION). Compare it with what they produce some weeks or months later to get an idea of their development.
- Language errors or a lack of fluency may be caused by the situation in which the students are working. Record some class discussions and some small group work and compare what happened. Are students more fluent and/or accurate when they are talking about particular topics? Is the size of the group important? Is small group work more effective for developing fluency?
- Make a note of the errors that you correct and notice when and how those errors come up again. Many teachers say that students make the same mistakes

time and time again because the students don't think before they speak/write. In truth, they are thinking about something else. What is it? Is the message more important to the students?

- Experiment with providing different levels of control and support over what the students speak/write. Do students produce more or less when a topic is left very open and language is not controlled? Try out different **OPEN-ENDED** and closed exercises and compare the results.

AtoZ GAMES

What and why?

At secondary school level, games are a lively way of maintaining students' interest in the language. Games in *CES* are an integral part of the course. They are fun but also part of the learning process and students should be encouraged to take them seriously. In general they need not be compulsory – students may prefer to do something else while another group plays a game. Most of the games in *CES* expect students to create some input before they play. This gives a sense of 'ownership' and extends the language learning element.

Practical ideas

- As with all **GROUPWORK**, the success of the game depends on the clear instruction to the students. Make sure that they understand the aim of the game and the rules before they start. (Initially, these are probably best explained in the **MOTHER TONGUE**).

- You will need to make sure that you have a supply of dice and counters permanently available.
- The best number of students for a game is probably four (six maximum) otherwise the game will move too slowly and the others will get bored while waiting for their turn.
- Students can choose a 'leader/referee' for the game before they start, to decide on disagreements.
- While they are playing you can be **MONITORING AND GUIDING**.
- Make sure they know how much time they have to play the game: 10–15 minutes is probably enough for most of the games in *CES*. Don't start a game 5 minutes before the end of a lesson! You can give students a 'five-minute warning' before the time is over so they can work towards the end.
- As the course progresses, you can get the students to invent their own games and design their own board.

AtoZ GRAMMAR

What and why?

An understanding of the grammar of English is crucial to the development of the students' language learning. By the time students reach secondary school age, they are able to handle and understand grammatical rules and descriptions. With the limited amount of time which the classroom provides for language learning, grammar can be a vital tool in speeding up the students' ability to produce 'correct', meaningful English. In order to see how the language 'jigsaw' fits together, it is also important that students learn to use words such as 'noun', 'verb', 'adjective' etc. This will enable the students to work things out for themselves (see **INDUCTIVE GRAMMAR**) and you, the teacher, to explain things to them.

Practical ideas

- The *Language Record* pages after the *Language focus* Units summarise the grammar points for the students. As the students fill it in, it provides a self created reference for revision.
- The *Revision and evaluation* Units give students an opportunity to reflect on grammar points which they

may still be uncertain about. In both Level 1 (Units 18, 23 and 33) and Level 2 (Units 12, 22 and 32), they can write their own tests as a creative practice to check their understanding.
- To make sure that students understand the metalanguage, they can write the main words – noun, verb, adjective, personal pronoun, etc. – on a poster on the wall with examples underneath to act as a reminder.
- As they discover the main grammatical rules and structures, students can construct a **POSTER** for the wall with example sentences underneath each main rule.
- The main rules can be written on a sheet by some of the students and placed in the class **EXERCISE BOX**.
- Grammar games are often a useful way of practising language. These can be combined with **PHYSICAL MOVEMENT**. For example, to practise the comparative forms, you can ask one of the students to come towards you saying 'Peter, please come here because you are smaller/bigger/prettier/younger/older, etc. than I am.' One of the other students then invites you to walk to them and gives a reason using the comparative form. That student then is invited by

another student, and so on. Similar games can be played which ask students to perform particular actions when they hear a noun, a verb or an adjective.

Researching the classroom

- How effective is explicit teaching of grammar? Some writers argue that grammar teaching has very little impact on the language that students produce spontaneously. Look carefully at the work that your students have written or record part of a lesson or some small group work. Can you trace the language structures that the students use *directly* to things that they have been taught? Are there some grammatical forms that they are using that they have not been taught?
- Choose an area of grammar from one of the *Language focus* Units, for example some Past simple irregular verbs or the use of 'enough'. Don't teach that area explicitly or ask the students to do any language focus exercises on that area, but otherwise carry on teaching as usual. After a couple of weeks, give the students a short test and include items on the area you chose to see if the students learned it 'naturally' anyway.
- Some areas of grammar seem to be acquired much later than other areas. Talk to teachers of students who have a higher level of English language ability or think about other classes you have. What 'typical errors' do higher level students make? Are they different from the 'typical errors' of lower level students? What areas are in common? When are those areas taught to the students? Can you experiment with changing the order in which language areas are taught?

AtoZ GROUPWORK

What and why?

Groupwork in *CES* is based on the idea that students can learn language and information from each other. The principle of cooperative learning is basic to classroom education. It also allows teachers the opportunity to help with individual problems, stronger and weak students to work at their own PACE (see MONITORING AND GUIDING) and more students to get more practice.

Practical ideas

- Before students begin groupwork, make sure they know exactly what they are expected to do. Make the focus clear with a definite outcome (for example, to write something, make a list of something).
- During the lesson note which students are working together so that you can encourage them to work with different people next time.
- After working in groups, students can be cross-grouped. This involves groups re-forming with representatives of the other groups (for example, if students are labelled A, B, C, and D in their groups, cross-groups can be formed by all the As coming together, all the Bs, all the Cs and so on). In their cross-groups, students can compare ideas.
- Three or four are probably the best numbers for groupwork.
- There are many ways to set up groups. Try to vary the basis on which you group students: i) students can choose who to work with; ii) they can turn round and work with the students behind/in front of /next to them; iii) they can be grouped according to ability; iv) they can be grouped alphabetically, according to birth months; v) they be can grouped to maintain a balance of boys and girls; vi) they can grouped by numbering students 1, 2, 3, 4 around the class; vii) you can cut up some postcards and distribute the pieces round the class. Students have to find who has the pieces which go with theirs and thus form a group; viii) you can give out cards with names of animals (four of each). Students have to walk around the class making the noise of the animal to find out who is in their group.

AtoZ HOMEWORK

What and why?

In *CES*, homework gives students time to absorb, process and practise what they have learnt at school (see also *Notes on the Workbook*, page 145). It also keeps the students involved between lessons and maintains their commitment to learning English. In most courses, the amount of time available in class is simply not sufficient for language learning to take place fast enough. Extra work outside class is essential.

Practical ideas

- Before you set homework make sure that the students know which exercises they have to do and how long they are expected to spend on their homework. (No more than half an hour is recommended.)
- There are no answers in the Workbook so their homework will have to be checked in the next lesson. You will need to allow some time for this and to build it in as part of the lesson.

- There are a number of ways in which you can correct homework (see *Notes on the Workbook*).
- If you set homework, but find that students do not do it, you need to consider why this is happening. There may be a number of possible reasons. It may be too difficult or too easy. They may not have time because of other commitments. They may not see the point of it. They may not have the book! They may have

other personal problems. You may be able to resolve these problems by talking to the students about it, agreeing with them when they can do their homework, discussing whether they find it too easy/difficult, and so on. Perhaps they can sometimes suggest something to do for homework. (Everybody doesn't always have to do the same thing.)

AtoZ IDEAS LIST

What and why?

The *Ideas list* is a list of the types of exercises on pages 150–151 in the Student's Book. The list is intended to help the students design their own practice exercises for themselves or for the **EXERCISE BOX**. Designing exercises increases the amount of **STUDENT INVOLVEMENT** with the course and their own learning, supports a general movement towards **AUTONOMY** and promotes deeper levels of understanding. The **EXERCISE BOX** is introduced in Unit 5 and, with it, the *Ideas list*.

Practical ideas

- Students can also use the *Ideas list* if they have **TIME TO SPARE**.
- You can encourage the students to bring in their own examples of English. They can then use the *Ideas list* to make some exercises for themselves and other students.
- The *Ideas list* is fairly short. Students may be able to add more examples to the list. (These can perhaps be put on the wall.) For example, students may be able to think of ideas to use with pictures, objects, listening passages, or writing.

AtoZ INDUCTIVE GRAMMAR

What and why?

GRAMMAR may be approached in two main ways: *deductively*, in which students are given a rule which they then practise (that is, they work using other people's deductions about the language), or *inductively*, in which they work out rules for themselves. Inductive grammar teaching is useful for a number of reasons. It can involve the students more fully as thinking people with ideas of their own and increase motivation. It can involve them more fully in understanding the language as they work out different rules for forming and using English and it can also help clear up misconceptions they have and make it clear to you, the teacher, what ideas they have about how grammar works. *CES* includes a number of inductive grammar tasks in the *Language focus* Units.

Practical ideas

- Some aspects of English grammar may be similar in the students' **MOTHER TONGUE**. Students can be asked to think about how things are expressed in their **MOTHER TONGUE** and when they use certain words, etc., before they are asked to think about English.
- Students can be given simple tables and asked to complete them (for example, sentences with 'don't' and 'doesn't' missing). They can then look through the Unit in the book to discover which word belongs with which subject pronoun.
- Students can briefly work in small groups/pairs to work out a rule before you ask for their ideas. If their ideas are incorrect, you can then present the correct rule or give some more examples which make them think about the rule further.

AtoZ INTERACTIVE WRITING

What and why?

Most often, the writing that students do in school is simply for the eyes of the teacher. Interactive writing involves students writing *to* and *with* other students. There are a number of reasons why this might be useful. Firstly, writing to other students can give the students a clear sense of purpose and audience for their writing –

they can **FEEDBACK** from the reader on how far their message has been understood. Secondly, writing with other students can give the students a clear focus for their work. Interactive writing will involve the students in asking each other about grammar, spelling, vocabulary, phrasing etc. and so give them the chance to learn in a non-threatening atmosphere.

Practical ideas

- While students are working in groups, you can circulate around the class, reading what they have written and helping with any problems.
- Discussion during interactive writing tasks may be in the MOTHER TONGUE. This may not be a problem since one of the purposes of interactive writing is to enable students to exchange ideas. An 'English only' rule may prevent this. The important point is to insist that the writing that they produce is in English.
- Writing can be a sensitive area and some students may not want to write with other students or their work to be seen by other students. In this case, students should be entitled to work alone if they wish.

AtoZ LANGUAGE RECORD

What and why?

There are *Language Record* pages at the end of the *Topic* and *Language focus* Units. These provide a record and easy reference of the language the students have covered. They are designed to be completed by the students in their own time either in class or at home.

Practical ideas

- As students finish the *Topic* Units and *Language focus* Units, direct them to the *Language Record* at the end of the Unit.

- Initially, allow time in class for students to complete it. They can also do it for HOMEWORK.
- Students don't have to wait until the end of the lesson to fill it in. If they have TIME TO SPARE, they can fill it in.
- While they are working on the *Language Record*, you can go round MONITORING AND GUIDING.
- Encourage students to think of their own examples for the sentences. This will support the *picture dictionary* sections in the Workbook.

AtoZ LEARNING STRATEGIES

What and why?

Learning strategies are the techniques individual students use to help themselves learn. Classroom research has identified three main types of strategies: *meta-cognitive* strategies, such as planning, evaluating and monitoring language use; *cognitive* strategies used in actually 'doing the learning', such as guessing words, repeating, learning things by heart, and working out rules; and *social* strategies, such as working with others, asking for help and so on. All students come to their English lessons with their own learning strategies. They learn many of these through their other schoolwork, through watching people, and by being told what to do. Learning strategies are very personal – what works for one person may not work for another person. Since the strategies students use are influenced by teaching and by others, students may not be using the best strategies for *them*. Teaching tends to emphasise particular approaches to learning (e.g. an emphasis on copying). Students are unlikely to be aware of what the alternatives might be and may assume that the way they learn and are taught is the only way.

Learning about learning is part of the process of education and provides an understanding which is transferable to other subjects, other areas of life and beyond school. It is also important in bringing about STUDENT INVOLVEMENT.

Practical ideas

- *CES* includes exercises which use various kinds of learning strategies. *Meta-cognitive* strategies are involved in the DECIDE and DO IT YOURSELF exercises, such as the 'Open Plan' at the end of each Theme of Level 2. *Cognitive* strategies are developed all through the materials and, in particular, in the *Help yourself* Units in the Workbook. *Social* strategies are involved in the numerous GROUPWORK and individual tasks, the encouragement to ask others and share ideas, and to use resources from outside the classroom.
- As you introduce a *Help yourself* Unit from the Workbook, discuss with students the strategies that they use. Encourage them to try a new strategy and discuss the results with them a few lessons later.
- Before giving a test, discuss with the students *how* they will revise.
- When they choose a *Decide* exercise ask them why they chose *that* one.
- You could make a *Help yourself* POSTER with ideas from the students about how they revise for tests, how they do their HOMEWORK, how they check their work, what they do to learn English in their free-time and so on.
- There are few 'right' or 'wrong' ways to learn a language. Some students may feel happier, for example, looking at a model before they write, while others prefer to 'write from the top of their heads'. The

important point is that students are aware of the possibilities. Every now and again, discuss with the students how they are going to do an exercise and allow a variety of learning approaches. In some cases, this may include looking at the answers *first,* for example.

AtoZ LISTENING

What and why?

In common with the other skills of WRITING, READING and SPEAKING, there are two main roles for listening in language teaching. The first is as a *goal* of teaching. It is important for students to develop the listening skill in order to understand spoken English, whether on TV, radio or in speaking to people. The second role, however, is as a *means* of learning. Listening can provide further sources of input and can help the students remember the words, phrases, grammar etc. that they are learning. By working on listening tasks, students can become closely involved with the language and, in doing so, develop their general language proficiency. Handled well, listening can thus form a very important element in the course.

Practical ideas

- In the early stages, the emphasis is probably best placed on listening as a *means* of learning rather than as a *goal* of learning. This means that rather than treating listening as 'comprehension' exercises, students can listen to texts they have read and discussed as a way of consolidating their learning. They can also look at the text while they are listening.

- For listening to work well, students have to be able to hear! If you are in a noisy classroom, close doors, windows, turn off fans, etc., while you are playing the cassette.
- With larger classes, students can listen in smaller groups while the other students are doing something else.
- Unless you are conducting a test, you can allow the students to listen again if they wish or to pause the tape to check the meaning. Listening in this case will be useful for learning English generally.
- Control of the cassette player can be passed to a student. Other students may then feel freer to ask for things to be replayed or paused.
- Before the end of a lesson, you can play the listening passage again as a way of recapping what you have done.
- If the students are doing a listening comprehension exercise, they can work in pairs with one of the students listening for answers to some of the questions and the other students listening for answers to the other questions. They can then compare afterwards.

AtoZ MIXED ABILITIES

What and why?

All classes are 'mixed-ability' classes. All classes consist of individual students with different personalities and interests. All students also, themselves, have 'mixed abilities'. For example, some students may find writing easier than speaking or vice versa. Some students find one particular task or approach more appealing than other tasks or approaches. It is also important to distinguish two aspects of 'ability': language ability and language learning ability. The first aspect refers to how much language the students actually know/understand at a particular point in time. The second aspect refers to their ability to learn. A student may be weak in English, for example, but given appropriate support may be able to learn quickly. This suggests that some 'mixed-ability' classes may be the result of particular approaches to teaching (the ability to learn or the ability to be taught?). For this reason, teachers need to adopt a flexible methodology that allows for a variety of learning styles and abilities (see LEARNING STRATEGIES).

Practical ideas

- One key principle in teaching mixed-ability groups is *transparency.* Try to make sure that *all* students understand what is happening in the lesson, for example by OVERVIEWING before beginning the lesson or a new task.
- There are a number of ways in which you can approach teaching groups of mixed language and learning ability: i) stronger/average/weaker students can be given completely different tasks at different levels of difficulty; ii) students can be given tasks on the same topic at varying levels of difficulty (see below); iii) students can be involved in OPEN-ENDED TASKS which allow them to respond at their own level of ability. In principle, approaches ii) and iii) are better, since they avoid students feeling left out. Approach iii), additionally, allows a student to develop more freely without being restricted by the tasks themselves.

- To provide tasks at varying levels of difficulty on the same topic, text, etc. Think about how a task can be made more challenging or how more support can be given. In the Teaching Notes for all the *Topic* and *Language focus* Units there are ideas for making these kinds of adjustments to the key exercises in the Units.
- At the back of this Teacher's Book, there are additional, photocopiable *Language worksheets* for each grammar point in the *Language focus* Units.
- The TIME TO SPARE? exercises at the end of each *Topic*

and *Language focus* Unit provide further tasks for varying levels of ability.
- The exercises in the *Decide* boxes encourage students to make choices about what they need to do and to work at their own pace.
- In GROUPWORK, try to mix students so that students of all abilities can work together.
- See further ideas under LISTENING, SPEAKING, READING and WRITING.

AtoZ MONITORING AND GUIDING

What and why?

In many of the activities in *CES*, students will be working in small groups or pairs. This way of working has many advantages, in that it gives students a chance to work at their own pace, to ask each other for help, to share ideas and to get more language practice. Small group work and PAIRWORK, however, can run the danger of students wasting their time together as they become distracted, talk about or do things other than requested, or produce work which is full of errors. For this reason, monitoring and guiding by the teacher is very important.

Practical ideas

- Before setting students to work in pairs/groups, check that they understand fully what they are going to do. You can go through one or two examples with the whole class first.

- While they are working, go round the class. You can check whether they are having any problems, check the work they have done, give extra ideas where necessary, and generally keep them on the task.
- While going round the class, you can also note down common errors that you notice. You can then spend a short time at the end of the lesson, going through a few of these.
- You also make a note of which students seem to be working well together and which seem to be having problems. Next time, you can vary the way you set up GROUPWORK accordingly.
- Before students start working, you can put some TASKS IN BLOCKS. Where students have finished the work, they can move on to something from the EXERCISE BOX, look back at previous Units, or choose to DO IT YOURSELF.

AtoZ MOTHER TONGUE

What and why?

The mother tongue plays an important role in all language learning. Firstly, it is an important tool for the teacher to clarify explanations, give instructions and provide translations. At the beginning of the course, many of the instructions about classroom activities will need to be given in the mother tongue to make sure that the students know what they are expected to do.

Secondly, the mother tongue is a primary learning tool for the students. As with all other kinds of learning, a large part of language learning involves relating what you are learning to what you already know, in this case the mother tongue. Studies show that all beginning students use the mother tongue as a resource consciously and subconsciously in language learning activities. Thus, the tasks and activities in the *CES* provide opportunities for the students to TRANSLATE sentences and texts into the

mother tongue so that they can compare the form and meaning of the two languages and ensure that the *correct* meanings are learned.

Practical ideas

- Students may also use the mother tongue because they feel embarrassed about speaking English in front of the whole class. In these cases, you can give them time to prepare what they are going to say (see PROCESSING TIME).
- If you feel the students use too much of the mother tongue (for example, in GROUPWORK), you will need to consider why this situation is arising and what you can do about it. It may be that the task is too difficult for them, not interesting enough, not clear to them, or too unstructured. You could try to discuss the problem with them, give clear examples of what they

have to do, or ask for suggestions from them.

- As you gradually introduce more English into your classroom management, encourage the students to reply in English to questions like 'Where is Peter today?' or 'Are you ready?'
- You will need to decide *when* you will use the mother tongue. You might for example limit yourself to

explanations of grammar and vocabulary and to when you are **MONITORING AND GUIDING**.

- You will also need to decide when you will accept the mother tongue from the students. For example, you may accept use of the mother tongue in **BRAINSTORMING** activities in which you translate their ideas and put them on the board.

A to Z MUSIC

What and why?

Potentially, music can have an important role in the classroom. The use of **SONGS** is already very familiar to most teachers. Music, however, plays a major role in many parts of our lives. We may, for example, listen to the radio while we are working, while we are driving or waiting for something. There may be background music while we are eating or reading. We may use music to relax or to mark a change of activity (such as 'coming home from work') and so on. In similar ways, music can be used to help make the classroom more welcoming.

Practical ideas

- Choose music for the atmosphere you want to create:

soft calm music if you want to calm the students down, energetic music if you want to wake them up, and so on.

- You can play music as they come into the classroom. This can help 'bring them into' English again, and relax them ready for work.
- You could use music regularly at set phases in your teaching – for example, when they are working on the *Activity* Units. Students could then suggest or bring in appropriate pieces of music.
- If there are a number of steps or phases in an activity, you can use music to mark the transition. For example, some fast music for a **BRAINSTORMING** phase and a slow, gentle piece of music for a writing phase.

A to Z OPEN-ENDED TASKS

What and why?

Open-ended tasks are tasks to which there is not a single absolutely correct answer or where a variety of answers are possible. They can be distinguished from 'closed tasks', where students have to answer in a particular way. An example of an open-ended task might be where the students are asked to imagine a person standing in a pair of shoes which they are shown and then to write a description of that person. A closed task using the same type of language might be one where they are given a description with certain words missing, which they have to supply. Both closed tasks and open-ended tasks are useful in language teaching. Where students are working in groups, for example, closed tasks can force the students to discuss more in order to find the correct answer. Open-ended tasks, however, are also very valuable for a number of reasons. Since there is no single correct answer, the students can often answer at the level of their ability. This means that in **MIXED-ABILITY** classes, students can be working on the same tasks at the same time. Open-ended tasks also allow for more **STUDENT INVOLVEMENT** since the students are asked to contribute more of their own personal ideas. This means that the outcome of classroom work will be richer – there will be a variety of ideas expressed which students can further compare and discuss. In this way, the students'

AUTONOMY in their own use of English can be developed. Open-ended tasks also allow you, the teacher, to get a good idea of what the students are capable of producing.

Practical ideas

- If, at the start of a course, you are uncertain how much English the students know, you can use the open-ended tasks in Unit 1 of both Level 1 and Level 2 of *CES*.
- You can set the students some open-ended writing tasks by asking them to write their ideas about some educationally broad **QUESTIONS**, particularly ones which require **PROBLEM SOLVING**.
- The students' answers to open-ended tasks can be included in a **PARCEL OF ENGLISH**. They will give the school or class that you send the parcel to a good idea of the range of abilities and interests in your class.
- Instead of asking the students conventional 'closed' comprehension questions about a text they have listened to or read, you can ask open-ended questions. For example, you can ask 'What do you think about …?', ' What would you do …?', 'Do you think it was good that …?', 'Why do you think he/she did that?', 'What do you think they said to each other?', 'What do you think he/she was thinking?' and so on.

AtoZ OPEN PLAN

See **DO IT YOURSELF**.

AtoZ OVERVIEWING

What and why?

A common experience of some students is that they often do not have a very clear idea of where they are in a lesson – they may have very little idea of what has just happened, an unclear idea of what they are supposed to be doing now, and no idea at all of what is going to happen next. As one teacher put it, for many students being in a classroom is rather like being put in a taxi without being told where you are going or what landmarks to look out for on the way. Overviewing is a technique which helps to give students a clearer idea of where they are in the lesson. That way, if they lose concentration for a short time, they won't lose their grip on the whole lesson (100% concentration during a whole 40–50 minute lesson requires a lot of mental effort!).

Practical ideas

- The *Take a look at Theme …* tasks on the Theme cover pages are intended to give the students an overview of what they will meet in the coming Units. The tasks require the students to look through the Theme and so familiarise themselves with its content.
- Before moving into an activity which has several steps, you can give the students an overview of what they will be doing. It will then be easier to move them on from one step to the next, once the activity has begun.
- You can place an overview of the lesson on the board at the start of the lesson, showing what they will be doing.
- You can give an overview of your next lesson, leaving open some period of time. They can then be asked to suggest ideas of things they would like to do (you could use a suggestion box for this). This will help create a feeling of **STUDENT INVOLVEMENT** in the lesson. (Have something planned, just in case!)

AtoZ PACE

What and why?

The **TIMING** and pace of any lesson are linked together. **TIMING** is concerned with the management of the time available for each class, that is, *when* certain things happen. Pace is more concerned with the rate at which the students work. All students work at a different pace and they thus need to be allowed to work at a rate at which they feel comfortable. *CES* provides a number of ways of preventing some students from falling behind because the pace is too fast and of preventing others from getting bored because the pace of the lessons is too slow.

Different types of classroom activities will naturally have a different pace. For example, oral discussion with the whole class may be experienced as 'faster' than individual writing. **PAIRWORK** may be experienced as more relaxed than questions and answers with the teacher. These differences in pace can be used to give variety to the shape of the lesson and thus sustain interest.

Practical ideas

- In large **MIXED-ABILITY** classes, different students can work on different tasks at the same time at their own pace.
- For most of the exercises, except the initial **BRAINSTORMING** and **OVERVIEWING** ones, students can work at their own pace (see **MONITORING AND GUIDING**).
- Certain parts of the course will allow students more opportunity to have direct control over their learning and thus their pace: the **TIME TO SPARE?** sections, the **EXERCISE BOX**, the **DECIDE EXERCISES**, the **DO IT YOURSELF** exercises and the use of **GROUPWORK** and **PAIRWORK**.
- If certain students are working at a very slow pace, you will need to ask yourself why this is and if you can or should do anything about it. For example, they may be tired, they may be confused, they may not understand the task, they may be bored, they may have things on their mind. You will then need to decide if you should intervene – for example, by encouraging them to work faster or by explaining things to them again.

AtoZ PAIRWORK

What and why?

Pairwork involves students working in pairs simultaneously. The reasons for the use of pairwork are similar to those of **GROUPWORK**. Pairwork allows more students to get more practice. It also provides a change of pace to a lesson and helps to sustain motivation. Students working in pairs are able to share ideas and help each other. However, pairwork can fail if it is not set up well. This can lead to students getting distracted, disenchanted with English, and, eventually, misbehaving.

Practical ideas

- Ensure that students know exactly what they have to do before they begin any pairwork activity. Run through a few examples with the whole class. Initially at least, pairwork tasks need to have a clear, concrete focus, for example on completing an exercise, doing PATTERNED PRACTICE, preparing some INTERACTIVE WRITING, preparing questions and so on.

- For variety, different students can be paired together. Students can be moved around the room or they can be put into pairs with students to their left or right, in front or behind.
- Give the students a time limit so that they know when they have to finish.
- Students can work in pairs to produce questions, exercises, etc. for other pairs to do.
- If the task does not actually *require* pairwork, the students can choose whether they want to work in pairs or alone.

AtoZ PARCEL OF ENGLISH

What and why?

A Parcel of English is a collection of pieces of work which the students can produce and send to another class (perhaps in another country) or display in their school. It is introduced in Unit 8 of Level 1 and Supplementary

Unit A of Level 2. Cambridge University Press offers a link-up scheme for classes to make contact with classes in other countries of the world. For further details see page 18 of this book and the registration card inside the book (or on the inside front cover).

AtoZ PARTICIPATION

What and why?

Particularly in large classes, some students may seem reluctant to participate orally and contribute to the lessons. There may be a number of reasons for this. There may, for example, be a number of negative factors such as being afraid to make mistakes in front of others, feeling that they will appear stupid, fearing that they will be corrected, or otherwise lacking in confidence in front of a large group. On the other hand, many students naturally say very little. They may feel that they learn best through listening and observing – silence is their preferred LEARNING STRATEGY. Before you insist on students participating orally in the lesson, it is best therefore to think about *why* they are not participating. What may seem a problem to you may not, in fact, be a problem to them. It is important to respect the personal preferences that different students may have. There are, however, a number of things that you can do to improve the chances of students participating.

Practical ideas

- If there are one or two students that are persistently quiet, you could talk to them after a lesson to find out what they think about it. Alternatively, you could make up a questionnaire which *all* students can answer.
- If possible, try to arrange the seating so that all the students can see you clearly and so that they can see each other. A horseshoe arrangement or circle is best, or try and push the desks together into pairs or groups.

- Accept that some students are quiet and may feel happier contributing in a less obvious way – perhaps by producing exercises and puzzles for the EXERCISE BOX, or helping to organise the PARCEL OF ENGLISH, or bringing in pictures and 'realia' for other activities.
- Some students may dominate the class by being over-noisy or always answering questions first. If this is a problem you could divide the class into four quarters and say that you will accept an answer from each group in turn.
- Some students may be reluctant to 'act out' in class. They may prefer to record a conversation on cassette at home for you to listen to later. Don't force students to speak out loud if they are not willing or ready.
- Make sure that the students understand that many of the activities in *CES* are open-ended so that a variety of answers are acceptable and 'right'. It is what *they* think that is important.
- Encourage students to understand the importance of everyone's contribution in GROUPWORK and that the work that the quiet students do often supports the work of the more dominant ones.
- Allow students to work at their own PACE (see also TASKS IN BLOCKS). This will give the more apprehensive students an opportunity to work without pressure.
- The DECIDE EXERCISES also allow students freedom to choose what they prefer to do. Give the quieter students encouragement while they work to build up confidence.

- You could make a particular point of praising weaker or quieter students and of accepting what they say (even if this contains many errors) in an effort to build up their confidence.

AtoZ PATTERN PRACTICE

What and why?

A key part in language learning is having the opportunity to use the language creatively to say real things. However, there is also an element in language learning which involves practising particular structures or forms so that the students can produce them effortlessly. One way in which this can be done is through pattern practice. Students produce sentences following a particular pattern and in doing so develop their ability to control the mechanical aspects of language production. Over-used, however, pattern practice can produce students who become bored and who find it difficult to use the language to actually communicate. For this reason, *CES* includes relatively few patterned exercises.

Practical ideas

- Pattern practice exercises can be done in small groups or pairs so that students get more opportunity to speak without having to wait for the rest of the class.
- The focus of pattern practice activities is on the *form* of what is said. This is the appropriate time to ensure that things are said accurately.
- Before getting students to work in pairs/groups on a patterned exercise, go through a few examples with the whole class so they know what is expected.
- While they are working, you can be MONITORING AND GUIDING.
- Oral pattern practice exercises can also be done in writing.

AtoZ PHYSICAL MOVEMENT

What and why?

Students in the early secondary years need physical activity. In school, they may often spend many hours confined to a desk as they have one lesson then another. This can lead to boredom and restlessness (with its effect on DISCIPLINE). Physical movement can also be important for other reasons. If students can be physically involved with English, it can lead to deeper, more long lasting learning as the language becomes more 'concrete' to them and involves them as whole persons.

Practical ideas

- 'Simon Says' games, in which students have to carry out actions upon the orders of the teacher/a student can be fun. Students must only do the action if the teacher/student says 'Simon says' first (For example: 'Simon says sit down', 'Simon says clap your hands'.)
- Basic verbs can be taught in this way, with the teacher first saying the verb and the students following the action and then the students doing the action as the teacher says the verb again.

- Students can also represent something in a group. For example, they might together form the shape of their country. They can then move to where they would like to be in their country and talk about why they want to go there. They could ask each other across the map: 'Peter, where are you?', 'I'm in Barcelona in the north east'. Students can similarly form maps of their town, maps of a jungle, and maps of their school.
- Mime is also useful. Students act out a word and the others have to guess what it is.
- You could have various items of clothing available such as hats, gloves, etc. to make role plays, acting out, mime, etc. more fun.
- Physical activity doesn't have to be related to language learning. You might start a lesson or break up a long lesson by getting the students to do something. For example shake their arms, change the shape of their face, or stand up and turn round a few times. You could combine this with MUSIC.

AtoZ POSTERS

What and why?

At various places in *CES* (particularly in the *Activity Units*), students are required to produce posters of their ideas. The production of posters is a useful technique in language teaching for a number of reasons. It gives the students a concrete focus for their work and also ensures that English (rather than only the MOTHER TONGUE) is produced as a result of their GROUPWORK. Poster production can also be a lively way of working. Students can design their posters, spend time on how they look and express their ideas graphically. They can form a welcome break from a linear presentation of ideas in which groups

FEEDBACK, one after the other, to the whole class. Posters allow all groups to **FEEDBACK** simultaneously, thus using the time more effectively. They also form a permanent record of the work that has been done that can be **DISPLAY**ed.

Practical ideas

- For poster production you – or the students – will need to have available supplies of large sheets of paper, coloured pens, scissors, glue or adhesive tape, and something to affix them to the wall.
- Coloured sheets mounted on a white background can make posters more attractive to look at.

- Students can be asked to work on parts of their posters for **HOMEWORK**, once they have decided in their group what they want to write.
- Encourage them to produce a draft before they put their writing on a poster.
- Once the students are ready with their posters, you can put them up on the wall or lay them out on the desks. Students can then walk around the class, looking at the posters. You could ask one member of each group to stay by their poster to explain what they have done.
- Posters can be photographed for permanent reference. A class photograph can be taken with their poster display.

AtoZ PROBLEM SOLVING

What and why?

Learning how to approach and solve problems, and accepting that there is often more than one answer to a question or more than one way of dealing with it is a key part of both education and language learning. The ability to determine the essence of a problem, and indeed to see that there *is* a problem, is a vital ingredient in learning. In *CES*, therefore, many tasks require the students to think things through not only in relation to the structure of the language but also by drawing on their existing knowledge to help understand new situations. For example, some exercises in which the students are asked to establish their own rules for a new grammatical structure require this kind of cognitive effort. Other exercises require students to think through *why* certain things happen or to work out an explanation for natural phenomena.

The benefits of a problem-solving approach to teaching and learning can be significant for a number of reasons. Firstly, involving the learner in thinking things through requires more involvement and produces greater depth of understanding. This kind of 'experiential knowledge' (that is, the knowledge gained through the experience of *doing* something) often lasts longer and is more significant to the learner than knowledge which is simply 'transmitted' by the teacher or the book. The students become involved in constructing their own *individual* systems of learning and understanding. Secondly, some recent research has suggested that where students are involved in using language to understand and formulate meanings, then language may be acquired more naturally, in much the same way as infants learn their first language.

Practical ideas

- When students ask you questions, you can, from time to time, insist that they find out for themselves, by using books, asking other people or figuring it out.
- Give hints or clues in answer to their questions rather than direct answers.
- You can set a 'problem of the week' for the students. Talk to other subject teachers in your school and ask for ideas about questions you could pose. 'What if ...' questions and 'How can ...' questions are often useful in stimulating thought. For example: 'What would happen if we had only three hours of light each day?', 'What would happen if we started teaching Chinese instead of English in school?', 'How can we make our classroom lighter and quieter?' Even: 'How can we best learn a language?' If you set such questions, you can discuss them at a specified time later.
- You can present 'language learning' as a 'problem' to be solved. Encourage students to think of their own ways of recording and learning new vocabulary. Let students discuss and compare in class the different methods they have tried. Encourage students to discuss grammar areas which they find difficult or easy to learn and use. Encourage the students to think about and investigate *how* they go about doing exercises, reading, how they revise for a test, etc.
- Students can be encouraged to bring puzzles and problems into class. They can also put these into the **EXERCISE BOX** and the **PARCEL OF ENGLISH**.

AtoZ PROCESSING TIME

What and why?

Learning – whether it is a foreign language or any other subject – often requires great mental effort. In any 40–50

minute lesson, a student may be required to absorb a lot of new information, make connections with what he or she already knows, and then be required to use it. Each of these processes takes time. Often, when students are asked a question and they fail to answer correctly, the problem is not that they don't know or haven't understood, it is simply that they haven't been given enough time to process the question and process an answer. If students are questioned with the whole class listening and waiting, there may be pressure on them to answer as quickly as possible. This can block their ability to process the question and an answer – that is, to think. The teacher may then feel under pressure to keep the lesson moving and so turns to another student. The same situation may repeat itself several times, until finally, a student who has not been put under this direct pressure and who has thus had enough time to process the question, is able to produce a satisfactory answer. This problem may be avoided by allowing all students processing time before you call for answers.

Practical ideas

- Allow students time to do an exercise by themselves/in pairs before you call for answers.
- Give students time to plan out what they are going to say, their ideas on a topic, etc. in writing before you discuss things with the whole class.
- Tell the students in advance what they will be doing. They can then prepare at home for the lesson.
- Choose 'larger' tasks which can be done in a large space of time (such as the majority of tasks in *CES*) rather than short 'item' tasks which require immediate responses (such as comprehension questions, gap filling exercises).

AtoZ PRONUNCIATION

What and why?

A correct and clear pronunciation is obviously of considerable importance in language learning. Without it, students may not be understood and may be poorly perceived by other English speakers. However, a good pronunciation is something which takes time to build up as there are many factors involved. Students need to hear a lot of English before they can develop a 'feel' for the sounds of English. They need to have confidence in their abilities, not feel shy and be ready to make a fool of themselves as they try to get round their tongues round the different sounds. Pronunciation is thus probably best dealt with a little at a time and in the context of learning new words, structures, etc. rather than in isolation.

Practical ideas

- The *Say it clearly!* reminders in the Student's Book are intended to draw attention to some sounds that the students may have difficulty with.
- It is better to spend very short periods running through pronunciation examples and exercises rather than one long session. Perhaps the same pronunciation exercise could be done in three or four different lessons for three minutes at a time.
- It is worth discovering which are the main pronunciation problems for students of your MOTHER TONGUE. You can then spend a little time focusing on them. A little pronunciation practice at this level goes a long way!
- Students may find stress and intonation practice easier and more interesting to respond to by doing some jazz chants or clapping as the words are stressed on the cassette. This can be done in small groups if they have the cassette recorder or briefly with all the students together.

- Students can be encouraged to do pronunciation practice at home. The *Topic* and *Language focus* Units in the Workbook contain pronunciation exercises. In addition, the Workbook contains *Help yourself with pronunciation* and presents some ideas they can use.
- READING aloud is a technique which is often used to check pronunciation. In our experience, however, reading aloud has very little effect in improving pronunciation. In the classroom, students typically make *more* mistakes when they read aloud than they do normally. It also wastes time for the students who have to listen and places the teacher in the role of having to correct the reader all the time. Turning the written word into sounds is quite a separate process from the production of a word in normal conversation.

Researching the classroom

- Personality and background can have a lot of influence on the way students see themselves as 'English speakers'. This will influence their pronunciation. Try to identify which of your students have the clearest pronunciation in English. Can you explain this in terms of their background or their personality? Do they have certain things in common? Are they, for example, quiet students or more extrovert? Have they travelled to English-speaking countries? Are they musical?
- Some pronunciation problems *may* originate in the difference between sounds in the MOTHER TONGUE and sounds in English. Is this true with your students? Can you identify which sounds these are? Try an experiment. Identify two sounds which you know are very different in English from the MOTHER TONGUE or which don't exist in the students' MOTHER TONGUE.

Give the students explicit practice in one of the sounds but do not pay any special attention to the other sound. After a few weeks, judge how well the students use each sound. Does explicit pronunciation practice always make a difference?

A to Z QUESTIONS

What and why?

Questions are important in language learning in three main ways. Firstly, and most obviously, the 'interrogative' is a grammatical form which students need to learn to master. For users of a foreign language, the ability to ask questions is essential. It provides the key to moving around in a new environment, integrating into a community and to finding essential information. Secondly, questions form one of the main 'tools' which teachers use to check students' comprehension and to get students to produce language. Thirdly, and more profoundly, the ability to generate questions is central to **AUTONOMY** in learning and to the students' personal *educational* development. Many types of questions used in classrooms, however, are *display questions* – that is, they require the students simply to show that they know something. This places the emphasis on reproducing isolated facts. Educational questions, on the other hand, require the students to think, to discuss, to share ideas or to investigate. They can bring about more **STUDENT INVOLVEMENT** with learning English and with their educational development in general. *CES* places particular emphasis on educational questions rather than display questions.

Practical ideas

- When beginning a new topic, you can get students to **BRAINSTORM** what they already know about it and what they would like to find out. You can get the students to produce a Question **POSTER** of things they can investigate/research over the next few weeks.
- Where possible, ask **OPEN-ENDED** questions, to which various answers are possible, rather than closed display questions where only one answer is correct. For example, after reading a text, instead of asking factual questions such as 'What did the man do in the shop?' (the answer to which is in the text), you could ask 'What do you think about what he did?', 'Why do you think that?'
- Before reading a text, or after reading part of a text, you can ask the students to predict what will happen next.
- If the students have a reading text with conventional comprehension questions, you can ask them to try to answer the questions *before* they read the text, using their imagination and what they already know. They can then approach the text more actively to check their answers.
- If you get students to produce questions for each other (perhaps for the **EXERCISE BOX**), you can ask them to formulate some educational questions rather than display questions.
- You can talk to teachers of other school subjects to find out what educational questions are relevant to the theme you are working on in *CES*. Students can then be asked to find answers to these questions over the next week or so. You can discuss what they have found out at a specified time.
- Rather than *telling* the students, you can ask them a series of questions so that they work things out for themselves. You can ask: 'Can you think of any other similar examples?', 'Why do you think it is like that?', 'When does this happen?', 'Where?', 'Does it always happen?', 'When doesn't it happen?', 'How do you think you can find out?', 'What books would you need to look in?', 'Who could you ask?' and so on.

A to Z READING

What and why?

Similar to **LISTENING**, **SPEAKING** and **WRITING**, there are two main roles for reading in language learning. The first is as a *goal* of learning: 'the skill of reading'. The second is as a *means* of learning: as a way of developing the students' language proficiency and educational depth. Secondary aged students need to develop the skill of reading in English. It is through reading that they will most likely come into contact with English, particularly if they go on to higher education or are employed in international work of some kind. But reading as a *means* of learning is also important. Reading can support their language learning through contextualising and extending vocabulary, creating a mental image of correct spellings, providing models for writing, and by developing a 'feel' for English – especially if they have very few classroom hours. Reading can also be a means for developing their learning beyond just English. Through reading, the students can learn more about the world and come into contact with different ideas. For these reasons, reading needs to be encouraged right from the start. There are a number of ways you can do this.

Practical ideas

- Students may not read very much in their **MOTHER TONGUE** so you may need to start by encouraging reading generally. You can do this by asking, perhaps at the start of every lesson, what they have read since the last lesson. This can be anything – a newspaper headline, a story, an advert, in the **MOTHER TONGUE** or in English. Gradually, you can suggest that they look for things to read in English which they can tell the class about. In this way, the students can begin to see reading as something of value to share.

- You can encourage extensive reading through readers or short stories. If possible, let the students choose what they want to read. Invite (rather than demand) them to tell other students (perhaps in small groups) what they have read. They don't need to report back on everything they read.

- You can allow time for silent reading in class. Some students may like to read if they finish an exercise early or if they chose to **DO IT YOURSELF** for the **DECIDE EXERCISES** in Level 2.

- Encourage students to read other students' creative work such as stories and poems.

- Encourage the students to guess the meaning of words they don't understand. Also, stress that they don't need to understand every word in order to read something.

- Show the students how to use a dictionary so that they can read alone. (At this level, a bilingual dictionary.)

- You can also teach the students other reading skills such as **SKIMMING AND SCANNING**.

- One common technique is to ask students to read aloud. In *CES*, this technique is not recommended. Reading aloud is, in fact, a separate skill from reading for comprehension. Students are unlikely to need this skill – unless they become newsreaders! In the classroom, students typically make *more* mistakes when they read aloud than they do normally (particularly in **PRONUNCIATION**). It also wastes time for the students who have to listen and places the teacher in the role of having to correct the reader all the time. Also, since the emphasis is on production, the main skills involved in reading – guessing words, working out meaning, predicting – are not utilised.

A to Z ROLE PLAY

What and why?

In a role play students take on the role of another person – a waiter, an adult, even a Martian or a monster. Often the situation is given (e.g. *You are in a restaurant. Order a meal.*) and perhaps some ideas of what to say. Role play is a popular method in language learning classrooms for a number of reasons. Students of this age find it fun and quiet students are often found to speak more openly in a 'role'. In a role play students are encouraged to use communication creatively and imaginatively and they get an opportunity to use language from 'outside' the classroom. In *CES*, there are role play tasks in many parts of the course, particularly in the *Out and about* sections.

Practical ideas

- The success of every role play depends on the students knowing exactly what they have to do. Make sure that the students know the role they are going to play, some language they can use and some ideas for content.

- In general, role play works better in groups of a maximum of three or four students.

- Discuss with students how long they need to prepare their roles and whether they can prepare in pairs or alone.

- Students can prepare either in 'complete' groups for the role play (that is, one student for each character) or in character groups (that is, in small groups they share ideas of what they will each say. They then join with other students when they are ready to act out the role play).

- Some students like to make notes of what they are going to say. This creates confidence in the preparation period but encourage students to speak without reading out their notes.

- As a role play is based on 'real life situations' if you have some 'realia' (real items) from an English speaking country these will make the role play more fun, e.g. real menus, real bus/train timetables, real/plastic English/American/Australian money etc. Younger students often like to have 'props' – handbags, shopping bags, purses, etc.

- During the preparation stage the role of the teacher is to circulate, answering questions, checking that everyone understands and making suggestions.

- You may need to remind students of some 'checking' and 'communication' phrases: 'Sorry? Could you say that again please?', 'What do you mean?', 'What's the word for ...?'.

- During the role play itself you can listen and write notes about points which can be discussed later. If a student gets stuck indicate to the others to help in any way they can. You can prepare a comments sheet like the one on the next page. The students who are listening to the role play can also make a note of their own comments.

Name:

To comment on	To praise
Grammar	
Vocabulary	
Pronunciation	
Communication	
Self-correction	
General comments	

- After the role play discuss with the class how they felt it went and then put general points on the board to avoid embarrassing individual students.
- Sometimes it is a good idea to record the role play on audio or video cassette so that you and the students can see/hear it again later.

AtoZ SKIMMING AND SCANNING

What and why?

'Skimming' and 'scanning' are two different READING skills. These are practised at the start of each theme, using the cover page tasks (*Take a look at Theme ...*). Skimming means looking at a text or chapter quickly in order to have a general idea of the contents. Scanning means looking at a text to find some particular information. For example, we skim through a report to have a rough idea of what it says but we scan a page of the telephone directory to find a particular name or number. As the students become more confident of their reading ability in the MOTHER TONGUE and in English they will learn how to approach texts with different reading skills, depending on the purpose of the text and the purpose they have for reading it. Students who find reading in English discouraging may be helped by knowing that they do not have to read and understand every word of a text.

Practical ideas

- Start by explaining the difference between skimming and scanning to the students (give them the example of a telephone directory and a chapter of a History/Science textbook).
- Before the students read a text ask them whether they think they need to skim or scan it depending on the task.
- Students often like having races. Occasionally ask students to see who can find the information in a text first.
- Make sure the students realise that understanding every word of a text is not always necessary.
- Allow time for students to read the texts quietly to themselves in class to practise their own technique. Texts do not need to be read out loud round the class.
- Encourage students to practise skimming and scanning when they read in their mother tongue.
- Ask the students who find the answers in the 'Skim' and 'Scan' section at the beginning of each *Topic* Unit to write some more questions for the rest of the class to do.

AtoZ SONGS

What and why?

In general, secondary school students like singing songs, particularly if they are melodic. They are a way of recycling language in a 'fun' format, they develop a natural sense of language achievement and can also bring about STUDENT INVOLVEMENT.

Practical ideas

- The songs in *CES* are on both the Class Cassette and the Workbook Cassette. You can point this out to the students and ask them to practise a song at home.
- You can ask the students to suggest a song that you can all sing. It is best if the song is one that they all know already so that everyone can sing. If you use songs regularly, students can take it in turns to bring

in a song or decide in their groups which song they would like to sing next time.
- It is probably best to sing the song either at the very beginning or the very end of a lesson.
- Make sure you allow enough time – 10 minutes at least – to give students a chance to listen and then to sing together at least twice.
- Some students may feel shy about singing, don't force them!
- Play the song through first, if you have it recorded – make sure students can hear. If the students have the words, they can read or sing while they listen.
- In some songs the students continue by making up words of their own.

Try to vary the presentation:

- Sometimes half the class or different groups can sing the verses and the other half sings the chorus.
- Sometimes half of the class sings alternate verses.
- Perhaps an extrovert has a wonderful voice and can sing a solo!
- Some students may have a guitar and would like to play the tune along with the music.
- Perhaps at the end of the term/year, the students could give a concert to the rest of the school.

The best thing to do with a song is to sing it! However, there are various teaching techniques that you can use from time to time with songs:

- Give the students the lyrics with some words missed out. The students have to listen and put in the words.
- If the song has a chorus or verses that are repeated, you can put the students into groups and give each student one sentence from the song. While they are listening, they have to put the sentences in the right order.
- Give them some questions about the song before they listen. Afterwards, they can tell you their answers.
- Sing all the verses except the last one. Give a choice of three verses for the last one, (you can modify/make up your own). Students have to read it and work out which one fits the tune best.

AtoZ SPEAKING

What and why?

One of the main aims of *CES* is to give students confidence in expressing themselves orally. The emphasis is, therefore, on spoken fluency rather than on spoken accuracy. This should encourage students to be confident and creative in their spoken English.

Practical ideas

- Before correcting a spoken error consider whether it could lead to misunderstanding. If not, there may be little reason to correct it. Too much ERROR CORRECTION can inhibit the students' desire to speak.
- Encourage students to give their reactions to the pictures and input at the start of a Unit. There is no need to insist on whole sentences – they may only manage a phrase or even a word. Try to react to *what* they have said rather than *how* they have said it.
- Allow space and time for the students to speak! You can record some of your lessons and calculate how much time *you* spend talking and how much time *the students* spend talking. If necessary, see if you can change the situation over the term.

- Students often find it difficult to provide a rapid spoken reply to a question without time to PROCESS an answer. Sometimes it may be useful to give the students in advance the questions you will ask them so they can prepare. At the beginning, it may be better to let students volunteer a reply rather than insist that they answer in turn.
- The quieter students may prefer to be given the choice of speaking on to a cassette at home. They could then, perhaps, give you the cassette to listen to.
- Try to ensure that different people speak each time. You can suggest that different people do the reporting back after GROUPWORK.
- If you have some students who never say anything, or who PARTICIPATE very little, you need to ask yourself why this is. It may be their preferred LEARNING STRATEGY/style (to listen and absorb), or they may feel shy, they may feel that they don't know enough, or they may feel that the lessons are dominated by other students. If the situation persists, you could talk to the students concerned to find out what they think about the situation. It may not be a problem for them at all!

AtoZ SPELLING

What and why?

Many students – and many native English speakers – find English spelling difficult. Since English has been influenced by many other languages, it does not have a completely consistent 'fit' between the way it is spoken and the way it is written. In addition, the invention of printing in the 15th century had the effect of 'fixing' the spelling of English at a time when the language was undergoing many changes.

'Good spelling' is important. It influences the way people think of you, and your ability to communicate clearly. However, it is important not to over-emphasise spelling. For many students, spelling is something that takes care of itself as they get more exposure to English. In the initial stages of learning, a stress on correct spelling may discourage students from using the language to try to express what they want to express. Some students may have problems in spelling in their own language, and drawing attention to this in English may strengthen their feeling of failure. The best approach is probably to draw the students' attention to spellings, and to do a little practice frequently.

Practical ideas

- There are two *Help yourself with spelling* Units in the Workbook.

- Ensure that the students understand that sometimes there is little or no relationship between pronunciation and spelling in English. You can make this fun by saying, for example, 'We say two /tuː/ but we write /twəʊ/.' You get them to count in 'spelling English': /əʊneɪ/, /twəʊ/, /t h reɪ/ and so on.
- If all your students share the same MOTHER TONGUE it is likely that they make the same spelling errors. Make a list of them and, if possible, put the correct version on a POSTER on the wall. Students can then refer to this when they are writing.
- You could give the students groups of words to learn, grouped around sounds. For example, [eː] words: sweet, feet, meat, heat, etc. Point out to students how the same sound is spelled in different ways.
- Do the spelling errors fall into groups? For example, perhaps they have trouble remembering the double consonant in some comparatives and superlatives, or perhaps they confuse 'ei' with 'ie'. With the students, you could draw up a checklist of their common errors. They can then use this checklist every time they write something.
- Encourage the students to check spellings in the *Wordlist/Index* at the back of their Student's Book.
- 'Good spelling' probably comes with READING. The more the students read, the more it may help their spelling. After the students have read a text, you could ask them to go back and focus on the words. Ask them to write down (or underline/circle) any words which they think they will have trouble spelling correctly later. Discuss with the group their choices and find out why they chose those words.
- To encourage students to look closely at common letter patterns, after they have read a text, write some two-, three- or four-letter patterns on the board (for example, '-ea-', '-ough-', '-th-'). Then individually or in teams ask them to find as many examples as possible in the text of those letter patterns.

- Students can test each other in groups.
- Play 'Spelling Snap!', in groups of three or four. Write on one side of some cards, words which they know but may find difficult. Make sure there are at least three examples of each of the letter patterns. Shuffle the cards. Each student has 10 or so cards. Students take it in turns to put one of their cards in the centre of the table and say the word on the card at the same time. If the card which follows has the same letter pattern they must shout 'Snap!'. The person with the most cards at the end is the winner.

Researching the classroom

- To find out if students who have problems with spelling in English also have problems in MOTHER TONGUE spelling, ask their other subject teachers if you can see some of their work. Alternatively, you can dictate a short text in the mother tongue to the students (perhaps about a *CES* Theme). Collect in the papers and make a note of the errors and the students who made them. Give another brief dictation in English and compare the results.
- To find out the nature of spelling problems that your students have, make a list of the words that they misspell when you correct their work. After a few weeks, see if you can put the words into groups. Are there particular sounds that they consistently misspell? Are there words that they confuse? (e.g. *right* and *write*)
- Does pressure of time affect the students' spelling? Give them a short period of time and ask them to write as much as they can about a topic. Some time later, suggest another topic and divide the time up: 15 minutes to write, five minutes to check and change. Compare the results.
- Are your students aware of their spelling difficulties? When they write something, ask them to underline the words they are not sure how to spell. Compare this with the mistakes they make.

AtoZ STUDENT INVOLVEMENT

What and why?

Student involvement is probably the single most important factor in language learning, especially with students in the early secondary school years. One of the greatest causes of drop-out and student failure in learning is that they do not feel part of their course. For this reason, the encouragement of student involvement is one of the key principles in *CES* (see the *Rationale*, pages 7–11). The aim is to involve the students as fully as possible in their English course, such that they feel it is *theirs* and one which is personally relevant to them. *CES* contains numerous practical ideas in relation to student

involvement. The following are some of the basic principles we have adopted.

Practical ideas

- Start from the students. When introducing a new topic, find out what the students already know about it and what they would like to know about it.
- Encourage regular EVALUATION of how they are learning and take steps accordingly.
- Provide choices between tasks. Students do not have to be doing the same things all the time. Allow them to DECIDE and make room for DO IT YOURSELF.

- Provide creative tasks which draw on the students' imagination, experience and personal views.
- Provide 'larger' **TASKS**, such as whole activities, where students can feel freer to work in their own way.
- Draw on the **MOTHER TONGUE** as a means of involving

the students' knowledge about how language works.
- Involve students in the production of **TESTS** and make tests less threatening.
- Focus on topics which are worth learning about in their own right, and which have **CURRICULUM LINKS**.

AtoZ TASKS

What and why?

The word 'task' is used in a variety of meanings in language teaching. One common use is in the sense of 'whole tasks', that is, a large classroom activity in which the students may be doing a variety of different things. In this sense, the *Activity* Units in *CES* are 'whole tasks'. The focus in 'whole task' work is usually on meaning, rather than the form of the language, although both are important (see **FLUENCY**). Many writers argue that teaching through 'whole tasks' is the most effective since students can learn the language through natural processes of acquisition.

In *CES*, however, the word 'task' is used in the same way as 'exercise', to refer to any structured language learning procedure. 'Task' in this sense will include everything from a gap-filling exercise to a poetry-writing activity. Tasks may be 'small' and may only take a few minutes

(such as doing a word puzzle) or 'large' (such as making a poster) which may take a whole lesson or more. In actual fact, 'large tasks' are likely to be made up of smaller tasks. Some of the key questions in language teaching are: 'What are the most effective kinds of tasks for language learning?', 'What makes a task more or less difficult for students?', 'How do different kinds of tasks affect classroom interaction?', 'How do different kinds of tasks shape **LEARNING STRATEGIES**?', 'What roles do different kinds of tasks place on teachers and students?'

Practical ideas

- See the A–Z entries on **TASKS IN BLOCKS, OPEN-ENDED TASKS, AUTONOMY, EXERCISE BOX, DECIDE EXERCISES, DO IT YOURSELF, PROBLEM SOLVING, MIXED ABILITIES, FLUENCY** and other cross-references.

AtoZ TASKS IN BLOCKS

What and why?

A situation which often arises in teaching is that students, working either in groups or alone, finish before each other. This may not be a problem. There is no particular reason, for example, why students should have to be kept 100% busy 100% of the time. In some cases, however, students may waste their time as they wait for others to catch up. This may lead to boredom, disenchantment with learning English and, in some cases, **DISCIPLINE** problems. Putting tasks in blocks is a technique which ensures that students have something to go on to when they finish their work.

Practical ideas

- Before students start working, you can put two or three tasks together 'in a block'. Go through the tasks, explaining what they have to do in each one. As students finish one task, they can move on to the next.
- You can also put some tasks in blocks with the **TIME TO SPARE?** sections and the **EXERCISE BOX**. Students will then have something to do when they finish the tasks.
- Putting tasks in blocks will give you more time for **MONITORING AND GUIDING.**
- You can give a time limit for the tasks. If they finish before, students can move on to anything else they wish, providing it is related to learning English (see **TIME TO SPARE?** and **EXERCISE BOX**).

AtoZ TESTS

What and why?

Tests can form a useful and important role in language learning. They can give both the students and the teacher a clear picture of how much the students have learned. They can also give the students a focus or something to work towards, and thus motivation for learning. However, tests can also have many negative consequences. Some students can become very anxious

about tests and this can prevent them from effective learning. Students may become so focused on the test that they lose sight of the wider goal – learning English. Learning can also become 'defensive' in which they learn something because of the fear of the test, but rapidly forget it once the test has passed. For these reasons, tests need to be handled carefully and made more 'friendly' to the students.

Practical ideas

- Before a test, give the students a clear list of what they will be tested on. They can then be asked to rate themselves on each area of the test and compare with the marks after the test.
- Try to view a test not so much as an indication of how much the students know/don't know but as an indication of how effective classroom language teaching is. If students perform badly, this may say more about what is happening/not happening in the classroom than it does about the students.
- In both Level 1 and Level 2, students can be involved in devising their own tests (see the *Revision and evaluation* Units). If you give a list of areas that you have covered over the last few lessons, pairs of students could make up parts of the test. You can then collect them in, correct them and assemble them into a complete test. Students can learn from the process of writing the test and seeing their own corrected version. The test is then also 'theirs' rather than 'yours' and so less threatening.
- Students can be given practice tests to do at home. (There are practice tests in the Workbook.) These give the students the opportunity to test themselves without anxiety.

AtoZ TIME TO SPARE?

What and why?

Students work at a different **PACE** and finish exercises more quickly or slowly than others. The *Time to spare?* sections (at the end of the *Topic* and *Language focus* Units) are designed to give students something to go on with if they finish ahead of the others.

Practical ideas

- The *Time to spare?* section contains extra exercises and the option of creating an exercise for the **EXERCISE BOX**. Students might also want to choose to **DO IT YOURSELF** (in Level 2).
- Students don't need to be kept 100% busy 100% of the time. If they do finish early, they can be given the option of just relaxing, as long as they don't disturb other students. Getting more work as a reward for working hard can be very demotivating!

AtoZ TIMING

What and why?

The timing and **PACE** of each lesson are linked together. However, timing refers mainly to *when* things are done in the lesson. The rhythm of the lesson needs to be maintained so that students use the class time productively and enjoyably. Your timing for new activities or steps in the lesson also needs to bear in mind what the students have just been doing and how much time is left in the lesson.

Practical ideas

- Look at the timing estimates in the Teaching Notes for each Unit before you start and write your own estimates.
- Make a note during the lesson of the actual time each exercise took with each class and, if appropriate, why you think it differed from your estimates.
- Before starting an exercise tell the students how long they have. Near the end of the time warn them that the time is almost over.
- Keep an eye on the clock during the lesson: don't start a new task just before the end of the lesson!
- If there are only a few minutes left at the end of the lesson the students can work on the **TIME TO SPARE?** exercises, fill in their **LANGUAGE RECORD**, do an exercise from the **EXERCISE BOX**, make an exercise, play a game, sing a song, or look back through the previous Units.

AtoZ TRANSLATION

What and why?

As a technique in language learning and teaching, translation used to be very popular. In recent years, however, it has fallen out of favour. There has been concern that an over-use of translation encourages the students to produce very strange sounding English. Too much translation can also prevent students from developing fluency in the language as they develop the habit of going through their **MOTHER TONGUE**. Yet, used appropriately, there are a number of reasons why translation, as a teaching technique, still offers considerable benefits. Students, especially in the initial stages *do* translate. It is, in fact, impossible to learn anything unless you find ways of integrating it into what you already know – for the beginning student this is the **MOTHER TONGUE**. It is thus important that the teacher is able to ensure that students have the *correct* translation in their minds. Translation can also help students be themselves – they can express what they want to say and then learn how to say those same things in English. It is also useful as a planning device (e.g. before writing) where trying to plan *in English* would prevent the flow of ideas.

Practical ideas

- You can deal with basic vocabulary problems through translation. This saves time compared with long explanations and ensures the correct meaning is understood.
- Students can play the translation game, where a 'non-English speaking' student says something in the

MOTHER TONGUE and another student has to interpret for him/her.

- BRAINSTORMING can be done in the MOTHER TONGUE, but as you put the ideas up on the board or a POSTER, you can translate them into English. Students can then learn from seeing *their* ideas in English.
- Before doing a ROLE PLAY, WRITING a passage, preparing QUESTIONS or an exercise, students can first plan things out in their MOTHER TONGUE, all the time thinking of what they are able to say in English. Planning in the MOTHER TONGUE can prevent language problems interfering with the generating of ideas.

AtoZ VIDEO

What and why?

In general, students find the use of videos motivating and stimulating. Videos are a useful vehicle for learning more about a topic, for making cross-cultural comparisons and for making the language more memorable. *CES* is accompanied by a set of videos. These can be used together with the coursebooks or on their own. The *CES* videos are not intended simply to provide 'language models'. They aim to enrich the students' knowledge and experience of language use in relation to the topics in the course by providing interesting extension material for each of the six Themes in the Levels. See the video packs themselves for further details of the *CES* videos and accompanying worksheets. The following notes apply to the use of videos in general.

Practical ideas

- Plan ahead! Book the video and cassette. Check if a technician will be available. Watch the video and read through the video script before the lesson so that you are aware of the language, characters, topic and content.
- Prepare the students before they see the video so that they have an idea of what they are going to see. Give them a general outline of what they will see. This will make it much easier for them to follow and learn.
- You can set some tasks before the students watch the video. These can be of a general nature, about what happens in the video. After the students have watched the extract from the video all the way through, you can follow this up with further detailed tasks which require the students to listen or look for detail.
- Tip: When you start the cassette put the counter on zero so that when you rewind and replay you will find the place more easily.

- Tip: Make sure that all the students can see the screen and hear.
- Keep the video session fairly short. Ten minutes of video frequently every week is more useful than 40 minutes every month.

Some ideas for exploiting videos:

- Play the video the first time without any sound. Ask the students what they think the people are saying.
- Students can watch the section all the way through. Rewind then play a part again. Then freeze the frame and ask them what they can remember comes next.
- Observation: the students can do this in teams. Give them a list of items before the viewing. They have to write down who had or did them, e.g. 'Who had a red car?', 'Who had glasses?', 'Who did Peter talk to?', etc.
- After viewing the video extract once, students can work in groups to write questions for each other. They can then exchange these and watch the video again to find the answers.
- Talk about cross-cultural aspects. Ask students to write down after the viewing four things they noticed which were different from their culture (objects, buildings, clothes, food, etc.) and four things which are the same. Put them on the board. Discuss why the things are the same or different.
- In advance, choose some sentences from the video script and ask what they think the video will be about, what they will learn about and so on. They can also guess who says the sentences, why, etc.
- Students can also be involved in making their own videos.

A to Z VOCABULARY

What and why?

Vocabulary is possibly the single most important area in language learning. With a large vocabulary, a person can communicate effectively even though he/she may be very weak in grammatical knowledge. In *CES*, vocabulary development is thus emphasised. This is achieved through various vocabulary related exercises, the **LANGUAGE RECORD** and the suggestions for making vocabulary exercises in the **IDEAS LIST** in the Student's Book, and the *Help yourself* Unit and *picture dictionary* in the Workbook. It can be expected, however, that the students' *passive* knowledge of vocabulary (their understanding) will always be greater than their *active* abilities (what they are able to produce). The same is likely to be true in the **MOTHER TONGUE**.

Practical ideas

- Writing vocabulary puzzles for the **EXERCISE BOX**, for the **PARCEL OF ENGLISH** or for their partner (see **IDEAS LIST**) also gives students time to absorb new words.
- Encourage students to compare new words with translations in the **MOTHER TONGUE**.
- Encourage students to guess new words in texts.
- Show the students how they can use a dictionary. This will help them build up their vocabulary outside of class time.
- You could encourage the students to keep a vocabulary notebook in which they note down words/phrases new to them and their meaning in their language.
- Students can be put into small groups to test each other on vocabulary or to devise a vocabulary test for the class.
- For each Theme, the students could gradually construct a large vocabulary puzzle. Decide in advance with the students what kind you will make (e.g. find the words, or one long word acting as the basis for all the words, a traditional crossword puzzle, a circular puzzle in which the last letter of one word is the first letter of the next, etc.) and put the plan on the wall. During the two or three weeks of the Theme each student puts a clue on the puzzle. At the end of the Theme, students write the clues and the blank puzzle in their books and do the puzzle together.
- 'I spy' is a lively vocabulary game which younger students like playing. (One student says 'I spy with my little eye something beginning with "w".' The object must be in the room. Students guess. The one to get it right has the next turn.)

Researching the classroom

Most research suggests that it is far easier to learn vocabulary in 'chunks' of meaning than as isolated words. This is one of the main reasons why *CES* is designed around Themes. This gives a context with which the students can associate language and thus makes it more memorable. You can see the effect of context, meaning and association with a few simple experiments with one of your classes.

- Give your students a list of 20 random words to learn and, at the same time, a short passage about something interesting. Test their ability to recall it in **WRITING**. Ask them to write down *anything* they remember from the list and *anything* from the passage (for the purposes of this experiment, ignore **SPELLING** mistakes). One week and two weeks later, test the students on both things again. Which do they remember most? How much is lost from the list and from the passage?
- Try a similar experiment but, this time, actively involve the students with the language in some way in order to build up associations with the language. For example, you could identify each word on the list with a part of the room (ask the students to imagine that the word 'street' is in the corner of the room, 'traffic' is near the window, 'airport' is near the door and so on). A week later, point to each part of the room and see if they can recall the word.
- You can try a similar experiment with remembering 'chunks' of text. Ask the students to act it out, perhaps in pairs as a dialogue. Or perhaps they could sing it or associate physical movement with each sentence.

A to Z WRITING

What and why?

In common with **LISTENING**, **READING** and **SPEAKING**, there are two main roles for writing in language teaching. The first is as a *goal* of teaching. It is important for students to develop the writing skill in order to express themselves in written English in letters, messages, stories, and so on.

The second role, however, is as a *means* of learning. Writing can provide further sources of practice and can help the students remember the words, phrases, grammar etc. that they are learning. By working on writing tasks, students can become closely involved with the language and, in doing so, develop their general language proficiency. Writing can thus form a very important element in the course.

Practical ideas

- Encourage the students to keep written records of what they learn. The **LANGUAGE RECORD** will be useful in this respect. Students can also keep 'Language Notebooks' in which they note down vocabulary, phrases, grammar points, etc. They can then look at these on the bus, while waiting somewhere, at home in bed, and so on.
- Before calling on the students to do any large oral activity, such as **ROLE PLAY**, students can be encouraged to plan in writing what they are going to say.
- Where students are involved in writing as a *goal* of language learning, encourage them to go through the various stages of collecting ideas, drafting, getting **FEEDBACK** from a reader, revising and final production.
- Where possible, give the students real life tasks which have a real audience. This could be writing a letter requesting information, the **PARCEL OF ENGLISH**, pen friends and so on. Writing to other students can also provide an audience (see **INTERACTIVE WRITING**).
- In correcting students' writing, try not to over-correct. A page full of red ink can be very demoralising! There are a number of alternative ways of approaching correction: ask the students to underline the things they are not sure of or where they would like your help – you need only then correct the things they have identified; limit yourself to no more than six to eight points for correction; rather than focusing on the form of what they have written, respond to the message. Write a brief reply to the ideas they have expressed; rather than correcting, give hints or clues and encourage the students to correct their own work. You can use a marking scheme (e.g. Sp = spelling, WW = wrong word, and so on).

Notes on the Workbook and Workbook answers

1 USING THE WORKBOOK

The Workbook and Workbook Cassette provide supplementary exercises for the work covered in the Student's Book.

As it is often difficult to do listening tasks and pronunciation work thoroughly and clearly in class, there is a cassette with the Workbook. This is optional but it is strongly recommended (all the exercises can be done without the cassette - except Unit 27. See below). The cassette contains listening tasks for comprehension, interactive dialogues during which the students respond to questions, pronunciation exercises and the songs from the Student's Book.

The Workbook exercises may be used in class or set for homework. For this, we anticipate that students will spend about half an hour on their homework after an English lesson. If the Workbook is set for homework it is important that it receives some attention during class time. If you vary the way this is done, you can help to sustain the students' commitment to homework (see also **AtoZ HOMEWORK**). There are a number of possible ways you can do this:

- Before you set Workbook exercises for homework, explain clearly what they have to do in each one. Write on the blackboard which exercises they are to do.
- After they have done the exercises, go through the answers with the class as a whole.
- Collect in the Workbooks periodically to check.
- Allow small groups of students to go through their answers together. During this time you can circulate around the class, helping out and checking.
- Provide an 'answer sheet' for students to check their own answers (this can be circulated around the class while they are doing some other activity, pinned up on the board for students to check after the lesson, or written on the blackboard).
- Get students to exchange books while you read out answers.
- Encourage students to do the Workbook exercises together with another student.
- Get them to record their answers to some exercises (interactive dialogues from the Workbook, for example, could be re-recorded by two pupils together).

2 SPECIAL NOTE ON THE 'HELP YOURSELF' UNITS

There are six *Help yourself* Units in the Workbook which cover the areas of Spelling (Units 6 and 22), Grammar (Unit 12), Vocabulary (Unit 17), Pronunciation (Unit 27) and Fluency (Unit 32). These are intended to give students practical ideas for learning English.

The Units have no 'right or wrong' answers which you can check since they are designed to be of direct use to the students in *how* they approach their learning and to support the general movement towards autonomy. The ideas presented are *suggestions* – whether or not students continue to use them will depend to a large extent on personal preference. However, students cannot make real decisions about how they learn unless they have experience to base it on: the Units are designed to give students that experience.

Although the Units are intended for the students to use alone, it is important, nevertheless, that they receive some attention in class. The Units are rather unusual in a

number of ways, so before the students do one of them, it is best if you go through (perhaps in the mother tongue) what the Unit is for and what they have to do. Additionally, you could:

- Discuss before they do a Unit, how they usually go about learning vocabulary, grammar, etc. (for example, in preparation for a test). Secondary aged students *do* have ways that they use to learn, although they may not be as efficient as they could be.
- Discuss, after they have done a Unit, what they thought about each of the ideas. If they haven't done them, discuss why this was.
- Set a test on a language area. They can then prepare for the test using the techniques. (For example, you could give a list of words to learn, a grammar area to revise, or some social situations to prepare for.) In this way, the students may see directly how the ideas in the *Help yourself* Units may help them.

3 WORKBOOK ANSWERS

Unit 1 Welcome to English!

1

```
F C A R S W I M
O j i A a e w g
O k q D D h m k
T l w I O r P t
B y r O W z I E
A r i W C T A I
L T E N I H X G
L W J L C I N H
M U S I C I O T
            E
```

2 1–7–13, 2–10–14, 3–6–15, 4–8–11, 5–9–12.

3 Example: This is my friend. Her name is Anna. She is 12 years old. She lives in … She can sing very well.

5
1 Fine thanks.
2 What's your name?
3 How do you spell 'car'?
4 I don't know.
5 How do you say this number in English?

6.2 Total is 279 divided by 2 = 139.5

Unit 2 Extension Around the world again

1.1
1 He is on a submarine. He has got a hat.
2 They are on a train. They have got a lot of books.
3 She is on a plane. She has got a lemonade.
4 He is in a helicopter. He has got a big suitcase.
5 They are in a hot air balloon. They have got two cameras.
6 They are in a car. They have got sunglasses.

3.1 A = Darwin. B = Alice Springs.

3.2 Example:

Sydney is in Australia. It is in the east of the country on the Pacific Ocean. There are three million people in Sydney. There are many factories which make cars and ships and there are a lot of beautiful beaches. People can go swimming all the time. The weather is warm in the summer and the winter. There are many big buildings. Sydney Opera House and Centrepoint Tower are famous. There are also many big bridges in Sydney.

4.1
1 false   4 true
2 false   5 false
3 false

5.2 Example: Ahmed has got black hair. It is straight and short. He has got black eyes. He is tall.

6.1
2 Portugal   4 Mexico
3 the United States of America

6.2 Examples:

1 This is London. It is the capital of England. They speak English there. Seven million people live in London. Buckingham Palace is in London.
2 This is Tokyo. It is the capital of Japan. They speak Japanese there. Eleven million people live there. The Meiji shrine is in Japan (Tokyo).

Theme A

Unit 3 Topic Around our school

1 Missing words: a farm, factory, market

2
a castle   e offices
b train station   f swimming pool
c bus station   g factories
d hospital

3 Example letter:

Dear Alice,
Here is a plan of my school. It is a very big school. It has got about 1,000 students. My classroom is on the fourth floor. The headteacher's office is on the first floor. The school canteen and the library are on the third floor. I have my lunch at school. A lot of students go home for lunch. We have got three computer rooms. They are on the second floor.

Write and tell me about your school,

Love,

…

5
1 subjects   6 because
2 favourite   7 bicycle
3 Maths   8 lessons
4 office   9 break
5 short
Word in the middle: timetable.

6
1 Saturday   5 Tuesday
2 Monday   6 Wednesday
3 Thursday   7 Friday
4 Sunday

Unit 4 Language focus

1.1
2 is in the north   6 is in the north east
3 is in the north west   7 is in the south east
4 is in the centre   8 is in the south east
5 is in the east

1.3 A1: river
A2, B4 and C1: picnic area
A3: airport
A4: Bird park
B1 and D1: museum
B2: hospital
B3: museum and information centre
C2: museum and horse racing
C3 and D3: woods
C4: theatre
D2: Sudeley Castle
D4: lake

2.1
1 beautiful   6 rich
2 small   7 straight
3 expensive   8 hot
4 important   9 new
5 curly
Word in the middle: favourite.

3
1 Impossible. Steve doesn't have time to play a musical instrument.
2 Impossible. Steve's brother goes to school by bus.
3 Possible.
4 Impossible. Steve lives in the city centre.
5 Impossible. Steve's family doesn't have a car.
6 Impossible. Steve doesn't like football.

5 Complete dialogue:

You:	Excuse me. How much are these jeans?
Shop assistant:	£250.
You:	That's expensive!
Shop assistant:	They're very good.
You:	How much are these jeans?
Shop assistant:	They're £15.
You:	How much is this bag?
Shop assistant:	That's £4.50.
You:	Can I pay for the jeans and the bag please?
Shop assistant:	That's £15 and £4.50. That's £19.50 please.
You:	Here you are.
Shop assistant:	Thank you.

Unit 7 Test yourself

2 Some examples:
Picture B hasn't got a cafe / many people.
There isn't a library in Picture B.
The school isn't next to a library in Picture B.
The clock isn't right / the clock doesn't say 4.30 in Picture B.
The bus isn't small in Picture B.

4.1 Monday: guitar lesson.
Tuesday: football at school.
Wednesday: supermarket.
Thursday: watch animal programme on television.
Friday: Sam here to play.

4.2 Example letter:

Dear Linda,

Thanks for your letter. We have a Maths test every Friday too!

I finish school at 4.00 p.m. and then I do different activities. On Monday I go to a guitar lesson. I can play a lot of different songs now. On Tuesday I go to play with my friend. My parents work late on Tuesdays. On Wednesday we finish school at 12 o'clock and I have got English lessons from 2–4 p.m. in a special school. On Thursdays I go swimming for an hour after school and on Friday I go and see my grandparents.

I go to bed at 9.00 p.m. I read for half an hour. What time do you go to bed?

Love,

…

5
1 How much is that mask, please?
2 That's expensive!
3 Let's try another shop.
4 Can I have that mask please?
5 Can I have that cloak, please?
6 Bye. Thanks.

7 Nouns: country, trumpet, years, chair, town, address.
Verbs: speak, sing, live, know.
Adjectives: blue, rich, big, straight, important, small.

Unit 8 Fluency practice A Parcel of English

3

```
u g e u m (L I B R A R Y) o l
n w e r t y u (A) o p (C) m j (F)
s t a h i o n (L) g h (A) n j (A)
j u i k l o p (R) g b (S) d c (C)
c d e r f t g (P) y b (T) n j (T)
(S C H O O L) s (O) r t (L) g h (O)
v f g t h y u (R) j k (E) j n (R)
f f i c e t g (T) (S H O P) k (Y)
```

6 Code says: Write us a letter.

A picture dictionary (1)

Label the picture: factory, hospital, school, park, library, cinema, river, house, flats, swimming pool, train station.
Names of subjects: Science, History, Biology, Mathematics.
Verbs: look, listen, swim, write, ride, paint, run, pay.
Adjectives: small, long, beautiful, expensive, old, new.
Nouns: breakfast, team, hill, map, offices, picture, boat, eye, hair, clock.

Theme B

Unit 9 Topic In the wild

1.1

```
(D O G) b c e f u e w
(P E O P L E) r s h (S)
x e m o g k e y w (H)
z h o r s t f o w (E)
w (C R O C O D I L E)
j k p r n k z (C) c (P)
(B) n (C A T) j k (O) o f
(E) m e f t i r (W) s d
(E) h s x e e p n d b
o w (E L E P H A N T)
```

2 Mammals: cats, whales, monkeys, horses, cows, lions, dolphins, tigers, bats, rhinoceroses.
Reptiles: crocodiles.
Fish: goldfish, salmon, flying fish, sharks.
Birds: ostriches, penguins, parrots.
Insects: bees, flies, mosquitoes.

3 's' sound: maps, books, shops.
'z' sound: leaves, rivers, farms, hours, towns.
'iz' sound: boxes, glasses, buses.

Unit 10 Language focus

1 Complete text: Humming birds are very _beautiful_. They _live in_ North America and _South_ America. They move their _wings_ very fast. They can stay in the same place in _the air_ for a long time. They drink from flowers. They also eat small _insects_.

2.1
1 Where do tigers live?
2 How long do tigers live?
3 When do tigers sleep?
4 What do tigers eat?
5 How much meat do tigers eat?
6 How many cubs do tigers have?
7 How long do the cubs live with their mother?

2.2 Example questions:
Have you got a dog?
Do you like cats?
Can you swim?
Do you like chocolate?
Can you play the guitar?
Can you dance?
Do you walk to school?
Can you paint?

3
2 her
3 his
4 their
5 our, his
6 my

4
A Is this your horse?
   [z] [s]   [s]
B No it isn't! I don't like horses!
   [z]   [iz]
A Well, whose horse is this?
   [z] [s] [z] [s]
B It's his horse.
   [s] [z] [s]
A Where does it live?
   [z]
B It lives in that house but it eats here!
   [z]   [s]   [s]

Unit 11 Fluency practice Animal world

1 1 – B, 2 – C, 3 – D, 4 – A.

2.1 Complete diagram information:
4,000 km, in Mexico: October to April;
Journey to Canada: April to July;
Journey from Canada: July to October;
Problem: They are in Canada only a few weeks.

2.2 Examples:
1 How many butterflies fly from Canada to Mexico every year?
2 How many kilometres do they fly every day?
3 When do they go to Mexico?
4 Why do they go to Mexico every year?
5 What do they do in Mexico?

Unit 13 Test yourself

1 Examples:
Dolphins live in the sea. They are mammals and they are very big. They live for about fifty years. They don't eat meat. They only eat fish. They sleep for about five hours at night and during the day.

3
1 our, my
2 my, our
3 her
4 their, his, my
5 its
6 their
7 our, our

A picture dictionary (2)

Label the animals: bird, giraffe, whale, horse, cow, kangaroo, fish, cat, baby, insect, dog.
Verbs: fly, sleep, eat, lay, ask, play, drink.
Adjectives: warm, clever, cold, easy.
Nouns: blood, wing, leg, skin, egg, bird, fruit, plant, meat, fish, flower, insect.

Theme C

Unit 14 Topic Food matters

1.1

F	I	S	H	t	g	C	g	s	R	f	r	h	n	u
e	r	g	a	f	t	H	v	r	I	s	M	E	A	T
B	U	T	T	E	R	E	a	w	C	q	v	n	m	h
i	d	o	r	j	u	E	u	i	E	o	p	l	m	d
C	E	R	E	A	L	S	s	u	q	z	E	G	G	S
B	e	r	d	f	g	E	j	s	w	q	z	x	d	f
R	e	M	f	h	k	v	P	O	T	A	T	O	E	S
E	r	I	t	i	g	F	R	U	I	T	l	i	p	n
A	y	L	t	e	d	t	u	i	o	p	l	m	d	s
D	w	K	r	V	E	G	E	T	A	B	L	E	S	g

1.2
1 Piece of toast with butter and jam: carbohydrates, fats, fibre, vitamins.
2 Vegetable soup and a bread roll: carbohydrates, fibre, water, minerals, vitamins, protein. Piece of cake: carbohydrates, fats, fibre.
3 Fish, boiled potatoes, runner beans: carbohydrates, fibre, water, protein, minerals, vitamins. Small salad: fibre, minerals, vitamins. Can of cola: water, carbohydrates.

3 Peter eats 707.5 kcals for breakfast.

Unit 15 Language focus

1
[C] I don't know. What do we need?
[E] Yes. Yes. We've got lots of sugar.
[A] Well, we've got about half a kilo.
[D] We've got some milk and eggs. Do we need them?
[B] Butter. Er … Oh no! We haven't got any butter!

2.1
3 There are some sweets and there are some bananas.
4 There is some milk but there isn't any sugar.
5 There is some cheese but there isn't any fruit.
6 There is some butter and there is some bread.
7 There isn't any rice and there isn't any flour.

2.2 A – 1, B – 4, C – 2, D – 3.

Unit 16 Fluency practice What do they think?

1   Graph B is correct.

2   Example:

We asked 20 people what they do in the evening. Eight of them stay at home, a fifth (four) go out with friends and a fifth (four) play sports. Two of them read and two of them do other things. Nobody works.

3

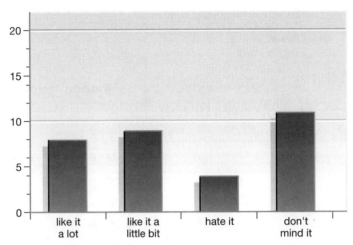

Unit 18 Revision Life on Earth

1   Example answers:
4   Foxes die because they eat rabbits.
5   Other animals die because there are no fish to eat.
6   Many animals have nothing to eat.

A picture dictionary (3)

Label the picture: rice, bread, fruit, juice, fizzy drinks, vegetables, eggs, cheese, butter, milk, potatoes, meat, fish.
Verbs: grow, clean, give, eat.
Nouns: breakfast, lunch, dinner, blood, bones, teeth, eyes, body, skin, hair.
Adjectives: fried, easy, strong, bored, horrible.

Theme D

Unit 19 Topic Into space

1.1   Sentences:
There are nine planets in our solar system. The smallest planet is Pluto. It is also the coldest. It is a long way from the sun.

2   3   True.
4   Wrong. It takes four and a half years.
5   True.
6   Wrong. They look the same because the moon is nearer.

3   Competition time answers:

There are nine planets.
No, nothing can live on the moon.
There isn't any air.
It is important for ships because it makes the tides.
The universe is expanding.
The first people on the moon were Neil Armstrong and Buzz Aldrin.

4   Anne Brown is on Planet Monz.

5   Example:

Dear Everyone,

Here I am on Planet Nevus! It is very hot and it is raining. I can see Earth and the moon. There are mountains and volcanoes.

See you soon,
Love,

…

Unit 20 Language focus

1   Paragraph order: 1–C, 2–D, 3–A, 4–B.

2.1   Examples:
2   She's walking on the moon.
3   She's opening a door.
4   She's running back to the rocket.
5   She's going back to Earth.

2.2   Example answers:
I think he's eating something.
I think he's cleaning/brushing his teeth.
I think she's writing something.
I think she's pouring something.

3.1   2   David is taller than Jane. Susan is the tallest.
3   Susan is stronger than David. Jane is the strongest.
4   David is better in Maths than Jane. Susan is the best.
5   Susan is worse in Science than David. Jane is the worst.

4   Student replies:
Can you tell me which bus goes to Minton?
What time does it go?
In the afternoon.
What time does it come back?
Thanks. How much is the ticket?
I'm 12.
Thanks very much.
Bye.

Unit 23 Revision The continents are moving!

1   1   planet   5   flag
2   expand   6   moon
3   sky   7   light
4   stars   8   ship

2   1   There are seven continents.
2   Asia, Africa, Europe, Antarctica, North America, South America and Australia.
3   They are moving.
4   Because India moved north and then it hit Asia.
5   We have earthquakes because the land is moving.

2.3   1   Wrong. (200 million years ago.)
2   No answer in the text.
3   Wrong.
4   Wrong.
5   Wrong. (They are in Asia.)
6   No answer in the text.

3
1 The biggest continent is Asia.
2 The coldest continent is Antarctica.
3 Wrong.
4 The highest mountain in the world is in Asia.
5 The biggest rainforest in the world is in America.
6 Your country is in …
7 The driest continent is Africa.
8 The smallest continent is Australia.
9 The biggest city in the world is in America.
10 The only continent without towns is Antarctica.

A picture dictionary (4)

Label the picture: sun, Earth, takes, nearest, star, moon, Gravity.
Verbs: leave, move, pull, put, take, drive, collect.
Nouns: planet, ladder, flag, picture, door, tide, sky.
Adjectives: small, hot, cold, high, low.

Theme E

Unit 24 Topic The weather

1
```
n o v a m z e (A) g (J) h
o (F) w t g h i (P) n (A) m
(D E C E M B E R) z (N) a
a (B) w (M A Y) v (I) y (U) p
q (R) e x (R (J U L Y (A) w
q (U) j (O C T O B E R) v
g (A) i l (H) u p f s (Y) y
q (R) b y k (J U N E) t f
d (Y) o u (A U G U S T) s
```

The missing months are September and November.

3
b It's a rainy day.
c It's a windy day.
d It's a chilly day.
e It's a foggy day.

4
3 Right.
4 Wrong. It becomes colder (because the air is thinner).
5 Wrong. Warm air rises.
6 Wrong. Snow is very cold water vapour.
7 Wrong. They are the same weight.

5
```
1 c o l d
2 a i r
3 a u g u s t
4 s h i n e s
5 w a t e r
6 s n o w
7 r a i n
8 w i n d
9 s t r o n g
```

Unit 25 Language focus

2
1 a lot of, much
2 many, a lot of
3 much, A lot, many
4 a lot of, much

3.1 Examples:
… more expensive …
… more beautiful …
… more beautiful to drive …
… longer …
… more comfortable …
… faster ….
… bigger inside …

Unit 26 Fluency practice It's windy, sunny, rainy, chilly and cloudy in Australia!

1
a False. Canberra is the capital of Australia.
b True.
c True.
d True.
e True.
f True.
g True.
h True.

2 It is 4,250 km from Perth to Brisbane and 3,000 km from Darwin to Adelaide. There are five rivers on the map. The longest river is the Darling. July is in the winter in Australia. The temperatures in Melbourne are usually about 10°C in July and 24°C in January.

3
a David is in Perth.
b It is in the winter, July.

Unit 28 Test yourself

1
a It's very windy!
b It's very sunny.
c It's very rainy.
d It's a sunnier day than yesterday.
e It's a windier day than yesterday.

4 Completed dialogue.
Pat: Hi, Anne! It's Pat.
Anne: Hi, Pat. What are you doing?
Pat: Well, I'm reading a magazine. There's a new fun park in town? Do you want to go?
Anne: Yes! But when?
Pat: Are you free tomorrow afternoon?
Anne: No. I'm going to my uncle's house. What about Wednesday?
Pat: Wednesday? That isn't any good. I've got a music lesson.
Anne: What about Saturday morning?
Pat: That's fine. What time?
Anne: Let me see. It opens at 10 o'clock and... Oh no!
Pat: What?
Anne: It costs £6 to get in!
Pat: What! Well, I can't go! I haven't got any money.

A picture dictionary (5)

Label the picture: thunder, lightening, snow, sun, wind, rain, water vapour, fog.
Verbs: rise, fall, shine, blow, rain, snow.
Nouns: garden, tree, ice(berg).
Adjectives: strong, windy, cold, hot, rainy, warm, sunny.

Theme F

Unit 29 Topic The cavepeople

1.1 exciting/boring, safe/dangerous, easy/difficult, happy/sad, wet/dry, inside/outside, horrible/nice, dead/alive.

1.2
1 boring
2 sleep
3 swim
4 travel
5 mammoth
6 born
7 frightened
8 brother
9 spear
Word in the middle: remembers.

2
1 It was a very cold day.
2 Ngoba and Mashan were very sad.
3 They were very cold.
4 They looked at the animal.
5 It was dead.
6 It was easy to cut the skin.
7 They were happy.
8 Ngoba and Mashan were warm.

3.1
2 David cleaned his teeth yesterday.
3 David walked to school yesterday.
4 David talked to his friends in the playground yesterday.
5 David played football yesterday.
6 David watched television yesterday.
7 David helped his brother and sister clean the car yesterday.

4

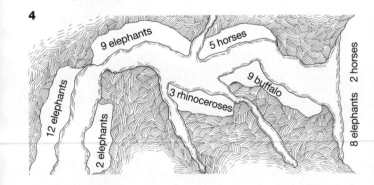

9 elephants 5 horses 2 horses 12 elephants 2 elephants 3 rhinoceroses 9 buffalo 8 elephants

5 Example:

Four boys, Jacques, Simon, Georges and Marcel were friends. In the summer of 1940 the weather was very hot. One day the boys went for a walk in the woods with their dog, Robot. The dog went into a hole in the ground. The boys looked for him. Then the four boys went into the hole and into the cave. Sudddenly they saw some pictures on the wall of the cave. The boys were very surprised.

Unit 30 Language focus:

1 listened, wanted, decided, jumped, cried, saw, dropped, washed, liked

L	I	S	T	E	N	E	D
W	A	N	T	E	D	C	E
D	E	P	M	U	J	R	C
D	E	H	S	A	W	I	I
x	D	R	O	P	P	E	D
D	E	K	L	A	W	D	E
L	I	K	E	D	x	x	D

2.1 was, were, was, were, was, were, was, was, was, was

2.2
Interviewer: Can you tell me what happened last Saturday?
Colin: Well, I didn't have any friends to play with.
Interviewer: Were they at the football match?
Colin: Yes, they were. So I went to the woods.
Interviewer: Was it very hot on Saturday?
Colin: Yes, it was. I had my lunch and then I saw a hole under a tree.
Interviewer: How big was it?
Colin: Oh very big. It went into a big cave.
Interviewer: Was it dark?
Colin: Yes. It was difficult to see. But there was a river on the left of the cave.
Interviewer: Was it deep?
Colin: I don't know! I decided to swim into the next cave.
Interviewer: Were there two caves then?
Colin: Yes, but when I was in the second cave all the stones came down from the wall!
Interviewer: Were you frightened?
Colin: Yes I was! I decided to try to find another hole at the end of the river.
Interviewer: How long were you in the river?
Colin: About three hours I think. Suddenly I saw the sun and the trees. I was very happy!

3 Washed /t/: helped, liked, asked, looked, watched
Lived /d/: stayed, changed, played
Started /ɪd/: wanted, decided, visited, studied

4 had, made, had, made, went, saw.

Unit 31 Fluency practice Family trees

1

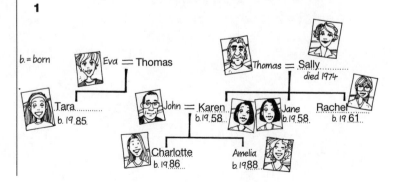

b. = born

Eva = Thomas   Thomas = Sally
                        died 1974

Tara   John = Karen   Jane   Rachel
b. 19.85   b. 19.58   b. 19.58 b. 19.61

         Charlotte   Amelia
         b. 19.86   b. 1988

2
  2 Thomas was a businessman but now he grows vegetables.
  3 Karen works in a library.
  4 John is a doctor.
  5 Jane works in a dress shop.
  6 Rachel is a pilot.

Unit 33 Revision: Dinosaurs

1
2	dark cave	**6**	dangerous jobs
3	wild animals	**7**	deep river
4	soft meat	**8**	poisonous fruit
5	wet walls		

3
1	false	**5**	false
2	false	**6**	true
3	true	**7**	true
4	true	**8**	false

A picture dictionary (6)

Label the pictures: cave painting, mammoth, river, skins, snow, fire, axe, bowl, brush, pot, bone.
Verbs: watched, saw, travelled, picked, painted, hunted, made, played.
Adjectives: bored, horrible, nice, dangerous, safe, hard, unhappy, happy, easy, difficult.
Nouns: hospital, doctor, sheep, light/lamp, tiger, bear, crops.

Supplementary worksheets

This section includes 18 supplementary worksheets which you may photocopy for your classes. There are two types of worksheets.

LANGUAGE WORKSHEETS

The *Language worksheets* give extra support to those students who need further practice with the grammar areas presented in the *Language focus* Units. There are two worksheets for each *Language focus* Unit: one for each area of grammar covered. The Worksheets have the same number as the *Language focus* unit. Worksheets 20.1 and 20.2, for example, give extra practice in the two language areas presented in Unit 20. There are also three worksheets for Unit 2. The worksheets can be done by students working alone, in pairs/groups or for homework.

The *Language worksheets* are:

Ws. 2.1: 'be', 'live', personal details, social language.
Ws. 2.2: 'There is/are', adjectives, negatives.
Ws. 2.3: adjectives, 'have/has got' 'be'.
Ws. 4.1: Present simple.
Ws. 4.2: Present simple negatives.
Ws. 10.1: Present simple questions.
Ws. 10.2: possessive adjectives.
Ws. 15.1: 'some' and 'any'.
Ws. 15.2: object pronouns.
Ws. 20.1: Present continuous.
Ws. 20.2: comparatives and superlatives (1).
Ws. 25.1: countables and uncountables / 'much' and 'many'.
Ws. 25.2: comparatives and superlatives (2).
Ws. 30.1: Past tense: 'was/were' and some regular verbs.
Ws. 30.2: Past tense: regular and irregular verbs.

SAY IT CLEARLY WORKSHEETS

The *Say it clearly worksheets* give extra practice in pronunciation. They focus on the sounds and words which appear frequently in the *Topic* and *Language focus* Units and which appear in the *Say it clearly!* exercises in the Workbook. You can use these worksheets with the whole class, with individual students or with a small group. You will need the Class Cassette and a cassette player.

The *Say it clearly worksheets* are:

SIC Ws. 1: /æm/and /aɪm/; /θ/ and /ð/; /s/, /z/ and /ɪz/.
SIC Ws. 2: /iː/; /e/; /eɪ/; /ɪŋ/.
SIC Ws. 3: /ə/; /ɪːə/ and /ɪəst/; /t/, /d/ and /ɪd/.

Note: On the Class Cassette, the recordings for each worksheet appear directly after the recordings for the relevant *Topic* and *Language focus* Units. Each worksheet contains material from two Themes of the book. For example, the recording for the first exercise in the first half (Theme A) of *Say it clearly!* worksheet 1 comes after the Unit 3 recordings; the recording for the second exercise comes after the Unit 4 recordings; the recordings for the second half of the worksheet come after the recordings for Unit 9.

Language worksheet 2.1 *Extension practice*

Summary

Can you complete the table?

'be', personal details, social language

I	am	
You	....	
He	....	
She	....	twelve years old.
It	....	very happy.
We	....	here!
You	....	
They	....	

1 How old are they?

Look at the table. Write about the people.

How old is Max? *He is eleven years old.*

How old are Steven and Susan?

....

How old is Anne?

....

How old are Kathy and Rick?

....

How old are you?

....

Anne	girl	11 years old
Max	boy	11 years old
Kathy	girl	12 years old
Rick	boy	12 years old
Steven	boy	13 years old
Susan	girl	13 years old

2 All about you

Complete the form with information about you.

PERSONAL DETAILS

Name: ....

Home address: ....

....

Telephone: ....

My age is: ....

My birthday is: ....

My hair is: ....

My eyes are: ....

School: ....

Address: ....

....

Pet's name: ....

Bicycle: ....

My favourite colour is: ....

Other important information: ....

....

3 What's the answer?

Choose the correct answer to each question.

1 How are you?   a I'm from England.

2 Where are you?   b My name's Steven.

3 What's your name?   c I'm twelve.

4 Where is your house? d Fine, thanks.

5 How old are you?   e I'm in here!

6 Where are you from?   f It's near my school.

PHOTOCOPIABLE

Language worksheet 2.2 *Extension practice*

Summary

'There is/are', adjectives, negatives

1 You can use 'There is' and 'There are' to say that something exists.

There are a lot of students in my school.   There is a big park near my school.

2 Adjectives in English come *before* the noun.

a big park   a new car   an old town   a small house

3 With 'have got', 'be', 'can' you can make a sentence negative with 'n't' (not).

I haven't got a bicycle.   There aren't any rivers in my town.   I can't hear you!

See also Pages 89–91 in your Workbook.

1 Right or wrong?

Look at the picture and read the sentences. Are they right or wrong? Correct the wrong sentences.

a There are two big parks in Newtown.

Wrong! There aren't two big parks. There is only one park. It is a small park.

b There is a train station.

Right!

c There are many tall buildings.

....

d There are a lot of shops.

....

e There is a big river in Newtown.

....

f There is a mountain in Newtown.

....

g There are four long beaches in Newton.

....

h There is a bridge in Newton.

....

i There are a lot of boats in Newton.

....

j There is a bus station.

....

2 Write some more sentences

Look at the picture again. Write six more 'Right or wrong?' sentences for another student. You can use these words.

an airport   cars   a football stadium   ships   a port
a sports centre

a *There* ....

b ....

c ....

d ....

e ....

f ....

PHOTOCOPIABLE

Language worksheet 2.3 *Extension practice*

Summary

Adjectives, 'have/has got'

When you speak, you can say 'have got'. (You can also say 'have' but 'have got' is more usual.)

Can you complete the table?

I	've got	
He	....	
She	....	blue eyes.
It	....	short hair.
You	....	a nice name.
They	....	
We	....	

Remember: adjectives in English come *before* the noun.

   short hair   blue eyes   short hair

Negatives and questions are easy.

   I haven't got a pen.   Have you got a pen?

See also pages 89–90 in your Workbook.

1   In the bank

You are in the town centre. You see two men in front of a bank. Look at the picture.

The men are robbers! On the TV, some people describe the man with the hat. Who is correct? Person A, B or C?

A
The man with a hat about 18 years old. He's got a small nose and a long face. He's got short straight hair. He hasn't got glasses.

B The man with a hat is about 40 years old. He's got a small nose and a long face. He's got a moustache and short curly hair. He's got glasses.

I think the man with a hat is about 25 years old. He's got a small face and a moustache. He's got glasses and long straight hair.

2   Tell the police!

Tell the police about the other man. Write a description.

....

....

....

PHOTOCOPIABLE

Language worksheet 4.1 *Present simple*

Summary

You can use the Present simple to talk about:

something that happens often   *and*   something that is true generally.

    I go to school at 9 o'clock.   We live in a big town.

Complete the table with the correct form of the verb.

I	swim every day.	He	....	every day.
You	ride a bicycle to school.	She	....	a bicycle to school.
We	play the guitar.	It	....	the guitar.
They	go to school at 8 o'clock.		....	go to school at 8 o'clock.

Be careful! swim ⟶ swim<u>s</u> **but** go ⟶ go<u>es</u>
See also page 91 in your Workbook.

1   At school in England

Read about school in England.

In England, children go to school from 9 a.m. to 3.30 p.m.
They don't go to school on Saturday. Boys and girls go
to the same school. They wear a school uniform and they eat
at school.

The children play in the playground when they arrive. Then
the bell rings. The children go into the classrooms.
The teacher has a list with the names of the students. The
teacher reads the names. The children say 'Yes, Miss', 'Yes,
Sir' or 'He's not here today, Miss' or 'She isn't here, Sir'.

True or false? Write T or F in the box.

a   English children go to school six days a week.   ☐

b   Children are in school for four hours a day.   ☐

b   The students say their names to the teacher.   ☐

c   The children eat at school.   ☐

d   The teacher reads the list of names.   ☐

2   School in your country

Write about school in your country.

In my country, children go to school from ....
....
....
....
....
....

3   Jill's week

Look at the pictures. Write about Jill's week. (Remember
the '-s'!)

Monday:
    On Monday, Jill plays football.

Tuesday:
....

Wednesday
....

Thursday:
....

Friday:
....

Saturday:
....

Sunday:
....

Language worksheet 4.2 *Present simple negatives*

Summary

You can make a negative sentence with 'don't' ('do not') or 'doesn't' ('does not').
Complete the table with 'don't' or 'doesn't'.

I	*don't*	live in a house. I live in a flat.
You	....	speak Chinese.
We	....	drink cola.
They	....	play the piano.
He	....	play football in the park.
She	....	have a television at home.
It	....	eat very much food.

See also page 91 in your Workbook.

1 Some questions and answers

Write about the students.

	Question	Yes	No
	1 Do you watch TV every day?	✓✓✓✓✓	✓
	2 Do you ride a bicycle to school?	✓	✓✓✓✓✓
	3 Do you live in the town centre?	✓	✓✓✓✓✓
	4 Do you go to school on Saturday?	✓	✓✓✓✓✓
	5 Do you have homework every day?	✓✓✓✓	✓✓
	6 Do you work on Saturdays?	✓	✓✓✓✓✓

1 *Five students watch TV every day. One student doesn't watch TV every day.*

2 One student..................... Five students don't ....

3 ....

4 ....

5 ....

6 ....

2 That's wrong!

Read these sentences. They are all wrong! Write a true sentence for each one.

a People in New Zealand speak Spanish.

Wrong! People in New Zealand don't speak Spanish. They speak English.

b Crocodiles live in the sea.

....

....

c Teachers work in shops.

....

....

d The President of the USA lives in France.

....

....

e Kangaroos come from England.

....

....

f A cow eats fish.

....

....

PHOTOCOPIABLE

Language worksheet 10.1 *Present simple questions*

Summary

Questions with 'Does' and 'Do'

You can make questions with 'be', 'have got' and 'can' like this:

You are tired.　　　You can swim.　　　You have got a bicycle

Are you hungry?　　Can you play the piano?　　Have you got a computer?

Other verbs use 'does' (for 'he', 'she' and 'it') or 'do' (for 'I', 'you', 'we', and 'they'):

You live in a big city.　　He likes football.　　They walk to school.

Do you live in a flat?　　Does he like swimming?　　Do they walk home?

See also pages 91–92 in your Workbook.

1　Make a question

Use the words to make a question. For example:

deserts? live Do in pandas ⟶ *Do pandas live in deserts?*

1　milk? spiders Do drink

....

2　dolphins? eggs lay Do

....

3　the monarch butterfly? India go Does to

....

4　eat lions Do grass?

....

5　flowers? nectar bees Do from take

....

6　night? Do koalas sleep at

....

2　Ask some more questions

Read the sentences and ask another question. For example:
Martin likes chocolate. *Does he like ice-cream?*

1　Giraffes eat leaves.

　Do they .... grass?

2　Kangaroos live in Australia.

　.. France?

3　Baby cows drink milk.

　.. water?

4　Maria plays tennis.

　.. football?

5　Steve and Sue know Mike.

　.. Jane?

6　You speak English.

　.. Spanish?

3　Question words

You can use question words in your questions.
For example:

How long does a snake sleep?
How much meat does a lion eat?
How many eggs do snakes lay?
Where do parrots live?
When do sharks sleep?
What do bats eat?

Choose a question word or phrase and make a question.

When　How long　How fast　How many　How much　Why

1　*How fast does* a tiger run?

2　.. birds fly south?

3　.................... kilometres .... monarch butterflies fly?

4　.. they fly to Mexico?

5　.. an elephant weigh?

6　.. elephant live?

4　Animal facts

Write some quiz questions for your friends. For example:

Sea crocodiles grow
to six metres.　⟶　*How long do sea crocodiles grow?*

1　...

　Bees fly at 22 kph.

2　...

　Polar bears live in the Arctic.

3　...

　Giraffes grow to 5.5 metres.

Language worksheet 10.2 *Possessive adjectives*

Summary

Questions with 'my, his, her, its, your, our, their'

Can you complete the sentences?

I live in this road and this is *my* house.

You live in this road and this is .... house.

She lives in this road and this is .... house.

This dog lives in this road and this is .... house.

We live in this road and this is .... house.

They live in this road and this is .... house.

Check your answers in your Workbook page 92.

1 What's the word?

Fill in the gaps with 'my, his, her, its, your, our', or 'their'.

1 I like Maria's cat but I don't like .... dog.

2 I can play Peter's guitar but I can't play .... piano.

3 .... name is Maria. What's .... name?

4 My parents work at home. .... office is upstairs.

5 We are in class 5. .... teacher's name is Mrs Brown.

6 My sister has got a new fish. .... name is Sinbad.

2 Angela's party

Put a circle around the right possessive adjective. For example:

ANGELA: Hi Matthew. My brother and I want to have a party on Saturday. Can you come to **his/its/our⃝** house then?

MATTHEW: Great! I'll ask **their/his/my⃝** mother.

MATTHEW: Mum?

MATTHEW'S MOTHER: Yes.

MATTHEW: Angela and Matthew want to have party on Saturday. Can I go to **his/their/your** house?

MATTHEW'S MOTHER: I'm sorry, Matthew. It's Grandad's birthday on Saturday. We are going to **my/his/our** house at one o'clock.

MATTHEW: Oh yes!

MATTHEW: Hi Angela

ANGELA: Yes.

MATTHEW: Sorry, I can't come to **her/your/their** house on Saturday. It's my Grandad's birthday.

ANGELA: Oh! It's Matthew's birthday on Saturday. He wants you to come to **my/our/his** party!

MATTHEW: What time is the party?

ANGELA: Six o'clock

MATTHEW: That's OK then. Grandad's party is at one clock. I can go to **her/his/our** party first and then I can go to **her/your/their** party in the evening. Great! Two parties on one day!

PHOTOCOPIABLE

Language worksheet 15.1 *'Some' and 'any'*

Summary

You use 'some' in positive sentences.

I've got some money in my pocket.

You use 'any' in questions and negative sentences.

Have you got any money?   I don't need any money.

See also page 92 in your Workbook.

1   Pancakes for breakfast

Read the sentences.
Put '+' next to the positive sentences.
Put '–' next to the negative sentences.
Put '?' next to the questions.

1   We can make .... pancakes for breakfast.

2   Have we got .... milk?

3   We've got .... flour

4   We don't need .... salt.

5   Do we need .... butter?

6   We don't need .... sugar.

7   Do we need .... water?

8   Oh no! We haven't got .... eggs.

Now write 'some' or 'any' in each sentence.

2   What's the answer?

Find the right reply (a–d) to each sentence (1–4). Write 'some' or 'any' in each space.

1   Has the dog got .... water?

2   Great! We haven't got .... History homework tonight!

3   I don't understand .... of this maths!

4   Is there .... milk in the fridge?

a   I know, but I've got ....Geography.

b   Yes you do. You got .... of them right.

c   No, he hasn't. I can give him ....

d   No, there isn't. There's .... on the table.

3   Things for the party

You and your friends want to have a party.
This is the list of things you need and the things you have (✓).

```
CDs,
cassettes ✓
videos ✓
cola
lemonade ✓
orange juice
milk ✓
bread
ice cream
fruit ✓
hamburgers ✓
cheese
cakes ✓
biscuits
```

Tell your friends what you have got. Ask them about the other things. Like this:

I've got some cassettes but I haven't got any CDs. Have you got any CDs?

1   ....
....

2   ....
....

3   ....
....

4   ....
....

Language worksheet 15.2 *Object pronouns*

Summary

> See also page 92 in your Workbook.
>
> Can you complete the sentences?
>
> | | |
> |---|---|
> | What do you think about Peter? | I like *him*. |
> | What do you think about Susanna? | I like .... |
> | What do you think about my cat? | I like .... |
> | What do you think about Henry and Kathy? | I like .... |
> | And what do you think about me?! | I like ....! |
>
> Check your answers on page 92 in your Workbook.

What do you think about Peter?

'me, you, him, her, it, us, you, them'

I like him.

2 What's the word?

Choose the correct word for each sentence

me   you   him   her   it   us   you   them

1 A: Do you like pancakes?

   B: Yes, I love .... I think they're great.

2 A: Do you know Maria?

   B: No, I don't know................ but I know her brother.

3 A: Have you got my book?

   B: Yes.

   A: Please give it to ....

4 A: Do you like football?

   B: No! I hate .... I like swimming.

5 A: Do you go to school with Peter?

   B: No,I don't go to school with .... I go to school with his sister.

6 A: Is that drink for me?

   B: No, it's not for .... It's for .... !

3 What comes next?

Match the two parts of the speech bubbles.

1 (This magazine is great.   Who wants to play with me?

2 (My brother is in England on holiday.   Can you show her the library?

3 (I've got a new camera   Do you like them?

4 (This bag is too heavy for me and my friend to carry.   Do you want to look at it?

5 (I like apples.   Here's a postcard from him.

6 (I've got a new game.   Can you help us?

7 (There's a new girl in school today.   Can I take a picture of you?

PHOTOCOPIABLE

© Cambridge University Press 1996

Language worksheet 20.1 *Present continuous*

Summary

'be' + '-ing'

You use the Present continuous to talk about something that is happening NOW.

- What are you doing?

- I am watching television.

You can also use it to talk about your plans.

- What are you doing tomorrow?

- I'm going to the cinema.

You make the present continuous with the verb 'be' ('am/is/are') + '-ing'. Like this:

What **is** he doing? He **is** walk**ing** on the moon.

Where **are** you going? I**'m** go**ing** to the shops.

See also page 93 in your Workbook.

1 On televison

You are a TV reporter. You are at the Olympics. It's a swimming race. Tell the people what is happening.

The five swimmers *are walking* (walk) to the swimming pool.
The American swimmer .... (stand) near lane two.
That's strange! He hasn't got a swimming hat. The Italian and the
Spanish swimmers .... (talk) to someone. The French
swimmer .... (do) some exercises and the German
swimmer .... (put) on his hat.

Now the judge .... (wave) his arm. Go! Oh no! The
American swimmer ....not (swim). He ....
(run) away from the pool. He's .... (go) to the end of
the pool. What .... he (do)? I know! He ....
(look) for his hat! Oh dear. The other swimmers ....
(swim) very fast. Everyone here .... (shout). The
Spanish and the Italian swimmers .... (win). What an
exciting race! A sad day for the American swimmer!

2 Grandma telephones Ben

Grandma is talking to Ben. Choose the correct answer for Ben.

GRANDMA: Hello, Ben. Are you doing your homework?

BEN: ....

GRANDMA: Is Anna watching television too?

BEN: ....

GRANDMA: In the park! It's raining here. What's your
father doing now?

BEN: ....

GRANDMA: And where is she?

BEN: ....

GRANDMA: Oh good!

BEN: ....

GRANDMA: I'm waiting for you! I'm at the train station.
I'm coming to the birthday party!

a He's making a cake for my mother's birthday.

b What are you doing, Grandma?

c No, she's playing in the park.

d No, I'm watching television.

e No, she's getting ready for her party.

PHOTOCOPIABLE

Language worksheet 20.2 *Comparatives and superlatives (1)*

Summary

Short adjectives + '-er', '-est'

You can compare things by putting '-er' and '-est' at the end of short adjectives. Short adjectives have one syllable.

  long tall big near fast old hot small

For example:

  The Sun is hotter than the Earth. The Sun is **the** hott**est** thing in the solar system.

  Vatican City is small**er** than Italy. It is the small**est** country in the world.

'Good' and 'bad' are different! Look:

  good ⟶ better ⟶ the best
  bad ⟶ worse ⟶ the worst

See also page 93 in your Workbook.

1 A puzzle

Look at the puzzle. Circle the word you find.

a (bigger)/ biggest   f smaller / smallest
b higher / highest   g taller / tallest
c longer / longest   h better / best
d older / oldest   i worse / worst
e shorter / shortest

```
S M A L L E R I W S
H L O N G E R P W H
F D H E G A N J H O
A D B I G G E R D R
W W U H A Q Y U I T
T H I G H E S T M E
H L O N G E S T G S
R Z O L D E S T Q T
```

2 Are you right?

Put the correct words from Exercise 1 in the sentences.

1 England is .... than America.

2 The River Nile is .... than the River Thames

3 China is .... than America.

4 Mount Everest is the .... mountain in the world.

5 In the Southern hemisphere, 21 June is the

   .... day of the year.

6 The............................... tree in the world is over 5,000 years old.

7 The Redwood trees in California, USA are the

   .... living things in the world. They are over 112 metres tall.

8 The south of England has a .... climate than the north of England.

9 The north of England has the .... weather in Europe. It rains nearly every day!

3 Two more puzzles

A Read the dates of birth. Are the sentences true ☐T☐ or false ☐F☐ ?

Alice: 15 February 1982	Daniel: 10 March 1983
Bob: 23 November 1982	Eva: 18 September 1983
Christina: 14 May 1983	

1 Alice is younger than Eva. ☐

2 Eva is older than Bob. ☐

3 Daniel is the oldest. ☐

4 Christina is the youngest. ☐

B Alice and Bob are older than Daniel. ☐

B Read about the Brown family.

There are five children in the Brown family. Anna is older than Ben and Chantal. She is younger than David and Ella. Ben is not the youngest and Chantal is not the oldest.

List the children from oldest to youngest.

1 ....

2 ....

3 ....

4 ....

5 ....

Language worksheet 25.1 *Countables and uncountables*

Summary

'much/many'; countables and uncountables

You use 'much' and 'many' in questions and negative sentences.

> How many people live in Mexico City?
>
> How much rain do they have in Saudi Arabia?

You use 'many' with things that you can count ('countables'). For example:

> people books cars houses pens

You use 'much' with things that you can't count ('uncountables'). For example:

> rain sugar milk petrol

For positive sentences, you can use 'a lot of', 'lots' and 'many'. For example:

> I've got a lot of friends.   There are lots of people in my school.
>
> It rains a lot in many countries

See also page 93 in your Workbook.

1 Countable or Uncountable?

Write 'C' (countable) or 'U' (uncountable) by each word or phrase.

rain ☐   books ☐   foggy days ☐   sunshine ☐

hours of sunshine ☐   ice-cream ☐   weeks ☐   time ☐

2 What's the word?

Complete the sentences with one of the words or phrases from Exercise 1.

1 In October in England we have a lot of *rain*.

2 We don't usually have much .... in an English winter.

3 How many .... have you got from the library?

4 How many .... does Sweden have in the summer?

5 In the summer the children eat a lot of ....

6 How much .... falls in the Sahara Desert?

7 I haven't got much .... to do my homework

8 How many .... holiday do you have every year?

3 Much or many?

Complete the sentences with 'much' or 'many'.

1 How .... rain does Iceland have in the spring?

2 How .... foggy days does Los Angeles have every year?

3 How .... ice would you like in your orange juice?

4 How .... sweets do you eat in a month?

5 How .... brothers and sisters have you got?

6 How .... money have you got?

7 How .... clouds can you see in the sky?

8 How .... snow falls every year in Antarctica?

4 School life

What questions does the girl ask? Use 'much' or 'many'.

ANNA: ....?

JOHN: There are about 600 students in my school.

ANNA: ....?

JOHN: I have eight lessons every day.

ANNA: ....?

JOHN: Homework? About one hour every evening.

ANNA: ....

JOHN: The bus to school costs 50p.

Language worksheet 25.2 *Comparatives and superlatives (2)*

Summary

You use 'more' and 'the most' to make comparisons with long adjectives.
Long adjectives have more than one syllable. For example:

expensive   A computer is **more** expensive than a calculator.

wonderful   My English teacher is **the most** wonderful teacher in the world!

Adjectives that end 'y' change to 'i'.

heavy   My brother is heavier than me.

happy   I'm the happiest person in the world!

See also page 94 in your Workbook.

1   More long adjectives

Look at these adjectives. Put 'L' next to the long adjectives. Put 'S' next to the short adjectives.

exciting ☐   new ☐   big ☐   difficult ☐

cold ☐   hot ☐   interesting ☐   long ☐

expensive ☐   near ☐   old ☐   modern ☐

slow ☐   dangerous ☐   small ☐   tall ☐

2   What's the word?

Complete the sentences with a long adjective from Exercise 1. Use 'more' and 'the most'.

1 Gold is *more expensive* than iron.

2 My camera is 10 years old. Your camera is one year old. It's

....

3 This is .... in the library. It's got a lot of

different information.

4 For an English person, it is .... to learn

Arabic than Spanish.

5 I think mountain climbing is .... than

skiing.

6 I think football is .... golf.

3   Some more sports

What do you think about these sports?

football   tennis   swimming   skiing   golf   table tennis
basketball

Write some sentences about them on another piece of paper. You can use these words:

dangerous   exciting   boring   interesting   difficult

For example:

Football is more exciting than golf but I think ski-ing is the most exciting sport.

4   Windier, sunnier, happier …

Look at the pictures.
Write a sentence about each one.

1

James is ....   Peter is ....

2

Yesterday ....   Today ....

3

Yesterday ....   Today ....

PHOTOCOPIABLE

Language worksheet 30.1 *Past tense*

Summary

'was/were' and some regular verbs

The past of 'be' ('am/is/are') is 'was' and 'were'.

> Were you at school yesterday?   Was Peter at school yesterday?

Can you complete the table?

I	was	
You	....	here yesterday.
He	....	happy last night.
She	....	12 last week.
It	....	
We	....	here yesterday.
You	....	happy last night.
They	....	12 last week.

See also page 94 in your Workbook.

1 Spot the differences

Can you find five more differences between now and one hour ago?

Write a sentence about each one.

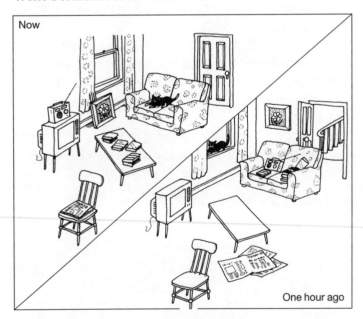

Now

One hour ago

a The books were on the table. Now they are on the sofa.

b ....

c ....

d ....

e ....

f ....

2 When Tom was a boy

Read about when Tom was a boy. Write 'was' or 'were' in the gaps.

When I .... a boy we lived in a village called Langton.

Langton .... an island. There .... water all round

Langton and there ....n't any schools in the village. In the

morning all the children walked to the end of the street. There

.... small boats at the end of the street. We ....

often late for school and the teachers .... sometimes

angry with us. My father .... a boatman. One day the

teacher asked him to write a letter when we .... late for

school. My father said: " There ....n't any schools when I

.... a boy so I can't read or write."

PHOTOCOPIABLE

Language worksheet 30.2 *Past tense*

Summary

Many verbs in English are 'regular'. They have '-ed' on the end in the past.

> We play**ed** tennis yesterday. I paint**ed** a picture last week. She watch**ed** a film last night.

Other verbs are different. Look:

> I **go** to school every day. I **went** to school yesterday.
> I usually **have** lunch at 1 o'clock. Yesterday, I **had** lunch at 2 o'clock.
> Peter **sees** Francis everyday at school. He **saw** him yesterday, too.
> Sometimes, I **make** breakfast for my parents. I **made** breakfast yesterday.

See also page 94 in your Workbook.

1 Jack's weekend

Use these verbs to write about Jack's weekend. They are all regular verbs.

Saturday: play tennis,   paint his room
   talk on the telephone   watch TV.

Sunday: cook breakfast,   repair his bicycle,
   play the guitar.

On Saturday, Jack played tennis. Then he..........................

....

....

....

....

....

2 Jack's birthday

Fill the gaps with the correct form of the verbs.

Monday *was* (be) a great day. It .... (be) my birthday! I
.... (go) to the cinema with my friend. We ....
(see) an excellent film. It .... (be) about life on other
planets. After the film, we .... (go) to a cafe. We
.... (have) something to eat and then we ....
(walk) home.

At home, I .... (open) my presents. I .... (have)
five presents. My favourite present .... (be) a model car
from my friend. I .... (make) the model with my friend in
the evening. After that, we .... (play) with my computer.
My friend .... (go) home at about 10 o'clock at night. At
school on Tuesday, we .... (be) very tired!

3 A puzzle

Read a story.

> **Hospital doctor cannot help young boy.**
> At ten o clock last night Mr Connor (aged 42) and his son, Michael, (aged 12) went home from a concert by car.
>   The journey was difficult because it was very dark and foggy. Suddenly they had a terrible accident with another car.
>   Mr Connor telephoned for an ambulance and they went to the hospital very quickly. Michael cried and cried. At the hospital they waited for the doctor. The doctor arrived and said " Oh no! I can't operate. This is my son!"

Question: How can Michael be the doctor's son? (Answer below.)

The doctor is Michael's mother.

PHOTOCOPIABLE

Say it clearly! worksheet 1

THEME A

1 Sounds practised in Unit 3

/aɪ æm/ **and** /aɪm/

1.1 What can you hear?

🔊 Listen. Underline what you hear. For example:

1 <u>I am</u> English.   I'm English.
2 I am cold.   I'm cold.
3 I am Italian.   I'm Italian.
4 I am 12.   I'm 12.
5 I am at school.   I'm at school.
6 I am in the football team.   I'm in the football team.

1.2 Answer the questions

Answer the questions with 'Yes, I am' or 'No, I'm not'.

Are you at home?
Are you English?
Are you hot?
Are you a student?
Are you a boy?
Are you in a football team?
Are you a good swimmer?
Are you happy?

Work in pairs. Ask your neighbour the questions.

2 Sounds practised in Unit 4

/θ/ **and** /ð/

🔊 Listen. Say the words.

birthday thirteen something thanks nothing these they're

Work in pairs. Read the dialogue.

A: It's my birthday today. I'm thirteen.
B: I know! Here's something for you.
A: Oh, thanks!
B: It's nothing.

A: These are my favourite sweets! They're great! Take one.
B: Thanks! Mmmmm. Can I take another one? Mmmmm. And another one ...
A: Hey!

🔊 Listen to the dialogue.

THEME B

3 Sounds practised in Unit 9

/s/, /z/ **and** /ɪz/

3.1 What's on the table?

Count the things on the table and then tell the class.

There are two ...., three ....,
four ...., five ...., six ....,
seven ...., eight ...., nine ....,
ten ....

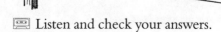

🔊 Listen and check your answers.

3.2 Put the words in columns

Say the words and then put them in the correct column.

watches sandwiches pens pencils books leaves balls bees cassettes

's' sound	'z' sound	'iz' sound
books	pens	watches

🔊 Listen and check your answers.

PHOTOCOPIABLE

Say it clearly! worksheet 2

THEME C

1 Sounds practised in Unit 14

/iː/

1.1 Say the words

🔊 Listen. Say the words. They all have the same vowel sound.

bee   monkey   eat   meat   cheese   sweet

1.2 Ask your neighbour

Work in pairs. Ask your neighbour the questions.

1   Does a monkey eat meat?
2   Does cheese come from milk?
3   Do bees like sweet things?
4   Do bees sleep?

2 Sounds practised in Unit 15

/e/

2.1 Say the words

🔊 Listen. Say the words. They all have the same vowel sound.

many   any   wet   get   pet   when   pen   ten   leg   egg

2.2 Ask your neighbour

Work in pairs. Ask your neighbour the questions.

1   Do reptiles lay eggs?
2   How many legs has a bird got?

3   What do elephants eat?
4   Do insects have ten legs?

2.3 One is different

🔊 Listen. Underline the word that has a different vowel sound. For example:

any   <u>money</u>   many

1   bee   many   cheese   4   get   let   eat
2   week   sleep   pen   5   insect   net   sleep
3   leg   any   meat   6   pet   sweet   egg

THEME D

3 Sounds practised in Unit 19

/eɪ/

3.1 Say the words

🔊 Listen. Say the words. Open your mouth!

name   same   day   say   play   take   cake   date   plate   hate

3.2 Count the sounds

Read and say the sentences. How many example of /eɪ/ can you find? Write the number in the box.

1   Take some cake from this plate.
2   What's the date today?
3   My name is the same as Jane's.
4   I hate playing football!

🔊 Listen and check your answers.

4 Sounds practised in Unit 20

/ɪŋ/

4.1 Say the words

🔊 Listen. Say the words.

painting   singing   dancing   drawing   running   jumping
playing   talking   reading   writing   eating

4.2 What are they doing?

Join the pictures. Say a sentence about each complete picture.

🔊 Listen and check your answers.

PHOTOCOPIABLE

Say it clearly! worksheet 3

THEME E

1 Sounds practised in Unit 24

/ə/

1.1 Put the words in the correct order.

Listen. Write the correct numbers beside each word. Notice how you often say '-er' in English.

	September		never		December
1	thunder		October		weather
	November		danger		water

Say the words in order. Be careful how you say '-er'.

1.2 The same sound, different spelling

We have the same sound in other words. Listen and say the words.

doctor actor vapour colour centre fire ear hear
vegetable portable

How many different spellings of /ə/ can you see?

Listen. Say the sentences.

These vegetables aren't portable.

Danger! The house is on fire!

Doctor! Doctor!
My ear is a strange colour!

2 Sounds practised in Unit 25

/ɪə/ and /ɪəst/

Listen. Say the words and sentences.

foggy foggier the foggiest
It's the foggiest day of the year!

pretty prettier the prettiest
That's the prettiest place I know!

silly sillier the silliest
He's the silliest person I know!

THEME F

3 Sounds practised in Unit 30

/t/, /ɪd/ and /d/

There are three ways to say '-ed' in English:
/t/, for example 'washed' /ɪd/, for example 'started'
/d/, for example 'lived'

Say the verbs and put them in the correct column.

used walked painted cooked cleaned visited hunted
helped stayed

Washed /t/	Started /ɪd/	Lived /d/

Listen and check your answers.

Listen. Say the sentences.

Cavepeople lived more than 30,000 years ago.
They used stones to make tools.
They hunted animals in big groups.
They painted pictures of the animals.

Classroom language

This section lists some useful classroom phrases which you can adapt as required.

Brainstorming

Our next topic is ...
What do you know about ...?
Write down some points/information about ...
Let's share some ideas about ...
Let's start by putting the topic in the circle.
What can you think of?
Can anyone think of anything else?
Can anyone add anything to that?
Think quietly for a moment or two.
Write down as many ideas as you can in two minutes.
Who wants to say something first?
Let's compare ideas.

Checking answers

Check your answers with your partner.
Give your writing/exercise to your neighbour to check.
The answers are on the board. Check them when you have finished this exercise
Let's go through your answers now.
There is an answer sheet here. Please pass it round and check your answers.
Work in small groups and check your answers together. I'll come round and help you.
If you have any problems put your hand up / ask me at the end of the lesson.
Did anyone get a different answer?
There are many different possible answers to this question. Let's see how many we can get.
Does everyone understand this exercise?

Discipline

Let's be quiet now, please.
Come on, come on, settle down now please.
Ssshhh please.
There's a lot of noise in here today.
Let's get down to some work now please.
I think we can all work better when it's quieter.
The pairwork is not going very well. Why do you think this is?
Perhaps we can discuss why there is so much noise today.
We've got a problem. Our groupwork isn't working. Why is that? Any ideas?
What can we do about it?
Any ideas?

Discussions

Who would like to start?
What would you like to say, X?
Take turns to speak.
Listen to the other students' ideas too.
Can you speak a little more loudly please?
Did everyone hear what X said?
Can anyone add anything to that?
Does everyone agree with that?
Who disagrees with that?
Don't worry if you make a mistake. We just want to know your ideas.
Use a word/phrase in (*mother tongue*) if you don't know what to say.
Say it in (*mother tongue*).

Error correction

Good/Well done/Excellent/ That's not bad. Can anyone think of another way to say that?
OK. Do you want to try again?
It's not easy to pronounce that word, is it? Listen to the cassette again.
I think it's probably better to write/say ...

Evaluation

What do you think about pairwork/groupwork?
How do you think you can do it better next time?
What do you think was the easiest part of the Unit/exercise?
What do you think would be a better way to do the task next time?

Encouragement

That's a good point.
Well done, that was quite a difficult exercise/word to pronounce/spell.
Yes, excellent!
That was difficult. Well done!

Feedback

I think there are a lot of good ideas.
Do you think it would be a good idea to leave this part out / say more about / move this word ...?
How/What about saying something about ...?
What about adding ...?

Games

Before you start to play, read the rules.
Would you like to check/translate the rules first?
Do you know what you have to do?
Choose a referee to settle the arguments.
Have you got dice and counters?
Do you think 10 minutes is enough time to play the game?
Don't forget to take turns!

Groupwork

Can you get into groups of three or four, please?
Would you like to work in a different group this time?
Find the group you were working with in the last lesson.
If you want to, you can work in groups for this task.

Homework

There are two exercises on ... in your Workbook. Choose
    one for homework.
Finish this exercise for homework, please.
Please do Exercise ... for homework.
Please do your homework for Thursday.
Shall we go through this homework in the lesson on Friday?
Exercises X and X in the Workbook give more practice
    with this vocabulary/grammar.
On Friday we are doing Unit X. Please read it through first.

Listening

Listen to the cassette.
Can you hear the cassette?
Would you like to hear it again?
Read the text first and then we'll listen to the cassette.
Would you like to listen to the cassette before/ while/after
    you read the text?
You can keep your books open while you listen to the
    cassette.
Do you want to close your books while you listen to the
    cassette?

Monitoring and guiding

How are you getting on with this ...?
Are there any problems with this ...?
Is it as easy/difficult as you thought?
Are you helping each other?
Would you like me to help you/suggest anything?
Shall I look at your work now or later?
Do you need more time to finish this?
What kind of mistakes do you think you are making here?

Mother tongue

If you don't know the word in English say it in ...
I'll put the English word on the board.
You can write down some ideas in our language first and
    then we can try to say them in English.
When shall we use (mother tongue)?
Think about when you use (our language). When you do
    pairwork or groupwork or in an activity, could you use
    English instead?

Pairwork

Work with your neighbour.
For this exercise you can work in pairs.
Work with a different partner this time.
Practise the dialogue together.
Check your answers with your neighbour.
Work together for five minutes.
Does everyone know what they have to do?
Has everyone got a partner?

Planning

We have 30 minutes to spare on Thursday. What would
    you like to do?
On ..., we are going to make ... You will need some ...
If you have any suggestions or requests, put them in the
    Suggestion Box.
What shall we try to finish this week?
When shall we collect the homework?

Pronunciation

Shall we say this sound/word together?
Is there a sound like this in our language?
Say it clearly!

Songs

Does anyone know this song/tune?
Let's listen to the song on the cassette first.
Look at the words in your book at the same time.
Do you know any other words for this song?
Can anyone play this on a guitar/violin, etc.?
This half of the class sing the verses and this half sing the
    chorus.
If you don't know the words yet, hum like this
    (mmmmmmm).
You can clap to the music first if you like.

Starting the lesson

In this lesson we are going to look at / finish Unit X.
Does anyone want to ask anything about the lesson
    yesterday?
Has everyone got their Workbook and Student's book?
If you haven't got your books, share with your partner.
Please turn to Unit X. Look at the pictures for a moment.
    What do you think the Unit is about?

Timing

We're going to work on ... now. How long do you think you
    need?
Let's work on this for 10 minutes and see how far you get.
Tell me when you have finished.
Do you need some more time to finish this?
When you have finished, move to the *Time to spare?* or
    the *Language Record* please.
See how much you can do in ten minutes.
There are five minutes left. Let's see if we can finish this.

Acknowledgements

The authors and publishers are grateful to the following illustrators and photographer:

Illustrators: Gecko Limited: DTP work on pp. 46, 161; Peter Kent: pp. 36, 155, 157*r*, 158, 159, 163*b*, 166l, 167*l*, 168, 169, 170, 171*t*; Steve Lach: pp. 39, 156, 157*l*, 160, 162, 163*t*, 165, 166*r*, 167*r*, 171*b*; Jan Lewis: p. 154; John Plumb: p. 51.

r = right   *l* = left   *t* = top   *b* = bottom

Photographer: Nigel Luckhurst: p. 60.

Cover design by Dunne & Scully based on an illustration by Felicity Roma Bowers.

Design and production by Gecko Limited, Bicester, Oxon.

ANIMALS

DISCOVER THE AMAZING DIVERSITY OF **NATURE**

PaRragon

Bath · New York · Cologne · Melbourne · Delhi
Hong Kong · Shenzhen · Singapore · Amsterdam

CONTENTS

INTRODUCTION

  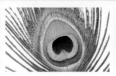  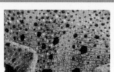  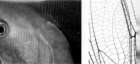

Welcome to the amazing world of animals! In this fascinating book you can explore the astonishing lives of some of the millions of species with which we share the planet Earth.

Every region of our planet has been colonized by animals. As scientific understanding of the animal world increases, so does our appreciation of the intimate relationships between humans and other animal species, and of the need to conserve the rich diversity of life on Earth, for the sake of our own survival as well as theirs.

Animals are classified into five main groups: Mammals, Birds, Reptiles, Fish and Amphibians, and Invertebrates. Mammals are the smallest group, but they include the largest animal, the blue whale. Easily the biggest group, with myriads of individual animals in millions of species, are the Invertebrates.

Mammals

From the frozen tundra to the tropical rainforests, the Earth is rich in mammals, animals of astonishing diversity that have occupied a wide range of environments. Mammals probably began to dominate the Earth about 65 million years ago. Without a doubt, modern humans are the most successful mammals – we have explored and colonized all the Earth's habitats. Our domestic coexistence with other species began around 10,000 years ago, when human culture shifted from nomadic hunter-gatherers to a society based on agriculture. Humans began to domesticate some mammals for work, meat and milk, and for useful products, such as wool and leather. These domestic animals included dogs, sheep, pigs, cows, goats and horses.

There are 5,416 known mammal species. Their diversity is evident in their adaptation to different environments. Mammal species can run, glide, fly, jump, swim and crawl. To survive the rigours of low temperatures, some cold-climate animals spend the winter in deep sleep to save energy. Most aquatic mammals have thick layers of body fat instead of hair, which in most land mammals serves to conserve heat. Seals, dolphins, bats and chimpanzees all have upper

COMMUNICATION
The ways in which cetaceans communicate with others of their kind are among the most sophisticated in the animal kingdom. Dolphins, for example, click with their mandibles when in trouble and whistle repeatedly when afraid or excited.

limbs with similar bones, but seals have flippers, dolphins have fins, bats have wings and chimpanzees have arms.

Birds

Birds never cease to amaze us. Avian abilities are varied, including diving, swimming and complex nest-building skills, but their ability to fly has long been envied by humans. Many birds fly enormous distances, crossing deserts and oceans to reach their breeding and feeding grounds. Much bird behaviour, such as the ability of migrants to find their way across continents and back, continues to be a mystery.

It is believed that there are approximately 9,700 bird species in the world. This makes birds the second largest vertebrate group of animals, after fish. Birds vary greatly in size: from a hummingbird weighing just 1.6 g ($^3/_{50}$ oz), to an ostrich weighing in at 150 kg (330 lb). Although most birds fly, there are some flightless birds – such as kiwis, penguins, rheas and ostriches. Other birds are adapted to aquatic life in oceans, rivers and lakes. The shape of birds' feet and bills reflects adaptations. Some aquatic species have bills modified to filter-feed on small particles in water, whereas birds of prey use hooked bills to hold down and tear apart prey. In many bird species, both males and females share nest making and the rearing of young, and some birds also display social behaviours in groups.

Reptiles

There are about 8,200 species of reptiles. They include turtles, lizards, snakes and crocodiles. Reptiles were the first vertebrates to be independent of water. An amniotic egg with a waterproof shell enabled them to breed and hatch on land, without the need to return to water. Because reptiles rely on external heat to regulate their body temperature, many spend hours in sunlight, warming themselves by infrared radiation.

Humans have long feared and respected reptiles. Snakes, crocodiles and mythical dragons are found in the legends of peoples throughout the world. Many reptile species have impressive abilities: they can scale walls, burrow, swim, climb slender stalks and even run across loose, hot sand dunes. These amazing animals with extraordinary traits have been around for many millions of years. Today, however, many species of reptiles are in danger of extinction, threatened by hunting and destruction of their habitat.

Fish and Amphibians

Among the first vertebrates (creatures with internal skeletons) were fish and amphibians, and each species has evolved to help it survive in a specific habitat. Fish are uniquely adapted to the watery world, with gills for breathing and fins for swimming. They can live in oceans, lakes and freshwater rivers and streams, while strange and little-known fish inhabit the cold, dark ocean depths. Many fish are valued as food by people, and the conservation of commercial fish stocks is a key issue for the future. Some fish remain elusive and even feared; few animals match the reputation in fact and fiction of the shark.

Way back in evolutionary prehistory, some species moved from water to dry land, breathing by means of lunglike air sacs. Fish with proto-limbs were able to exploit new food sources and, over time, adapted to life

GREEN TREE PYTHON
This tree-dwelling green python usually coils around a branch and waits with its head hanging down, ready to attack. It eats small mammals and birds.

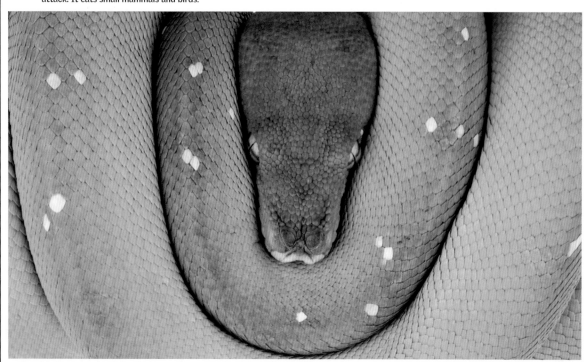

OWL
As a group, birds have exceptional eyesight – they have the largest eyes in relation to their bodies. This
Cape eagle owl, *Bubo capensis*, is native to Africa. It feeds on birds and mammals.

on land. This evolutionary change –
from water-dwelling to land-dwelling
animals – constituted a revolution
for life on Earth. Some land-dwelling
animals retained a link with water
through breeding behaviour; these
are the amphibians, such as frogs and
toads. The living amphibians are a tiny
fraction of a once-numerous class that
appeared during the Devonian period
of prehistory, but most became extinct
during the later Triassic period.

Invertebrates
The most ancient forms of animal life
on Earth are the invertebrates. They
are also by far the most numerous. With
more than 1.5 million known species,
it is estimated that 97 per cent of all
animal species are invertebrates. This
fascinating group of creatures offers
amazing examples of adaptation and
habits. Many invertebrates play a vital
role in food chains and ecosystems,
so they are very important to other
species. Others are useful controls:
without spiders as expert predators, the
world might be overrun by insect pests.

Conserving the Natural World
We may wonder at the thousands of
species of animals alive today. Yet it
is thought that 99.9 per cent of all the
animal species that have ever existed
are now extinct. Extinctions happen
naturally, but human actions can also
lead to species being lost forever.
Modern science is showing us how
all living things are interconnected in
complex ecosystems. By learning more
about animals, we will be better able
to conserve the natural world and to
protect the Earth's amazing wildlife
for future generations.

What Is a Mammal?

Mammals share a series of characteristics that distinguish their class: a body covered by hair, the birth of live young and the feeding of newborns on milk produced by the females' mammary glands. All breathe through lungs, and all possess a closed, double circulatory system and the most developed nervous systems in the animal kingdom. The ability to maintain a constant body temperature has allowed them to spread out and conquer every corner of Earth, from the coldest climates to hot deserts and from the mountains to the oceans.

GORILLA
Gorilla gorilla

A Body for Every Environment

Mammals have skin covered with hair and sweat glands, which helps create and maintain a constant body temperature. Eyes placed on each side of the head give monocular vision (except in the primates, which have binocular vision) but allow important angles of sight. The four limbs, ending in either feet or hands, vary in structure depending on the part of the foot used for walking. In aquatic mammals, the limbs have evolved into fins; in bats, into wings. Hunters are equipped with powerful claws, and unguligrades (such as horses) have strong hooves that support the whole body when running.

AMAZING FACT

Gorillas share around 98 per cent of their genetic make-up with humans, but chimpanzees are even closer relatives, with nearly 99 per cent.

BOTTLENOSE DOLPHIN
Tursiops truncatus

Hair

Body hair is unique to mammals and absent in other classes of animals. Sirenians, with little hair, and cetaceans are exceptions; in both cases, the absence of hair is a result of the mammal's adaptation to an aquatic environment.

Teeth

Most mammals change their dentition in their passage to adulthood. Teeth are specialized for each function: molars for chewing, canines for tearing and incisors for gnawing. In rodents, such as chipmunks, the teeth are renewed by continuous growth.

CHIPMUNK
Tamias sp.

Close Relatives

Humans belong to the primate group. The great apes (orangutans, gorillas and chimpanzees) are the largest of our primate relatives, weighing between 48 and 270 kg (105–595 lb). In general, males are larger than females, with robust bodies and well-developed arms. Like humans, their vertical posture differentiates their skeletons from those of other primates. Gorillas inhabit only the equatorial jungles of western Africa. They support themselves on their forelimbs while walking. Normally their height varies between 1.2 and 1.8 m (4–6 ft), but, if they raise their forelimbs and stand erect, they can be over 2 m (6½ ft) tall.

Homeothermy

Mammals keep their body temperature relatively constant, independent of the ambient temperature. Hibernating species are the exception; they must lower their body temperature to enter this state of reduced metabolic activity. Contrary to popular belief, bears do not truly hibernate but rather enter into a period of deep sleep during winter.

BROWN BEAR (GRIZZLY BEAR)
Ursus arctos

CRANIUM
Relatively large compared to the size of the body. And the brain is more developed and more complex than that of any other animal.

ALWAYS 37°C (98°F)
The ability to maintain a constant body temperature is not a characteristic unique to mammals: birds also have this ability.

AN EAR OF BONES
The tiny bones of the ear form a system for sensing and transmitting sound.

LOWER JAW
Formed by a single bone, called the 'dentary', and teeth specialized for each function. The entire skull has a very simplified bone structure.

Limbs

Mammals have four limbs that are adapted for moving about. The exceptions are the cetaceans, so adapted to marine life that their vestigial hind limbs are hidden inside their bodies. Forelimbs may have other abilities (such as seals' flippers for swimming, or hands for manipulation).

ELEPHANT SEAL
Mirounga sp.

5,416

IS THE NUMBER OF MAMMAL SPECIES ESTIMATED TO EXIST ON EARTH.

Take Habitat into Account

Between every mammal and its natural habitat there is a relationship that exists and is expressed in the animal's physical characteristics. Just as the flippers of the elephant seal are used to swim and hunt fish, mimicry and running are vital for deer. Physiology is a special instrument of adaptation to the environment, as in the case of the camel.

| Aquatic | Temperate forests | Desert | Meadow or pastureland |

| Tropical savanna | Tropical rainforest | Taiga | Tundra |

MAMMARY GLANDS
Secrete milk with which the females feed their young during their first months of life. These glands give the class its name.

A THICK SKIN
Formed by an outer layer (epidermis), another deeper layer (dermis) and a layer of fatty tissue that stores energy and helps regulate temperature.

AN UNCOMMON PRIMATE

Humans have adapted to almost all habitats through their ability to modify certain elements of their habitat to their advantage. They often create tools to help them adapt to their environment. In this way, they do not need to rely on natural evolution alone. Humans have adapted to almost all habitats.

Life Cycles

Birth, maturity, reproduction and death: this life cycle has certain particularities among mammals. As a general rule, the larger a mammal, the longer the members of its species tend to live, but the fewer offspring are born to a single female per litter or reproductive season. Most mammals, including humans, are placental mammals; the young's vital functions are fully developed inside the body of the mother.

100 Years

IS THE AVERAGE LIFE SPAN OF A BOWHEAD WHALE – THE GREATEST OF ANY LIVING MAMMAL.

Placental Mammals

This is the largest group of mammals, the one that has multiplied most on the planet, although its form of gestation and lactation produces great wear and tear on females, making them less prolific. They are generally polygamous: a few males (the most competitive) fertilize many females, while other males have no offspring. Only 3 per cent of mammals are monogamous in each season. In these cases, males participate in rearing young, as they also do when resources are scarce. If resources are abundant, the females take care of the young alone, and the males mate with other females.

They make use of natural caves or dig underground.

Weaning
35 TO 40 DAYS

Young rabbits remain with their mother even after nursing ends for protection and the inculcation of species-specific behaviour.

Sexual Maturity
5 TO 7 MONTHS

The better rabbits are fed, the more quickly they become capable of reproducing. They are considered adults at 8 or 9 months, when they weigh around 900 g (2 lb).

Females have four to five pairs of teats.

Female rabbits can mate at any time.

Lactation
25 TO 30 DAYS

The young are fed on milk, although they can digest solid food after 20 days. They abandon the burrow after 35 or 40 days but remain in the area where they were raised.

Gestation
28 TO 33 DAYS

They spend it in a collective burrow (warren) dug in the ground and covered with vegetation and fur. The female will abandon the burrow as soon as lactation ends.

10 cm (4 in)

Rabbits are born without fur, with translucent skin.

EASTERN COTTONTAIL RABBIT
Sylvilagus floridanus

Longevity 4 to 10 years

AT BIRTH
The young weigh some 40–50 g (1½–1¾ oz). They do not open their eyes until the tenth day.

NUMBER OF OFFSPRING

In general, it is inversely proportional to the species' size.

COW	1 offspring
GOAT	2–3 offspring
DOG	5–7 offspring
RAT	6–12 offspring

3 to 9 young
PER LITTER, AND FROM 5 TO 7 LITTERS PER YEAR

Marsupials

After a very short gestation period, the young develop in a partially open pouch (called a 'marsupium'), which the female carries on her belly. The majority of the roughly 300 known species of marsupials are solitary, except during mating periods. In general, they are promiscuous animals, although some, such as wallabies (small kangaroos), tend to mate with the same female throughout their life.

Lactation
22 WEEKS

A muscle inside the pouch prevents the infant from falling out. At 22 weeks, it opens its eyes, and a type of pap produced by its mother is added to its diet, which will prepare it for a herbivorous diet.

Gestation
35 DAYS

With its extremities and functional organs barely developed at birth, the newborn must crawl by itself from the cloaca to the pouch to continue its development.

2 cm
(³/₄ in)

1 offspring
1 BIRTH PER YEAR

The young animal fastens itself to its mother and is carried around by her, clinging to her shoulders.

BANISHED OFFSPRING
Dominant males keep the offspring and other young males apart.

Dominant males mate with all the females.

Some females leave to look for strong males.

KOALA
Phascolarctos cinereus

By the end of lactation, fur covers the whole body.

Leaving the Pouch
1 YEAR

The offspring reaches a size that allows it to fend for itself. It has already incorporated herbivorous food into its diet. The mother can become pregnant again, but the young will remain nearby.

Sexual Maturity
3 TO 4 YEARS

At two years, koalas already have developed sexual organs (females earlier than males). But they do not start mating until one or two years later.

Longevity
15 to 20 years

LONGEVITY

HUMANS	70 years
ELEPHANTS	70
HORSES	40
GIRAFFES	20
CATS	15
DOGS	15
HAMSTERS	3

GESTATION PERIODS

ANIMAL	MONTHS
Elephants	23
Giraffes	17
Gibbons	9
Lions	7
Dogs	2

COMPARISON OF EGG SIZE

The shell is soft and facilitates the offspring's birth. Unlike birds, they do not have beaks.

CHICKEN

ECHIDNA

Monotremes

Mammals whose females lay eggs are generally solitary species for most of the year. Platypuses are seen as couples only when they mate. Although they have a period of courtship for one to three months, the males have no relationship with the females after copulation or with the offspring. Short-beaked echidna females may be pursued by 'trains' of up to ten males in the mating season.

Incubation
12 DAYS

Eggs gestate for a month before hatching. They incubate within a pouch for about ten days to remain at the proper temperature until the young are born.

Newborn offspring

Shell

15 mm
(½ in)

1 to 3
EGGS AT A TIME

In the Pouch
2 TO 3 MONTHS

After breaking the shell, the young are suckled while they remain in a pouch on the female's belly.

Undeveloped limbs

Underground cave or burrow among rocks

The fur is already spiny.

Weaning
4 TO 6 MONTHS

After three months, the offspring can leave the burrow or remain in it alone for up to a day and a half before finally separating from the mother.

Longevity
50 years

SHORT-BEAKED ECHIDNA
Tachyglossus aculeatus

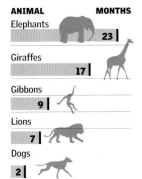

Developed Senses

Dogs have inherited from wolves great hearing and an excellent sense of smell. Both perform an essential role in their relationship with their surroundings and their social activities. Whereas humans often remember other people as images, dogs do so with smell, their most important sense. They have 44 times more olfactory cells than humans, and they can discern one molecule out of a million others. They can hear sounds so quiet that they are imperceptible to people.

AMAZING FACT

Dogs have at least 18 muscles that control the movements of their ears, allowing them to focus precisely on the source of a sound.

Hearing

The auditory ability of dogs is four times greater than that of human beings, and it is highly developed. Their ability depends on the shape and orientation of their ears, which allow them to locate and pay closer attention to sounds, although this varies by breed. They can hear sharper tones and much softer sounds, and they can directly locate the spatial reference point where a noise was produced. Dogs hear sounds of up to 40 kilohertz, whereas the upper limit for human hearing is 20 kilohertz.

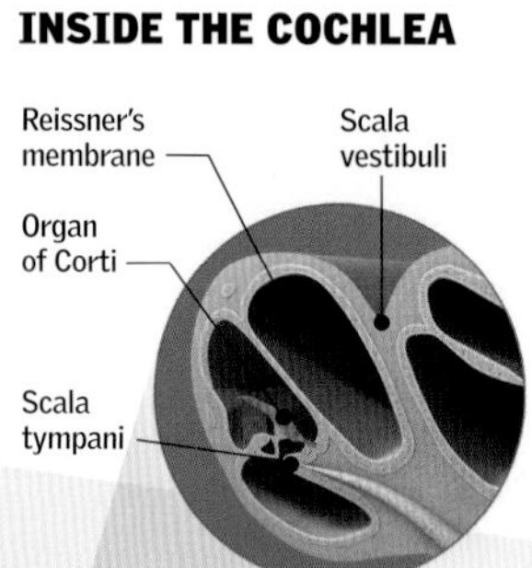

INSIDE THE COCHLEA

Reissner's membrane
Scala vestibuli
Organ of Corti
Scala tympani

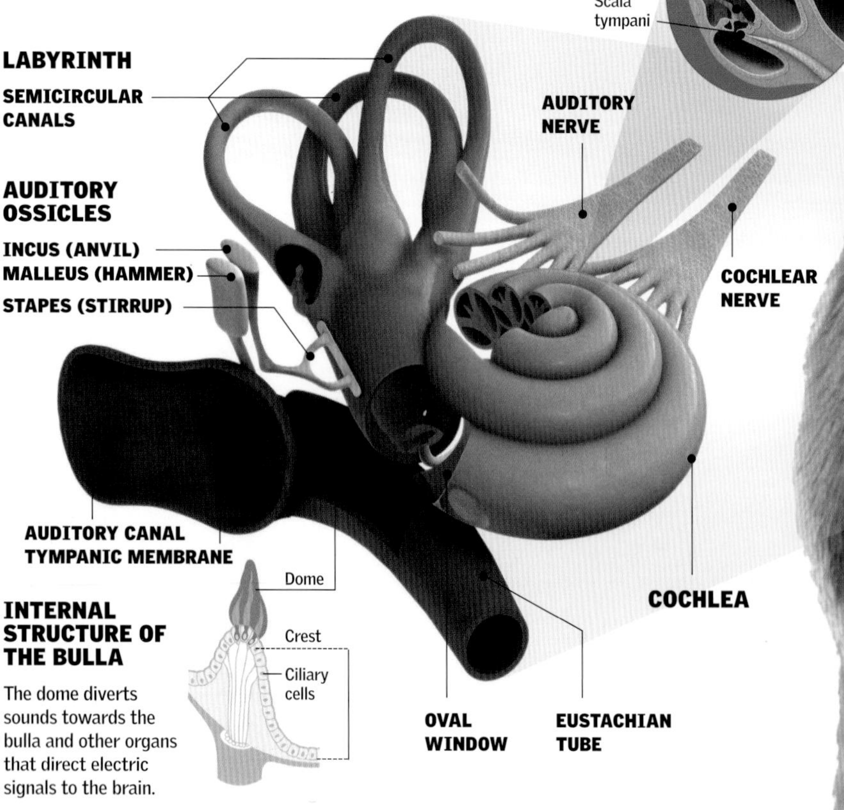

AURICULAR CARTILAGE

LABYRINTH
SEMICIRCULAR CANALS

AUDITORY NERVE

AUDITORY CANAL

AUDITORY OSSICLES

INCUS (ANVIL)
MALLEUS (HAMMER)
STAPES (STIRRUP)

MIDDLE EAR

COCHLEAR NERVE

COCHLEA

AUDITORY CANAL
TYMPANIC MEMBRANE

COCHLEA

INTERNAL STRUCTURE OF THE BULLA

Dome
Crest
Ciliary cells

The dome diverts sounds towards the bulla and other organs that direct electric signals to the brain.

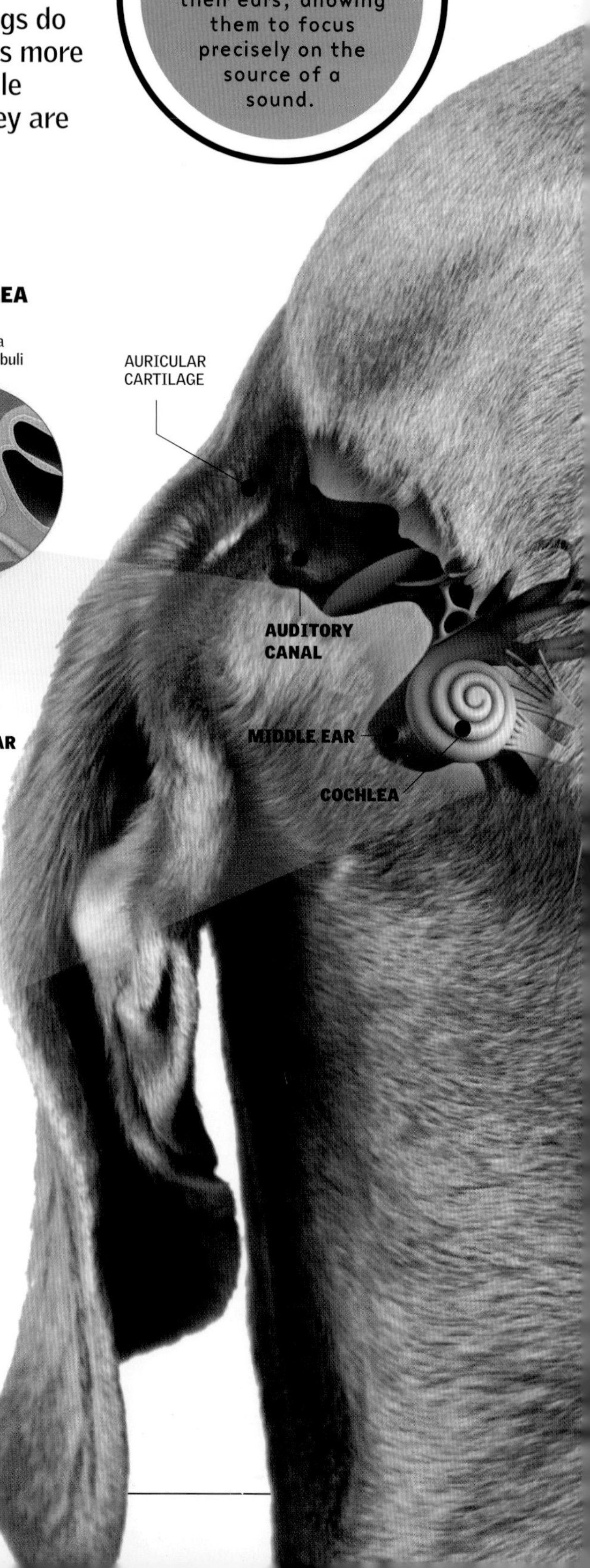

OVAL WINDOW
EUSTACHIAN TUBE

AUDITORY LEVELS

	0 hertz	1	10	100	1,000	10,000	20,000	40,000
HUMANS								
FOXES								
MICE								
BATS								
FROGS								
ELEPHANTS								
BIRDS								

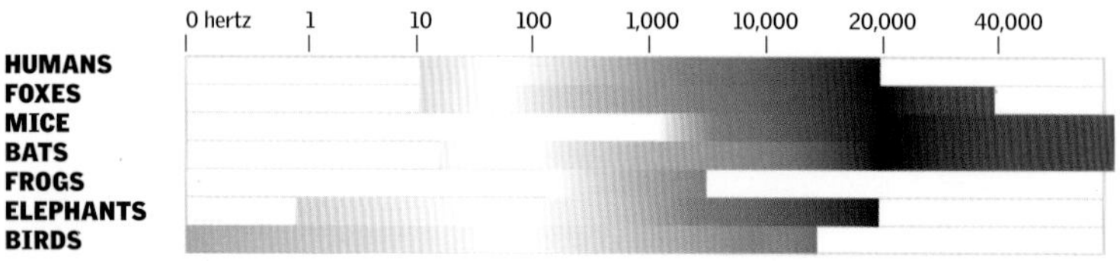

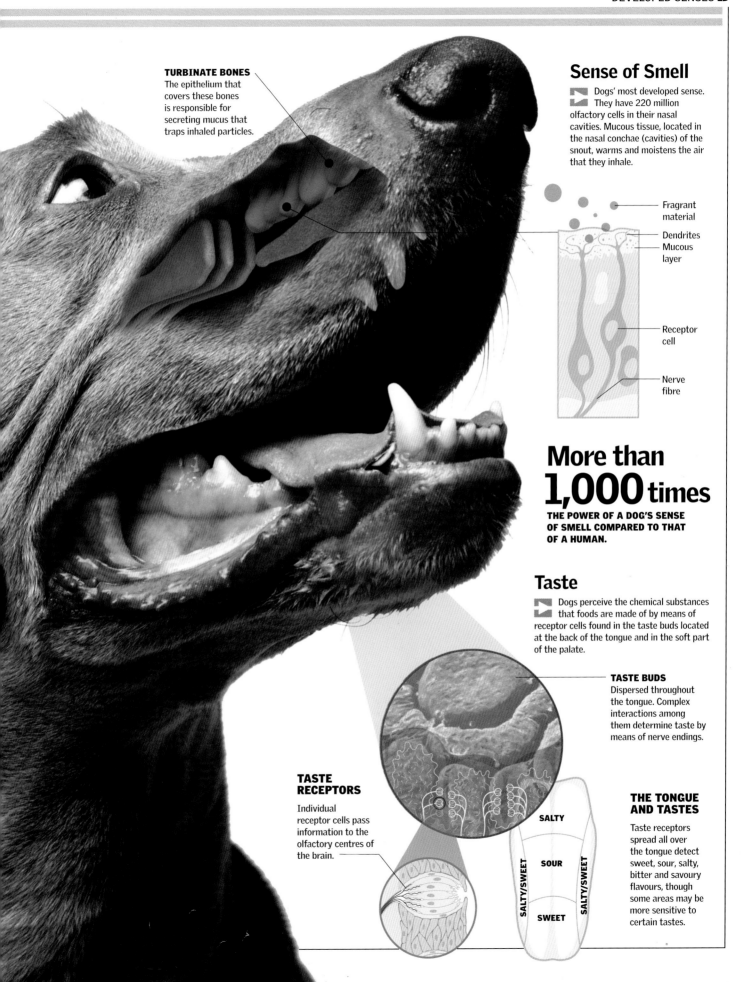

TURBINATE BONES
The epithelium that covers these bones is responsible for secreting mucus that traps inhaled particles.

Sense of Smell

Dogs' most developed sense. They have 220 million olfactory cells in their nasal cavities. Mucous tissue, located in the nasal conchae (cavities) of the snout, warms and moistens the air that they inhale.

Fragrant material

Dendrites

Mucous layer

Receptor cell

Nerve fibre

More than 1,000 times

THE POWER OF A DOG'S SENSE OF SMELL COMPARED TO THAT OF A HUMAN.

Taste

Dogs perceive the chemical substances that foods are made of by means of receptor cells found in the taste buds located at the back of the tongue and in the soft part of the palate.

TASTE BUDS
Dispersed throughout the tongue. Complex interactions among them determine taste by means of nerve endings.

TASTE RECEPTORS

Individual receptor cells pass information to the olfactory centres of the brain.

SALTY

SALTY/SWEET

SOUR

SALTY/SWEET

SWEET

THE TONGUE AND TASTES

Taste receptors spread all over the tongue detect sweet, sour, salty, bitter and savoury flavours, though some areas may be more sensitive to certain tastes.

Speed and Agility

They are meteors of flesh, bone and hot blood. Cheetahs are members of the Felidae family and the fastest of all land animals, using their keen vision and great speed to hunt. They can reach 115 kilometres per hour (70 mph) in short runs and accelerate to 72 km/h (45 mph) in an average of only 2 seconds. They are also agile at high speed, making swift turns to catch their prey. They look like leopards, but their physical characteristics are different: they are built for speed, with long tails, slender bodies and limbs, and small, rounded heads.

TAKE-OFF
From the top of a tree, the flying squirrel jumps towards another, shorter tree.

Cheetahs

 Whereas tigers prefer to lie in wait for prey and then jump on it, the cheetah uses explosive speed of more than 100 km/h (60 mph) to run its prey down.

 Start
The cheetah begins running by lengthening its stride and extending its four legs.

 Spinal Contraction
Then it gathers its legs under its body, contracting its cervical spine to the maximum.

NOSTRILS
Very wide, they allow it to receive more oxygen as it runs.

ORDER	Carnivora
FAMILY	Felidae
SPECIES	*Acinonyx jubatus* (Africa)
	Acinonyx venaticus (Asia)

FIRST POINT OF CONTACT
As it runs, only one leg touches the ground at a time, but during the cervical contraction, the entire body lifts from the ground.

SECOND POINT OF CONTACT
Extending its four legs again, it picks up more momentum, supporting itself on only one back leg.

Bipeds versus Quadrupeds

29 KM/H (18 MPH)
SIX-LINED RACERUNNER
Cnemidophorus sexlineatus
Lizard endemic to the USA.

37 KM/H (23 MPH)
HUMAN BEING
Track record: Usain Bolt (Jamaica), 100 m (110 yds) in 9.58 seconds.

67 KM/H (42 MPH)
GREYHOUND
A dog with a light skeleton and aerodynamic anatomy.

80 KM/H (50 MPH)
HORSE
Anatomy designed for running, with powerful musculature.

115 KM/H (70 MPH)
CHEETAH
It only takes 2 seconds to reach a speed of 72 km/h (45 mph).

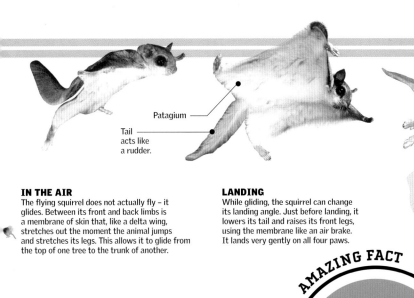

Patagium

Tail acts like a rudder.

IN THE AIR
The flying squirrel does not actually fly – it glides. Between its front and back limbs is a membrane of skin that, like a delta wing, stretches out the moment the animal jumps and stretches its legs. This allows it to glide from the top of one tree to the trunk of another.

LANDING
While gliding, the squirrel can change its landing angle. Just before landing, it lowers its tail and raises its front legs, using the membrane like an air brake. It lands very gently on all four paws.

TOES
Upon landing, it grabs on to the surface with its toes.

Siberian Flying Squirrel
Flying squirrels (*Pteromys volans*) belong to the same rodent family as common squirrels, to which they are similar in both appearance and way of life. They live in the mixed forests of northern Europe, across Siberia and into East Asia.

3 ## Extending the Spine
In a counterthrust opposing the contraction, the spine extends, creating forward momentum. The cheetah can cover 8 m (26 ft) in a single stride.

AMAZING FACT

Cheetahs can't roar but are quite vocal: they communicate through chirping, churring, growling, hissing and purring.

SHOULDER
The extensive flexion of the shoulder allows it to take very long leaps.

HEAD
Small and aerodynamic, with low air resistance.

TAIL
Large compared to the rest of the body, it acts as a pivot used to change direction suddenly.

LIMBS
Long and agile. It has a powerful, flexible skeleton and musculature.

115 km/h
(70 mph)
MAXIMUM SPEED, BUT CAN BE MAINTAINED FOR ONLY 500 M (550 YDS).

ZIGZAGGING AT HIGH SPEED

1 Cheetahs can make sharp turns while running at high speed.

2 These movements are possible because cheetahs grip the ground firmly with their claws.

PAWS

DIGITS
5 in forepaws
4 in hind paws

CLAWS
Unlike other felines, their claws are not fully retractable, allowing them to grip the ground better.

Sloth
These animals are notable for their extremely slow metabolism. They take half a minute to move a limb. They are also somewhat shortsighted, their hearing is mediocre, and their sense of smell barely serves to distinguish the plants on which they feed. They are the extreme opposite of cheetahs. However, since they live practically all their lives perched in trees, they do not need to move or see or hear precisely. They are perfectly adapted to their way of life.

THREE-TOED SLOTH
Native to the Amazon River basin.

Meat Eaters

The carnivore group is composed of species whose diet is based on hunting other animals. The kinds of teeth they have help them efficiently cut and tear the flesh of their captured prey. Lions, the most sociable of the felines, have good vision and sharp hearing; they are the only cats to live in packs, and when they go hunting, they do so as a group.

Lions

are characterized by a strong, muscular physique. A male requires 7 kg (15½ lb) of meat a day, whereas a female needs 5 kg (11 lb). They have a short digestive tract, which rapidly absorbs nutrients from the meat they eat.

Teeth

UPPER PREMOLARS

UPPER INCISORS

UPPER CANINE

CARNASSIAL PAIR

They are very large, and the dental crowns are two long blades arranged as shears that fit into each other. Together they slice and cut flesh to perfection.

ANTERIOR PREMOLARS

LOWER CANINE

LOWER INCISORS

The Hunt

1 **LYING IN AMBUSH**
Hidden in the grass, the lioness silently approaches the prey. Other females wait in hiding.

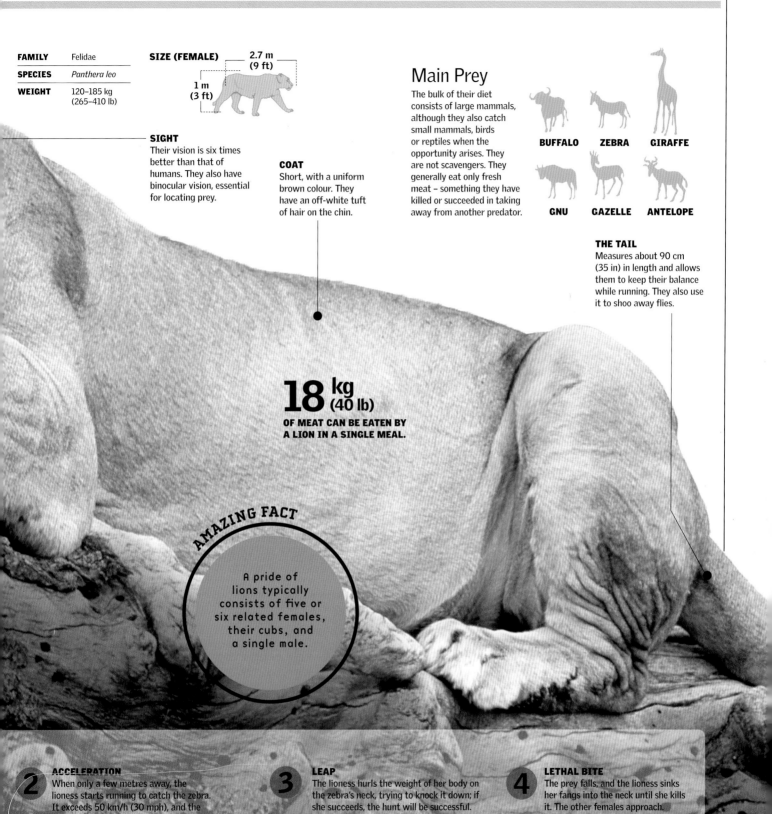

FAMILY	Felidae
SPECIES	*Panthera leo*
WEIGHT	120–185 kg (265–410 lb)

SIZE (FEMALE)
2.7 m (9 ft)
1 m (3 ft)

SIGHT
Their vision is six times better than that of humans. They also have binocular vision, essential for locating prey.

COAT
Short, with a uniform brown colour. They have an off-white tuft of hair on the chin.

Main Prey
The bulk of their diet consists of large mammals, although they also catch small mammals, birds or reptiles when the opportunity arises. They are not scavengers. They generally eat only fresh meat – something they have killed or succeeded in taking away from another predator.

BUFFALO **ZEBRA** **GIRAFFE**

GNU **GAZELLE** **ANTELOPE**

THE TAIL
Measures about 90 cm (35 in) in length and allows them to keep their balance while running. They also use it to shoo away flies.

18 kg (40 lb)
OF MEAT CAN BE EATEN BY A LION IN A SINGLE MEAL.

AMAZING FACT
A pride of lions typically consists of five or six related females, their cubs, and a single male.

2 ACCELERATION
When only a few metres away, the lioness starts running to catch the zebra. It exceeds 50 km/h (30 mph), and the others cooperate in the hunt.

3 LEAP
The lioness hurls the weight of her body on the zebra's neck, trying to knock it down; if she succeeds, the hunt will be successful.

4 LETHAL BITE
The prey falls, and the lioness sinks her fangs into the neck until she kills it. The other females approach.

Herbivores

Ruminants, such as cows, sheep and deer, have stomachs made up of four chambers with which they carry out a unique kind of digestion. Because these animals need to eat large quantities of grass very quickly in the wild – or else become easy targets for predators – they have developed a digestive system that allows them to swallow food, store it and then return it to the mouth to chew calmly. When animals carry out this activity, they are said to ruminate, or chew the cud.

KEY

▬▬▬ INGESTION AND FERMENTATION

▬▬▬ RUMINATION

▬▬▬ REABSORPTION OF NUTRIENTS

▬▬▬ ACID DIGESTION

▬▬▬ DIGESTION AND ABSORPTION

▬▬▬ FERMENTATION AND DIGESTION

Teeth

Herbivorous animals, such as horses and cows, have molars with a large flat surface that reduces food to pulp, as well as incisors for cutting grass. Grinding is also done by the molars.

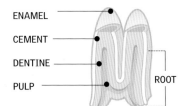

ENAMEL

CEMENT

DENTINE

PULP

ROOT

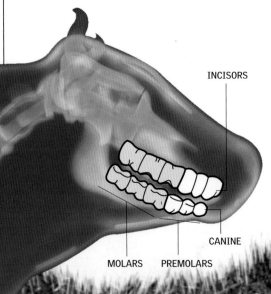

INCISORS

MOLARS PREMOLARS CANINE

Cows wrap their tongues around the food.

Then they chew it with lateral movements.

 1

Cows lightly chew grass and ingest it into their first two stomachs: the rumen and the reticulum. Food passes continually from the rumen to the reticulum (nearly once every minute). There, various bacteria colonies begin fermenting the food.

THE RUMINATION PROCESS

helps ruminants reduce the size of the ingested food particles. It is part of the process that allows them to obtain energy from plant cell walls, also called fibre.

2

When cows feel satiated, they regurgitate balls of food from the rumen and chew them again in the mouth. This is called rumination; it stimulates salivation, and, as digestion is a very slow process, cows make use of rumination to improve their own digestion together with the intervention of anaerobic micro-organisms, such as protozoa, bacteria and fungi.

150 litres (40 gallons)

OF SALIVA ARE PRODUCED DAILY IN THE PROCESS.

Ⓐ ——→ Ⓑ ——→ Ⓒ ——→ Ⓓ

REGURGITATION   REMASTICATION   REINSALIVATION   REINGESTION

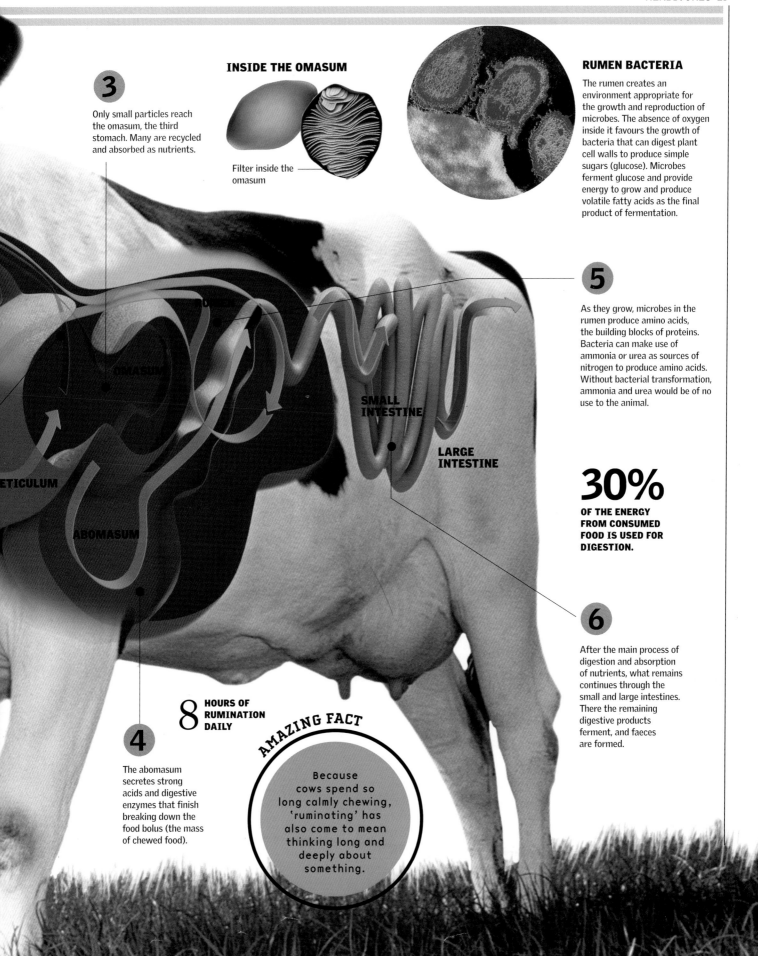

3

Only small particles reach the omasum, the third stomach. Many are recycled and absorbed as nutrients.

INSIDE THE OMASUM

Filter inside the omasum

RUMEN BACTERIA

The rumen creates an environment appropriate for the growth and reproduction of microbes. The absence of oxygen inside it favours the growth of bacteria that can digest plant cell walls to produce simple sugars (glucose). Microbes ferment glucose and provide energy to grow and produce volatile fatty acids as the final product of fermentation.

5

As they grow, microbes in the rumen produce amino acids, the building blocks of proteins. Bacteria can make use of ammonia or urea as sources of nitrogen to produce amino acids. Without bacterial transformation, ammonia and urea would be of no use to the animal.

OMASUM

ETICULUM

ABOMASUM

SMALL INTESTINE

LARGE INTESTINE

30%
OF THE ENERGY FROM CONSUMED FOOD IS USED FOR DIGESTION.

6

After the main process of digestion and absorption of nutrients, what remains continues through the small and large intestines. There the remaining digestive products ferment, and faeces are formed.

8 HOURS OF RUMINATION DAILY

4

The abomasum secretes strong acids and digestive enzymes that finish breaking down the food bolus (the mass of chewed food).

AMAZING FACT

Because cows spend so long calmly chewing, 'ruminating' has also come to mean thinking long and deeply about something.

One for All

Meerkats are small mammals that live in underground colonies, posting guards while the mothers take care of their young. During the day, they go above ground to feed, and at night they go into the burrow to take refuge from the cold. In this large family, made up of dozens of members, each one fulfils a function. When faced with danger, they employ various tactics to defend themselves. One of these is the squeal that lookouts emit in the face of even slight dangers.

MEERKAT
Suricata suricatta

FAMILY	Herpestidae
HABITAT	Africa
OFFSPRING	2 to 7

30 cm
(12 in)

Weight
1 kg
(2 lb)

About
30 IS THE NUMBER OF INDIVIDUALS A GROUP CAN HAVE.

Social Structure

The social structure is extensive and well defined, ensuring that everyone has a role to fulfil. The lookouts (which may be female or male) take turns to sound the alarm over the arrival of strangers; one that is better fed replaces another that needs to eat. Meerkats are carnivorous: they eat small mammals, as well as insects and spiders.

FEMALES
must dedicate all their energy to the process of reproducing and feeding and raising young.

YOUNG
When the adult standing guard gives the cry of danger, all run to hide in the burrow.

BLACK-BACKED JACKAL
The meerkats' largest predator. To detect one before it is seen is of prime importance for the colony.

MARTIAL EAGLE
The most dangerous enemy they have and the one that kills the greatest number of meerkats.

Lookout

When a predator is detected, the lookout warns its group so that all of them can take cover in a nearby hole. This role rotates among different members of the group, and the warning is given by a very wide repertoire of sounds, each of which has a distinct meaning.

MEERKATS ALSO USE VOCALIZATIONS TO COMMUNICATE.

Defence

1 SURROUNDING THE ENEMY
They emit a type of squeal. They rock back and forth. They try to appear larger and more ferocious than they are.

2 ON THEIR BACKS
If this tactic fails, they throw themselves down on their backs to protect their necks, showing their fangs and claws.

3 PROTECTION
When it is an aerial predator, they run to hide. If taken by surprise, adults protect the young.

SIGHT
Binocular and in colour, it allows them to locate their greatest predators, birds of prey.

HEAD
is kept permanently erect, observing the burrow's surroundings.

VIGILANCE FROM ABOVE
It is common to see them at the highest spots of their territory, on rocks or tree branches.

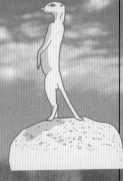

MALES
defend their territory and stand watch. The dominant male is the reproducer.

FRONT PAWS
They have strong claws, which they use for digging or to defend themselves.

AMAZING FACT

Females without offspring act as babysitters for the young in the group while their mother is foraging for food.

Territory

The area defended provides the food necessary for the group's subsistence. Males devote themselves to defence, and when resources run out the group migrates to another area.

BURROWS
They dig them with their sharp claws and leave them only during the day.

HIND FEET
They can support themselves on their hind feet when standing upright to keep watch.

TRIPOD TAIL
Meerkats use it to balance themselves when they are in an upright position.

Record Breath-Holders

Sperm whales are unique animals whose species is remarkable for many reasons. They have the ability to dive to a maximum depth of 3,300 m (10,000 ft) and remain underwater without oxygen for up to two hours. They are able to do this by means of a complex physiological mechanism that, for example, can decrease their heart rate, store and use air in the muscles and prioritize the delivery of oxygen to certain vital organs, such as the heart and lungs. They are the largest whales to have teeth, which are found only on the lower jaw and fit into sockets in the upper jaw.

Up to 120 minutes

IS THE LENGTH OF TIME THEY CAN SPEND UNDERWATER WITHOUT BREATHING.

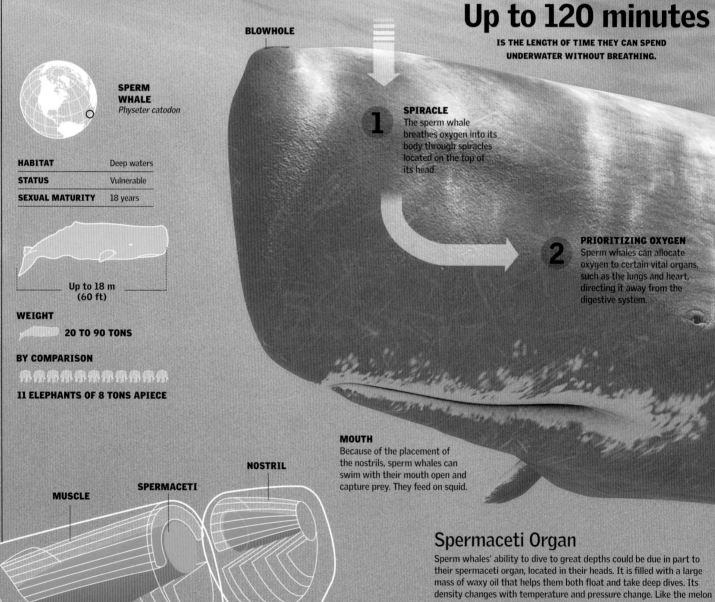

BLOWHOLE

SPERM WHALE
Physeter catodon

HABITAT	Deep waters
STATUS	Vulnerable
SEXUAL MATURITY	18 years

Up to 18 m
(60 ft)

WEIGHT

20 TO 90 TONS

BY COMPARISON

11 ELEPHANTS OF 8 TONS APIECE

1 SPIRACLE
The sperm whale breathes oxygen into its body through spiracles located on the top of its head.

2 PRIORITIZING OXYGEN
Sperm whales can allocate oxygen to certain vital organs, such as the lungs and heart, directing it away from the digestive system.

MOUTH
Because of the placement of the nostrils, sperm whales can swim with their mouth open and capture prey. They feed on squid.

MUSCLE   SPERMACETI   NOSTRIL

MANDIBULAR BONE

TEETH
They have 18 to 20 conical teeth, each weighing up to 1 kg (2 lb), on each side of the lower jaw.

Spermaceti Organ

Sperm whales' ability to dive to great depths could be due in part to their spermaceti organ, located in their heads. It is filled with a large mass of waxy oil that helps them both float and take deep dives. Its density changes with temperature and pressure change. Like the melon of a dolphin, it directs sound, focusing clicks, because the whale's eyes are of little use when far from light.

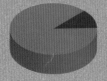

COMPOSITION
90% SPERMACETI OIL
It is made up of esters and triglycerides.

Adaptation in Respiration

When they dive to great depths, sperm whales activate an entire physiological mechanism that makes maximum use of their oxygen reserves. This produces what is called a thoracic and pulmonary collapse, causing air to pass from the lungs to the trachea, reducing the absorption of the toxin nitrogen. They also rapidly transmit nitrogen from the blood to the lungs at the end of the dive, thus reducing the circulation of blood to the muscles. Sperm whales' muscles contain a large amount of myoglobin, a protein that stores oxygen, allowing the whales to stay underwater much longer.

BLOWHOLE
Upon submerging, it fills with water, which cools the spermaceti oil and makes it denser.

HEART
The heart rate slows down during the dive, limiting oxygen consumption.

BLOOD
An ample blood flow, rich in haemoglobin, transports elevated levels of oxygen to the body and brain.

ON THE SURFACE
The blowhole remains open, allowing the whales to breathe as much oxygen as they can before diving.

WHEN THEY DIVE
Powerful muscles tightly close the opening of the blowhole, keeping water from entering.

RETIA MIRABILIA
The retia is a network of blood vessels (mirabilia) that filter the blood entering the brain.

LUNGS
absorb oxygen very efficiently.

TAIL
is large and horizontal and is the whale's main means of propulsion.

3 **BRADYCARDIA**
During a dive, the heart rate drops (a condition known as bradycardia), which lowers oxygen consumption.

AMAZING FACT

From the eighteenth century, sperm whales were hunted for spermaceti oil, in demand for making candles, ointments and cosmetics.

Dive

True diving champions, sperm whales can dive to depths of 3,300 m (10,000 ft), descending up to 3 m (10 ft) per second in search of squid. As a general rule, their dives last about 50 minutes, but they can remain underwater for up to two hours. Before beginning a deep dive, they lift their caudal (tail) fin completely out of the water. They do not have a dorsal fin, but they do have a few triangular humps on the posterior part of their body.

0 M (0 FT)
ON THE SURFACE
They inhale oxygen through the blowhole located at the top of the head.

+ 1,000 M
(3,300 FT)
90 MINUTES
They store 90 per cent of their oxygen in their muscles, so they can stay submerged for a long time.

0 M (0 FT)
ON THE SURFACE
They exhale all the air from their lungs; this is called spouting, or blowing.

Making Use of Oxygen

Sperm whales can dive deeper and stay submerged longer than any other mammal, because they have various ways of saving oxygen: an ability to store it in their muscles, a metabolism that can function anaerobically, and the inducement of bradycardia during a dive.

15%
OF AIR REPLACED IN ONE BREATH

85%
OF AIR REPLACED IN ONE BREATH

Underwater Language

The ways in which cetaceans communicate with others of their kind are among the most sophisticated in the animal kingdom. Dolphins, for example, click when in trouble and whistle repeatedly when afraid or excited. During courtship and mating, they touch and caress each other. They also communicate through visual signals – such as leaping – to show that food is close by. They have a wide variety of ways to transmit important information.

HAVING FUN

Play for dolphins, as with other mammals, fulfils an essential role in the formation of social strata.

COMMON NAME	Bottlenose dolphin
FAMILY	Delphinidae
SPECIES	*Tursiops truncatus*
ADULT WEIGHT	150–650 kg (330–1,400 lb)
LONGEVITY	30–40 years

2–4 m (7–13 ft)

THEY REACH 35 KM/H (22 MPH)

MELON

An organ filled with low-density lipids that concentrate and direct the pulses emitted, sending waves forwards. The shape of the melon can be varied to better focus the sounds.

SPIRACLE LIP

NASAL AIR SAC

DORSAL FIN allows dolphins to maintain their equilibrium in the water.

LARYNX

CAUDAL FIN has a horizontal axis (unlike that of fish), which serves to propel dolphins forwards.

PECTORAL FIN

1 Emission

Sounds are generated by air passing through the respiratory chambers. But it is in the melon that resonance is generated and amplified. Greater frequencies and intensities are achieved in this way.

HOW THE SOUND IS PRODUCED

1 INHALATION The spiracle opens so oxygen can enter.

SPIRACLE

Air to the lungs

2 The nasal air sacs begin to inflate.

They can go for 12 minutes without taking in oxygen.

Air in the lungs

4 The nasal air sacs deflate

Melon

SOUND

3 EXHALATION Air resonates in the nasal sacs and the produced sound is directed through the melon.

Brain

MANDIBLE

The lower mandible plays a very important role in the transmission of sounds to the inner ear.

3 Reception and Interpretation

The middle ear sends the message to the brain. Dolphins hear frequencies from 100 hertz up to 150 kilohertz (the human ear can hear only up to 20 kilohertz). Low-frequency signals (whistles, snores, grunts, clicking) are key in the social life of dolphins, cetaceans that cannot live alone.

1.4 kg
(3 lb)
HUMAN BRAIN

1.7 kg
(4 lb)
DOLPHIN BRAIN

MORE NEURONS

A dolphin's brain, which processes the signals, has at least double the convolutions of those of humans, as well as nearly 50 per cent more neurons.

MIDDLE EAR

2 Message

Low-frequency signals are used for communication with other dolphins, and high-frequency signals are used as sonar.

1.5 km per second
(1 mile/sec)
SOUND WAVES TRAVEL 4.5 TIMES FASTER IN WATER THAN IN AIR.

AMAZING FACT

Cetacean mothers use echolocation while diving to keep track of their young calves, who need to stay nearer the surface to breathe.

Echolocation

A The dolphin emits a series of clicking sounds from the nasal cavity.

B The melon concentrates the clicks and projects them forwards.

C These waves bounce off objects they encounter in their way.

E The intensity, pitch and return time of the echo indicate the size, position and direction of the obstacle.

D Part of the signal bounces back and returns to the dolphin in the form of an echo.

SIGNAL WITH ECHO

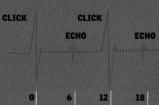

CLICK   CLICK

ECHO   ECHO

0   6   12   18

SECONDS

Nocturnal Flight

Bats are the only mammals that can fly. Scientists call them Chiroptera, a term derived from Greek words meaning 'winged hands'. Their forelimbs have been transformed into hands with very long fingers, joined together by a membrane (the patagium) that forms the surface of the wing. These mammals' senses are so sensitive that they can move and hunt quickly and accurately in the dark.

AMAZING FACT

Bats are found all over the world, and they make up around 20 per cent of all classified mammal species.

Expert Pilots

Moved by their chest and back muscles, bats' wings push downwards and backwards, generating both thrust and lift. Then the wings spread sideways and upwards. Finally, they move forwards until the tips almost rub the bat's head. Many of these flying mammals can drift through the air, gliding without flapping and manoeuvring by folding their wings.

Their Radar

Most of the time bats fly at night in near-total darkness. Instead of light, they use a natural system similar to sonar or radar to guide themselves. This system uses acoustical signals the bats themselves emit while flying. It allows them to recognize the location of any object in front of them or of prey, along with its direction, size or speed. It is as if they were seeing without light.

1 The animal emits an acoustical vibration imperceptible to the human ear because of its high frequency (up to 80 kilohertz). The signal strikes the objects around it.

2 When the signal bounces back, the bat perceives its intensity and phase difference – the faster and more intense the return signal, the nearer the object or prey.

97 km per hour (60 mph) IS THE SPEED SOME BATS MAY REACH DURING FLIGHT.

Hibernation

These bats spend the winter in a lethargic state hanging by their feet, heads down, in caves and other dark places. Bats are warm-blooded animals while they are active and become similar to cold-blooded creatures when they are asleep. They enter a state of hibernation more rapidly and easily than any other mammal, and they can survive in cold temperatures for many months – even inside refrigerators – without needing to feed.

HUMERUS

RADIUS

THUMB

SECOND FINGER

FOURTH FINGER

THIRD FINGER

FRUIT BAT (FRANQUET'S EPAULETTED BAT)
Epomops franqueti

HABITAT	Forests of Ghana and Congo
FAMILY	Pteropodidae
LENGTH OF WINGSPAN	36 cm (14 in)

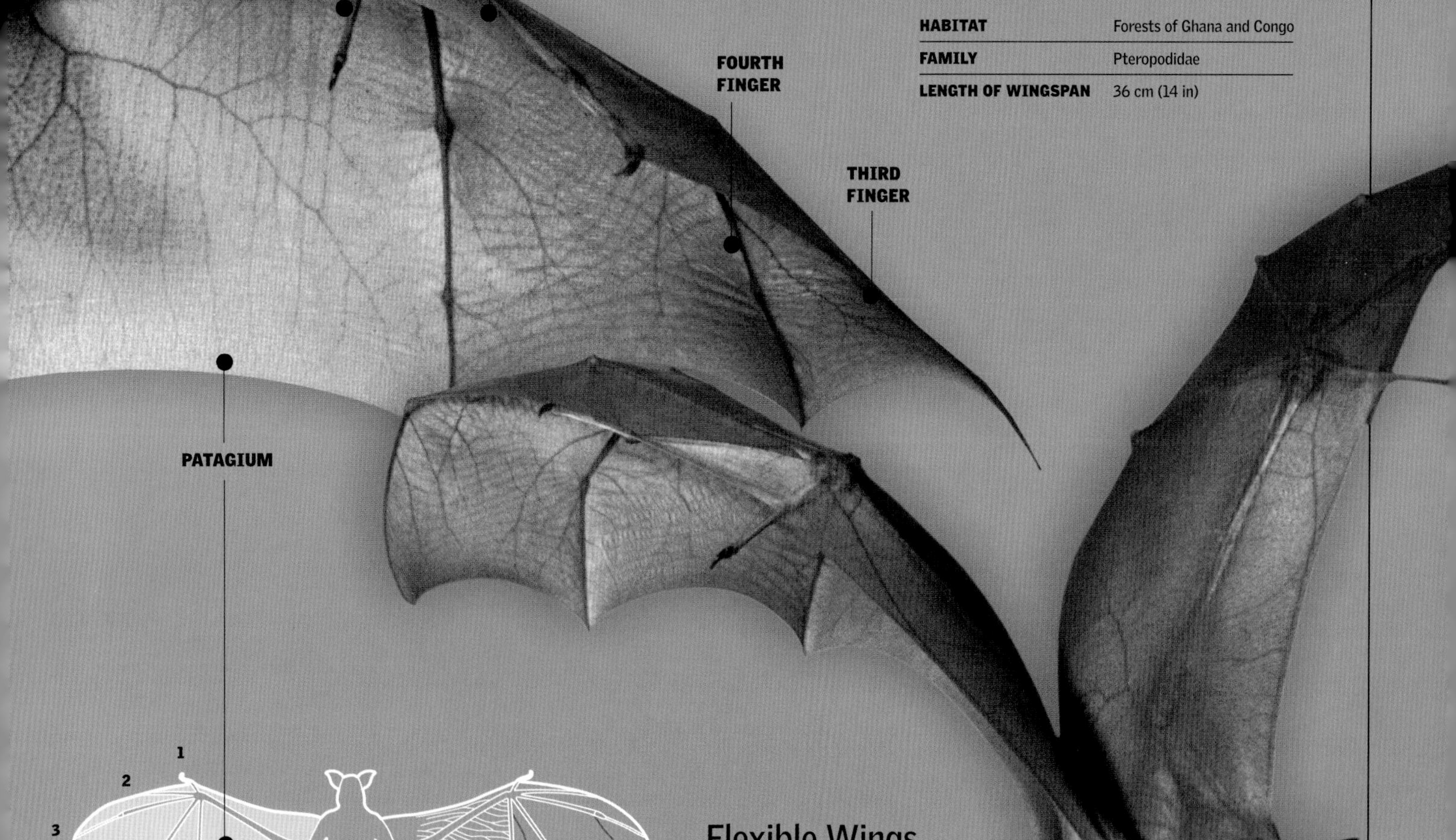

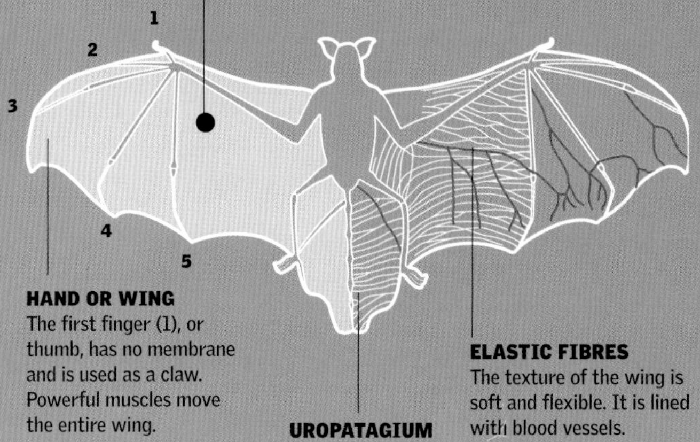

PATAGIUM

1
2
3
4
5

HAND OR WING
The first finger (1), or thumb, has no membrane and is used as a claw. Powerful muscles move the entire wing.

UROPATAGIUM

ELASTIC FIBRES
The texture of the wing is soft and flexible. It is lined with blood vessels.

Flexible Wings

The patagium is formed by the membranes between the digits. In some species, the wings are also extended by an additional membrane (uropatagium), which joins the hind limbs to the tail. Their wings are not only used for flying (pushing the air as if they were oars in water) but also help to maintain a constant body temperature and, in insect-eating species, to trap prey.

Life in the Air

Both lightweight and resistant, the skeleton of birds underwent important changes in order to adapt to flight. Some bones, like those of the skull and wings, fused to become lighter. Birds have fewer bones than other vertebrates. Because their bones are hollow, containing internal air chambers, the total weight of their skeleton is less than that of their feathers. Birds' spines tend to be very flexible in the cervical region and rigid near the ribcage, which joins a large, curved frontal bone called the 'sternum'. The sternum features a large keel, to which the pectoral muscles attach. These large, strong muscles are used for flapping the wings. In contrast, running birds, such as ostriches, have more developed muscles in their legs.

EYE SOCKE

Flapping Wings

Flying demands an enormous amount of energy and strength. Consequently, the muscles responsible for flapping the wings become very large, easily comprising 15 per cent of the weight of a flying bird. Two pairs of pectorals, in which one muscle of the pair is bigger than the other, work to raise and lower the wings. They function symmetrically and in opposition to each other: when one contracts, the other relaxes. Their placement within the thoracic cavity corresponds roughly to the bird's centre of gravity. The motion of the wings also requires strong tendons.

HUMMINGBIRD
Because of its adaptation to stationary flight, its pectoral muscles account for as much as 40 per cent of its total weight.

SKULL
Light because of the fusing of bones, the skull does not have teeth, a bony jaw or grinding muscles.

UPPER MANDIBLE OF BILL
In some species, it is flexible.

LOWER MANDIBLE OF BILL
It is flexible, allowing birds to open their mouths wide.

FURCULA (COLLARBONE)
Also known as the wishbone, it is unique to birds and results from the fusion of the collarbones.

STERNUM
Hyperdeveloped in flying birds, the sternum's long keel facilitates the attachment of the pectorals.

DOWNWARD FLAP

Right wing · Humerus · Tendon · Left wing · Coracoids

1 THE LARGER PECTORALS CONTRACT.

Keel · Legs · **THE SMALLER PECTORALS RELAX.**

2 THE DESCENDING FLAPPING OF THE WINGS TAKES PLACE.

UPWARD FLAP

Tendon · Right wing · Coracoids · Left wing · Humerus

1 THE LARGER PECTORAL MUSCLES RELAX.

Legs

2 THE SMALLER PECTORALS CONTRACT AND DRAW THE WINGS INWARDS.

WINGS

Without doubt, wings are the greatest adaptation of birds. Strong tendons travel through the wings and merge into the hand bones, where the feathers are attached.

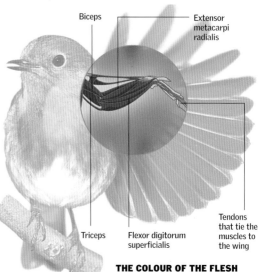

Biceps · Extensor metacarpi radialis

Triceps · Flexor digitorum superficialis · Tendons that tie the muscles to the wing

THE COLOUR OF THE FLESH
depends on the blood circulation in the muscles: the more circulation, the redder the flesh. Flying birds have red flesh, while non-flying birds, such as chickens, have white flesh.

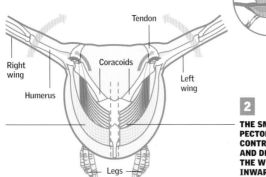

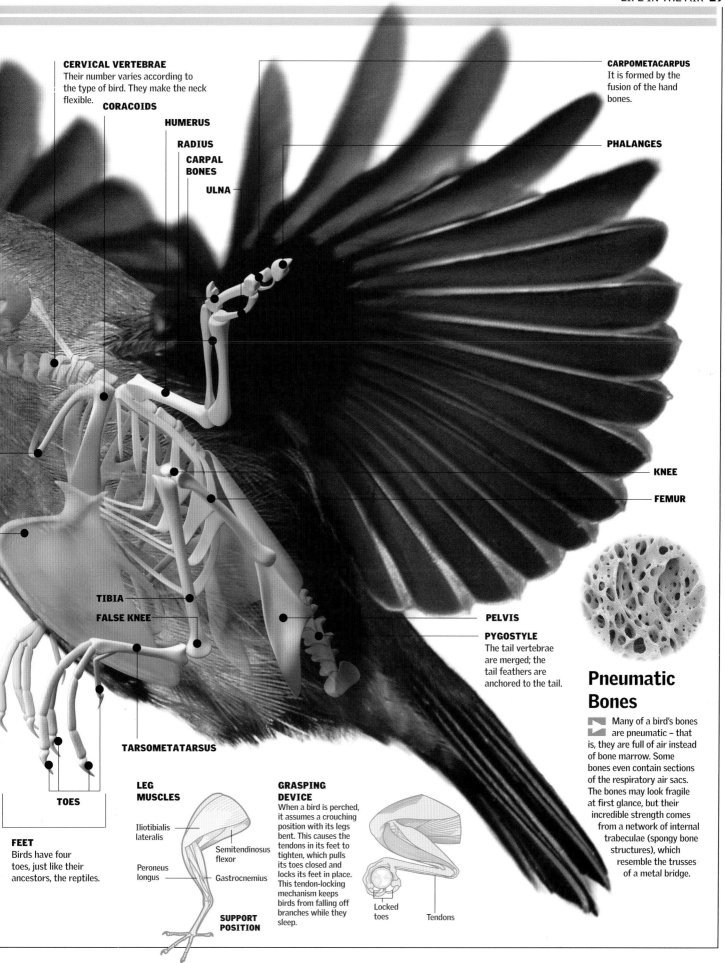

CERVICAL VERTEBRAE
Their number varies according to the type of bird. They make the neck flexible.

CORACOIDS

HUMERUS

RADIUS

CARPAL BONES

ULNA

CARPOMETACARPUS
It is formed by the fusion of the hand bones.

PHALANGES

KNEE

FEMUR

TIBIA

FALSE KNEE

PELVIS

PYGOSTYLE
The tail vertebrae are merged; the tail feathers are anchored to the tail.

TARSOMETATARSUS

TOES

FEET
Birds have four toes, just like their ancestors, the reptiles.

Pneumatic Bones

Many of a bird's bones are pneumatic – that is, they are full of air instead of bone marrow. Some bones even contain sections of the respiratory air sacs. The bones may look fragile at first glance, but their incredible strength comes from a network of internal trabeculae (spongy bone structures), which resemble the trusses of a metal bridge.

LEG MUSCLES

Iliotibialis lateralis

Semitendinosus flexor

Peroneus longus

Gastrocnemius

SUPPORT POSITION

GRASPING DEVICE
When a bird is perched, it assumes a crouching position with its legs bent. This causes the tendons in its feet to tighten, which pulls its toes closed and locks its feet in place. This tendon-locking mechanism keeps birds from falling off branches while they sleep.

Locked toes

Tendons

Feathers

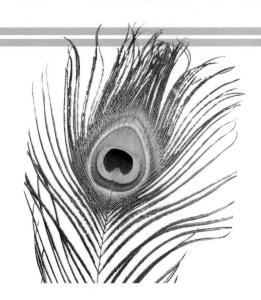

Feathers are the feature that distinguishes birds from all other animals. They make birds strikingly colourful, protect them against cold and intense heat, enable them to move easily through the air and water and hide them from enemies. Feathers are also one of the reasons why human beings have domesticated, caught and hunted birds. A bird's set of feathers is called its 'plumage', and its colour is essential for reproductive success.

Structure

 The structure of a feather has two parts: a shaft and a blade. The shaft is called the rachis, and the part connected to the bird's skin is called the calamus, or quill. The movement of a feather is generated in the rachis. The blade is composed of barbs that branch into barbules. The feather's blade, in which the barbules have a series of barbicels, or hooklets, at the tip, is called a vane. The interlocking hooklets in the vane create a network that adds rigidity and resistance to the feather. It also defines the characteristic aerodynamic shape of feathers and helps make the feather waterproof. When feathers wear out, birds have the ability to replace them with new ones.

1 A swelling, or papilla, develops in the bird's skin.

2 In the papilla, special skin cells form a follicle.

3 A tube that will extend from its base and become a feather grows in the follicle.

EDGE
The edge presents an excellent aerodynamic profile for flying.

RACHIS
A feather's main shaft, similar to a hollow rod

HOLLOW INTERIOR

INNER PULP OF THE SHAFT

INFERIOR UMBILICUS
The orifice at the base of the calamus, into which the dermic papilla penetrates. New feathers receive nourishment through it.

CALAMUS
It provides the necessary nutrients for feathers to grow. Nerve endings that stimulate the feather's movement are found at its base. This allows the bird to detect changes in its surroundings.

SUPERIOR UMBILICUS
It contains some loose barbs. Some feathers have a secondary rachis, the hyporachis.

BARBS
are slim, straight filaments that grow perpendicular to the rachis.

Types of Feathers

 There are three main types of feathers, classified according to placement: those closest to the body are down, or underlying feathers; those at the top are contour feathers; and those on the wings and tail are flight feathers, often referred to as remiges (on the wings) and rectrices (on the tail).

DOWN
These light and silky feathers protect the bird against the cold. They have a short rachis, or none at all. Their barbs are long, and their barbules lack hooklets. In general, down is the first type of feather that birds develop when they hatch.

CONTOUR
Also called covert feathers, they are short and rounded. They are more rigid than down feathers. Because they cover the body, wings and tail, they give birds their shape as they fly.

What Is Keratin?

Keratin is a protein that forms part of the outermost layer of a bird's skin, just as it does in other vertebrate animal groups. Keratin is the main component of feathers, hair and scales. Its distinct resistance helps keep the hooklets woven together in the vane. This allows birds' feathers to maintain their shape in spite of the pressure exerted by the air during flight.

BARBS

BARBULES

HOOKLETS, OR BARBICELS

VANE, OR BLADE
Its outer portion contains a great number of barbicels.

25,000

THE NUMBER OF FEATHERS THAT LARGE BIRDS, SUCH AS SWANS, CAN HAVE.
In contrast, the number of feathers small birds, such as songbirds, can have varies between 2,000 and 4,000.

TRAILING EDGE NOTCH
The turbulence during flight is reduced by this notch, found near the tip of the wing.

PREENING THE PLUMAGE
Birds need to preen their feathers with their bills not only to keep them clean and free of parasites but also to keep them lubricated, which helps birds resist wet weather. Birds touch their uropygial, or preen, glands with their bills. Then they distribute the oil and wax this gland produces all over their plumage. This task is a matter of survival.

SELF-CLEANING WITH ANTS
Some birds, such as certain tanagers, catch ants with their bills and grind them. They then oil their feathers with the ground-up ants. It is believed that the acid juices from the squashed ants work as a repellent against lice and other external parasites.

DUST BATH
Birds such as pheasants, partridges, ostriches, pigeons and sparrows perform dust baths to control the amount of grease on their feathers.

PTERYLAE AND APTERIA
At first glance, a bird's body is covered with feathers. However, feathers do not grow all over the body but rather in particular areas called 'pterylae'. This is where the papillae, which create new feathers, are found. The shape and placement of pterylae vary according to species. Pterylae are surrounded by naked areas, called 'apteria', in which feathers do not grow. Penguins are the only birds whose bodies are completely covered with feathers. This characteristic makes it possible for them to live in cold regions.

IMPERIAL HERON
Powder down keeps its plumage waterproof.

SPECIAL FEATHERS

Vibrissae are formed of only one filament, sometimes with loose barbs at the base. They perform a tactile function and are located around the bill of insect-eating species. Filoplumes are hairlike feathers that may be sensory or decorative and are usually blended with contour feathers.

Filoplumes

Vibrissae

POWDER DOWN

This special type of feather can be found on some aquatic birds. The feathers grow constantly and break off at the tip into small waxy scales. This 'powder' is preened into the plumage to provide protection.

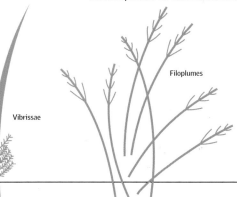

First, the Egg

Birds may have inherited their reproductive method from their predecessors, the theropod reptiles. In general, they lay as many eggs as they can care for until the chicks become independent. Highly adapted to the environment, the eggs of the same species have varying shapes and colours. These variations help keep them safe from predators. They also vary greatly in size: the egg of an ostrich is 2,000 times bigger than that of a hummingbird.

How It Forms

Birds have only one functional ovary, the left one, which grows dramatically during the mating season. The ovule can descend and form what are known as unfertilized eggs (the type used in cooking). If the egg is fertilized, embryonic development begins. The ovule, fertilized or not, descends to the cloaca in a few hours or days. The eggshell begins to be formed at the isthmus, through the secretion of calcium. At first soft, the shell hardens when it comes in contact with the air.

3 Most birds' organs are formed in the first hours of incubation.

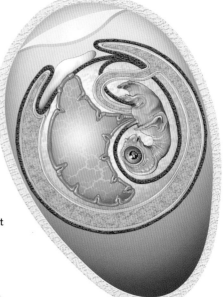

2 As it feeds to grow, the embryo produces waste that is kept in a special sac.

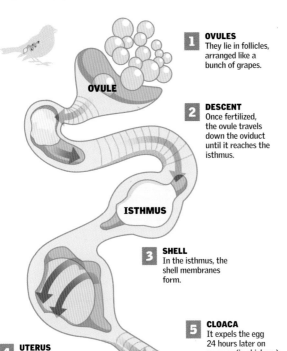

1 OVULES
They lie in follicles, arranged like a bunch of grapes.

OVULE

2 DESCENT
Once fertilized, the ovule travels down the oviduct until it reaches the isthmus.

ISTHMUS

3 SHELL
In the isthmus, the shell membranes form.

5 CLOACA
It expels the egg 24 hours later on average (in chickens).

4 UTERUS
The egg becomes pigmented, and the shell hardens.

CLOACA

WASTE SAC

CHORION
protects and contains the embryo and its food.

YOLK

YOLK SAC

ALBUMEN

1 The egg contains an embryo in one side of the yolk. The yolk is held in the middle of the white (albumen) by two protein cords, isolating it from the outside world.

EMBRYO

PROTEIN CORD (CHALAZA)

CLUTCH

A group of eggs laid at one time is called a 'clutch'. During the mating season, a sparrow can have several clutches. If some eggs are removed, the sparrow can replace them without difficulty.

SHAPE

It depends on the pressure exerted by the oviduct walls. The large end emerges first.

Oval: The most frequent

Conical: Prevents falling

Spherical: Reduces the surface area

COLOUR AND TEXTURE

Both texture and colour help parents locate their eggs.

Light Egg

Dark Egg

Speckled Egg

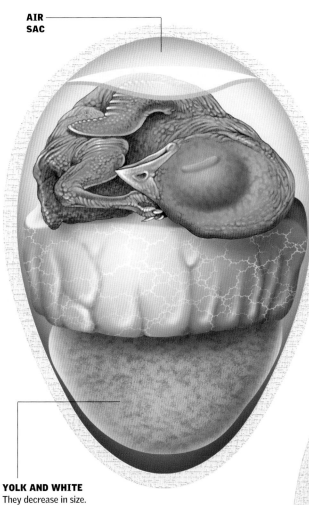

AIR SAC

YOLK AND WHITE
They decrease in size.

THE SHELL

Formed by a solid layer of calcium carbonate (calcite), it has pores that enable the chick to breathe. Bacteria are kept out by two semipermeable membranes that line the shell.

PORE   SHELL   OUTER AND INNER MEMBRANES

OXYGEN

CO_2 AND WATER VAPOUR

8%

IS THE PROPORTION OF AN EGG TAKEN UP BY THE EGGSHELL.

The bill and scales of the legs harden towards the end, when the chick is formed and reaches a size similar to that of the egg. At that point, rotation begins so that the chick will be positioned to break its shell.

SIZE

There is no exact proportion between the size of a bird and its egg.

500 g
(1 lb)
KIWI'S EGG

60 g
(2 oz)
CHICKEN'S EGG

5

By the time the chick is ready to break the shell, it is taking up all the space inside the egg. The chick is cramped with its legs against its chest. This enables it to open the shell with small movements and with the help of a hard point at the tip of its bill, called an "egg tooth."

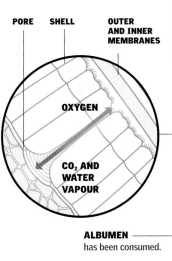

ALBUMEN
has been consumed.

YOLK
disappears into the body.

No Flying Allowed

A few birds have lost their ability to fly. Their main characteristic is wing loss or reduction, although for some a remarkable size may be the cause of their inability to fly. Flightless bird species include runners (ostriches, cassowaries, emus, rheas, kiwis); extremely fast birds that live in remote areas of New Zealand; and swimmers, such as penguins, that have developed extraordinary aquatic abilities.

AFRICAN OSTRICH
A single species inhabits eastern and southern Africa. Adults reach a height of 2.75 m (9 ft) and a weight of 150 kg (330 lb).

Super Swimmers

Penguins' bodies are covered with three layers of small, overlapping feathers. A penguin has small limbs and a hydrodynamic shape that helps it swim with agility and speed. Dense, waterproof plumage and a layer of fat insulate the bird from the low temperatures of the regions where it lives. Because its bones are rigid and compact, it is able to submerge itself easily. This adaptation distinguishes it from flying birds, whose bones are light and hollow.

AMAZING FACT

The dodo was a flightless bird endemic to Mauritius that was hunted to extinction by sailors in the seventeenth century.

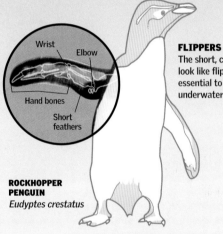

Wrist
Elbow
Hand bones
Short feathers

ROCKHOPPER PENGUIN
Eudyptes crestatus

FLIPPERS
The short, compact wings look like flippers. They are essential to the penguin's underwater movements.

SMALL HEAD

LONG NECK

ATROPHIED WINGS

PELVIS

FLAT STERNUM

ROBUST BONE

PENGUIN HEADING TO THE WATER

HUNTING
The wings work like flippers. The foot – with four joined toes pointing backwards – and the tail steer the direction of the dive.

BREATHING
When looking for food, penguins need to leave the water and take a breath between plunges.

RELAXING
When resting in the water, they move slowly. They float on the surface with their heads up and balance their bodies with their wings and feet.

RUNNER'S CHEST

The keel-shaped sternum of flying and swimming birds offers a larger surface for attachment of the pectoral muscles. The flat sternum of running birds has a smaller surface and, consequently, less mobility.

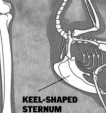

KEEL-SHAPED STERNUM

The Ratites

Running birds belong to the group of the ratites (*rata* = raft, an allusion to the flat sternum). The forelimbs are either atrophied or have functions unrelated to flying. The hind limbs have very strong muscles as well as sturdy, vigorous bones. Another difference is found in the sternum. It is a flat bone without a keel, which flying and swimming birds possess. Wild ratites can be found only in the Southern Hemisphere. The Tinamidae (tinamous), native to Central and South America, belong to this group.

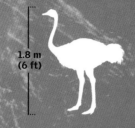

1.8 m (6 ft)

1.2 m (4 ft)

1.4 m (4½ ft)

0.4 m (1¼ ft)

STRUTHIONIFORMES
The ostrich is the only species in this group. It uses its wings for balance when running fast. It has only two toes on each foot. The adult male can weigh up to 150 kg (330 lb).

RHEIFORMES
Rheas are common in South American countries, such as Argentina. They look like ostriches but are smaller. Their three-toed feet allow them to chase prey. Their long necks and excellent eyesight make them skilful hunters.

CASUARIIFORMES
Cassowaries are agile runners and swimmers. The colours on their necks and heads are distinctive. A bony hoof protects them from vegetation when they run. They have long, sharp talons on their feet.

APTERYGIFORMES
Kiwis. These birds have four toes on each foot, and their feathers look like fur because they do not have barbules. They use their keen sense of smell to find insects, usually at night. They lay only one large egg.

MAORI HEN
Gallirallus australis

ASIA

OCEANIA

AUSTRALIA NEW ZEALAND

0.6 m (2 ft)

Running and Kicking

Ostriches usually run to escape from predators or to hunt small lizards and rodents. In both cases, because of their strong legs, they are able to reach a speed of 72 km/h (45 mph) and to maintain it for 20 minutes. When running is not enough to protect the bird, it may resort to kicking to discourage its attacker. In courtship displays, forceful stamping is also used to win over females.

GREATER DIVERSITY
Running birds can be found in many parts of the world, largely because of human intervention. The area where flightless birds have diversified the most is Oceania (including Australia, New Zealand and Papua New Guinea), due to continental isolation.

18
VERTEBRAE IN THE NECK OF AN OSTRICH.

Other Walkers

More than 260 species belong to the order Galliformes, which includes chickens, turkeys and pheasants. The birds in this group have keels, and they will perform abrupt and fast flights, but only in extreme situations. Their feet are suitable for walking, running and scratching the ground. This group includes the birds that human beings use the most. In general, females are in charge of incubating and raising the young.

TARSUS METATARSUS

PHALANGEAL CUSHION

PHALANGES

TOE

CLAW

PLANTAR CUSHION

ON TWO TOES
With just two toes, the contact surface between the foot and the ground is relatively small. This is an advantage when moving on land.

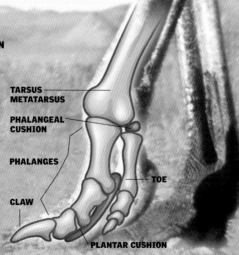

1 Taking a run and jump

2 Clumsy and flapping fast

3 Emergency landing

Freshwater Birds

This group includes birds that vary greatly – from common kingfishers to ducks to storks – and covers a wide spectrum. Freshwater birds live in rivers, lakes and ponds for at least part of the year and are perfectly adapted to aquatic life. Some are excellent swimmers, whereas others are great divers. An important group with long legs wades in watercourses as they fish. Freshwater birds have a varied diet and are mostly omnivorous.

Ducks and Distant Cousins

The order Anseriformes includes birds that are very familiar to humans: ducks, geese and swans, for example. They have short, webbed feet and wide, flat bills lined with lamellae (combs) that enable them to filter their food, catch fish and scrape the beds of rivers and ponds. Most are omnivorous and aquatic (either staying on the surface or diving), although some species spend more time on land. They are widely distributed, and the plumage of males becomes very colourful during the courtship season.

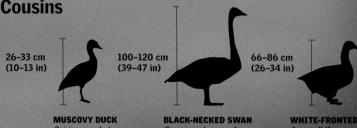

26–33 cm
(10–13 in)

MUSCOVY DUCK
Cairina moschata

100–120 cm
(39–47 in)

BLACK-NECKED SWAN
Cygnus melancoryphus

66–86 cm
(26–34 in)

WHITE-FRONTED GOOSE
Anser albifrons

FOLDED WEB

UNFOLDED WEB

HOW THEY USE THEIR FEET TO SWIM

A duck moves its feet in two ways. To advance, it spreads out its toes and uses its webbed feet to row. It closes the toes before bringing the foot forward again. If the bird wants to turn, only one foot pushes to the side.

A DUCK'S DIET

1 It swims on the surface, looking for food underneath the water.

2 It sticks its head into the water, abruptly pushes back its feet, and turns its neck downwards.

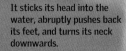

3 It floats face down and pokes around on the bottom with its bill.

ORIFICES
Open and oval

LAMELLAE
Comblike structures
around the inside
edges of the bill

DUCK BILLS

are flat, wide and slightly depressed towards the middle.
In general, their shape does not vary much, but there are
species with tiny bills (the mandarin duck, for example).

5–10 cm
(2–4 in)

2.7 cm (just
over 1 in)

SHOVEL-SHAPED BILL:
Typical of many ducks. The
size varies.

MANDARIN DUCK BILL:
One of the smallest-billed
species.

**FULVOUS
WHISTLING
DUCK**
*Dendrocygna
bicolor*

Wading Birds

These birds belong to an artificial order since,
from a genetic perspective, the species are
not related. They are grouped together because
adaptation to the same habitat has caused them
to develop similar shapes: long bills and necks to
perform skilful movements and thin legs designed
to wade across the water as they fish. Herons form
a special group because they are cosmopolitan and
because they have powder down in their plumage. Ibis
and storks also occur in many parts of the world. Birds
that have spoon- and hammer-shaped bills are found
primarily in Africa.

Divers and Other Fishers

Diving birds such as grebes feed on fish and aquatic insects. They are
excellent swimmers but clumsy on land as their legs are set so far back
on their body. Kingfishers find their prey by watching the water closely from
a perch above it, then diving in to spear the fish with their bills. Curlews,
sandpipers and their relatives are shorebirds, wandering along the water's
edge in search of food. Their long legs keep their bodies out of the water. They
are not swimmers.

30–40 cm
(12–16 in)

40 cm
(16 in)

18 cm
(7 in)

GREBE
Podiceps sp.

STONE CURLEW
Burhinus oedicnemus

**COMMON
KINGFISHER**
Alcedo atthis
(Also known as the
Eurasian Kingfisher)

AMAZING FACT

Pelicans
have long bills
with lower mandibles
that open into huge
expandable pouches,
which they use to
scoop up fish as
they swim.

**THE BILL OF
AN IBIS**
is long and thin,
ideal to stick in
the mud to look
for food.

WHITE IBIS
Edocimus albus

THE LEGS OF AN IBIS
keep the bird above the water
but close enough to fish. Ibis
also stir up the beds of lakes
and ponds.

IBIS (*Ibis* sp.):
Some filtrate, and others fish.

STORK (*Ciconia* sp.):
It fishes with its long bill.

SHOEBILL (*Balaeniceps rex*):
It eats among floating sedges.

HERON (*Egretta* sp.):
It fishes with its sharp bill.

COMMON SPOONBILL
(*Platalea leucorodia*): It eats
several types of aquatic animals.

HAMMERKOP (*Scopus
umbretta*): It fishes and hunts
small animals.

Armed to Hunt

Birds of prey are hunters and are carnivorous by nature. They are perfectly equipped to eat living animals. Their eyesight is far sharper than that of human beings; their ears are designed to determine the precise status of their prey; they have strong, sharp talons; and they can kill a small mammal with the pressure of their talons alone. Their hook-shaped bills can kill prey by tearing its neck with a single peck. Eagles, falcons, vultures and owls are examples of birds of prey. Birds of prey can be diurnal or nocturnal, and they are always on the lookout.

Diurnal and Nocturnal

Eagles, falcons and vultures are diurnal birds of prey, whereas owls are nocturnal – that is, they are active during the night. The two groups are not closely related. These birds' main prey includes small mammals, reptiles and insects. Once they locate the victim, they glide towards it. Nocturnal birds of prey are specially adapted: their eyesight is highly developed, their eyes are oriented forwards, and their hearing is sharp. The feathers on their wings are arranged in such a way that they make no noise when the bird is flying. In order to protect themselves while sleeping during the day, they have dull plumage, which helps them blend in with their surroundings.

EURASIAN EAGLE OWL
Bubo bubo
Its ears are asymmetrical and can determine the location of prey with great precision.

BALD EAGLE
Haliaeetus leucocephalus
It has a visual field of 220 degrees and a bifocal vision of 50 degrees.

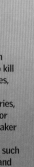

CERE
Fleshy formation, somewhat thick and soft

TIP
Where the tooth is located

NOSTRIL
Olfactory canals

Zone-tailed Hawk
Buteo albonotatus

Bills

The bills of birds of prey are hook-shaped. Some species have a tooth that works like a knife, allowing them to kill their prey, tear its skin and muscle tissues, and get to the food easily. The structure and shape of the bills of birds of prey varies, depending on the species. Scavengers (for example, vultures and condors) have weaker bills because the tissues of animals in decomposition are softer. Other species, such as falcons, catch prey with their talons and use their bills to finish it off with a violent stab to the neck, breaking its spine.

BALD EAGLE
Its hooked bill is a shape common to many birds of prey.

SPARROW HAWK
Its thin bill enables it to extract snails from their shells.

FALCON
It can break the spine of its prey with its upper bill.

GOSHAWK
Its strong bill means that it can catch prey as large as hares.

OWL PELLETS

Owls produce pellets. They swallow their prey whole and regurgitate the indigestible substances. The study of pellets makes it possible to determine the fauna of small areas with great precision.

DIMENSIONS

The wings of birds of prey are adapted to suit their flying requirements. They can measure up to 3 m (10 ft).

CONDORS
0.95–2.9 m (3–9½ ft)

EAGLES
1.35–2.45 m (4½–8 ft)

BUZZARDS
1.2–1.5 m (4–5 ft)

KITES
0.8–1.95 m (2½–6½ ft)

RED-BACKED HAWK
1.05–1.35 m (3½–4½ feet)

FALCONS
0.67–1.25 m (2¼–4 ft)

HOW VULTURES HUNT

1 Vultures feed mainly on carrion, although they are able to attack a living animal if it is vulnerable and the situation presents itself.

2 Thanks to their ability to glide on thermals, vultures can find carcasses on which to feed without wasting energy.

3 Once they find food, they must analyse the territory to know if they will be able to take flight again soon.

AMAZING FACT

The eyesight of raptors is up to eight times sharper than ours, and a golden eagle can spot its prey from 1.6 km (1 mile) away.

Feet

Most birds of prey catch and kill their prey with their talons and tear away the meat with their bills. For this reason, birds' feet constitute one of the morphological characteristics of a species. The toes end in strong, sharp claws that the bird uses as pincers to catch its prey in flight. The osprey also has barbs on its feet, which help it to grip slippery fish.

GRIFFON VULTURE
Its long toes do not have a good grasp.

FISH HAWK
Its toes have rough scales like barbs, which help it to catch and hold on to fish.

GOSHAWK
It has calluses at the tips of its toes.

SPARROW HAWK
Its feet have tarsi and short, strong toes.

The Perchers Club

Passerines – perching birds – form the largest, most diverse order of birds. What distinguishes them? Their feet are suited for perching and, therefore, for living among trees, although they can also stroll on the ground and through brush. They inhabit terrestrial environments all over the world, from deserts to woodlands. Their complex sounds and songs originate from a very well-developed vocal organ called a 'syrinx'. Their chicks are nidicolous – that is, naked and blind at birth. In youth, they are agile and vivacious, with very attractive, abundant and colourful plumage.

AMAZING FACT

The songbird's syrinx is at the base of the trachea, where it forks into the lungs, allowing some birds to produce more than one sound at a time.

The Smallest

Passerines are small in comparison with other birds. They range in size from tiny bee hummingbirds (*Mellisuga helenae*) to the heavily built common raven (*Corvus corax*).

HUMMINGBIRDS
5 CM (2 IN)
They get so much energy from nectar that they can double their body weight by eating. However, they use this energy up during their frantic flights.

SWALLOWS
19 CM (7 IN)
Swallows have great agility and skill. These popular migratory birds have bodies suited for long journeys.

RAVENS
65 CM (26 IN)
They eat everything: fruits, insects, reptiles, small mammals and birds. They are skilful robbers of all kinds of food.

PASSERIFORMES

Passerines have been classified into 79 families, with more than 5,400 different species.

50%

THE PERCENTAGE OF BIRDS INCLUDED IN THE ORDER PASSERIFORMES.

Family Album

Four basic groups have been established to facilitate the study of families: broadbills, passerines with wide bills; ovenbirds, with dull, brown plumage, noted for the great care they take in building their nests; lyrebirds, whose tails have two showy external feathers that are longer than the others; and songbirds, with their elaborate and pleasant singing. Songbirds form the most numerous and varied group, which includes swallows, goldfinches, canaries, vireos and ravens.

LYREBIRDS
There are only two species of these Passeriformes, and they are found only in Australia. They are very melodic and are excellent imitators of other birds. They can even imitate the sound of inanimate objects, such as motors or mobile phones.

HARD, SHORT BILL
The bill of a swallow is very short and tough. The swallow can use it to catch insects in flight.

SINGER
This blue-and-white swallow (*Notiochelidon cyanoleuca*) intones its pleasant and trilling chant in flight and while perching. Larks, goldfinches, canaries and other passerines delight us with their trills and songs.

SYRINX
This organ is the equivalent of the human larynx, but has no vocal cords. The syrinx muscles move the bronchial walls, which, as air passes through, produce the melodic sounds that characterize songbirds.

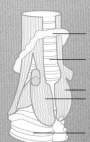

SYRINGEAL CARTILAGE

TRACHEAL RING

BRONCHIAL MUSCLES

BRONCHIAL RING

LIVING AT THE EXTREMES

Swallows range from one hemisphere to the other. They raise their chicks in the north and fly to the south to spend winter there. Their sense of direction is remarkable. They can find and reuse their nests after returning from a migration.

A In the summer, during the reproductive season, they live in the Northern Hemisphere. In general, neotropical migratory birds are those that reproduce above the Tropic of Cancer.

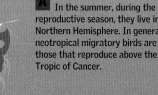

BARN SWALLOW
(*Hirundo rustica*)
Swallows spend most of their time travelling to temperate zones.

B When winter arrives in the Northern Hemisphere, they perform a mass migration to the south. The American barn swallow travels 22,000 km (14,000 miles) during its migratory trip from the United States to southern Argentina.

PERCHING FOOT
Three toes project forwards, and the well-developed hallux projects backwards. This type of foot allows the bird to hold on tightly to branches.

BROADBILLS
They are native to Africa and Asia and inhabit tropical zones with dense vegetation. They eat insects and fruits. They produce non-vocal sounds with the flapping of their wings. They do this during courtship, and the sound can be heard 60 m (200 ft) away.

OVENBIRDS AND THEIR RELATIVES
Ovenbird nests are completely covered structures, built from clay. Other members of this family build nests with leaves and straw, weaving interesting baskets. Still others dig tunnels in the ground.

Skin with Scales

Reptiles are vertebrates, meaning that they are animals with a spinal column. Their skin is hard, dry and flaky. Like birds, most reptiles are born from eggs deposited on land. The offspring hatch fully formed without passing through a larval stage. The first reptiles appeared during the height of the Carboniferous period in the Palaeozoic era. During the Mesozoic era, they evolved and flourished, which is why this period is also known as the age of reptiles. Only 5 of the 23 orders that existed then have living representatives today.

SOLOMON ISLAND SKINK
Corucia zebrata

EMBRIONIC MEMBRANES
All reptiles develop two: a protective amnion (egg sac) and a respiratory allantois (vascular foetal membrane).

EYES
are almost always small. In diurnal animals, the pupil is rounded.

NICTITATING MEMBRANE
It extends from the internal angle of the eye to cover the eyeball.

4,765
SPECIES OF LIZARDS EXIST.

Habitat

Reptiles have a great capacity to adapt, because they can occupy an incredible variety of environments. They live on every continent except Antarctica, and most countries have at least one species of terrestrial reptile. They can be found in the driest and hottest deserts, as well as the steamiest, most humid rainforests. They are especially common in the tropical and subtropical regions of Africa, Asia, Australia and the Americas, where high temperatures and a great diversity of prey allow them to thrive.

BLACK CAIMAN
Melanosuchus niger

Crocodiles

are distinguished by their usually large size. From neck to tail, their backs are covered in rows of bony plates, which can resemble spikes or teeth. Crocodiles appeared towards the end of the Triassic period, and they are the closest living relatives to both dinosaurs and birds. Their hearts are divided into four chambers, their brains show a high degree of development, and the musculature of their abdomens is so developed that it resembles the gizzards of birds. The larger species are very dangerous.

OVIPAROUS
Most reptiles are oviparous (they lay eggs); however, many species of snakes and lizards are ovoviviparous (they produce eggs that develop within the mother's body and give birth to live offspring).

THORAX AND ABDOMEN
are not separated by a diaphragm. Alligators breathe with the help of muscles on the walls of their body.

AMERICAN ALLIGATOR
Alligator mississippiensis

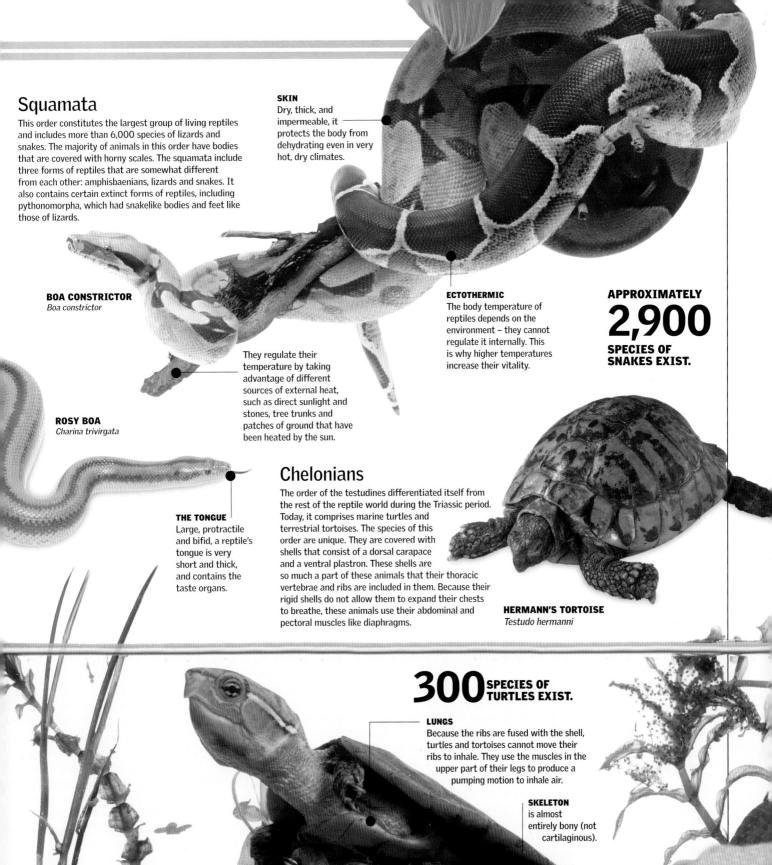

Squamata

This order constitutes the largest group of living reptiles and includes more than 6,000 species of lizards and snakes. The majority of animals in this order have bodies that are covered with horny scales. The squamata include three forms of reptiles that are somewhat different from each other: amphisbaenians, lizards and snakes. It also contains certain extinct forms of reptiles, including pythonomorpha, which had snakelike bodies and feet like those of lizards.

SKIN
Dry, thick, and impermeable, it protects the body from dehydrating even in very hot, dry climates.

ECTOTHERMIC
The body temperature of reptiles depends on the environment – they cannot regulate it internally. This is why higher temperatures increase their vitality.

BOA CONSTRICTOR
Boa constrictor

They regulate their temperature by taking advantage of different sources of external heat, such as direct sunlight and stones, tree trunks and patches of ground that have been heated by the sun.

ROSY BOA
Charina trivirgata

THE TONGUE
Large, protractile and bifid, a reptile's tongue is very short and thick, and contains the taste organs.

APPROXIMATELY
2,900
SPECIES OF SNAKES EXIST.

Chelonians

The order of the testudines differentiated itself from the rest of the reptile world during the Triassic period. Today, it comprises marine turtles and terrestrial tortoises. The species of this order are unique. They are covered with shells that consist of a dorsal carapace and a ventral plastron. These shells are so much a part of these animals that their thoracic vertebrae and ribs are included in them. Because their rigid shells do not allow them to expand their chests to breathe, these animals use their abdominal and pectoral muscles like diaphragms.

HERMANN'S TORTOISE
Testudo hermanni

300 SPECIES OF TURTLES EXIST.

LUNGS
Because the ribs are fused with the shell, turtles and tortoises cannot move their ribs to inhale. They use the muscles in the upper part of their legs to produce a pumping motion to inhale air.

SKELETON
is almost entirely bony (not cartilaginous).

CENTRAL AMERICAN RIVER TURTLE
Dermatemys mawii

Lizards

Lizards are the largest group of reptiles. They live in most environments except for extremely cold regions, because they cannot regulate their own body temperatures. There are land-dwelling, underground, tree-dwelling and even semiaquatic lizards. They can walk, climb, dig, run and even glide. Most lizards have differentiated heads, movable eyelids, a rigid lower jaw, four five-toed feet, a long body covered with scales and a long tail. Some can even shed their tails when threatened.

AMAZING FACT

If a lizard sheds its tail to escape a predator, the tail goes on wiggling to fool the attacker into thinking it is still holding the whole lizard.

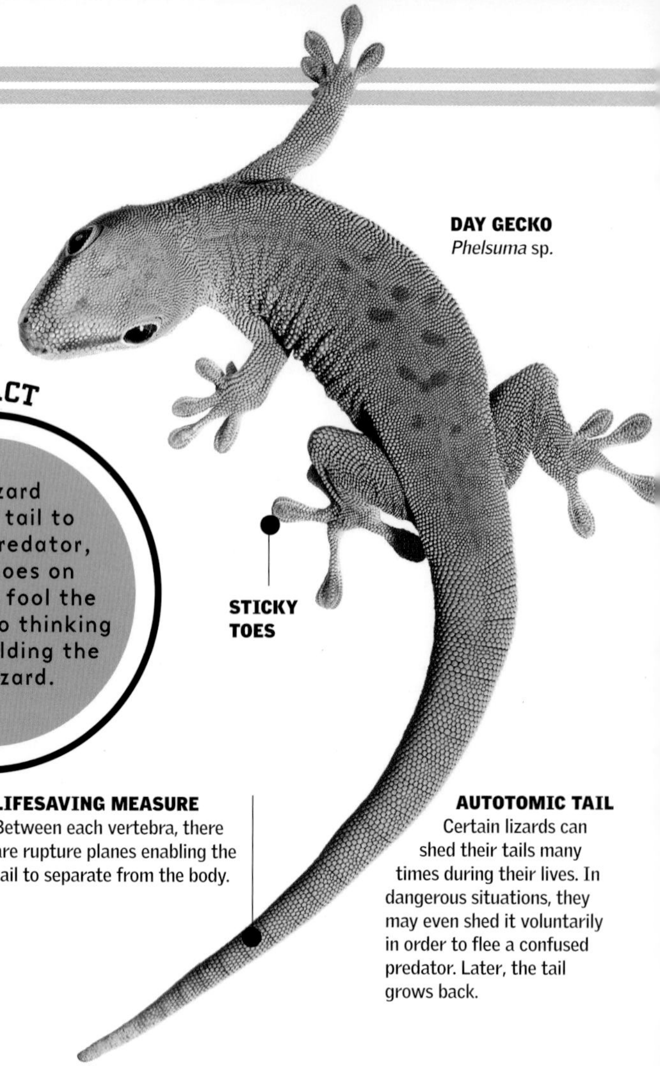

DAY GECKO
Phelsuma sp.

STICKY TOES

Chameleons

live in Africa, especially in southeastern regions and on Madagascar. They live in forests, where they use their prehensile tails and toes to climb trees. Their well-known ability to change colour is important when they face danger or during courtship.

Camouflage

is an adaptive advantage. By blending in with the vegetation surrounding them, lizards can escape the notice of both their predators and their prey.

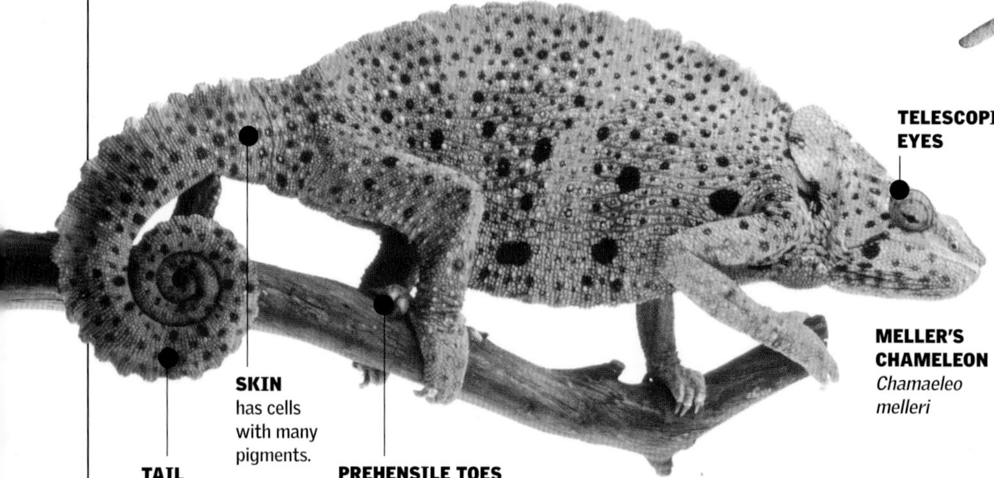

LIFESAVING MEASURE
Between each vertebra, there are rupture planes enabling the tail to separate from the body.

AUTOTOMIC TAIL
Certain lizards can shed their tails many times during their lives. In dangerous situations, they may even shed it voluntarily in order to flee a confused predator. Later, the tail grows back.

TELESCOPIC EYES

Geckos and Skinks

are lizardlike animals of the family Gekkonidae that live in warm regions. Their limbs are very small, or even nonexistent in some species. Their bodies are covered with smooth, shiny scales.

MELLER'S CHAMELEON
Chamaeleo melleri

SKIN
has cells with many pigments.

TAIL
curls up when necessary.

PREHENSILE TOES
can surround a branch and hold on tight.

CLAW

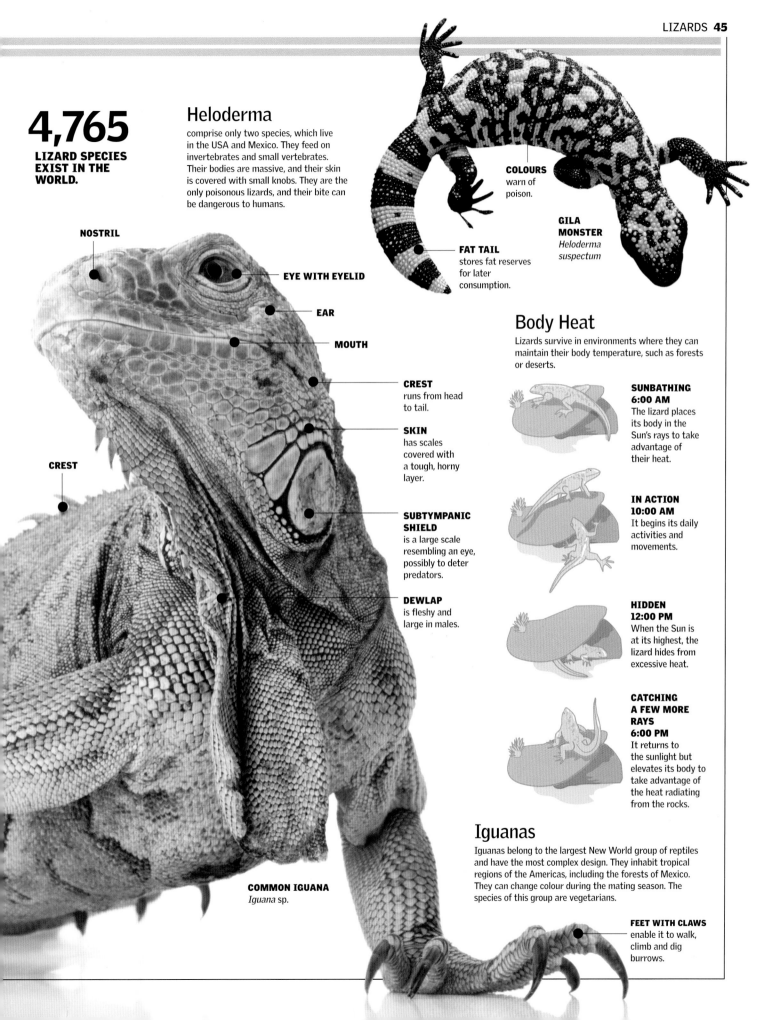

4,765
LIZARD SPECIES EXIST IN THE WORLD.

Heloderma

comprise only two species, which live in the USA and Mexico. They feed on invertebrates and small vertebrates. Their bodies are massive, and their skin is covered with small knobs. They are the only poisonous lizards, and their bite can be dangerous to humans.

COLOURS warn of poison.

GILA MONSTER *Heloderma suspectum*

FAT TAIL stores fat reserves for later consumption.

NOSTRIL

EYE WITH EYELID

EAR

MOUTH

CREST runs from head to tail.

SKIN has scales covered with a tough, horny layer.

SUBTYMPANIC SHIELD is a large scale resembling an eye, possibly to deter predators.

DEWLAP is fleshy and large in males.

CREST

COMMON IGUANA *Iguana* sp.

Body Heat

Lizards survive in environments where they can maintain their body temperature, such as forests or deserts.

SUNBATHING 6:00 AM
The lizard places its body in the Sun's rays to take advantage of their heat.

IN ACTION 10:00 AM
It begins its daily activities and movements.

HIDDEN 12:00 PM
When the Sun is at its highest, the lizard hides from excessive heat.

CATCHING A FEW MORE RAYS 6:00 PM
It returns to the sunlight but elevates its body to take advantage of the heat radiating from the rocks.

Iguanas

Iguanas belong to the largest New World group of reptiles and have the most complex design. They inhabit tropical regions of the Americas, including the forests of Mexico. They can change colour during the mating season. The species of this group are vegetarians.

FEET WITH CLAWS enable it to walk, climb and dig burrows.

Venerated and Feared

Crocodiles – along with their relatives, the alligators, caimans and gharials – are very ancient animals. They belong to the same group that included the dinosaurs and have changed very little in the last 65 million years. They can go for long periods without moving; during these times, they sun themselves or rest in the water. However, they can also swim, jump and even run at high speed to attack with force and precision. In spite of their ferocity, female crocodilians provide more care for their young than any other living group of reptiles.

LOWER JAW
The lower teeth are invisible when the mouth is closed.

SCALES
are flat on the tail.

GHARIAL
Gavialis gangeticus

HABITAT	Fresh water
NUMBER OF TYPES	One
DEGREE OF DANGER	Harmless

4–7 m (13–23 ft)

GHARIAL
has a long, narrow snout, with long front teeth.

CROCODILE
has a V-shaped snout, narrower than the alligator's.

ALLIGATOR
has a wide, short, U-shaped nose.

The Gharial

is the strangest of all crocodilians. Its long, narrow snout, with small, sharp teeth, sweeps through the water. Its interlocked, outward-curving teeth are perfect for catching slippery fish. Adult males drive away their rivals with loud buzzing sounds that they make by exhaling air through a bump on their nose.

SNOUT
Long, narrow nose

TEETH
are longest in front.

1 It moves forward with its four limbs.

The front legs begin the movement.

2 Its legs are suspended.

Then the hind legs come into action.

3 The cycle starts again.

The tail is raised to avoid acting as a brake.

15 km per hour (9 mph)
IS THE SPEED THEY CAN REACH AT A FULL RUN.

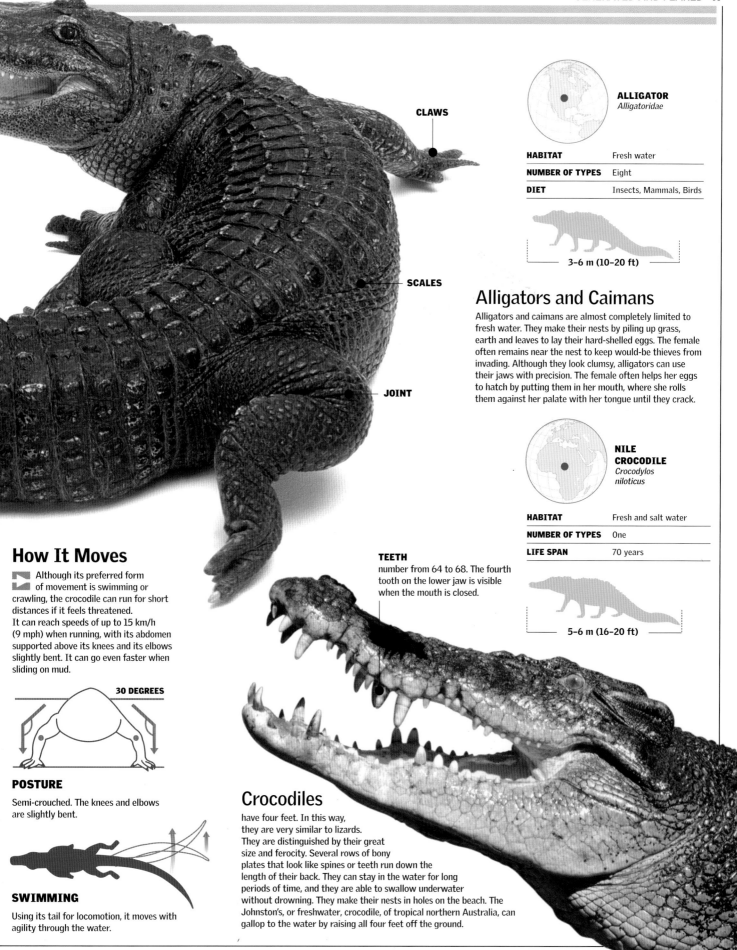

CLAWS

SCALES

JOINT

ALLIGATOR
Alligatoridae

HABITAT	Fresh water
NUMBER OF TYPES	Eight
DIET	Insects, Mammals, Birds

3–6 m (10–20 ft)

Alligators and Caimans

Alligators and caimans are almost completely limited to fresh water. They make their nests by piling up grass, earth and leaves to lay their hard-shelled eggs. The female often remains near the nest to keep would-be thieves from invading. Although they look clumsy, alligators can use their jaws with precision. The female often helps her eggs to hatch by putting them in her mouth, where she rolls them against her palate with her tongue until they crack.

NILE CROCODILE
Crocodylos niloticus

HABITAT	Fresh and salt water
NUMBER OF TYPES	One
LIFE SPAN	70 years

5–6 m (16–20 ft)

TEETH
number from 64 to 68. The fourth tooth on the lower jaw is visible when the mouth is closed.

How It Moves

Although its preferred form of movement is swimming or crawling, the crocodile can run for short distances if it feels threatened. It can reach speeds of up to 15 km/h (9 mph) when running, with its abdomen supported above its knees and its elbows slightly bent. It can go even faster when sliding on mud.

30 DEGREES

POSTURE

Semi-crouched. The knees and elbows are slightly bent.

SWIMMING

Using its tail for locomotion, it moves with agility through the water.

Crocodiles

have four feet. In this way, they are very similar to lizards. They are distinguished by their great size and ferocity. Several rows of bony plates that look like spines or teeth run down the length of their back. They can stay in the water for long periods of time, and they are able to swallow underwater without drowning. They make their nests in holes on the beach. The Johnston's, or freshwater, crocodile, of tropical northern Australia, can gallop to the water by raising all four feet off the ground.

Dangerous Coils

Snakes are scaly reptiles with long bodies and no legs. Some are poisonous, but others are not. Like all reptiles, they have a skeletal structure and a spinal column composed of a system of vertebrae. The anatomical differences between species reveal information about their habitats and diets – climbing snakes are long and thin, burrowing snakes are shorter and thicker, and sea snakes have flat tails that they use as fins.

COLD-BLOODED
Their temperature varies according to the environment. They do not generate their own body heat.

HEART
The ventricle has an incomplete partition.

OESOPHAGUS

LUNG

EMERALD TREE BOA
Corallus caninus

LARGE INTESTINE

TREE BRANCH
Boas can change colour to imitate the branch they are curled around.

Primitive Snakes

Boas and pythons were the first snake species to appear on Earth. Many have claws or spurs as vestiges of the ancient limbs of their ancestors. They are not poisonous, but they are the largest and strongest snakes. They live in trees, and some, such as the anaconda – a South American boa – live in rivers.

10 m
(33 ft)
THE LENGTH OF A PYTHON.

SPOTTED PYTHON
Antaresia maculosa
inhabits the forests of Australia.

THE SPINAL COLUMN
is composed of an assembly of jointed vertebrae with prolongations that protect the nerves and arteries. The system makes them enormously flexible.

VERTEBRAE

NEURAL ARCH

BODY OF THE VERTEBRA

HEMAL KEEL

FLOATING RIBS
allow the body to increase in size.

VERTEBRA

FLOATING RIB

RANGE OF MOTION OF THE RIBS

400 vertebrae
THE NUMBER A SNAKE CAN HAVE.

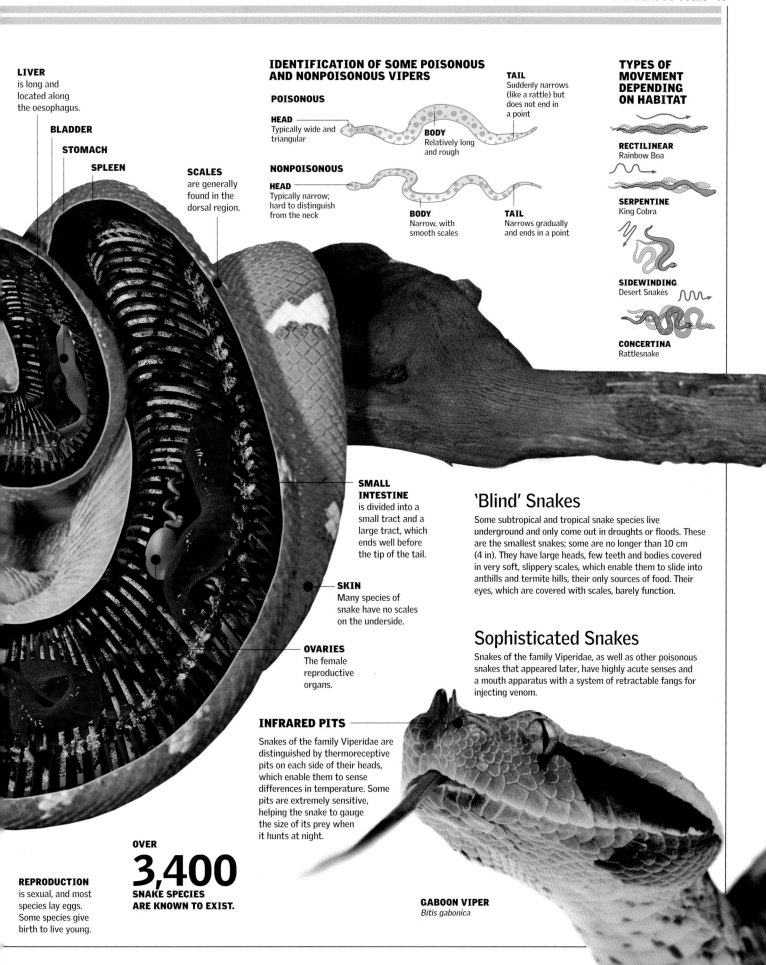

LIVER
is long and located along the oesophagus.

BLADDER

STOMACH

SPLEEN

SCALES
are generally found in the dorsal region.

IDENTIFICATION OF SOME POISONOUS AND NONPOISONOUS VIPERS

POISONOUS

HEAD
Typically wide and triangular

BODY
Relatively long and rough

TAIL
Suddenly narrows (like a rattle) but does not end in a point

NONPOISONOUS

HEAD
Typically narrow; hard to distinguish from the neck

BODY
Narrow, with smooth scales

TAIL
Narrows gradually and ends in a point

TYPES OF MOVEMENT DEPENDING ON HABITAT

RECTILINEAR
Rainbow Boa

SERPENTINE
King Cobra

SIDEWINDING
Desert Snakes

CONCERTINA
Rattlesnake

SMALL INTESTINE
is divided into a small tract and a large tract, which ends well before the tip of the tail.

SKIN
Many species of snake have no scales on the underside.

OVARIES
The female reproductive organs.

INFRARED PITS

Snakes of the family Viperidae are distinguished by thermoreceptive pits on each side of their heads, which enable them to sense differences in temperature. Some pits are extremely sensitive, helping the snake to gauge the size of its prey when it hunts at night.

'Blind' Snakes

Some subtropical and tropical snake species live underground and only come out in droughts or floods. These are the smallest snakes; some are no longer than 10 cm (4 in). They have large heads, few teeth and bodies covered in very soft, slippery scales, which enable them to slide into anthills and termite hills, their only sources of food. Their eyes, which are covered with scales, barely function.

Sophisticated Snakes

Snakes of the family Viperidae, as well as other poisonous snakes that appeared later, have highly acute senses and a mouth apparatus with a system of retractable fangs for injecting venom.

GABOON VIPER
Bitis gabonica

REPRODUCTION
is sexual, and most species lay eggs. Some species give birth to live young.

OVER
3,400
SNAKE SPECIES ARE KNOWN TO EXIST.

Fishy Features

Similar characteristics define nearly all fish, with a few rare exceptions. These aquatic animals are designed to live underwater; they have a jawbone and lidless eyes and are cold-blooded. They breathe through gills and are vertebrates – that is, they have a spinal column. They live in the oceans, from the poles to the Equator, as well as in bodies of fresh water and in streams. Some fish migrate, but very few can pass from salt water to fresh water or vice versa. Their fins enable them to swim and move in different directions. Marine animals such as dolphins, seals and whales are at times mistaken for fish, but they are actually mammals.

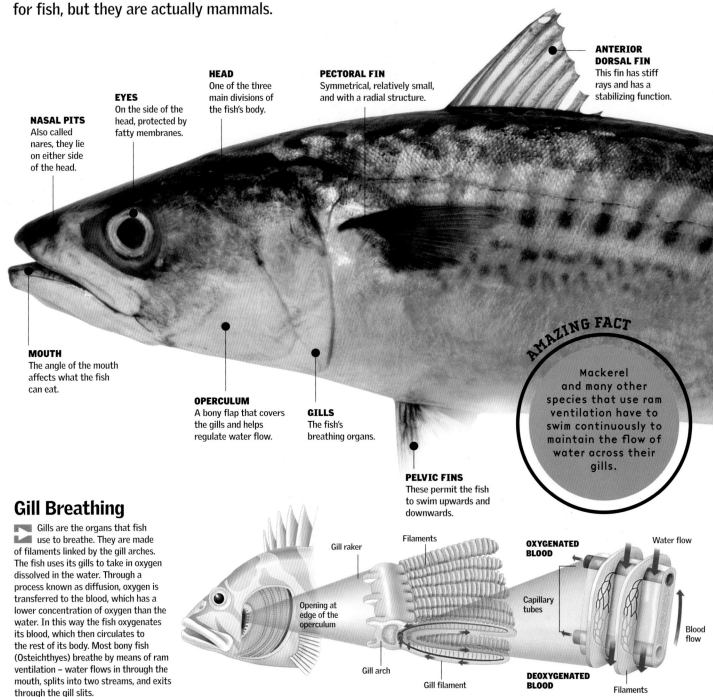

NASAL PITS
Also called nares, they lie on either side of the head.

EYES
On the side of the head, protected by fatty membranes.

HEAD
One of the three main divisions of the fish's body.

PECTORAL FIN
Symmetrical, relatively small, and with a radial structure.

ANTERIOR DORSAL FIN
This fin has stiff rays and has a stabilizing function.

MOUTH
The angle of the mouth affects what the fish can eat.

OPERCULUM
A bony flap that covers the gills and helps regulate water flow.

GILLS
The fish's breathing organs.

PELVIC FINS
These permit the fish to swim upwards and downwards.

AMAZING FACT

Mackerel and many other species that use ram ventilation have to swim continuously to maintain the flow of water across their gills.

Gill Breathing

Gills are the organs that fish use to breathe. They are made of filaments linked by the gill arches. The fish uses its gills to take in oxygen dissolved in the water. Through a process known as diffusion, oxygen is transferred to the blood, which has a lower concentration of oxygen than the water. In this way the fish oxygenates its blood, which then circulates to the rest of its body. Most bony fish (Osteichthyes) breathe by means of ram ventilation – water flows in through the mouth, splits into two streams, and exits through the gill slits.

Gill raker

Filaments

Opening at edge of the operculum

Gill arch

Gill filament

OXYGENATED BLOOD

Capillary tubes

DEOXYGENATED BLOOD

Water flow

Blood flow

Filaments

Near-fossils

Choanichthyes (Sarcopterygii) are archaic bony fish with fleshy fins. Some of them were the first animals to have lungs. Only a few species survive.

COELACANTH
Latimeria chalumnae
This species was thought to have become extinct millions of years ago, until one was discovered alive off the coast of South Africa in 1938; more of these fish were found later.

Jawless Fish

Of the ancient Agnathans, considered the first living vertebrates, only lampreys and hagfish are left.

SEA LAMPREY
Lampetra sp.
Its round, toothed mouth allows it to suck the blood of fish of various species. There are also freshwater lampreys.

SCALES
The scales are imbricate – that is, they overlap one another.

POSTERIOR DORSAL FIN
This soft-structured fin is located between the dorsal fin and the tail.

Just Cartilage

Cartilaginous fish, such as rays and sharks, have extremely flexible skeletons with little or no bone.

RAY
Raja miraletus
Its large fins send currents of water carrying plankton and small fish to its mouth. The ray is very fast.

LATERAL LINE
Fish have sensory organs all along this line.

With Spines

Osteichthyes is the most numerous class of fish. The skeleton has some level of calcification.

ATLANTIC MACKEREL
Scomber scombrus
This fish has no teeth. It lives in temperate waters, and its meat is considered delicious. It can live for more than ten years.

ANAL FIN
Soft, with a row of finlets.

TAIL MUSCLE
This is the strongest muscle in the fish.

CAUDAL FIN
It moves from side to side, propelling the fish forwards.

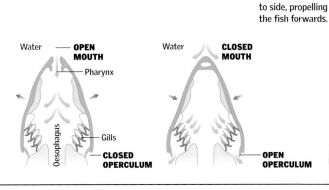

IN ACTION
Water enters the mouth and flows over the gills. After the gills extract oxygen, the water is expelled through the gill slits.

OPERCULUM
Opens and closes the openings where water exits

Water — **OPEN MOUTH**
Pharynx
Oesophagus
Gills
CLOSED OPERCULUM

Water **CLOSED MOUTH**
OPEN OPERCULUM

OVER
28,000
IS THE NUMBER OF KNOWN FISH SPECIES, MAKING UP NEARLY ONE HALF OF ALL CHORDATE SPECIES.

The Art of Swimming

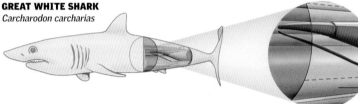

To swim, fish move in three dimensions: forwards and back, left and right, and up and down. The main control surfaces that fish use for manoeuvring are the fins, including the tail, or caudal, fin. To change direction, the fish tilts the control surfaces at an angle to the water current. The fish must also keep its balance in the water; it accomplishes this by moving its paired and unpaired fins.

UPSIDE-DOWN CATFISH
Synodontis nigriventris
This fish swims upside down, seeking food sources that are less accessible to other species.

MUSCLES

The tail has powerful muscles that enable it to move like an oar.

GREAT WHITE SHARK
Carcharodon carcharias

RED MUSCLES
are for slow or regular movements.

LARGER WHITE MUSCLES
are for moving with speed, but they tire easily.

1 Starting Out

The movement of a fish through the water is like that of a slithering snake. Its body goes through a series of wavelike movements similar to an S curve. This process begins when the fish moves its head slightly from side to side.

The crest of the body's wave moves from back to front.

In its side-to-side movement, the tail displaces the water.

At first, the tail is even with the head.

Streamlined Shape

Like the keel of a ship, the rounded contours of a fish are instrumental. In addition, most of a fish's volume is in the front part of its body. As the fish swims, its shape causes the density of the water ahead to be reduced relative to the density of the water behind. This reduces the water's resistance.

The head moves from side to side.

THE FISH'S KEEL

A ship has a heavy keel in the lower part to keep it from capsizing. Fish, on the other hand, have the keel on top. If the paired fins stop functioning to keep the fish balanced, the fish turns over because its heaviest part tends to sink, which happens when fish die.

KEEL

LIVE FISH **DEAD FISH**

THE FASTEST

The powerful caudal fin displaces large amounts of water.

SAILFISH
Istiophorus platypterus

The unfurled dorsal fin can be up to 150 per cent of the width of the fish's body.

Its long upper jaw enables it to slice through the water, aiding this fish's hydrodynamics.

109 km per hour
(70 mph) THE MAXIMUM SWIMMING SPEED IT ATTAINS.

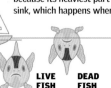

Forward Motion

results from the synchronized S-curve movement of the muscles surrounding the spinal column. These muscles usually make alternating lateral motions. Fish with large pectoral fins use them like oars for propulsion.

The oarlike movement of the tail is the main force used for forward motion.

THE DORSAL FIN keeps the fish upright.

THE PECTORAL FINS maintain balance and can act as brakes.

THE VENTRAL FINS stabilize the fish for proper balance.

Balance

When the fish is moving slowly or is still in the water, the fins can be seen making small movements to keep the body in balance.

Upwards and Downwards

The angle of the fins relative to the body allows the fish to move up or down. The paired fins, located in front of the centre of gravity, are used for this upward or downward movement.

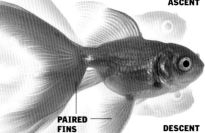

ASCENT

PAIRED FINS

DESCENT

 ## 2 Forceful Stroke

Muscles on both sides of the spinal column, especially the tail muscles, contract in an alternating pattern. These contractions power the wavelike movement that propels the fish forwards. The crest of the wave reaches the pelvic and dorsal fins.

When the crest reaches the area between the two dorsal fins, the tail fin begins its push to the right.

 ## 3 Complete Cycle

When the tail moves back towards the other side and reaches the far right, the head will once again turn to the right to begin a new cycle.

1 second

THE TIME IT TAKES FOR THIS SHARK TO COMPLETE ONE SWIMMING CYCLE.

The crest of the wave passes to the first dorsal fins.

CAT SHARK
Scyliorhinus sp.

The resulting impulse moves the fish forwards.

4 cubic km
(1 cubic mile)
THE AREA THAT CAN BE TAKEN UP BY A SCHOOL OF HERRING.

SCHOOL
A group of fish, usually of the same species, that swim together in a coordinated manner and with specific individual roles.

Swimming in Groups

 Only bony fish can swim in highly coordinated groups. Schools or shoals of fish include thousands of individuals that move harmoniously as if they were a single fish. To coordinate their motion, they use their sight, hearing and lateral line senses. Swimming in groups has its advantages: it is harder to be caught by a predator, and it is easier to find companions or food.

AMAZING FACT

Imaging technology called Ocean Acoustic Waveguide Remote Sensing has detected megashoals of hundreds of millions of herring in the Atlantic.

The fish on the outside, guided by those in the middle, are in charge of keeping the group safe.

The fish in the middle control the group.

Deadly Weapon

One of the greatest predators in the ocean is the great white shark, easily identified by its distinctive white colouring, black eyes and fierce teeth and jaws. Many biologists believe that attacks on humans result from the shark's exploratory behaviour, because these fish often lift their heads above the water and explore things by biting them. This activity is often lethal because of the sharpness of the sharks' teeth and the strength of their jaws. Great white sharks are implicated in most fatal shark attacks on humans, especially on surfers and divers.

Senses

Sharks have senses that most animals lack. The ampullae of Lorenzini are small clefts in the shark's head that detect electricity. This sense helps them find prey hidden in the sand. The lateral line is used to detect movement or sound underwater. Smell is their most advanced sense, and it occupies two thirds of their brain. They also have a highly developed sense of hearing, which allows them to detect very low-frequency sounds.

NASAL PITS

EYES
Sharks have poor vision and use their sense of smell to hunt.

JAW
During an attack, it stretches forwards.

UNPROVOKED ATTACKS BY WHITE SHARKS 1876–2013

26 MEDITERRANEAN

101 WEST COAST OF UNITED STATES

7 EAST COAST OF UNITED STATES

1 RUSSIA

2 JAPAN

1 SOUTH KOREA

1 HAWAII, UNITED STATES

1 MEXICO

1 CARIBBEAN ISLANDS

3 SOUTH AMERICA

59 SOUTH AFRICA

64 AUSTRALIA

11 NEW ZEALAND

280
INCLUDING 77 FATAL ATTACKS.

HEARING
Detects sounds of very low frequency.

AMPULLAE OF LORENZINI
Detect nerve impulses.

LATERAL LINE
Detects movements or sounds underwater.

NOSE
The most highly developed sense is smell; it takes up two thirds of the brain.

ELECTRIC RADAR

DORSAL FIN

CAUDAL FIN
The great white shark has a large heterocercal caudal fin.

ANAL FIN

PECTORAL FIN
Highly developed and very important for swimming.

PELVIC FIN

GREAT WHITE SHARK
Carcharodon carcharias

HABITAT	Oceans
WEIGHT	2,000 kg (4,400 lb)
LENGTH	7 m (23 ft)
LIFE SPAN	30–40 years

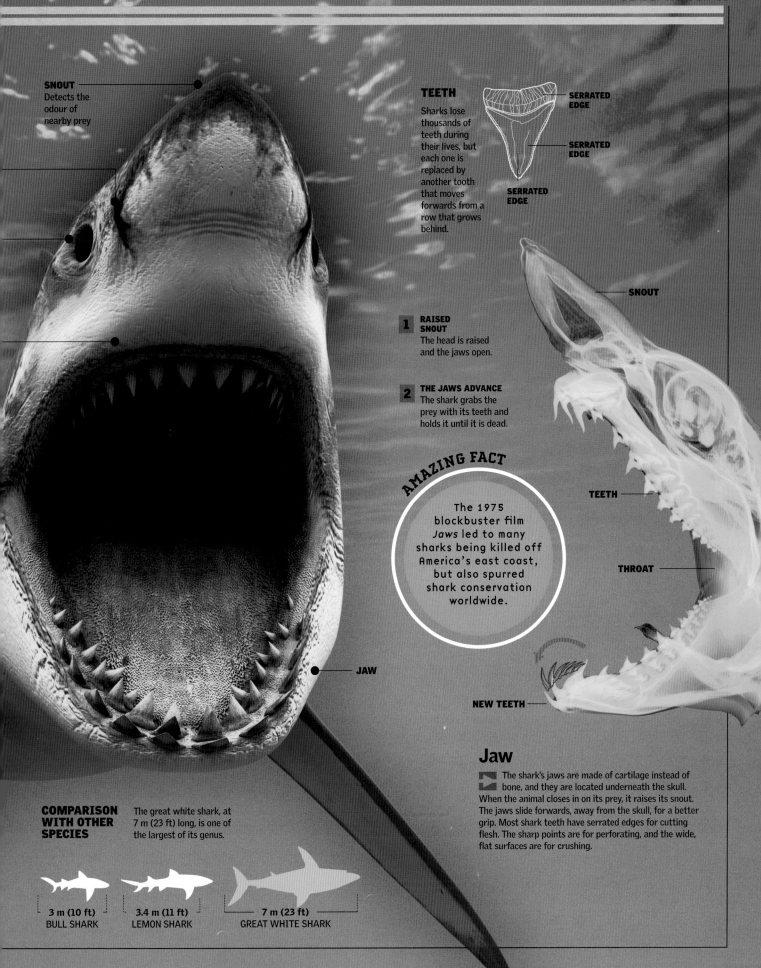

SNOUT
Detects the odour of nearby prey

TEETH
Sharks lose thousands of teeth during their lives, but each one is replaced by another tooth that moves forwards from a row that grows behind.

SERRATED EDGE

SERRATED EDGE

SERRATED EDGE

SNOUT

1 RAISED SNOUT
The head is raised and the jaws open.

2 THE JAWS ADVANCE
The shark grabs the prey with its teeth and holds it until it is dead.

AMAZING FACT

The 1975 blockbuster film *Jaws* led to many sharks being killed off America's east coast, but also spurred shark conservation worldwide.

TEETH

THROAT

JAW

NEW TEETH

Jaw

The shark's jaws are made of cartilage instead of bone, and they are located underneath the skull. When the animal closes in on its prey, it raises its snout. The jaws slide forwards, away from the skull, for a better grip. Most shark teeth have serrated edges for cutting flesh. The sharp points are for perforating, and the wide, flat surfaces are for crushing.

COMPARISON WITH OTHER SPECIES
The great white shark, at 7 m (23 ft) long, is one of the largest of its genus.

3 m (10 ft)
BULL SHARK

3.4 m (11 ft)
LEMON SHARK

7 m (23 ft)
GREAT WHITE SHARK

The Journey Home

After living in the ocean for five or six years, the Pacific red salmon (*Oncorhynchus nerka*) returns to the river where it was born to reproduce. The journey lasts around three months, and demands a great deal of energy. The salmon must swim against the current, climb waterfalls and evade predators, including bears and eagles. Once the salmon reach the river, the female lays her eggs, and the male fertilizes them. Typically, the same locations in specific rivers are sought year after year. This species of salmon dies after completing the reproductive cycle, unlike the Atlantic salmon, which repeats the cycle three or four times. Once the eggs hatch, the cycle begins anew.

ASIA   ALASKA   UNITED STATES

The Route

There are six species of salmon in the Pacific Ocean and one in the Atlantic. The red salmon (*Oncorhynchus nerka*) migrates from the Pacific Ocean to the rivers of the USA and Canada on one side and to the rivers of Alaska and eastern Asia on the other.

AMAZING FACT

The adult salmon's journey back to the river where it was born takes an estimated three months.

1 Strenuous Race

Salmon swim upstream from the ocean to the river. On the way, many fall prey to bears.

Neither waterfalls nor strong currents can stop salmon in their journey.

5 Fry

Only 40 per cent of the eggs laid each autumn hatch. The fry remain in the river for up to two years and then migrate to the ocean.

6 Death

Adult salmon die a few days after spawning, exhausted by the work they have done. Their bodies decompose along the riverbank.

2 Red River

The salmon returns to its birthplace to spawn. Males have intense coloration with a green head.

Seen from above, salmon appear as a large red spot.

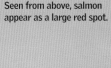

Survival

Of the more than 7,500 eggs that two females might lay, only two hatched fish will remain at the end of the life cycle of two years. Many eggs die before hatching, and after hatching, salmon fry are easy prey for other fish.

EGGS		7,500
FRY		4,500
FRY		650
FRY		200
SALMON		50
ADULT SALMON		4
EGG SPAWNING		2

6-Year Cycle
FROM SPAWNING TO ADULTHOOD.

5,000
THE QUANTITY OF EGGS A FEMALE CAN LAY.

3 The Couple

While females are busy preparing nests in the sand to deposit their eggs, males compete for mates.

BACK
A hump develops in the dorsal section of the body.

COLOUR
The blue-backed salmon turns a fiery red.

MOUTH
During the mating season, the lower jaw of the male curves upwards.

4 Spawning

The female deposits between 2,500 and 5,000 eggs in a series of nests. The male fertilizes them as they fall between the rocks.

Kings of Darkness

In depths below 2,500 m (8,200 ft), where barely any light penetrates, live rare species known as abyssal fish. In this environment, life is possible near hydrothermal vents in the seabed that warm the nearby waters. In spite of this natural warmth, in many areas the temperature never rises above 2°C (36°F). At this depth, fish have peculiar shapes, with large heads and strong teeth for eating other fish, because no vegetation can grow there. To attract their prey, many have 'lure' organs made of photophores that shine in the darkness. The fish are usually black or dark brown for purposes of camouflage.

2,500 m
(8,200 ft) DEPTH OF WATER.

SLOANE'S VIPERFISH
Chauliodus sloani
Between 30 and 50 cm (12–20 in) long, it is dark blue or silvery in colour and lives in warm tropical waters.

SHARP, POINTED TEETH
It gulps down its prey after grabbing them with its enormous teeth and its strong suction force.

LANTERN
Like most abyssal fish, it has a lure organ.

EYES FOR SEEING IN DIM LIGHT

TAPETUM
reflects light like a mirror. Each ray hits the retina twice, doubling its sensitivity.

RAY OF LIGHT

RETINA
Blind to red light. It registers only blue light waves, which travel better in the water.

FANGTOOTH
Anoplogaster cornuta
This fearsome hunter kills its prey by seizing it with its jaw and strong teeth.

FANFIN SEADEVIL
Caulophryne jordani
This dark brown fish uses the photophore organ on its head to penetrate the darkness.

FILAMENTS
cover its entire body for protection.

DRAGONFISH
Bathophilus sp.
Found in most tropical regions of the world, it has photophores along both sides of its body.

CHIN APPENDAGE
shines in the darkness.

LANTERN
produces bluish light, which reaches farthest underwater.

FUMAROLE
Openings in the Earth's surface that discharge geothermal water and minerals. As the water cools, these minerals solidify.

2°C (36°F)
TEMPERATURE OF WATER HEATED BY FUMAROLES.

TUBE-WORM TENTACLES
Tube worms have neither mouths nor digestive tracts. They feed on organic molecules formed from elements in the water by chemosynthetic bacteria that live inside the worms.

GLOWING LURE
produces light to attract prey.

DIMENSIONS

Weight
300 g (10½ oz)

10 cm (4 in)

HUMPBACK ANGLERFISH
Melanocetus johnsoni
15 cm (6 in) long. Its small fins are insufficient to enable fast manoeuvring.

1 cu m
(1.3 cu
yds) of
water

= 1,000 kg
(1.1 tons)

HYDROSTATIC PRESSURE
The weight of a column of water: the pressure of the water increases with depth. In the Mariana Trench (the deepest undersea trench on the planet), every square centimetre bears the weight of 1.1 tonnes (7¾ tons per sq in) of water.

SKIN
Dark colours are likely to make it invisible to attackers.

KILLER JAWS
In the ocean's depths, only the best hunter survives.

CHIN APPENDAGE
produces light to attract prey.

ILLUMINATED NETDEVIL
Linophryne arborifera
has a glowing lure on the end of its nose and a branching beard that also glows to attract prey. The male is smaller than the female and lives off her like a parasite.

TAILS AND FINS
contain luminous cells.

GLOWING LURE
gives off light to attract prey.

ATLANTIC FOOTBALL FISH
Himantolophus groenlandicus
The females can reach up to 60 cm (24 in) long, whereas the males barely reach 4 cm (1½ in) long and live as parasites on their mates.

Between Land and Water

As indicated by their name (*amphi*, 'both', and *bios*, 'life'), amphibians lead a double existence. When young, they live in the water, and when they become adults they live outside it. However, many species need to remain near water or in very humid places to keep from drying out. This is because these animals also breathe through their skin, and only moist skin can absorb oxygen. Some typical characteristics of adult frogs and toads include a tailless body, long hind limbs and large eyes that often bulge.

Amphibian Anatomy

Their anatomy has several peculiarities. Larvae, such as tadpoles, have a respiratory system with gills. Most species develop lungs when they reach adulthood. They also have a trachea, pharynx and saclike lungs, even though skin breathing is at times more important than lung breathing. The heart has two auricles and one ventricle, and the digestive and excretory systems are similar to those of mammals.

VOCAL SACS

Both toads and frogs sing. The sound is originally produced by their vocal cords, but in males it is amplified by means of inflatable sacs on each side of the larynx.

The Skin

Amphibians breathe through their skin, which is clean and smooth, without hair or scales. They must always keep it moist, because it has a strong tendency to dry out. Even though they have mucous glands that help maintain moisture, amphibians must live in damp places. The skin of most amphibians protects them from possible predators and has poisonous glands that secrete unpleasant and even toxic substances.

Carbon dioxide

Oxygen

Blood vessel that carries deoxygenated blood

Blood vessel that carries oxygenated blood

Poison gland

Mucous gland

HIND LIMBS

The muscular leg and foot have five long fingers joined by a webbed membrane that aids swimming.

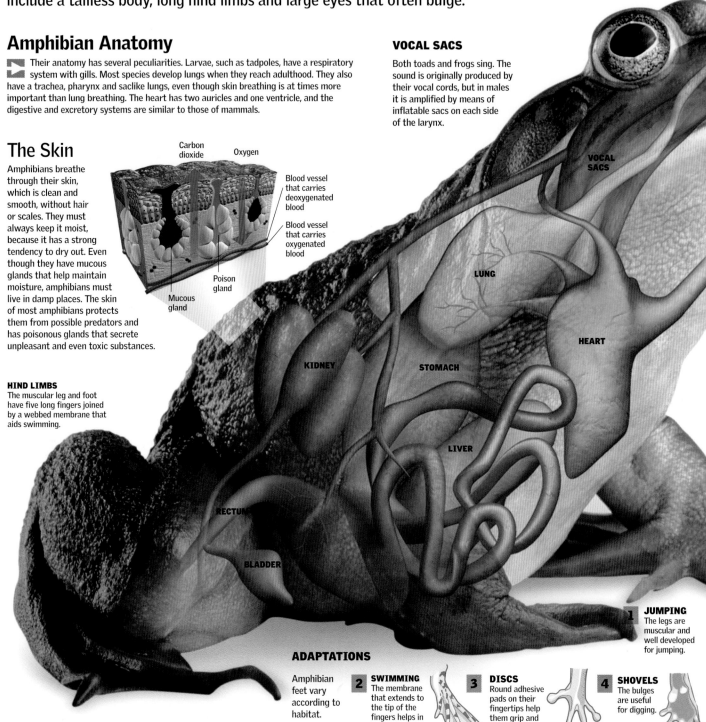

VOCAL SACS

LUNG

HEART

KIDNEY

STOMACH

LIVER

RECTUM

BLADDER

1 JUMPING
The legs are muscular and well developed for jumping.

ADAPTATIONS

Amphibian feet vary according to habitat.

2 SWIMMING
The membrane that extends to the tip of the fingers helps in swimming.

3 DISCS
Round adhesive pads on their fingertips help them grip and climb.

4 SHOVELS
The bulges are useful for digging.

Differences Between Frogs and Toads

Because of their similar shape, frogs and toads are often confused, but they are actually quite different animals. Toads have wrinkled skin and short legs, and they are land animals. Frogs are smaller, have webbed feet, and live in the water and in trees.

SKIN
Soft and smooth, with strong, bright colours

EYES
Frogs have horizontal pupils.

EYES
The pupil is usually horizontal, although some toads have vertical pupils.

SKIN
The skin of a toad is wrinkled, hard, rough and dry. It is sometimes used as leather.

COMMON TOAD
Bufo bufo

REED FROG
Hyperolius tuberilinguis

POSTURE
Toads are terrestrial species, slow-moving, and wider than frogs. Frogs live mainly in water, which is why they have webbed toes adapted for swimming.

LEGS
are long and are adapted for jumping. Frogs have webbed toes to help with swimming.

LEGS
are shorter and wider than those of frogs and are adapted for walking.

CATCHING PREY
Toads gulp down their prey, swallowing it whole.

SWALLOWING
Eye retraction, where the toad closes and turns its eyes inwards, increases pressure in the mouth, pushing food down the oesophagus.

Nutrition

During the larval stage, nutrition is based on plants, whereas in the adult stage the main food sources are arthropods (such as beetles and spiders) and other invertebrates, such as butterfly caterpillars and earthworms.

Types of Amphibians

Amphibians are divided into three groups that are differentiated on the basis of tail and legs. Newts and salamanders have tails. They belong to the order Urodela. Frogs and toads, which have no tail except as tadpoles, belong to the Anura group. Caecilians, which have no tail or legs, are similar to worms and belong to the Apoda group.

1
ANURA
Tailless

EUROPEAN TREE FROG
Hyla arborea
A small docile species that lives near buildings.

2
APODA
Without legs

RINGED CAECILIAN
Siphonops annulatus
Resembles a large, thick worm.

Legs

Frogs and toads have four fingers on each front leg and five on each hind leg. Water frogs have webbed feet; tree frogs have adhesive discs on the tips of their fingers to hold on to vertical surfaces; and burrowing frogs have callous protuberances (called 'tubercules') on their hind legs, which they use for digging.

3
URODELA
With a tail

TIGER SALAMANDER
Ambystoma tigrinum
One of the most colourful in North America.

Metamorphosis

Metamorphosis is the process of transformation experienced by anurans (it can also be observed in amphibians from the order Urodela and caecilians), starting with the egg and ending at the adult stage. Amphibians leave the egg in a larval form. They then undergo very important changes in their anatomy, diet and lifestyle, slowly mutating from their first stage, which is completely aquatic, until they transform into animals adapted to life on land.

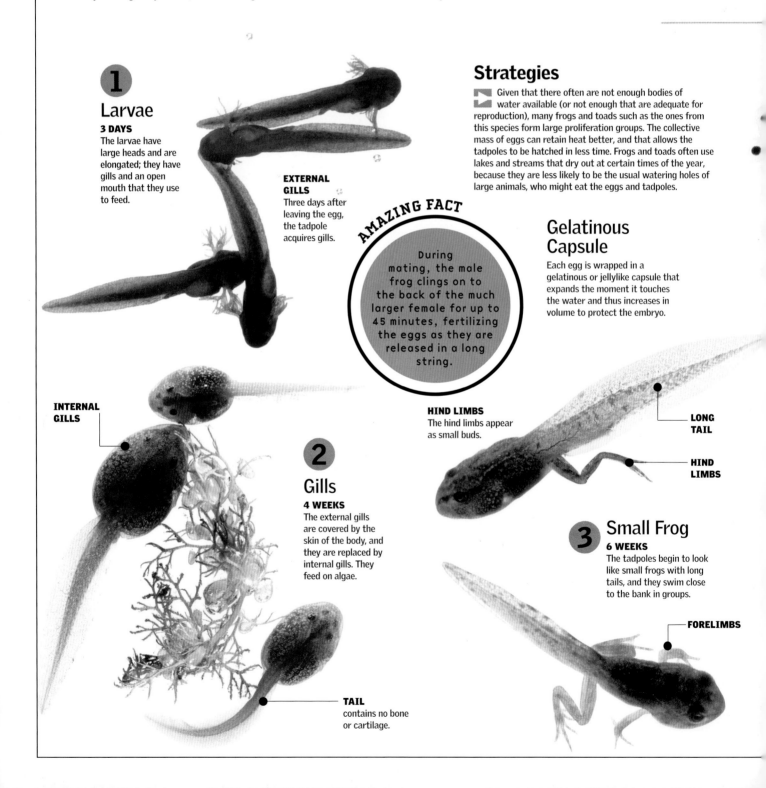

1 Larvae

3 DAYS
The larvae have large heads and are elongated; they have gills and an open mouth that they use to feed.

EXTERNAL GILLS
Three days after leaving the egg, the tadpole acquires gills.

INTERNAL GILLS

2 Gills

4 WEEKS
The external gills are covered by the skin of the body, and they are replaced by internal gills. They feed on algae.

TAIL
contains no bone or cartilage.

AMAZING FACT

During mating, the male frog clings on to the back of the much larger female for up to 45 minutes, fertilizing the eggs as they are released in a long string.

Strategies

Given that there often are not enough bodies of water available (or not enough that are adequate for reproduction), many frogs and toads such as the ones from this species form large proliferation groups. The collective mass of eggs can retain heat better, and that allows the tadpoles to be hatched in less time. Frogs and toads often use lakes and streams that dry out at certain times of the year, because they are less likely to be the usual watering holes of large animals, who might eat the eggs and tadpoles.

Gelatinous Capsule

Each egg is wrapped in a gelatinous or jellylike capsule that expands the moment it touches the water and thus increases in volume to protect the embryo.

HIND LIMBS
The hind limbs appear as small buds.

LONG TAIL

HIND LIMBS

3 Small Frog

6 WEEKS
The tadpoles begin to look like small frogs with long tails, and they swim close to the bank in groups.

FORELIMBS

Cycle
METAMORPHOSIS

The development of the common
European frog from egg to adult
takes approximately 16 weeks.

Mother Frog and Her Eggs

Despite the fact that the survival instinct of anurans is not fully
developed, frogs and toads somehow take care of their future
young. Laying eggs in great quantities ensures that many tadpoles
will be able to escape predators who feed on the eggs. The gelatinous
layer also protects the eggs from other predators. In one species, the
Surinam toad, the mother cares for her tadpoles by nestling them in
special pouches on her back.

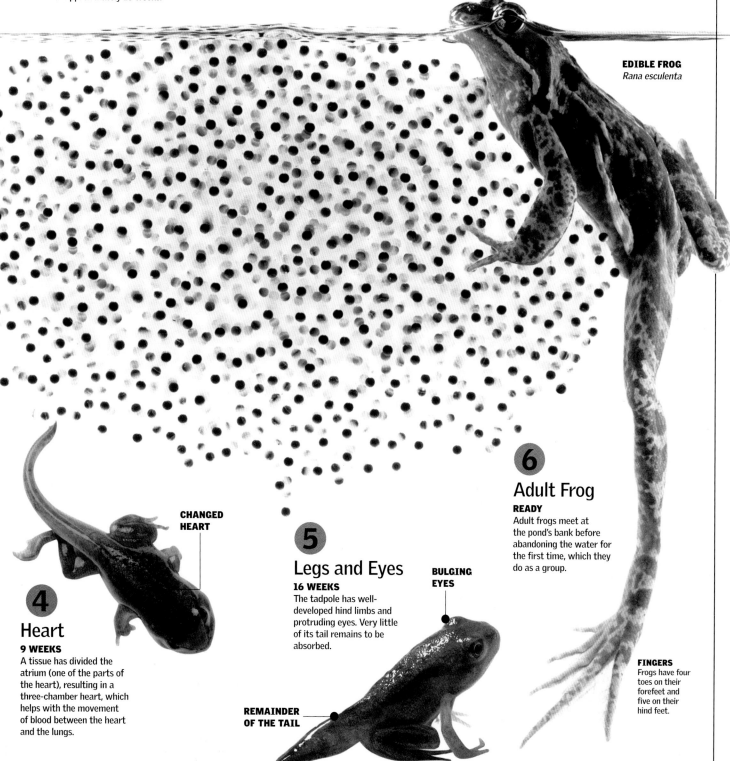

EDIBLE FROG
Rana esculenta

**CHANGED
HEART**

4
Heart
9 WEEKS
A tissue has divided the
atrium (one of the parts of
the heart), resulting in a
three-chamber heart, which
helps with the movement
of blood between the heart
and the lungs.

5
Legs and Eyes
16 WEEKS
The tadpole has well-
developed hind limbs and
protruding eyes. Very little
of its tail remains to be
absorbed.

**REMAINDER
OF THE TAIL**

**BULGING
EYES**

6
Adult Frog
READY
Adult frogs meet at
the pond's bank before
abandoning the water for
the first time, which they
do as a group.

FINGERS
Frogs have four
toes on their
forefeet and
five on their
hind feet.

Jointless

The body of most molluscs is soft, extremely flexible and without joints, but many have a large, hard shell. Most species live in the ocean, but they are also found in lakes and land environments. All modern molluscs have bilateral symmetry, one cephalopod foot with sensory organs and locomotion, a visceral mass and a covering – the mantle – that secretes the shell. They feed by means of a unique rasplike mouth structure called a radula.

INTESTINE

GONAD

DIGESTIVE GLAND

LUNG

Gastropods

These molluscs are characterized by their large ventral foot, whose wavelike motions are used to move from place to place. The group comprises snails and slugs, and they can live on land, in the ocean and in fresh water. When these animals have a shell, it is a single spiral-shaped piece, and the extreme flexibility of the rest of the body allows the gastropod to draw itself up completely within the shell. Gastropods have eyes and one or two pairs of tentacles on their head.

KIDNEY HEART

SALIVARY GLAND

OESOPHAGUS

FEMALE SEXUAL ORGAN

PROSOBRANCHIA

This mollusc subclass mainly includes marine animals. Some have mother-of-pearl on the inside of their shell, whereas others have a substance similar to porcelain.

LUNGED

Snails, land slugs and freshwater slugs have lungs, and their lung sacs allow them to breathe oxygen in the atmosphere.

BENDING OF THE SNAIL

In snails, bending is a phenomenon that moves the cavity of the mantle from the rear towards the front of the body. The visceral organs rotate 180 degrees, and the digestive tube and the nervous connections cross in a figure of eight.

OPISTHOBRANCHIA

are sea slugs, which are characterized by having a very small shell or no shell at all.

Gills

Nervous system

Digestive tract

SEA ANGEL
Candida sp.

Bivalves

Molluscs with a shell divided into two halves. The two parts of the shell are joined by an elastic ligament that opens the shell, abductor muscles that close the shell, and the umbo, a system of ridges that helps the shell shut tightly. Almost all bivalves feed on microorganisms. Some bury themselves in wet sand, digging small tunnels that let in water and food. The tunnels can be from a fraction of a centimetre to over a metre long.

SCALLOP
Pecten jacobaeus

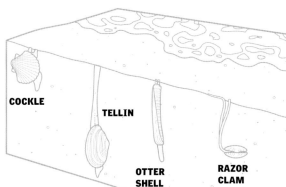

COCKLE

TELLIN

OTTER SHELL

RAZOR CLAM

LAMELLIBRANCHIATA

include most bivalves. They use gills to breathe and to feed. They have no differentiated head, eyes or extremities. They can grow up to 13 cm (5 in) long, and they rest on the ocean floor.

GREEN MUSSEL
Perna viridis

PROTOBRANCHIA

This class includes bivalves with a split lower foot, called a 'sole'. Bivalves use their gills only to breathe. This subclass includes small bivalves 13 mm (½ in) wide, called nutclams (*Nucula nitidosa*).

BROWN GARDEN SNAIL
Helix aspersa

Under the Sand

Many molluscs live buried under the sand in order to hide from predators and the effects of waves, wind and sudden changes in temperature.

100,000

THE NUMBER OF LIVING MOLLUSC SPECIES; AS MANY MORE HAVE BECOME EXTINCT.

Cephalopods

Cuttlefish, octopus, squid and nautilus are called cephalopods because their extremities, or tentacles, are attached directly to their heads. These predators are adapted to life in the oceans, and they have quite complex nervous, sensory and motion systems. Their tentacles surround their mouths, which have a radula and a powerful beak. Cephalopods range from 1 cm (⅓ in) to several metres long.

RADULA

NAUTILUS
Nautilus sp.

COLEOIDEA

Cephalopods of this class have a very small internal shell, or none at all, and only two gills. Except for the nautilus, this class includes all cephalopods alive today – octopus, cuttlefish and squid.

COMMON CUTTLEFISH
Sepia officinalis

NAUTILOIDEA

This subclass populated the oceans of the Palaeozoic and Mesozoic periods, but today only one genus – *Nautilus* – survives. A nautilus has an outer shell, four gills and ten tentacles. Its shell is made from calcium, is spiral in shape, and is divided into chambers.

Colourful Armour

E ven though they inhabit all known environments, crustaceans are most closely identified with the aquatic environment. That is where they were transformed into arthropods with the most evolutionary success. Their bodies are divided into three parts: the cephalothorax, with antennae and strong mandibles; the abdomen, or pleon; and the back (telson). Some crustaceans are very small: sea lice, for instance, are no larger than 0.25 mm ($\frac{1}{100}$ in). The Japanese spider crab, on the other hand, is more than 3 m (9 ft) long with outstretched legs, because it has legs in both its abdomen and its thorax, in addition to two pairs of antennae.

WOODLOUSE

Armadillidium vulgare
This invertebrate, belonging to the order Isopoda, is one of the few terrestrial crustaceans, and it is probably the one best adapted to life out of water. When it feels threatened, it rolls itself up, leaving only its exoskeleton exposed. Even though it can reproduce and develop away from water, it breathes through gills. The gills are found in its abdominal appendages and for this reason must be kept at specific humidity levels. That is also why the woodlouse seeks dark and humid environments, such as under rocks, on dead or fallen leaves and in fallen tree trunks.

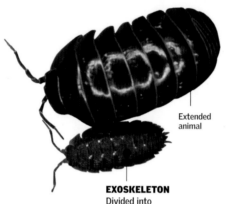

Extended animal

EXOSKELETON
Divided into independent parts

Rolled-up animal

Antennae

Head

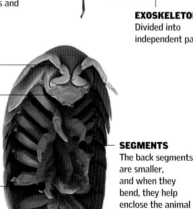

LEGS
This species has seven pairs of legs.

SEGMENTS
The back segments are smaller, and when they bend, they help enclose the animal completely.

Anus

Malacostraca

■ is the name given to the class of crustaceans that groups crabs together with sea lobsters, shrimps, woodlice and sea lice. The term comes from Greek, and means 'soft-shelled'. Sea and river crabs have ten legs, and one pair of these legs is modified in a pincer form. Malacostraca are omnivorous and have adapted to a great variety of environments; the number of segments of their exoskeleton varies from a minimum of 16 to more than 60.

APPENDAGES
consist of a lower region from which two segmented branches grow, one internal (endopod) and the other external (exopod).

THE PACIFIC SPIDER CRAB CAN WEIGH UP TO

20 kg
(45 lb).

BARNACLES WITHOUT A SHELL

BARNACLE COLONY

Together Forever

At birth, barnacles (*Pollicipes cornucopia*) are microscopic larvae that travel through the sea until they reach a rocky coast. There they attach themselves to the shore by means of a stalk, which they develop by the modification of their antennae, and then form a shell. Once they are attached, they remain in one spot for the rest of their lives, absorbing food from the water. Barnacles are edible.

BARNACLE TRANSVERSAL CUT

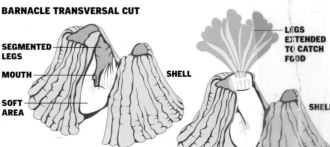

SEGMENTED LEGS

MOUTH

SOFT AREA

SHELL

LEGS EXTENDED TO CATCH FOOD

SHELL

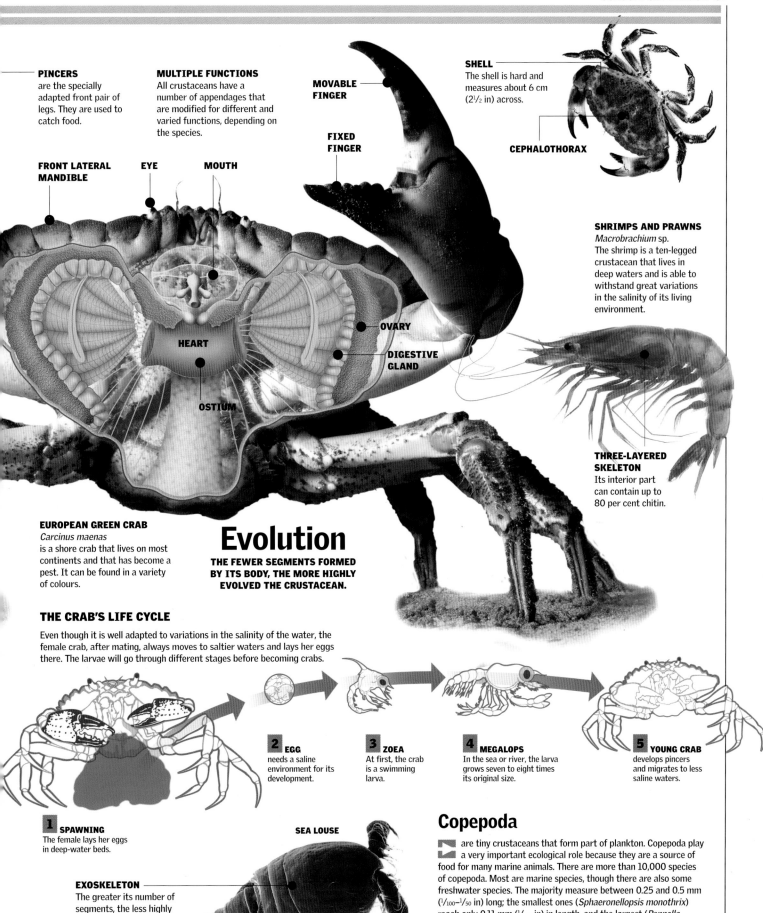

PINCERS
are the specially adapted front pair of legs. They are used to catch food.

MULTIPLE FUNCTIONS
All crustaceans have a number of appendages that are modified for different and varied functions, depending on the species.

MOVABLE FINGER

FIXED FINGER

SHELL
The shell is hard and measures about 6 cm (2¹/₂ in) across.

CEPHALOTHORAX

FRONT LATERAL MANDIBLE

EYE

MOUTH

HEART

OSTIUM

OVARY

DIGESTIVE GLAND

SHRIMPS AND PRAWNS
Macrobrachium sp.
The shrimp is a ten-legged crustacean that lives in deep waters and is able to withstand great variations in the salinity of its living environment.

THREE-LAYERED SKELETON
Its interior part can contain up to 80 per cent chitin.

EUROPEAN GREEN CRAB
Carcinus maenas
is a shore crab that lives on most continents and that has become a pest. It can be found in a variety of colours.

Evolution
THE FEWER SEGMENTS FORMED BY ITS BODY, THE MORE HIGHLY EVOLVED THE CRUSTACEAN.

THE CRAB'S LIFE CYCLE

Even though it is well adapted to variations in the salinity of the water, the female crab, after mating, always moves to saltier waters and lays her eggs there. The larvae will go through different stages before becoming crabs.

1 SPAWNING
The female lays her eggs in deep-water beds.

2 EGG
needs a saline environment for its development.

3 ZOEA
At first, the crab is a swimming larva.

4 MEGALOPS
In the sea or river, the larva grows seven to eight times its original size.

5 YOUNG CRAB
develops pincers and migrates to less saline waters.

SEA LOUSE

EXOSKELETON
The greater its number of segments, the less highly evolved the species.

Copepoda

are tiny crustaceans that form part of plankton. Copepoda play a very important ecological role because they are a source of food for many marine animals. There are more than 10,000 species of copepoda. Most are marine species, though there are also some freshwater species. The majority measure between 0.25 and 0.5 mm (¹/₁₀₀–¹/₅₀ in) long; the smallest ones (*Sphaeronellopsis monothrix*) reach only 0.11 mm (¹/₂₅₀ in) in length, and the largest (*Pennella balaenopterae*) are 32 cm (13 in) long.

Eight Legs

Arachnids make up the largest and most important class of Chelicerata. Among them are spiders, scorpions, fleas, ticks and mites. Arachnids were the first arthropods to migrate from the oceans and colonize terrestrial environments, and nearly all species now live on land. The best-known arachnids are the scorpions and spiders, both found on every continent except Antarctica.

AMAZING FACT

Fossil scorpions dating from the Silurian period, 430 million years ago, show that these animals have changed little in form and behaviour.

The female can transport up to 30 offspring on her back.

GIANT HOUSEHOLD SPIDER
Tegenaria duellica
This spider is distinguished by its long legs in relation to its body.

PEDIPALPS
The terminal pedipalp forms a copulating organ through which the male inseminates the female. Pedipalps also act as sensory organs and manipulate food.

Scorpions

Long feared by people, the scorpion is characterized by the fact that its chelicerae (mouth parts that are large in scorpions) and pedipalps form pincers. The body is covered with a chitinous exoskeleton that includes the cephalothorax and abdomen.

EMPEROR SCORPION
Pandinus imperator
Like other scorpions, it has a stinger crisscrossed by venomous glands. It measures between 12 and 18 cm (5–7 in) long, although some have reached a length of 20 cm (8 in).

The claws hold the prey and immobilize it.

CHELICERAE
move up and down and are used as sensors. In the more primitive spiders (such as tarantulas), they move from side to side like pincers.

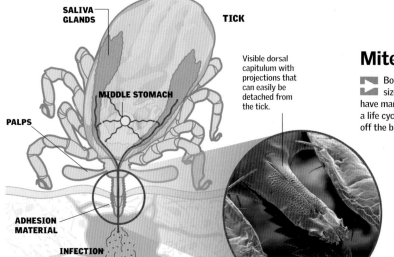

SALIVA GLANDS

TICK

Visible dorsal capitulum with projections that can easily be detached from the tick.

MIDDLE STOMACH

PALPS

ADHESION MATERIAL

INFECTION

Mites and Ticks

Both are members of the Acari order and are chiefly differentiated by their size. Mites are smaller; ticks may measure up to 2.5 cm (1 in) in length. Mites have many diverse forms and are parasites of animals and plants. Most ticks have a life cycle of three stages: larva, nymph and adult, during each of which they live off the blood of their hosts and are vectors of a number of infectious diseases.

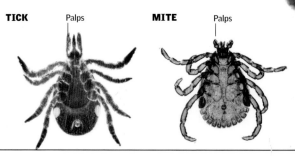

TICK   Palps

MITE   Palps

100,000

IS THE NUMBER OF SPECIES OF ARACHNIDS THOUGHT TO EXIST IN THE WORLD.

EXOSKELETON

Growth happens through moulting, a process by which the spider gets rid of its old exoskeleton. In its youth the spider grows through successive moultings (up to four a year), and once it reaches adulthood, it goes through a yearly change.

1 The front edge of the shell comes off, and the tegument separates from the abdomen.

2 The spider raises and lowers its legs until the skin slips off.

3 It discards the old exoskeleton, and the new one hardens on contact with the air.

CEPHALOTHORAX (PROSOMA)

ABDOMEN (OPISTHOSOMA)

HEART

CHELICERAE

SIMPLE EYE

CLOACA

VENOM GLAND

INTESTINE

STOMACH

OVARIES

LUNG

GENITAL ORIFICE

SILK GLAND

FEMUR

PATELLA

TIBIA

WALKING LEGS
The spider has four pairs of legs for walking. The hairs help it to recognize terrain.

METATARSUS

TARSUS

WITH ITS LEGS SPREAD OUT, A SPIDER CAN MEASURE

30 cm
(12 in) IN LENGTH.

Spiders

are the most common arthropods. They have the surprising property of secreting a substance that, on contact with the air, creates very fine threads that spiders skilfully manage for diverse purposes. Once a female spider mates, she deposits her eggs inside a cocoon of special silk, called an 'egg sac'. The appearance of spiders is unmistakable: the two main sections of the body, the thorax (also called a prosoma) and the abdomen (also called an opisthosoma), are united by a narrow stalk (the pedicel). Spiders have four pairs of eyes, whose distinctive size and placement help characterize different families of spiders. Their chelicerae end in fangs that carry conduits from venom glands. Spiders kill their prey by using their chelicerae to apply venom.

Amblypygi

Whip spiders are small arachnids that measure between 4 and 45 mm ($^1/_5$ –2 in). The chelicerae are not as large, although the pedipalps are strong and are used to capture prey. The first pair of legs are long and thin and used as sensors, while the last three take care of movement. Because the whip spider's body is flattened, its gait is similar to that of a crab.

SOUTH AMERICAN CAVE SPIDER
Phryna grossetaitai

Secrets of Success

Sensory antennae, highly developed eyes on the sides of the head, pairs of jointed legs with functions that depend on the species – all are outstanding features of insects and myriapods. Insects, also called hexapods, have six legs attached to the thorax. Myriapods (millipedes and centipedes) are multisegmented arthropods that have developed only on land.

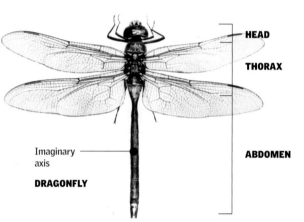

HEAD

THORAX

ABDOMEN

Imaginary axis

DRAGONFLY

BILATERAL SYMMETRY

The entire body of insects and myriapods is composed of pairs, arranged along an imaginary axis that passes from the head to the lower end of the abdomen.

Two Pairs of Wings

Some ancient species had three pairs of wings. Today, however, insects have one or two pairs. Butterflies, dragonflies, bees and wasps use two pairs to fly, but other insects fly with only one pair.

OPEN CIRCULATION

A tubular heart pumps the haemolymph (blood) through the dorsal aorta. Accessory contracting organs help push the blood into the wings and legs.

HIND WINGS

AT REST
Dragonflies can place their wings against their bodies.

APPENDAGE
contains the genital organs.

SEGMENTED REGIONS

Insects' bodies are divided into three parts: the head (6 segments), the thorax (3 segments), and the abdomen (up to 11 segments).

SPIRACLES
Small entrances to the tracheae.

1 million
KNOWN INSECT SPECIES

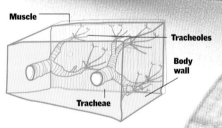

RESPIRATORY SYSTEM

Land-dwelling arthropods breathe with tracheae. Through branching tubes (tracheoles), air containing oxygen is brought directly to each cell, and carbon dioxide is eliminated.

Muscle

Tracheoles

Body wall

Tracheae

STRUCTURE
gives the wings great stability.

Legs Adapted for Type of Use

The shape of the arthropod legs shown here is closely related to their use and to the arthropod's habitat. Some species have taste and touch receptors on their legs.

Sacs

LEGS

WALKING
Cockroach

JUMPING
Grasshopper

SWIMMING
Water scorpion

DIGGING
Mole cricket

GATHERING
Bee

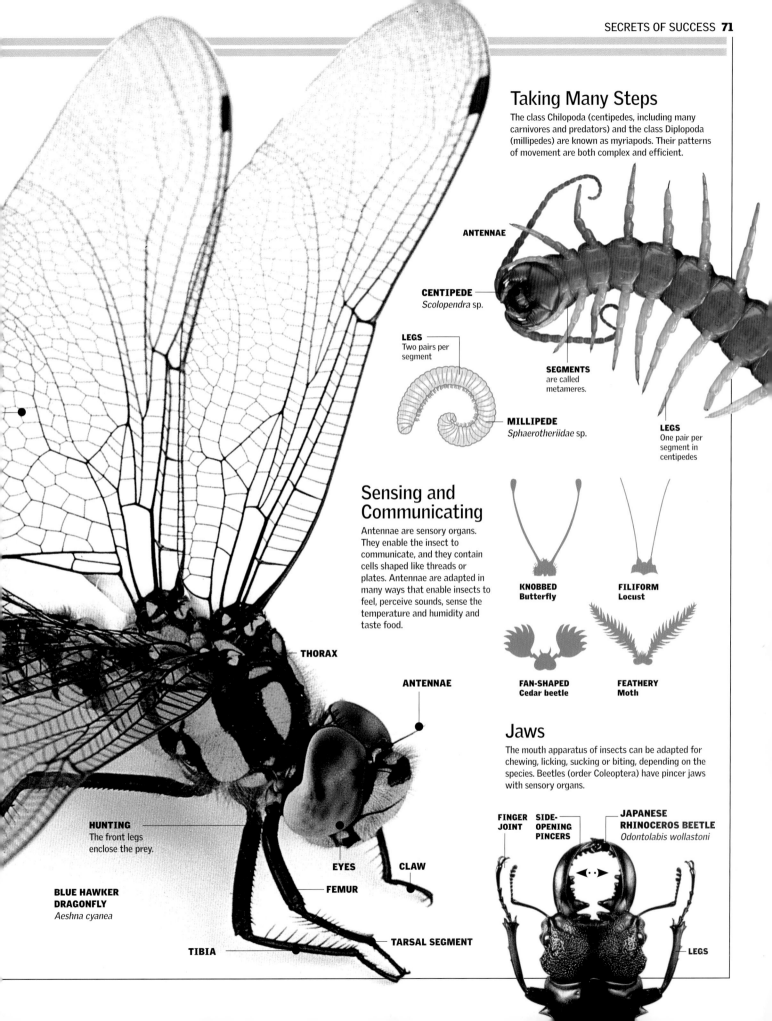

SECRETS OF SUCCESS **71**

Taking Many Steps

The class Chilopoda (centipedes, including many carnivores and predators) and the class Diplopoda (millipedes) are known as myriapods. Their patterns of movement are both complex and efficient.

ANTENNAE

CENTIPEDE
Scolopendra sp.

LEGS
Two pairs per segment

SEGMENTS
are called metameres.

MILLIPEDE
Sphaerotheriidae sp.

LEGS
One pair per segment in centipedes

Sensing and Communicating

Antennae are sensory organs. They enable the insect to communicate, and they contain cells shaped like threads or plates. Antennae are adapted in many ways that enable insects to feel, perceive sounds, sense the temperature and humidity and taste food.

KNOBBED
Butterfly

FILIFORM
Locust

FAN-SHAPED
Cedar beetle

FEATHERY
Moth

THORAX

ANTENNAE

Jaws

The mouth apparatus of insects can be adapted for chewing, licking, sucking or biting, depending on the species. Beetles (order Coleoptera) have pincer jaws with sensory organs.

HUNTING
The front legs enclose the prey.

FINGER JOINT

SIDE-OPENING PINCERS

JAPANESE RHINOCEROS BEETLE
Odontolabis wollastoni

EYES

CLAW

BLUE HAWKER DRAGONFLY
Aeshna cyanea

FEMUR

TIBIA

TARSAL SEGMENT

LEGS

The Art of Flying

One of the most basic adaptations of insects has been their ability to fly. Most have two pairs of wings. Beetles (order Coleoptera) use one pair to fly and one pair for protection. For example, the rounded body of a ladybird is nothing more than the covering for a very sophisticated flight system. It makes these small beetles, which are harmless to humans, great hunters in the insect world.

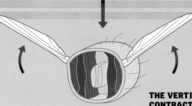

THE VERTICAL MUSCLE CONTRACTS AND THE WINGS MOVE UPWARDS.

THE HORIZONTAL MUSCLE CONTRACTS AND THE WINGS MOVE DOWNWARDS.

THORAX

WING

'Ladies' of Land and Air

Some 4,500 species of these beetles live throughout the world. Almost all are brightly coloured, with black spots on a red, yellow or orange background. These colours warn off predators, who usually associate bright colours with poison. In fact, some ladybirds are actually poisonous for small predators, such as lizards and small birds. Ladybirds pose the greatest danger to agricultural pests, such as plant lice and gadflies, so they are often used as a natural biological pest control.

3

Flight

With the elytra open and spread like aeroplane wings, the second pair of wings is free to move. The muscles at their base control the direction of flight.

2

Take-off

Although the colourful elytra are not used in flying, the insect needs to lift them in order to unfold its wings, which are seen only during flight.

Raised elytra

FRONT VIEW OF ELYTRA

1–2 m
per second
(40-80 in/s)
IS THE AVERAGE SPEED OF FLIGHT.

SEVEN-SPOTTED LADYBIRD
Coccinella septempunctata
Thanks to their help in destroying pests, during the Middle Ages these beetles were considered instruments of divine intervention from the Virgin Mary, so became known as 'Our Lady's bird'.

The insect is between 0.1 and 1 cm ($1/25$–$1/2$ in) long.

1

Preparation

The elytra, or modified front wings, can separate from the rest of the body. They protect the thorax, and also the wings when folded inside.

WINGS PREPARED FOR FLIGHT

BACK VIEW

RAISED ELYTRON

VISIBLE WING

APOSEMATISM
The opposite of mimetism: these insects use their bright colours to scare away predators.

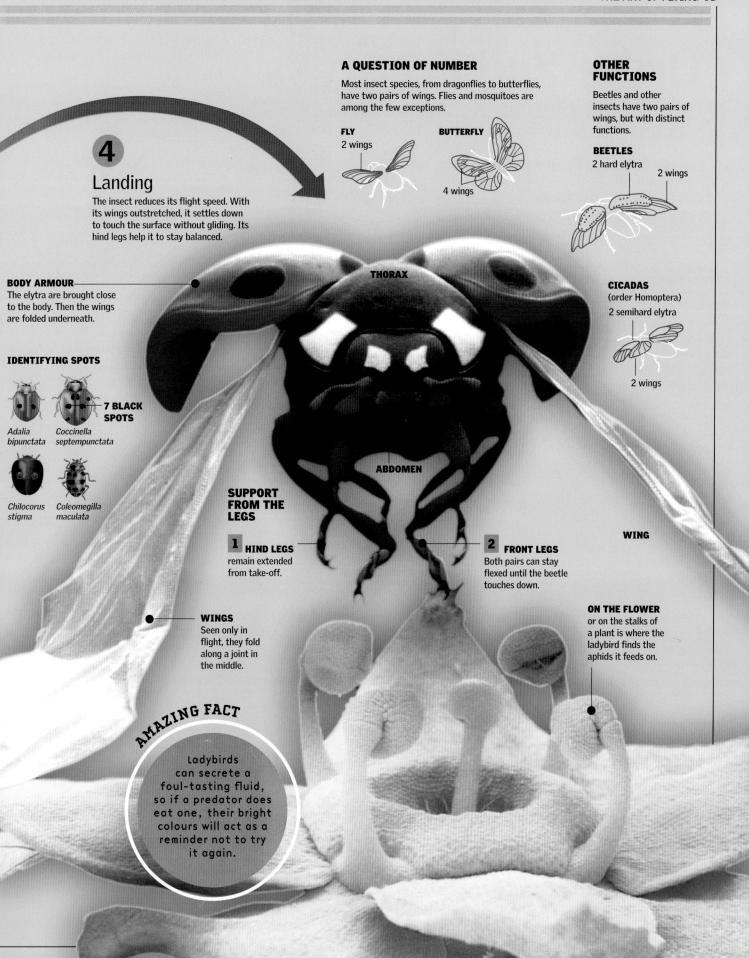

A QUESTION OF NUMBER

Most insect species, from dragonflies to butterflies, have two pairs of wings. Flies and mosquitoes are among the few exceptions.

FLY
2 wings

BUTTERFLY
4 wings

OTHER FUNCTIONS

Beetles and other insects have two pairs of wings, but with distinct functions.

BEETLES
2 hard elytra
2 wings

CICADAS
(order Homoptera)
2 semihard elytra
2 wings

4
Landing

The insect reduces its flight speed. With its wings outstretched, it settles down to touch the surface without gliding. Its hind legs help it to stay balanced.

BODY ARMOUR
The elytra are brought close to the body. Then the wings are folded underneath.

IDENTIFYING SPOTS

Adalia
bipunctata

Coccinella
septempunctata
7 BLACK SPOTS

Chilocorus
stigma

Coleomegilla
maculata

THORAX

ABDOMEN

WING

SUPPORT FROM THE LEGS

1 HIND LEGS
remain extended from take-off.

2 FRONT LEGS
Both pairs can stay flexed until the beetle touches down.

WINGS
Seen only in flight, they fold along a joint in the middle.

ON THE FLOWER
or on the stalks of a plant is where the ladybird finds the aphids it feeds on.

AMAZING FACT

Ladybirds can secrete a foul-tasting fluid, so if a predator does eat one, their bright colours will act as a reminder not to try it again.

Order and Progress

Ants are one of the insects with the highest social organization. In the anthill, each inhabitant has a job to do. The head of the family is the queen, the only one that reproduces. All the rest of the ants are her offspring. During mating, queens and drones (males) from various colonies mate on the wing. The queens need to mate several times, because the sperm they receive will have to last their lifetime. There are about 10,000 different ant species.

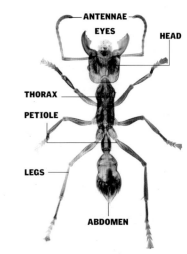

ANTENNAE
EYES
HEAD
THORAX
PETIOLE
LEGS
ABDOMEN

BLACK GARDEN ANT
Lasius niger

MAIN ENTRANCE

The Anthill

After mating, the queen loses her wings and chooses a place to lay eggs. At first she lives on reserves derived from the muscle mass of her wings and some of the first eggs she has laid. She takes charge of raising the first generation of worker ants, which will then take on the task of finding food while the queen focuses exclusively on laying eggs.

COMMUNICATION

An ant communicates using its antennae through chemical means, by capturing particles of certain substances (pheromones) that enable it to recognize another ant from the same colony. Ants do not have a well-developed sense for perceiving sound.

FOOD STORAGE
Honeypot ants coordinate the food supply.

METAMORPHOSIS

In the egg stage, the future ant remains near the queen but leaves her during the larval stage. Other ants then take care of the larva, until it becomes a nymph and forms a cocoon from which it will emerge as an adult.

EGGS   **LARVAE**   **NYMPHS**   **COCOON**

AMAZING FACT

The total weight of all the ants in the world is roughly equal to the weight of all the humans in the world.

UNUSED TUNNEL

3 NYMPHS
are fed and taken care of in another area.

2 LARVAE
are carried to another chamber to grow.

1 EGGS
are laid by the queen in the lowest area.

4 COCOONS
The new ants hatch ready to work.

QUEEN ANT

YOUNG ANTS

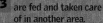

The Castes

Each ant plays a role in the nest and is assigned its role at birth. Drone, soldier, worker and replete worker (specialized to store food reserves) are the castes that distinguish what chores each ant will have.

Four wings

QUEEN
The largest ant. She lays the eggs that will become workers, drones and new queens.

Two wings

DRONE
His only function is mating; afterwards he dies.

WORKER
The worker ant may have the role of gathering food, cleaning or protecting the anthill.

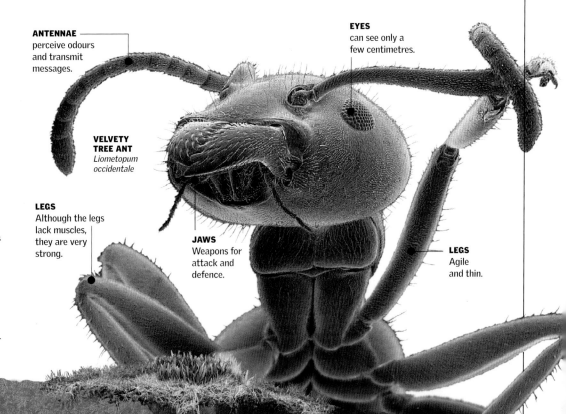

ANTENNAE
perceive odours and transmit messages.

VELVETY TREE ANT
Liometopum occidentale

EYES
can see only a few centimetres.

LEGS
Although the legs lack muscles, they are very strong.

JAWS
Weapons for attack and defence.

LEGS
Agile and thin.

Feeding

Ants cannot eat solid food. The plants and animals they eat are mixed with saliva to form a paste, which is used to feed the whole colony.

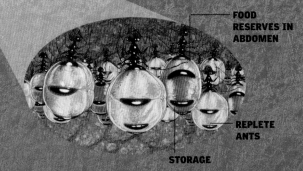

FOOD RESERVES IN ABDOMEN

REPLETE ANTS

STORAGE

INTERCHANGE OF FOOD

Having two stomachs, an ant can share food. The transfer begins when the receiving ant uses its front legs to touch the lip of the donor ant.

CROP
Social pouch

STOMACH
Individual pouch

Defence

The most widely used defence is biting and spraying jets of formic acid. Soldier ants have the job of scaring away the enemy because they have larger heads than worker ants.

JAW

The jaw is the ant's main weapon of defence, with a bite that can scare away or harm a rival. The jaw is also used for hunting and feeding.

AMERICAN FARMER ANT

CLAMPING JAW

VENOM

may contain formic acid and can kill or paralyse the prey. It comes from special glands in the lower abdomen.

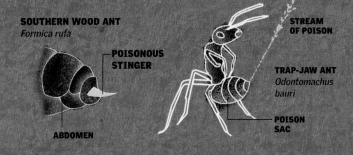

SOUTHERN WOOD ANT
Formica rufa

POISONOUS STINGER

ABDOMEN

STREAM OF POISON

TRAP-JAW ANT
Odontomachus bauri

POISON SAC

Survival Strategies

Evolution has moulded some striking traits into living beings. In particular, some insects, disguised as branches or leaves, can escape notice so they can hunt or hide from predators. To avoid being attacked, other insects develop colours and shapes that deceive other animals and put them off attacking. Hiding and showing off are two opposite strategies that have been favouring the survival of the fittest for millions of years.

BRIMSTONE BUTTERFLY
Gonepteryx sp.
The profile of the wings resembles the shape of cut leaves.

PEACOCK BUTTERFLY
Inachis io
The flashy, aposematic (warning) coloration keeps predators away by warning of the danger the insect poses.

WINGS
These wings look like leaves, with a similar colour, shape and structure.

FALSE EYE
The scales are pigmented to look like eyes.

Masters of Simulation

Camouflage, or crypsis, is a phenomenon in which animals use amazing disguises as advantageous adaptations. Camouflage is used both by hunters and by potential prey. Insects' bodies may be disguised to match soil, rock or parts of trees, such as bark or leaves. These masking techniques are a convenient way for the insect to fade into the background.

Disguise

Some insects use survival strategies designed to keep predators from seeing them. This disguise is their only means of defence.

DOUBLE PROTECTION
Caligo sp.
Owl butterflies combine Batesian and Müllerian mimicry. Predators may confuse the owl butterfly with leaves, but if a predator succeeds in finding it, the butterfly folds its wings to look like the shape and eyes of an owl. The predator, confused, backs off from attacking.

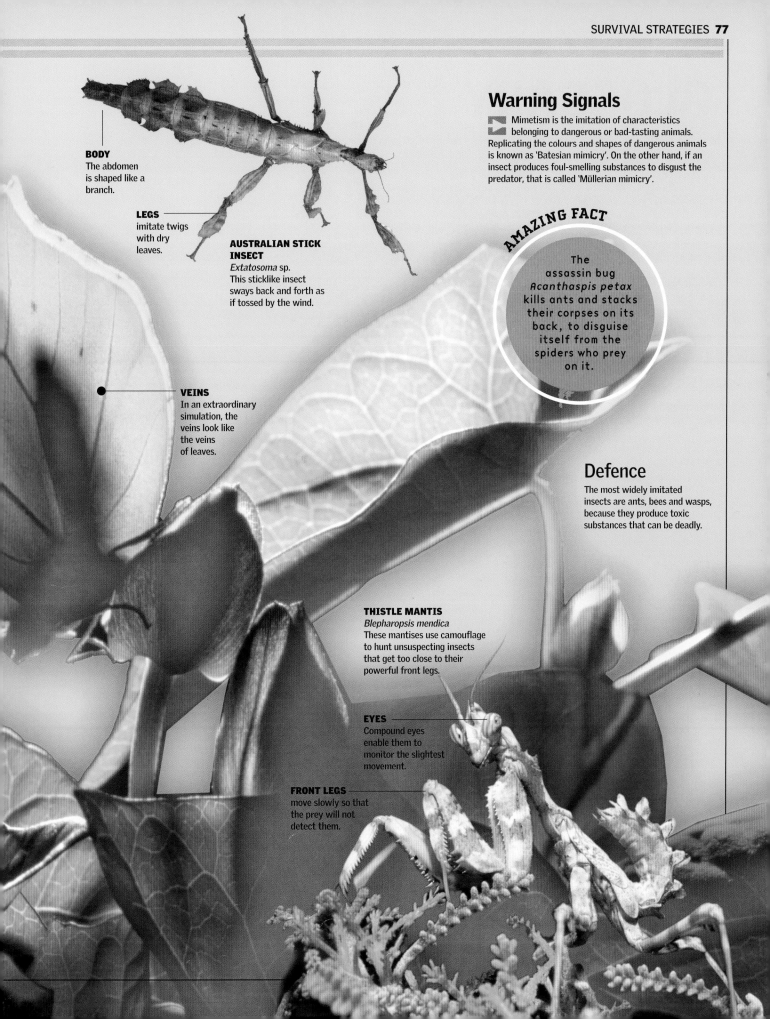

BODY
The abdomen is shaped like a branch.

LEGS
imitate twigs with dry leaves.

AUSTRALIAN STICK INSECT
Extatosoma sp.
This sticklike insect sways back and forth as if tossed by the wind.

VEINS
In an extraordinary simulation, the veins look like the veins of leaves.

Warning Signals

Mimetism is the imitation of characteristics belonging to dangerous or bad-tasting animals. Replicating the colours and shapes of dangerous animals is known as 'Batesian mimicry'. On the other hand, if an insect produces foul-smelling substances to disgust the predator, that is called 'Müllerian mimicry'.

AMAZING FACT

The assassin bug *Acanthaspis petax* kills ants and stacks their corpses on its back, to disguise itself from the spiders who prey on it.

Defence

The most widely imitated insects are ants, bees and wasps, because they produce toxic substances that can be deadly.

THISTLE MANTIS
Blepharopsis mendica
These mantises use camouflage to hunt unsuspecting insects that get too close to their powerful front legs.

EYES
Compound eyes enable them to monitor the slightest movement.

FRONT LEGS
move slowly so that the prey will not detect them.

GLOSSARY

Adaptation
A structural, physiological or behavioural trait that allows an organism to live in its environment.

Aerodynamic
Having an appropriate shape to decrease resistance to the air.

Amino Acid
Organic molecule from which proteins are produced.

Amphibians
Group including frogs, toads and salamanders, in which the young live in water and the adults on land.

Anaerobic
Breathing process that does not require oxygen.

Antennae
A pair of long sensory appendages on the head of many arthropods.

Aorta
Main artery in blood circulation systems. It sends blood to other tissues.

Arthropod
An animal with articulated appendages and a segmented body, covered by an exoskeleton.

Bilateral Symmetry
Corporeal form whereby the right and left halves are approximate mirror images of each other.

Biped
Animal that stands upright, walks or runs using only the two hind limbs.

Bony Fish
Fish with bony skeletons and jaws. They have flexible fins that allow precise control of their movements.

Calcite
A form of the chemical compound calcium carbonate.

Cartilaginous Fish
Fish with skeletons made of cartilage, such as sharks and rays.

Carrion
The remains of dead animals used as food by some birds or other animals.

Caste
A social group that carries out specific tasks, characteristic of ants and bees.

Cephalopod
A class of exclusively marine molluscs with tentacles or legs attached to the head. These appendages have rows of suckers that are used for capturing prey and copulation.

Cephalothorax
The head and thorax combined in one single body segment.

Chelicera
First pair of appendages in crabs, sea spiders and arachnids, usually in the form of pincers or fangs.

Chitin
Durable polysaccharide that contains nitrogen and is found in the exoskeleton of arthropods or other surface structures of many invertebrates.

Chordate
Animal with a spinal cord, whether throughout its development or only in certain stages.

Cloaca
Open chamber into which the urinary and reproductive ducts empty.

Cochlea
A structure like a coiled spiral tube, located in the inner ear of mammals.

Cocoon
A protective sheath, usually of silk, made by insects to protect themselves during the pupa stage.

Cold-blooded
Organism whose body temperature is mainly controlled by external heat sources.

Colony
A group of animals of the same species that live and work together to survive.

Convolution
Each of the slight folds that mark the surface of the cerebral cortex.

Crustacean
An animal of the arthropod group, with antennae and articulated appendages, that uses gills to breathe and has a body protected by a thick covering.

Crop
Sac that communicates with a bird's oesophagus, where food is softened.

Dendrite
The branched elongation of a nerve cell through which it receives stimuli.

Dermis
The inner layer of the skin, located under the epidermis.

Dewlap
Fold of skin hanging below the chin and extending to the chest in some lizards and other tetrapods.

Display
Behaviour directed at attracting the attention of a partner. It can also be done to threaten or distract predators.

Distribution
All the places where a species is located. It includes areas that the species occupies in different seasons.

Diversity
Degree to which the total number of individual organisms in an ecosystem is distributed among different species.

Echolocation
The ability to orient by emitting sounds and interpreting their echoes.

Embryo
The first stage of development of a multicellular animal or plant.

Epidermis
The outer layer of the skin.

Evolution
Gradual process of change of a species to adjust to its environment.

Exoskeleton
The external covering supporting the body, commonly found in arthropods.

Family
A category in taxonomy lower than an order and higher than a genus.

Fertilization
Union of male and female reproductive cells that will create a new individual.

Follicle
A small organ in the form of a sac located in skin or mucous membranes.

Fossil
Remains of various types of ancient life forms, both plants and animals, in a rocky substrate.

Fry
Newly hatched fish whose shape resembles that of adults.

Gene
Unit of information in a chromosome; sequence of nucleotides in DNA that carries out a specific function.

Genus
A category in taxonomy that groups species together.

Gestation
The state of an embryo inside a female mammal from conception until birth.

Gizzard
Muscular stomach of a bird. It is very robust, especially in granivores, and is used to grind and soften food.

Gland
Group of cells that produce secretions, organized inside a membrane to form an organ whose function is to synthesize and excrete molecules.

Gonad
Gland that produces reproductive sex cells.

Habitat
The set of geophysical conditions in which an individual species or a community of animals or plants lives.

Herbivore
Animal that feeds exclusively on plants.

Heterocercal
Tail fin in which the spine curves upwards, forming a large upper lobe.

Hibernation
The physiological state that occurs in certain mammals as an adaptation to extreme winter conditions, exhibited as a drop in body temperature and a general decrease in metabolic function.

Homeothermy
Thermoregulation characteristic of animals that maintain a constant internal temperature, regardless of external conditions.

Incubation
The act of keeping eggs warm so that the embryos inside can grow and hatch.

Invertebrate
Animal without a spinal column, such as worms and arthropods.

Keel
Ridge or fleshy border along the sides of the caudal peduncle.

Keratin
A protein rich in sulphur, the chief element of the outermost layers of mammals' epidermises, including hair, horns, nails and hooves.

Lactation
The period in mammals' lives when they feed solely on maternal milk.

Larva
Animal in a developmental stage, after leaving the egg. It can feed itself but has not yet acquired the shape and structure of the adults of its species.

Lateral Line
Line along the sides of the fish's body consisting of a series of pores.

Lipids
Water-insoluble substances including fats, oils, waxes, steroids, glycolipids, phospholipids and carotenes.

Mandible
Appendage just below the antennae, used to trap, hold, bite or chew food.

Mantle
In molluscs, the outer layer of the body wall or a soft extension of it. It usually secretes a shell.

Marsupial
Mammals whose females give birth to unviable infants, which are then incubated in the ventral pouch, where the mammary glands are located.

Metabolism
The sum of all the physical and chemical transformations that occur within a cell or organism.

Metacarpus
The set of elongated bones that make up the skeleton of the anterior limbs of certain animals and of the human hand.

Metamorphosis
Abrupt transition from the larval form to the adult form.

Microorganism
Organism that can be seen only with a microscope.

Mimetism
Property of certain animals and plants to resemble living things or inanimate objects that live nearby.

Mimicry
Ability of certain organisms to modify their appearance to resemble elements of their habitat or other species.

Molars
Group of teeth that crush or grind food.

Mollusc
Invertebrate with a soft body divided into a head, foot and visceral mass.

Morphology
Study of the form of an object.

Moulting
Removal of all or part of the outer covering of an organism; in arthropods, a periodic changing of the exoskeleton.

Neuron
A differentiated cell of the nervous system capable of transmitting nerve impulses. It is composed of a receptor site, dendrites and a transmission (or release) site – the axon, or neurite.

Nidicolous
Descriptive of a chick that depends on its parents' care after birth.

Order
Taxonomic category lower than a class and higher than a family.

Organ
Body part made of various tissues grouped into a functional unit.

Organism
Any living creature, whether single-celled or multicellular.

Ovary
Organ that produces female sex cells.

Oviduct
The duct through which the ova leave the ovary to be fertilized.

Papillae
Small conical elevations on skin or mucous membranes, especially those on the tongue used to taste.

Parasite
Organism that lives at the expense of another and typically obtains nutrients already processed by the host.

Pheromones
Chemical substances secreted by the reproductive glands of animals to attract individuals of the opposite sex.

Photophore
Mucous glands modified for the production of light, from either symbiotic phosphorescent bacteria or oxidation processes within the tissues.

Phylum
Taxonomic category lower than a kingdom and higher than a class.

Pigment
Substance that colours skin, feathers or tissues of animals and plants.

Placenta
The spongy tissue that completely surrounds the embryo and whose function is to allow the exchange of substances through the blood.

Plankton
Group of small plants (phytoplankton) or animals (zooplankton) that live suspended in water.

Polyandry
Copulation by a female with various males during one breeding period.

Protein
Macromolecule composed of one or more chains of amino acids.

Protractile
Describes a type of reptilian tongue that can be voluntarily hurled outwards in a rapid, precise movement.

Reef
Hard bank that barely reaches above the ocean surface or that lies in very shallow waters. It can be inorganic or result from the growth of coral.

Retina
The inner membrane of the eyes, where light sensations are transformed into nerve impulses.

Salinity
Measurement of the amount of common salt in water or soil.

Scales
Small bony plates that grow from the skin and overlap each other.

Scavenger
Animal that eats organic forms of life that have already died.

School
Transient grouping of fish of the same population or species, brought together by similar behaviour.

Spawning
Action of producing or laying eggs.

Species
A group of individuals that recognize one another as belonging to the same reproductive unit.

Spiracle
One of the external openings of the respiratory system in terrestrial arthropods.

Substrate
The surface that constitutes an organism's habitat or life support.

Thermal
Hot air current that rises. Many birds use it to gain height effortlessly.

Thorax
In crustaceans and insects, the fused segments located between the head and the abdomen to which the legs are attached.

Tissue
Group of identical cells that carry out a common function.

Trachea
In insects and some other terrestrial arthropods, the system of air conduits covered with chitin.

Tundra
Vast treeless plains in Arctic regions.

Vertebrates
Animals that have a spinal column, such as birds, fish, reptiles, amphibians and mammals.

Viviparous
Refers to animals in which the embryonic development of offspring occurs inside the mother's body and the offspring emerge as viable young.

Weaning
The process by which a mammal ceases to receive maternal milk as its subsistence.

INDEX